I0418882

New Floating World

Contemporary Japanese Art and Illustration

GINGKO PRESS

New Floating World
Contemporary Japanese Art and Illustration

First Published in the USA in 2025 by

GINGKO PRESS

Gingko Press, Inc.
217 W. Richmond Ave, Suite B
Richmond, CA 94801 USA
Email: books@gingkopress.com
www.gingkopress.com

ISBN 978-1-58423-801-0

By arrangement with
Sandu Publishing Co., Ltd.

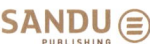

Copyright © 2025 by Sandu Publishing Co., Ltd.
First co-published in 2025 by Sandu Publishing Co., Ltd.

Edited and produced by Sandu Publishing Co., Ltd.
Editors: Zhiqing Zhang, Anton Tan
Designer: Yuhua Pan
Cover Design by Yuhua Pan
Front cover artwork by Sakuma Yuka
Back cover artwork by Miki Katoh
Book block artwork by Tsubonari

info@sandupublishing.com
sales@sandupublishing.com
www.sandupublishing.com

All rights reserved. No part of this publication may be reproduced or transmitted in any form or by any means, electronic or mechanical, including photocopy, recording or any information storage and retrieval system, without prior permission in writing from the publisher.

Printed and bound in China

CONTENT

PREFACE

New "Japanese Beauty" Rising

by Miki Katoh

Unlike perception, the evolution of the imagination, which allows us to imagine things that do not exist, has enabled humans to engage in the complex creative activity of art. Art materializes some meaning and can be considered an "embodied meaning." Artists (expressers) create works of art in the real world through perception and action. In this creative process, some kind of meaningful idea is generated in the world of the imagination, forming the basis of artistic expression.

As an island nation, Japan has had limited exchange with the world and has developed its own culture and social structure. Its traditional culture has produced epic stories and is the source of contemporary artistic creation. Since ancient times, Japan has worshipped nature and has built a primitive religion in which gods, who are personified or deified, appear in numerous myths and fables. This idea of nature worship is deeply connected to animism, which worships the souls and spirits that reside in all things. Even in the stage of transition to higher religions such as Buddhism, it presents the cycle of life, in which reincarnation is the norm, and a view of life and death in the form of reincarnation.

It is an irrefutable fact that Japanese painting is characterized by spatial expression using contour lines. Whether it is ancient records such as sliding screen paintings and picture scrolls, ukiyo-e that flourished as popular culture in the Edo period, or modern manga and animation, the most important element is the "line." At the end of the 19th century, Japanese art made a big impact on Western art, where shading was the norm, sparking a Great Japan Boom called "Japonism." This movement absorbed and inspired each other's merits and advantages, and was sublimated into today's contemporary art.

Using the new "Japanese beauty" as a platform, this publication creates an opportunity for up-and-coming artists to gather and gain clues for creating the future through artistic expression that connects Japan's past and present. Each work, which sheds light on the complex phenomenon of artistic expression from a different perspective, is a free expression in which anyone can be themselves and is the crystallization of outstanding creativity that presents diverse values that allow you to spend a rich time filled with new discoveries.

The main focus of these works is on important items that reflect Japanese culture, such as the traditional Japanese national dress, the kimono, samurais and warriors, swords, Shinto and Buddhist implements, sailor suits, Japanese school uniforms, Lolita fashion, cosplay, etc. These items are then given new life as creative works embodied in the real world by the artists' imagination.

It is expected that this publication will serve as a medium for connecting the inner worlds of artists and their works, for dialogue between the outer worlds of the viewers and the artists, and for the formation of a cycle of expression and perception. It is also expected that artists will be inspired by the works of others, evoking new images and ideas, and heightening emotions and motivation, which will trigger a process of inducing new creations. This publication, which embodies and supports a cycle model of "inspiring artistic communication," can be regarded as a compass that leads to the door of new creations.

From the perspective of diversity and inclusion, all people can come into contact with the works in this publication and feel the creativity of a culture that respects diversity. Yes, it is no exaggeration to say that this publication provides a new alternative space for "Japanese beauty." Gender balance has been progressing in the art world for a long time, ahead of other industries, and has supported and nurtured the evolution of the sensibility of humanity. This publication also incorporates these results, creating a unique and diverse collection using a variety of methods. Each work deepens the "Japanese beauty" by depicting the flow of modern and contemporary Japanese art in a novel way, mixing social contexts and global perspectives. These works also present an opportunity to discover new values by coming into contact with the transition from Japan's past to the present and the perspectives and ways of thinking of a rapidly changing and diverse society.

Art has always pioneered new paths, driven by a free spirit and creativity, and the works it produces sometimes have the potential to change people's lives.

As one of the authors, it would be my greatest joy if readers who pick up this publication experience a new world of "Japanese beauty" and use it as a milestone in their lives.

"

The contemporary artworks usually combine traditional Japanese cultural imagery, either realistically presented, or combined with trendy elements to create unconstrained ideas. They all present the unique side of Japanese culture as well as the spiritual traits and aesthetic concepts of the Japanese people.

"

SAILOR SUITS AND SWEET DREAMS

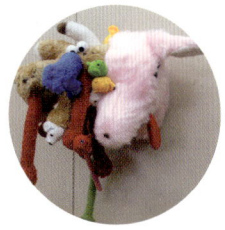

Kazuhiro Hori

He was born in 1969 and is heavily influenced by Japanese manga and anime. In his works, girls in sailor suits are the main characters. At the same time, He depicts a world full of kawaii motifs such as sweets and stuffed animals that many of these girls like. By depicting the contemporary situation and psychology of these girls, the artist brings to light social issues and other problems.

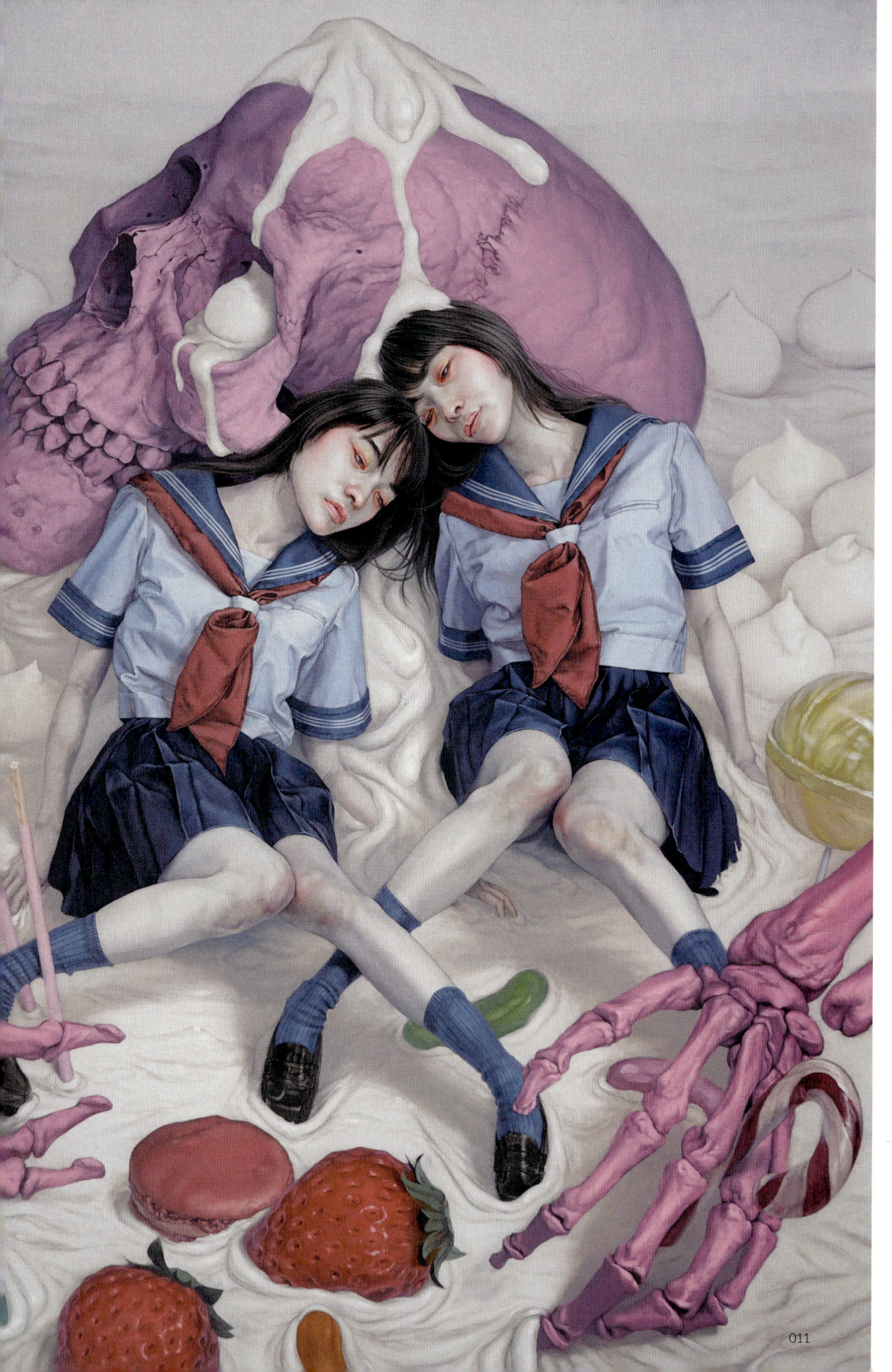

• DEPENDENCE •

Q: Can you introduce your artistic background? Which courses or experiences have had a significant impact or helped shape your artistic career?

KH: My first encounter with painting and oil painting was in my first year of high school. I had always loved manga and anime, so I had always drawn illustrations, but later I also worked hard at sketching in order to go to art school. In college, I majored in oil painting, and my studies at that time had a great influence on me. The way I paint today is an extension of the techniques I acquired as a student. I think that it was the publication of my works on Instagram that led me to exhibit my works outside of Japan.

Q: You mentioned your work is influenced by Japanese manga and anime. Could you specifically discuss in what aspects these influences are reflected? Do you have any particular favorite manga artists or works?

KH: Not only me, but many Japanese children grow up surrounded by anime and manga. I was not good at sports and socializing, and I loved to draw, so I copied those characters and others every day. My childhood dream was to become a manga artist, and my favorite manga artists as a teenager were Akira Toriyama, Katsuhiro Otomo, and Masamune Shirou. I also think that the slightly darker themes of my works are largely influenced by Japanese subcultures. For example, many Japanese animations express the dark side of human nature.

Q: The themes of your paintings often revolve around sailor suits, desserts, and plush toys, with a prevalent use of pink tones, symbolizing cuteness and sweetness. However, the girls in your works are often depicted as being trapped, restrained, or even threatened by these sweet items, rather than being in a happy and safe environment.

Could you discuss the significance of this combination of good and bad?

KH: The girl tries to fill her world with pretty things she loves. At first glance, this space appears to be a paradise or sanctuary. However, that space is a fiction, and once she steps outside, she must face a reality that can be described as cruel in order to survive. The delicate relationships with friends, the unknowable adult world, the choices and actions that come with responsibility, and becoming adults themselves. Of course, they are aware of this and accept it. But they want to be able to perceive, at least for a moment, that the world around them is a fuller place.

Q: In your work *Pietà* (P021), you mentioned that the inspiration comes from Michelangelo Buonarroti's *Pietà* and Katsushika Hokusai's ukiyo-e. How do these classic pieces influence your creation? How do you integrate them into your works?

KH: My works are not limited to *Pietà*, but I often take my inspiration from classical paintings. In the past, I have used Da Vinci's *Mona Lisa*, Hieronymus Bosch's *Ship of Fools*, and Rogier van der Weyden's *Altarpiece* when the images strike me. Famous works can be catchy icons in their own right. However, there is little thematic connection. I just hope that people who recognize the origin will chuckle at it.

Q: In your works, girls wearing sailor suits are the main characters. Why did you choose this particular character image to express your artistic ideas, especially in pieces such as *Dependence, Empty, Necrosis, Temptation*, and *Sweet Life*, where you depict the emptiness and struggles beneath the sweet exterior of the girls? How do you reveal the inner states of individuals and

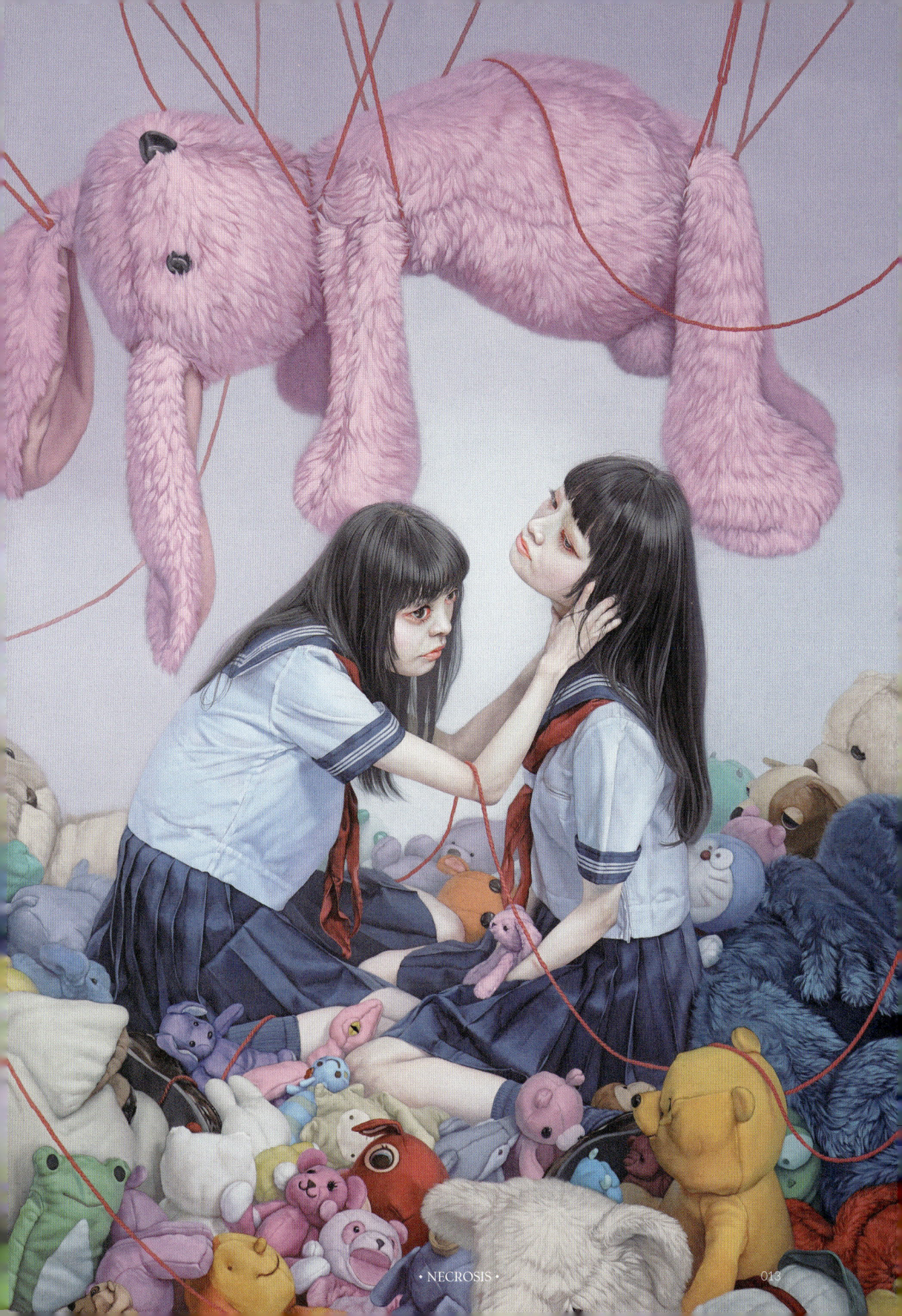

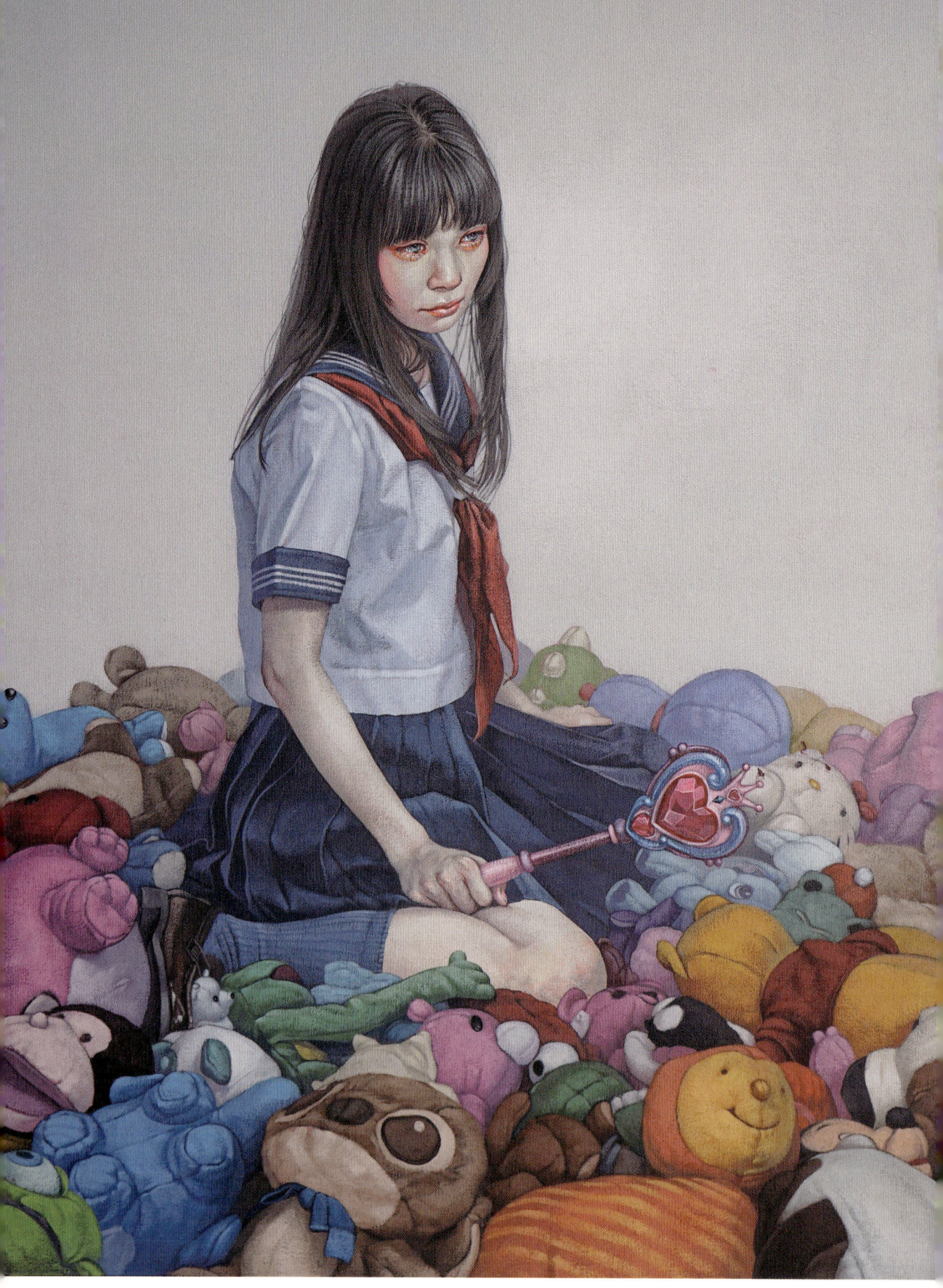

• EMPTY •

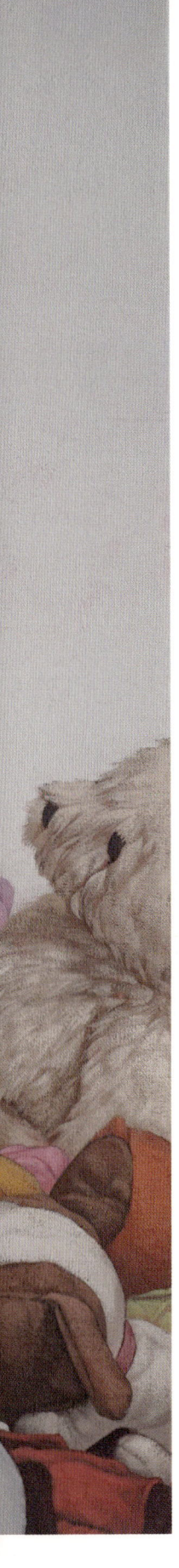

address the psychological and social issues they face in modern society through these works? What reflections and insights do you hope the audience will gain from them?

KH: The sailor suit is an icon that any Japanese can guess the age it represents and the situation and feelings of these girls in the present day. *Seifuku* is an institution enforced by society, but at the same time, it is a protective armor that allows and protects one's belonging to that society. In their groups, standing out from the crowd is frowned upon, and belonging to a group is granted only if one is in sync with the group. The absence of a group to which they belong can make them feel as if they are denied the meaning of their existence. The image associated with the sailor suit is that of a young girl, innocent and at the same time an item that arouses desire. Such a complex image is a true icon of the girl. As the author, I am a man, I can only fantasize about the feelings of these girls, but I think I can express them critically by relating them to contemporary society. Of course, the protagonists of my works are girls, but I believe that there are aspects of universal issues that transcend age and gender. Although I approach the theme of each work from a slightly different aspect, the underlying concept is common.

Q: Have there been any turning points or interesting and challenging events in your creative process?

KH: I changed my style of expression 15 years ago. Before that, I deformed the human body in my paintings, applied thick layers of paint, and used darker colors. I was more conscious of social issues than I am now. However, I wanted to return to figurative expression, which is how I originally started painting. This was a major turning point to me, and I changed my motif to girls.

Q: With 30k followers on Instagram, how do you showcase your works on social media? How does this help with your creative process and promotion?

KH: I don't think that the number of followers is a fair reflection of the appreciation of my work. In fact, the number of "nice" votes for each post is not as large as the number of followers, so I am not very active on social networks. I only post when I announce a group show or a solo exhibition. I also don't like to expose myself more than my work. Still, I think it is useful to have a tool that allows me to communicate with the world.

Q: You've primarily used acrylic as your medium. What do you find special about this medium? Would you consider exploring new mediums to showcase your work?

KH: As mentioned above, my painting career began with oils. The reason I switched to acrylics was initially time constraints. After all, the speed at which paint dries is definitely faster with acrylics. When I started using acrylics, I found that I could achieve a light and bright expression in a good sense, and I was able to get a feeling that I could get closer to the expression I was aiming for at the time, I have continued to work with them ever since. Recently, however, I have been trying to work with oil paints again.

Q: What are your expectations and plans for future creations? What new themes or emotions do you hope to convey through your future works?

KH: I don't plan too far in advance. Thankfully, I have been getting a steady stream of offers lately, so I've been busy with that. If I had to say, I would like to spend a little more time on each piece to increase the density.

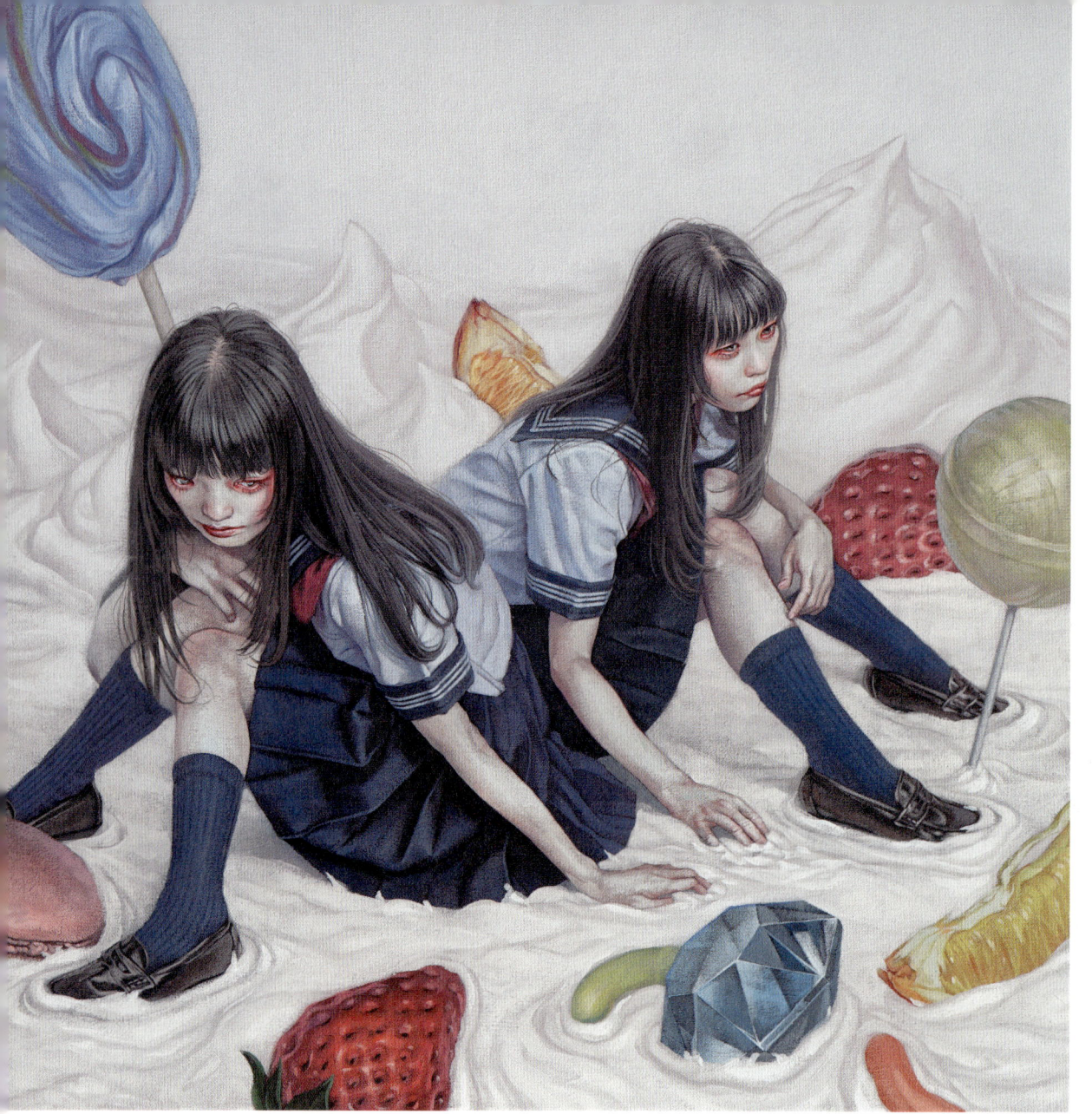

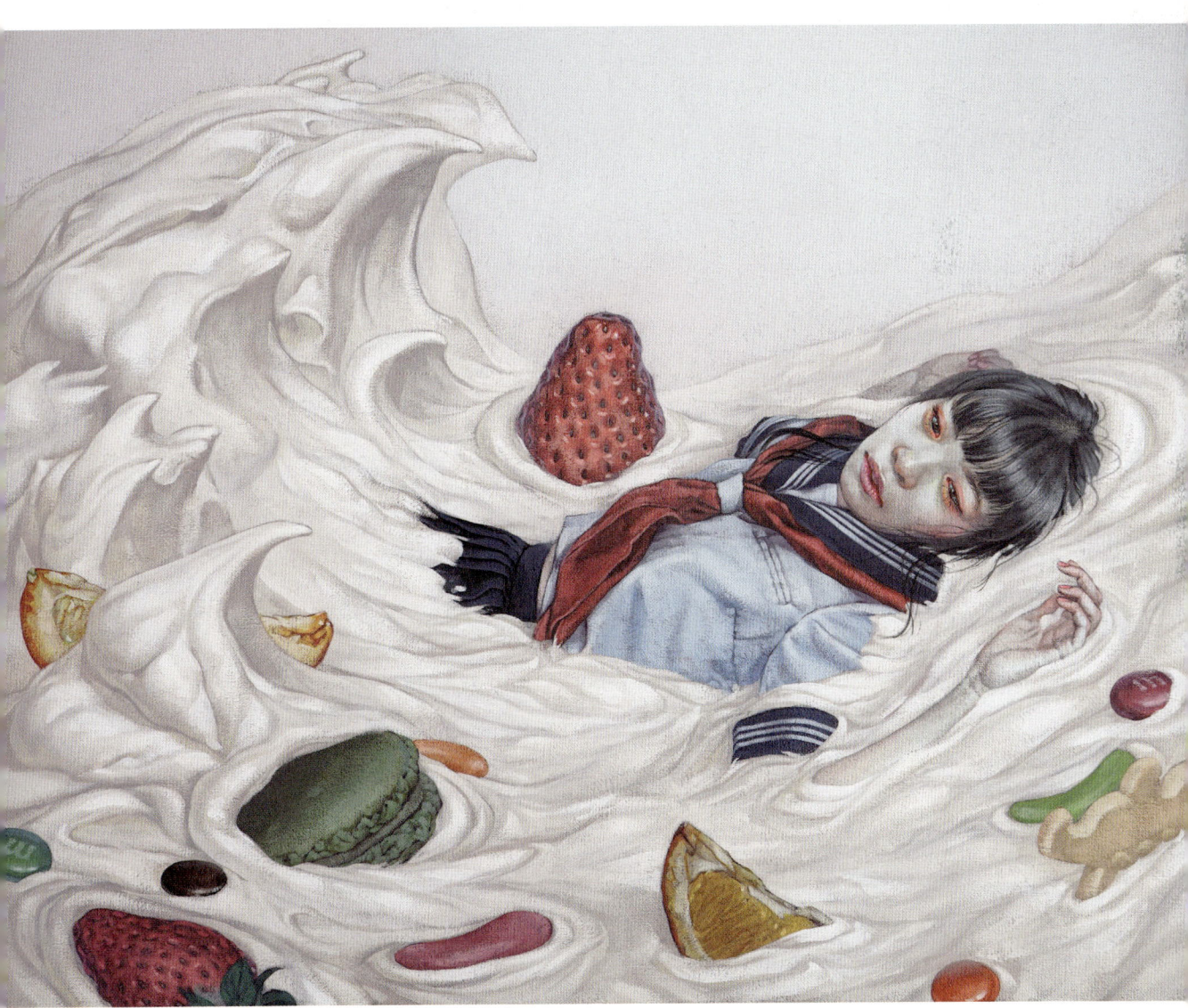

" *The girl tries to fill her world with pretty things she loves. At first glance, this space appears to be a paradise or sanctuary. However, that space is a fiction, and once she steps outside, she must face a reality that can be described as cruel in order to survive.* "

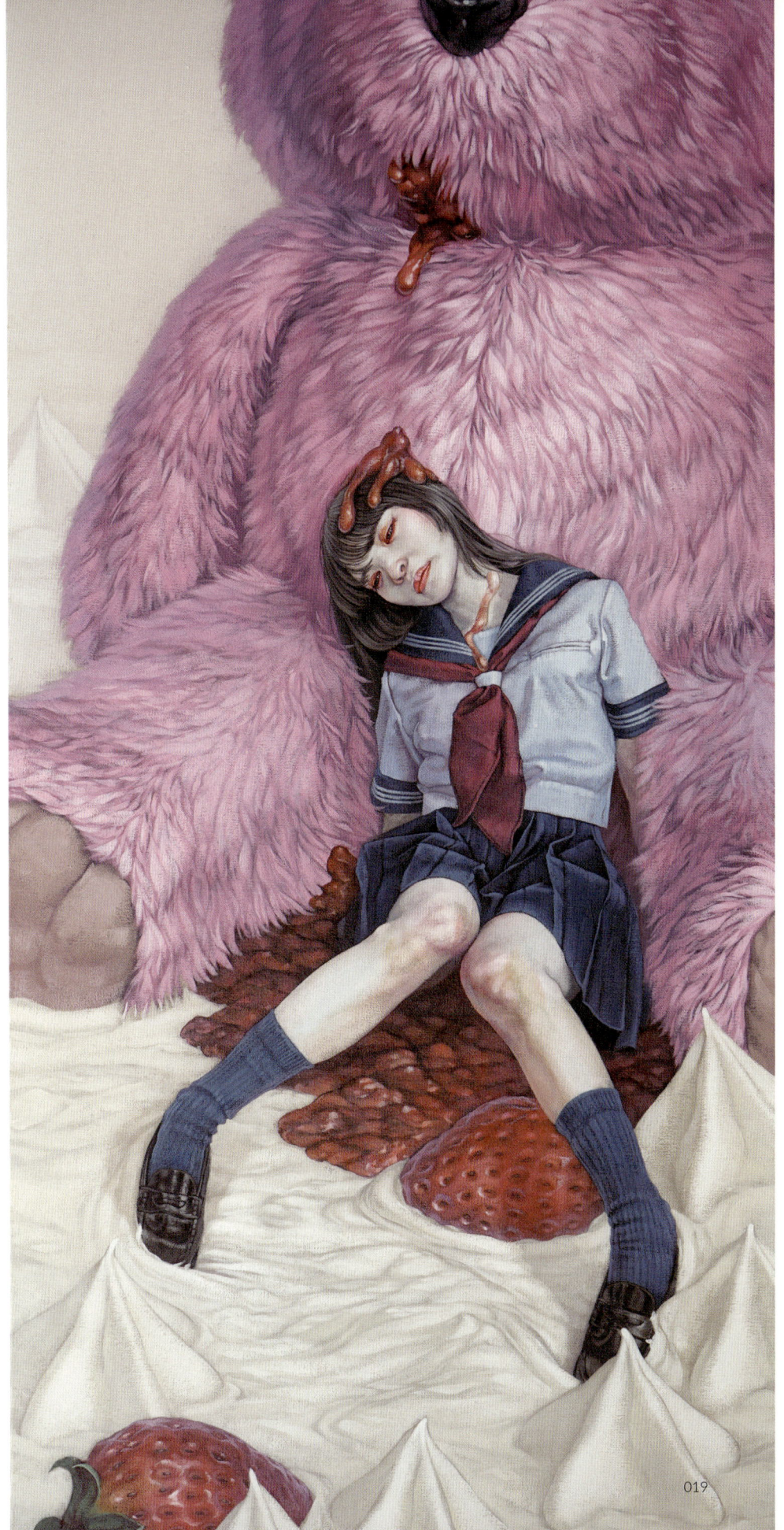

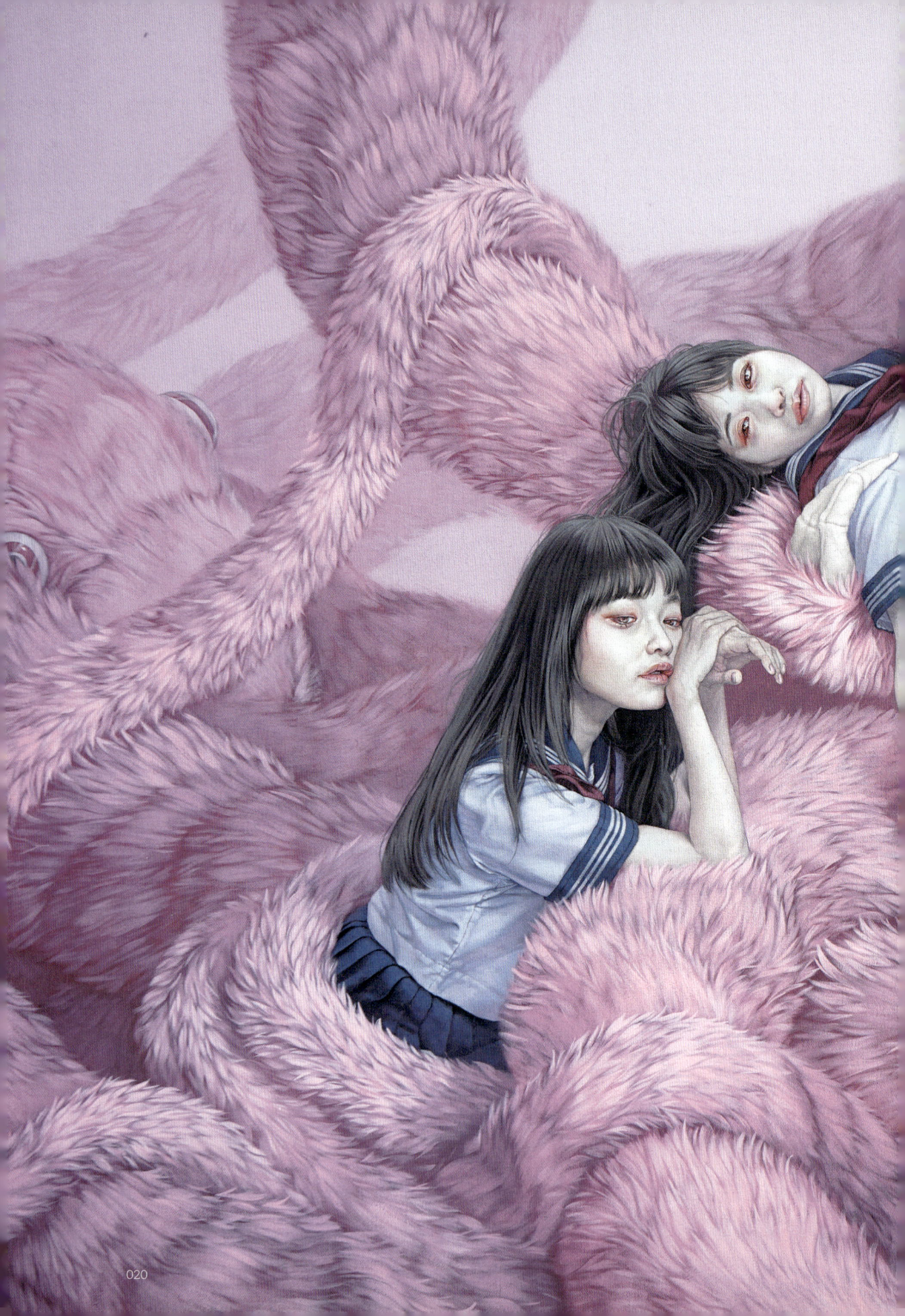

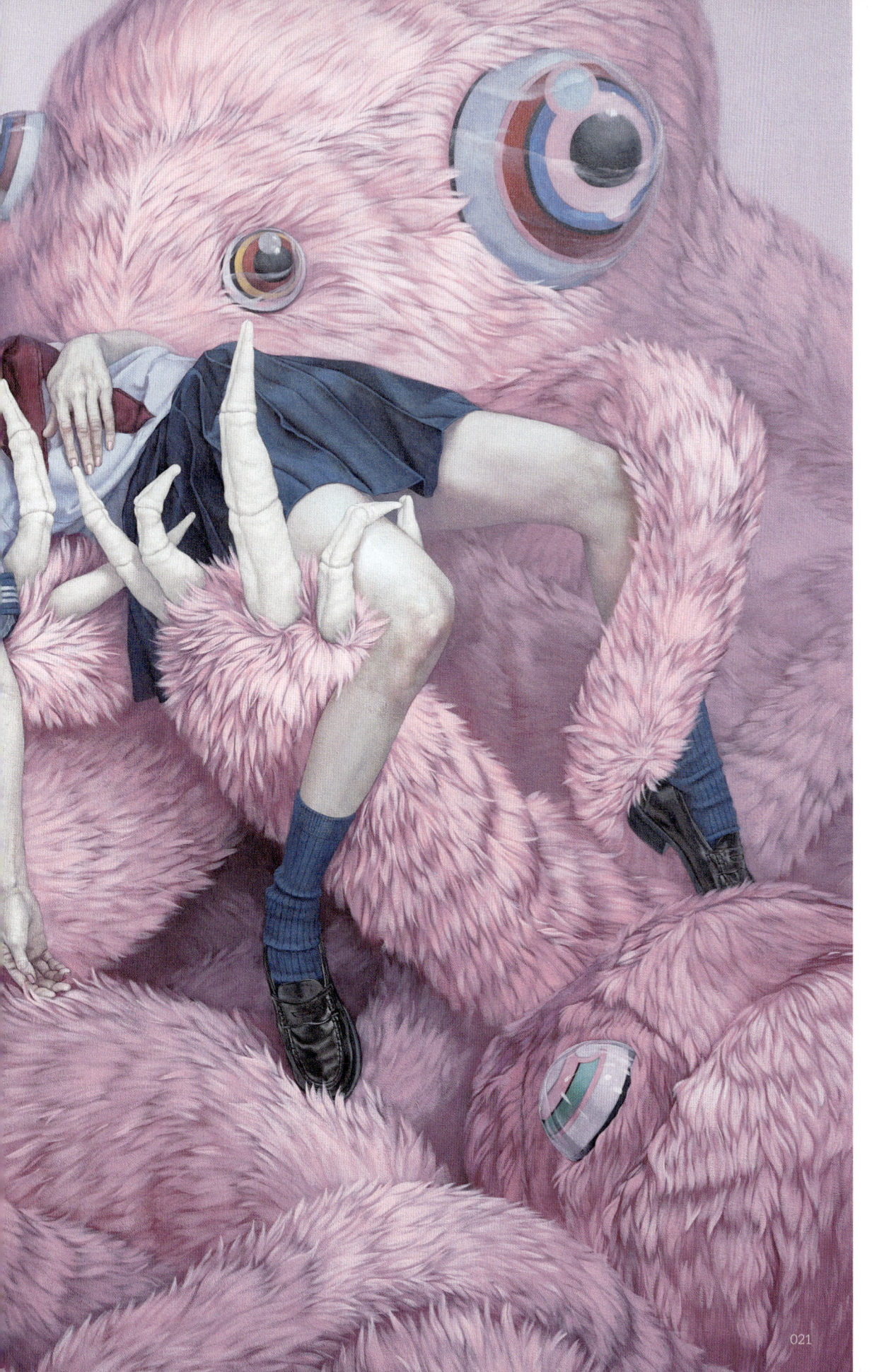

CRAFTING THE OTHERNESS

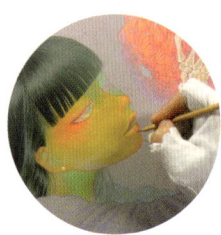

Fuco Ueda

In 2003, Fuco Ueda completed graduate school at Tokyo Polytechnic University. She began her career as a painter while she was still in school. In 2001 she held a solo exhibition "Ueda Fuco Exhibition." From around 2006 she has held many solo and group exhibitions, both in Japan and abroad, mainly overseas. Ueda uses girls, goldfish, animals, and plants as motifs, and develops her works based on her unique worldview.

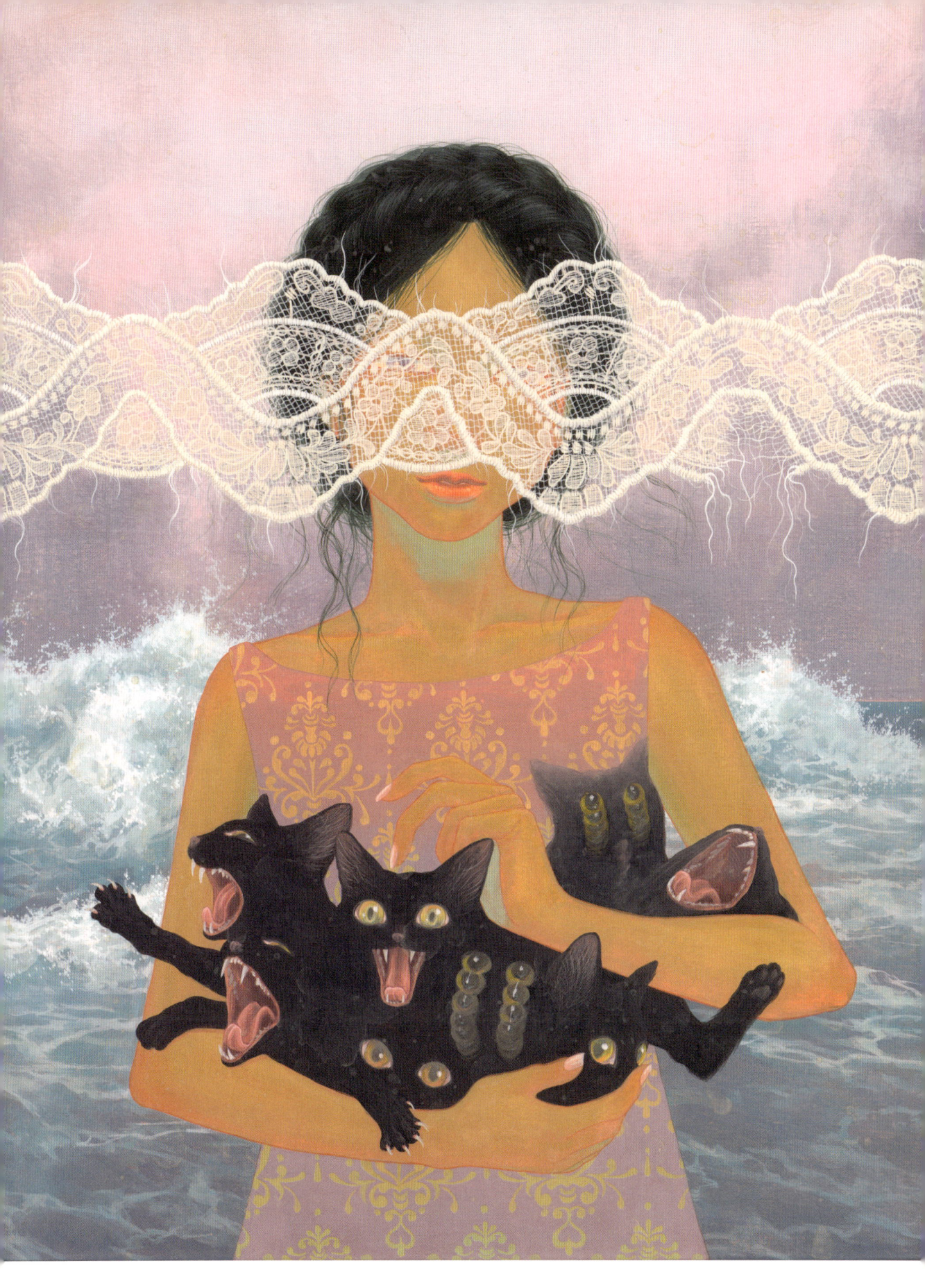

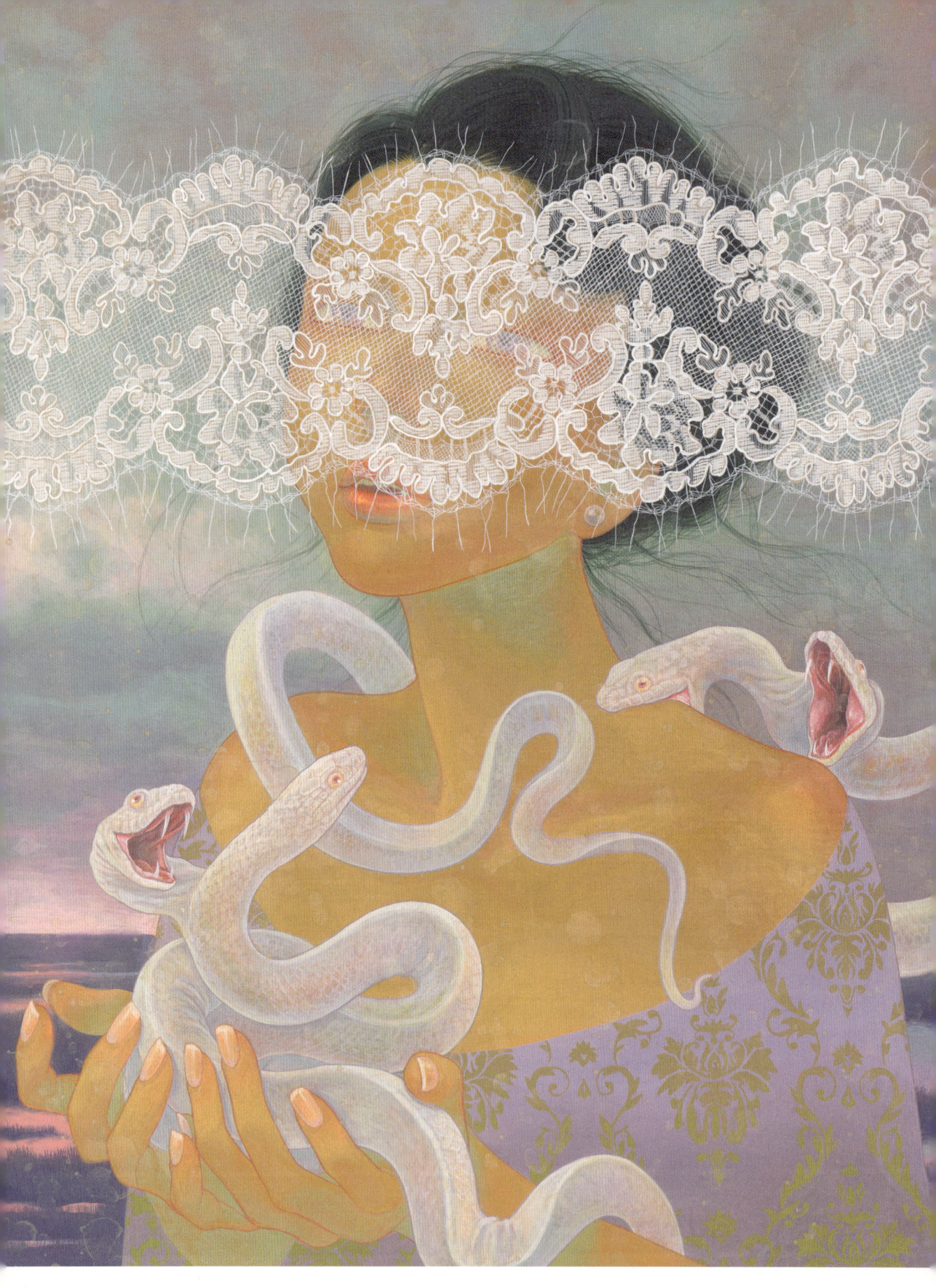

· THE VISITOR I ·

Q: Please tell us a little about your artistic background. How did you get interested in art?

FU: I have loved books since I was a child and aspired to be a novelist or manga artist. I longed for something with a story. I became interested in the world of art by looking at various art books at the library.

Q: What inspires your works that showcase distinctive female characters and elements? Are there any specific experiences or cultural influences that have shaped your creations?

FU: In various classical arts, themes of women and beauty are universal. At the same time, I treat women as equals to plants, animals, and minerals. It may be some kind of utopia. I incorporate the concept of coexistence in my own way.

Q: You mix acrylic and shell white to paint. Such a technique gives your works a unique visual impact. How do you decide to use this particular material and technique?

FU: I learned oil painting when I was a teenager. Then, I majored in design at art school and began using acrylic paints. At first, I painted with acrylic paint on paper, but after researching traditional Japanese paintings and oil painting supports, I arrived at my current technique. I still want to improve it.

Q: Your works often present a fiery, fantastical atmosphere, with female characters seemingly inhabiting the border between dreams and reality. What does this expression of emotion and atmosphere mean to you?

FU: I'm not interested in things that are easy to understand or realistic. It is often said that it is like looking into the underworld from this world. Maybe unconsciously I want to express a sense of otherness that we can never understand.

Q: In your work, characters appear to possess various emotions, sometimes sweet, other times with elements of provocation and seduction. How do you shape these characters?

FU: This also applies to the above answer, but even when a person thinks they understand something, the other person may have completely different feelings. Even if you sense a provocation or temptation, the other person may not have the slightest intention of doing so. I'm interested in that kind of miscommunication. Just as adults try to understand the innocence and naivety of children by stereotyping them. If it's a novel or a movie, the story might start from there.

Q: How do you stay inspired? What drives your creative motivation? During the creative process, what aspects do you particularly focus on or pay attention to?

FU: It is important to be inspired by art from various genres: novels, manga, movies, stage plays, music, design, etc. Enjoying, being excited and moved by art makes me who I am.

Q: Your paintings are delicate and full of detail. Which one of your works is your favorite or holds the deepest significance for you?

FU: That's a very difficult question. One thing I can say is that in my career of over 20 years, there are works that can only be created at that age. The works I created when I was 19 were possible because I was that age. I would not have been able to create the work I do now in the past. I think it's important to always do your best.

Q: How has Japanese culture influenced your work? Which aspects have had the most impact on your work?

FU: This is also a difficult question. Even if you are unconscious, you will not be able to escape from Japanese culture. A country or a culture is something that cannot be separated from the people who live there. I also think that the environment in which one is raised has a great influence on an artist. My family lived on a farm, and when I was a child, I spent time with more kinds of animals than humans. It was a place rich in nature. They probably have had a big influence on my work as well.

Q: You have participated in many solo and group exhibitions. How have these exhibitions impacted your career?

FU: A solo exhibition is like your own big stage, and it is fun to be able to freely set up and direct the space. Group exhibitions are also fun because collaborating with other artists brings unexpected effects and encounters. As an artist, continuing to hold solo exhibitions has helped shape my career.

Q: Finally, what's your new plan or project? Do you intend to continue exploring the themes and styles in your work, or do you have other new directions and challenges in mind?

FU: I am answering this question in May 2024, but I am currently participating in an art exhibition that is touring three museums in Japan. Additionally, in October 2024, a three-person exhibition will be held at an art museum in Shizuoka Prefecture, Japan. In 2007, I exhibited works with the motif of the deep sea and deep-sea fish, and since I will be exhibiting them at a museum near a fishing port, I am planning to create new works with those themes again.

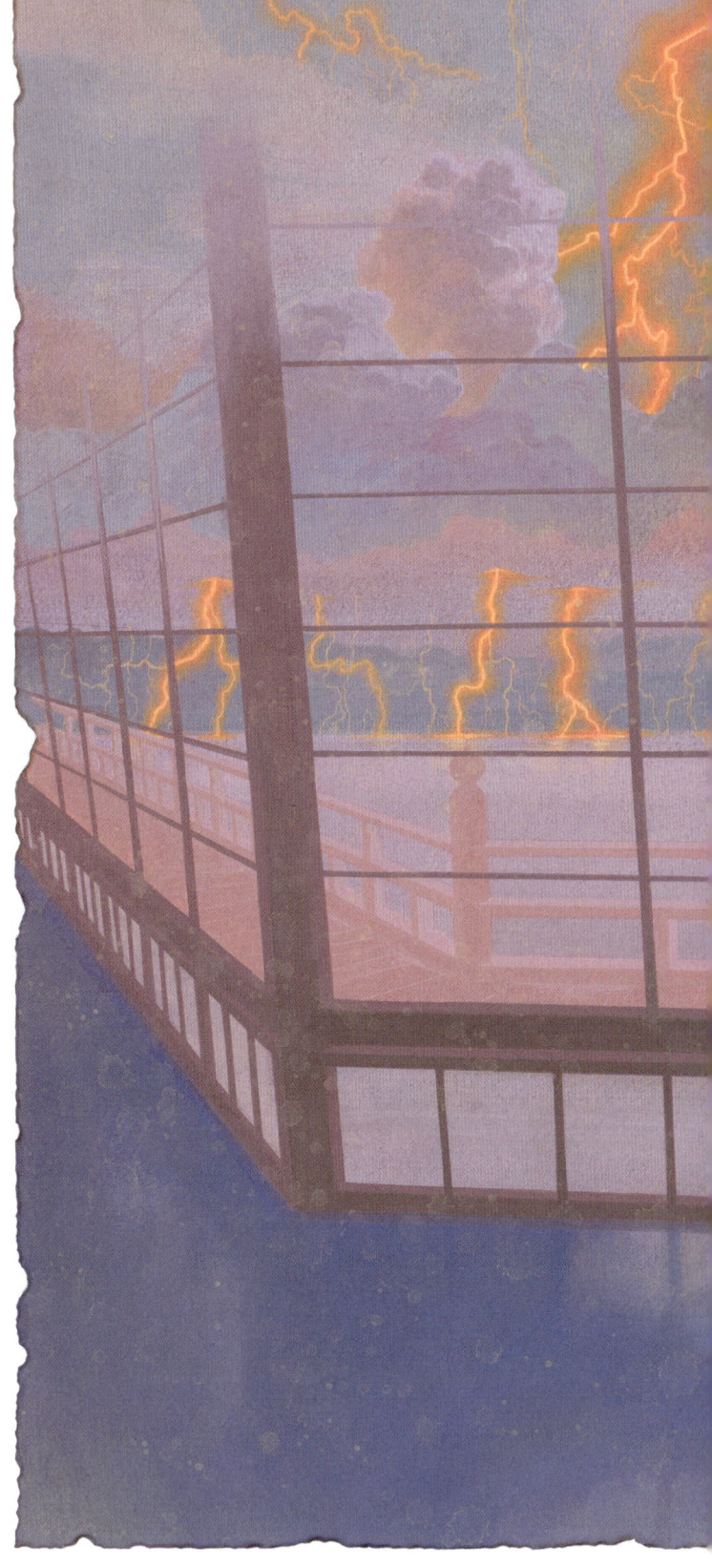

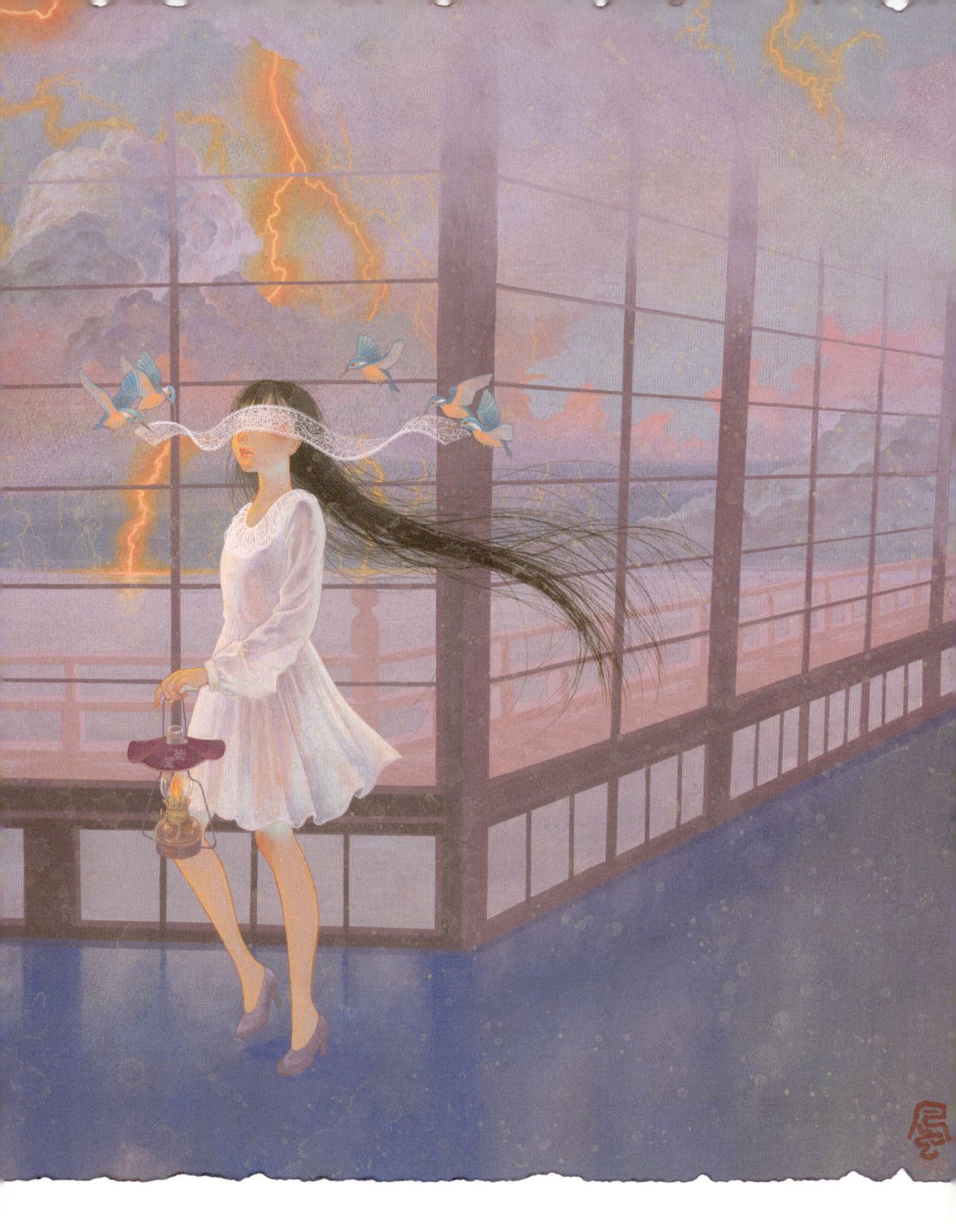

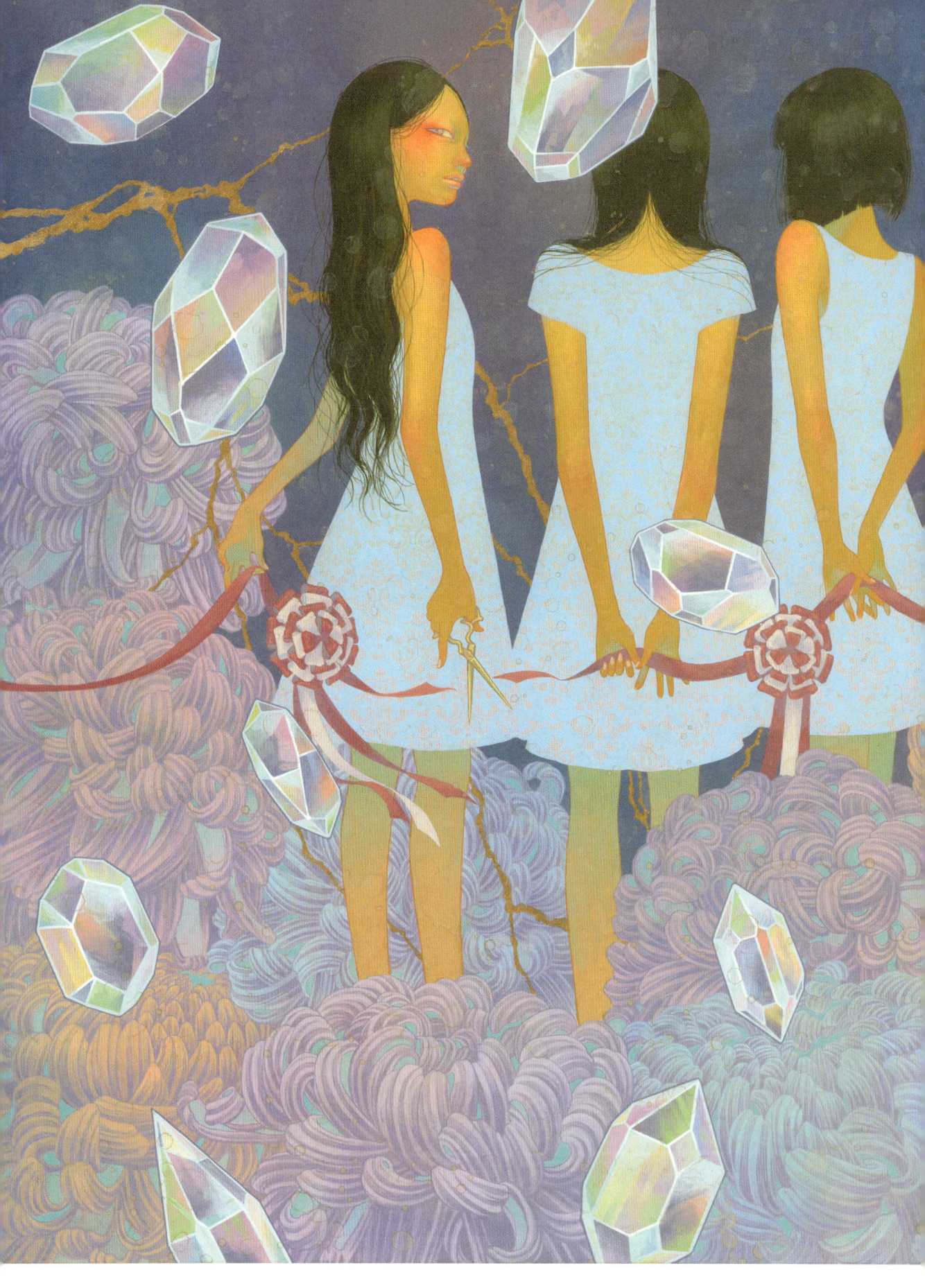

• FEEL DIZZY AND FEEL REAL •

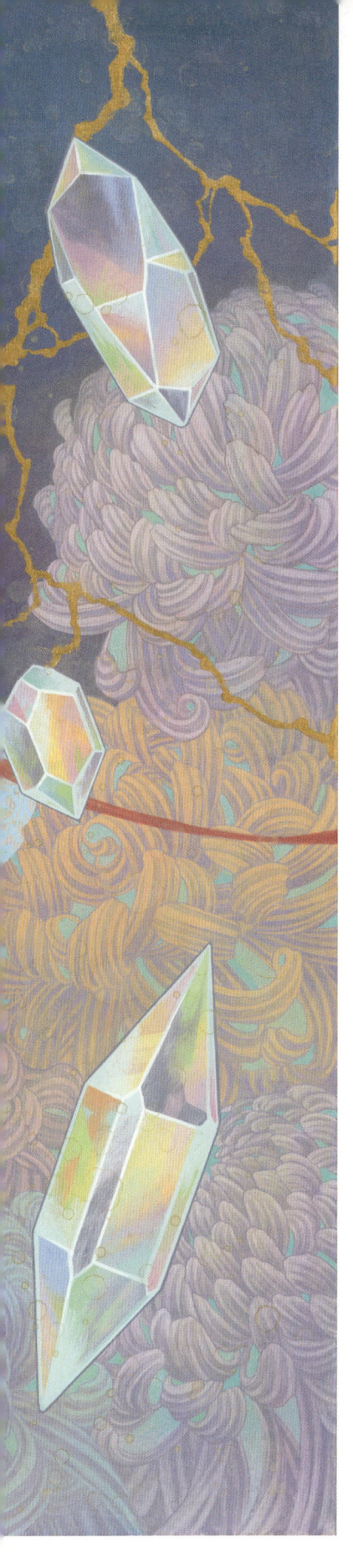

" *Even if you are unconscious, you will not be able to escape from Japanese culture. A country or a culture is something that cannot be separated from the people who live there. I also think that the environment in which one is raised has a great influence on an artist.* "

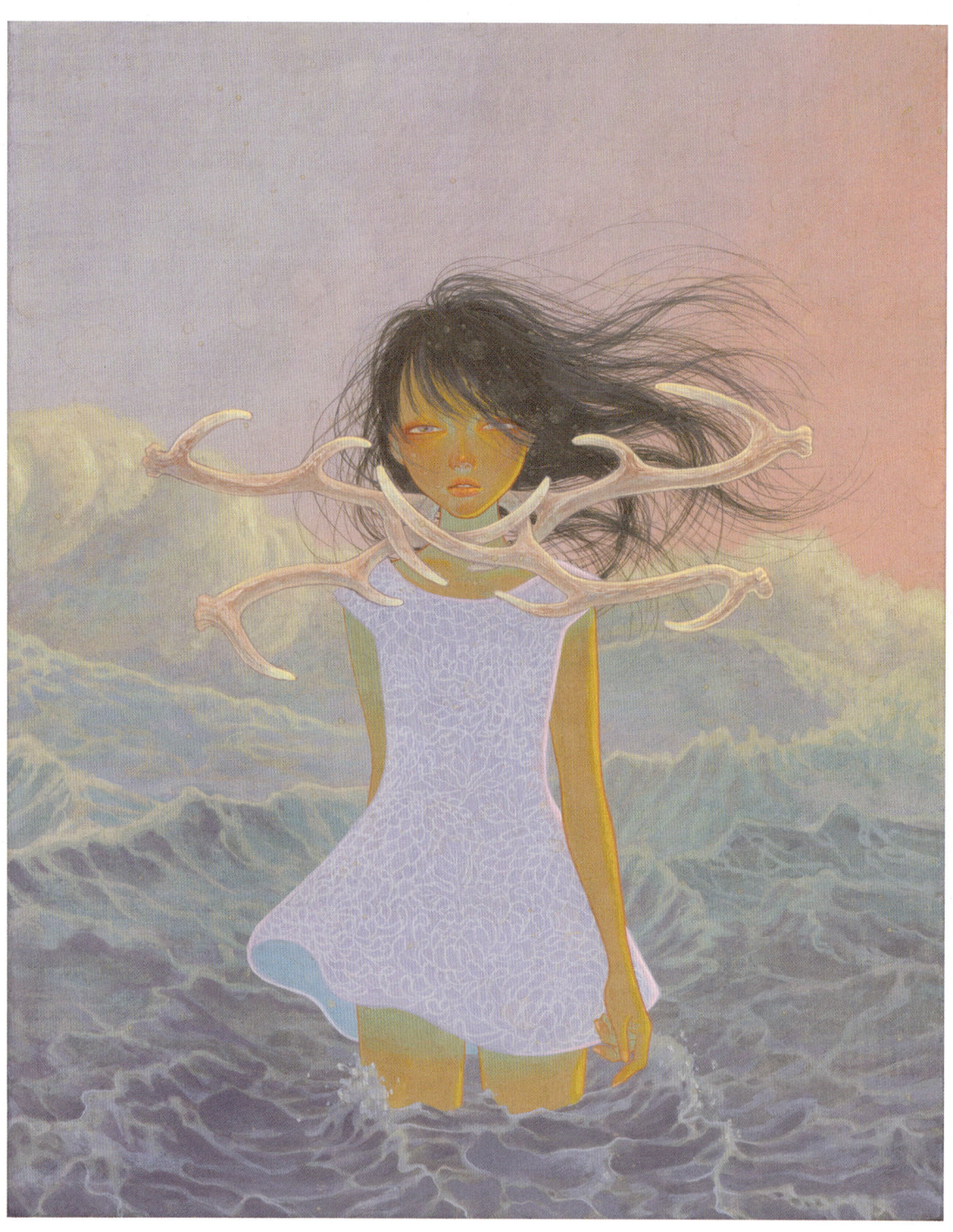

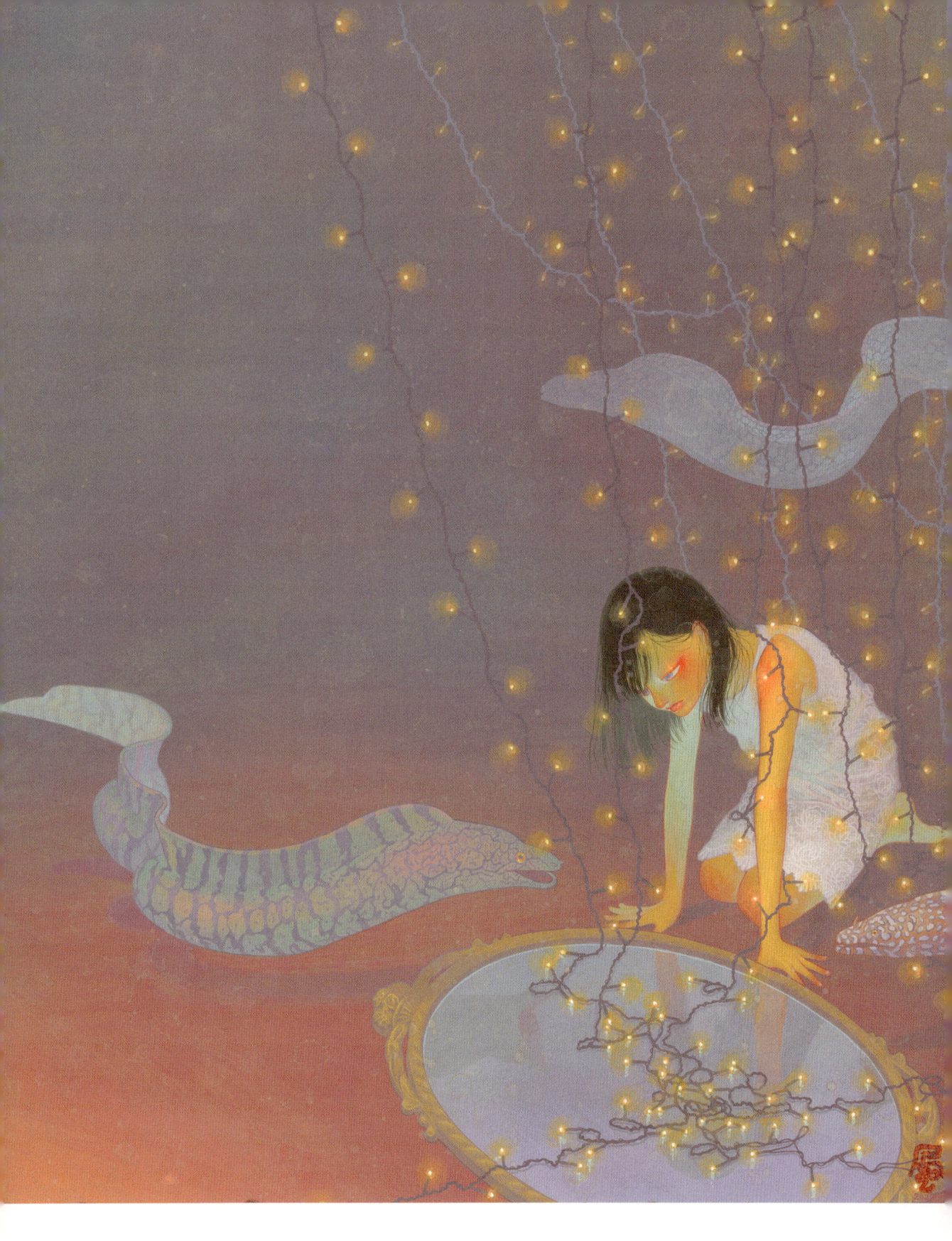

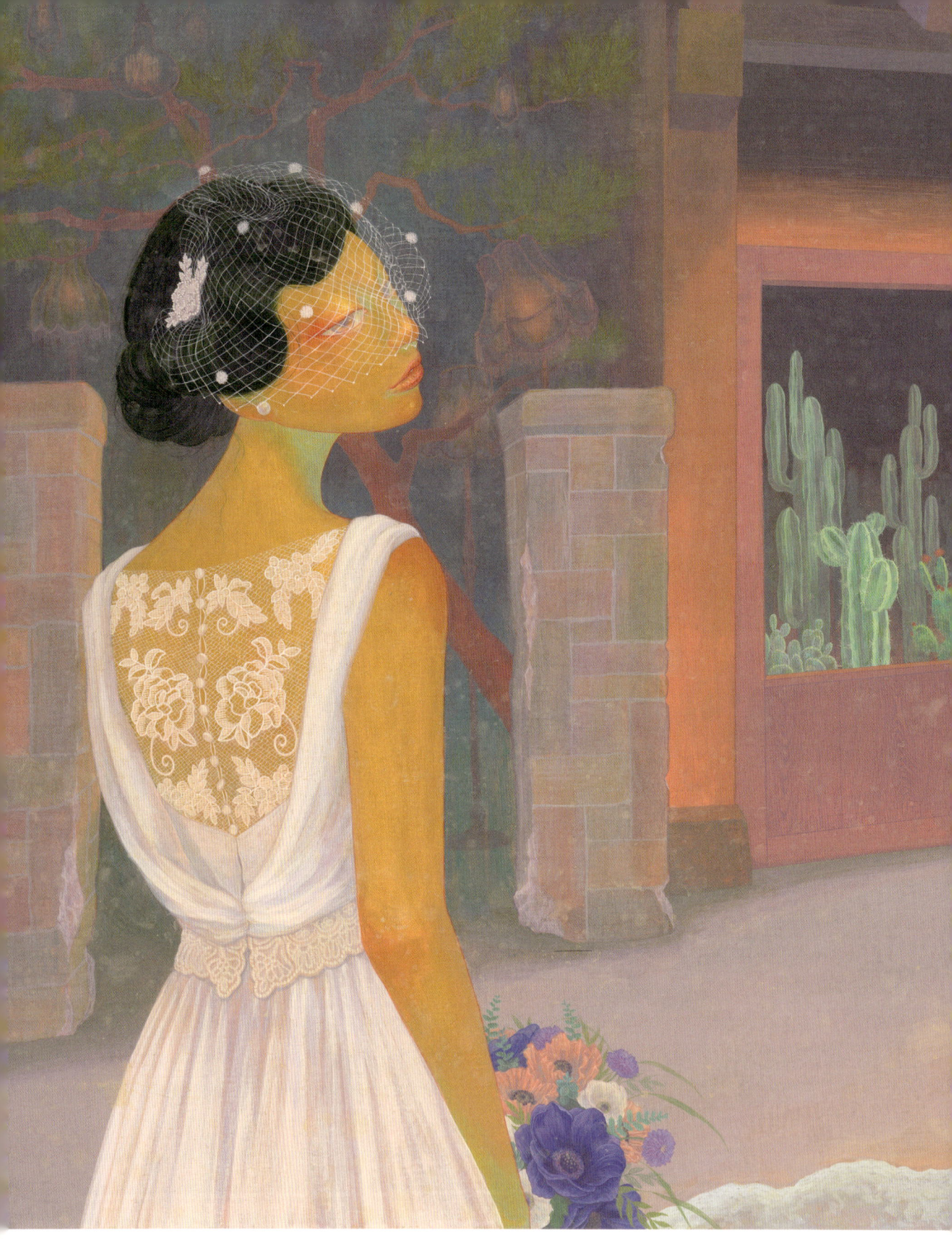

• THE VISITOR III •

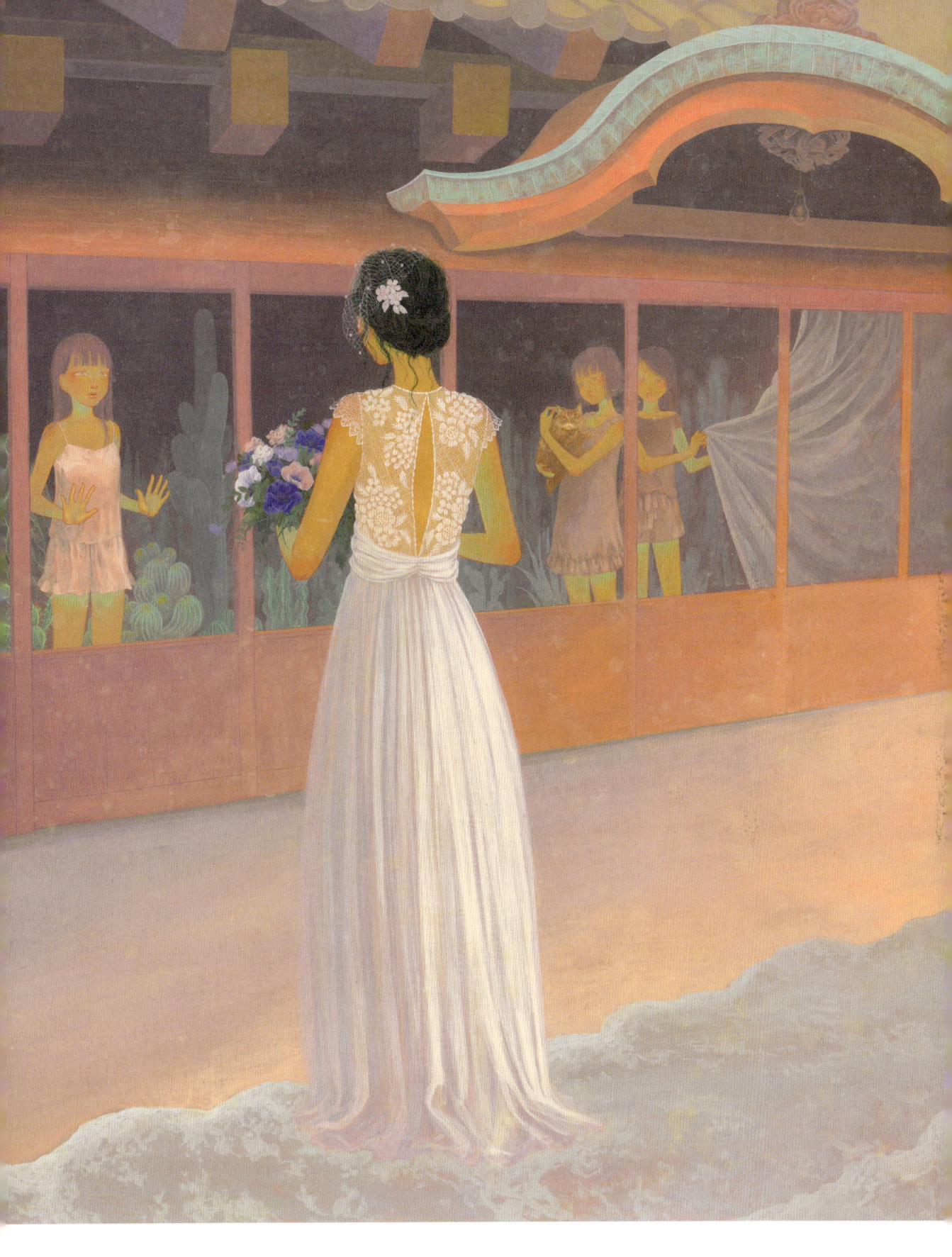

HOPES WITH FEMININITY

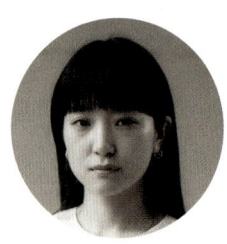

Sakuma Yuka

Sakuma Yuka is a painter and illustrator based in Nagoya. The "little girl," the motif of Yuka Sakuma's own work, is no longer seen today as something fragile and to be protected, but rather as something superhuman, invincible, and the strongest.

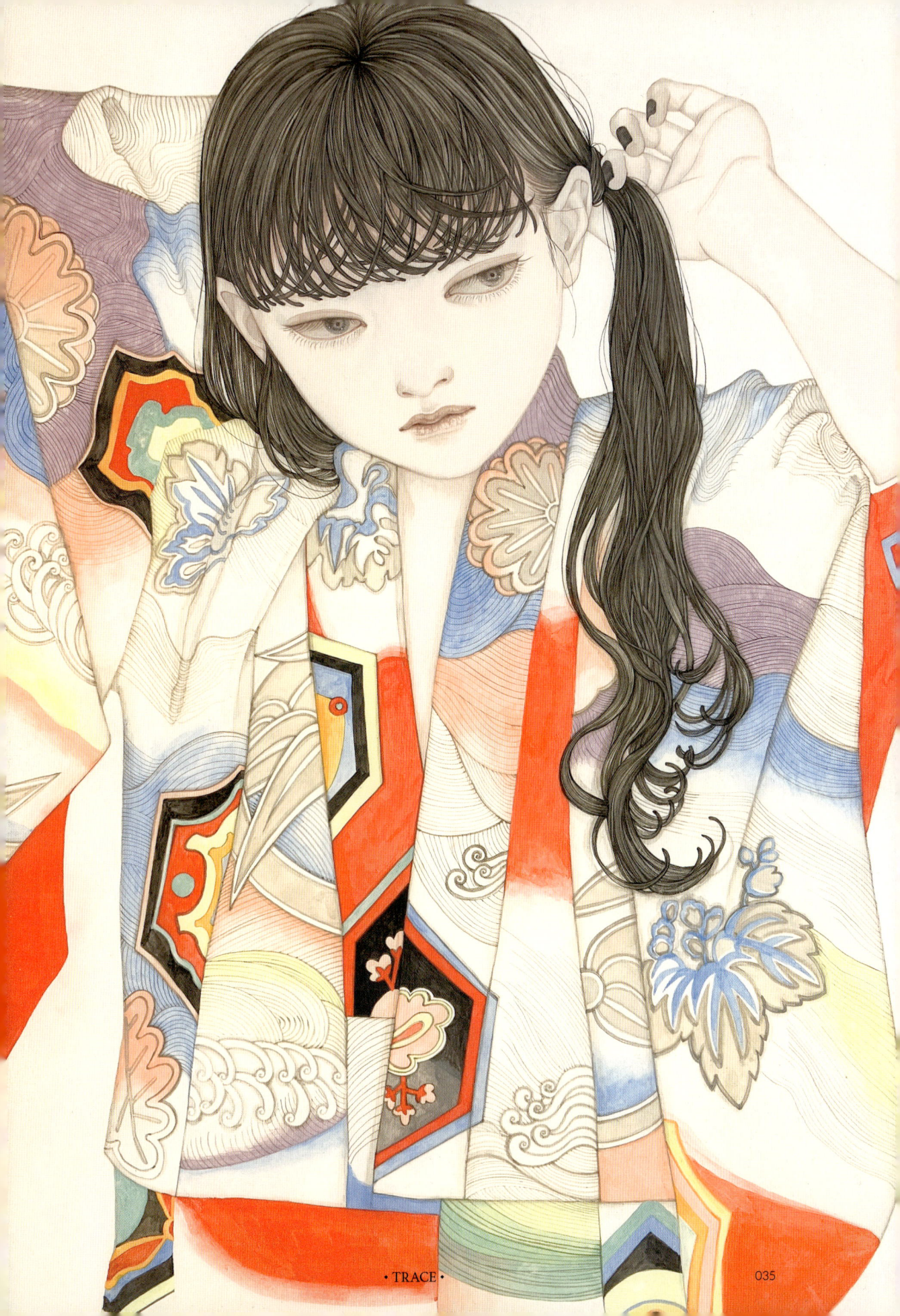

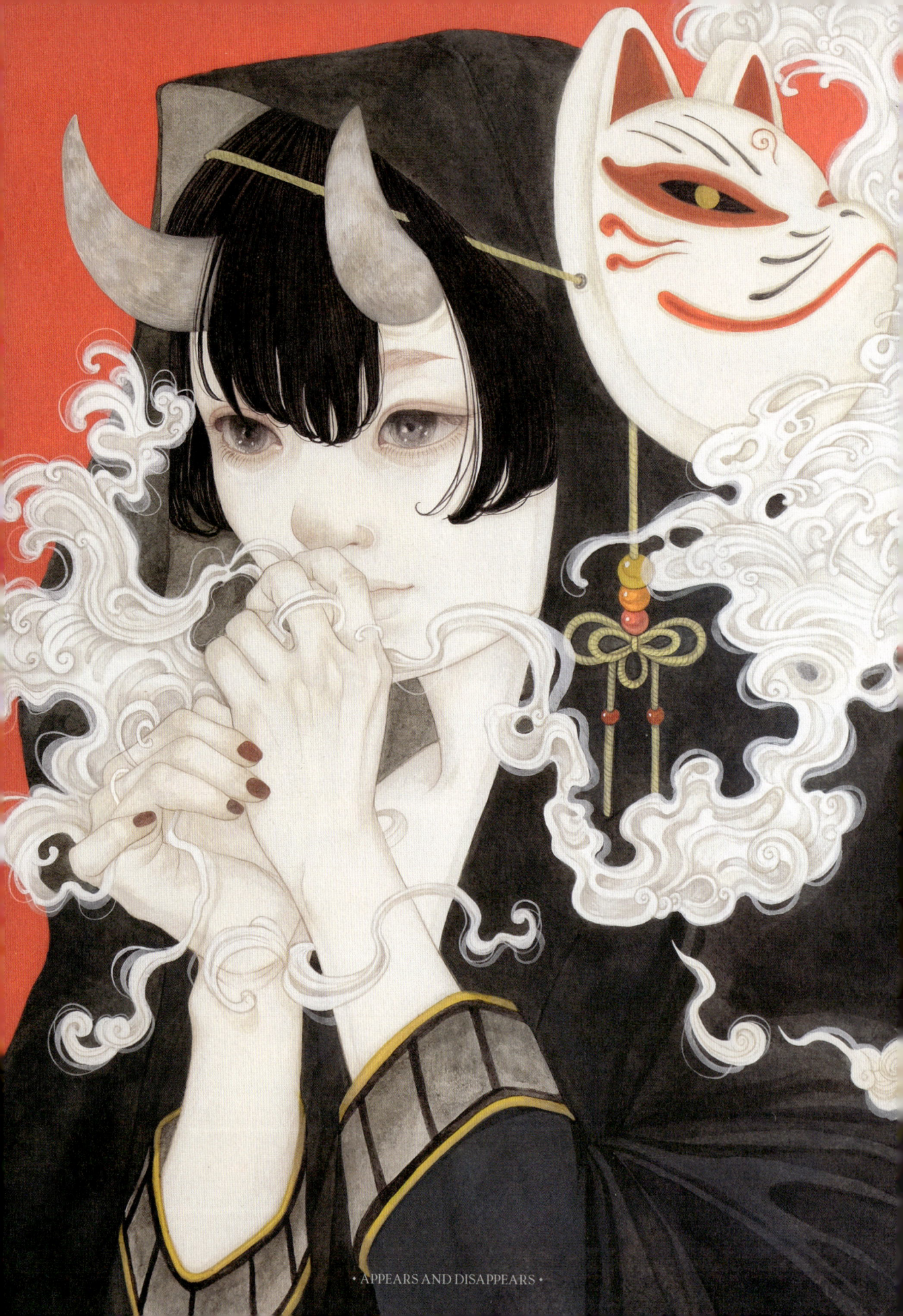

APPEARS AND DISAPPEARS

Q: Can you say something about why you choose pale girls as your creation main character?

SY: Ever since women have been depicted as a motif in Japanese style painting, their skin has been painted white like clouds in a blue sky on a sunny day, or snow piled up on the ground. In my work, the girl is my motif of choice as a symbol of innocence. Therefore, the girl's translucent white skin is indispensable.

Q: How do you think the traits of femininity play a role in your paintings? How do you incorporate these traits into your creations?

SY: The symbol of femininity is hair. Long, beautifully grown hair provides a wide variety of compositional options. And it also helps to show off the beauty of the lines drawn with a brush.

Q: Your major is Japanese painting and you keep exploring it. How has your university's course provided help with your creation?

SY: It takes a great deal of time and experience to become proficient in the use of Japanese-style painting materials. I learned about those basics in college. However, many unexpected things happen while I am still creating. I believe that enjoying those coincidences is also important in the creation of Japanese-style paintings.

Q: In your works, you often use traditional Japanese painting mediums such as crushed mineral pigments and Japanese ink. How do you apply these mediums to express your artwork?

SY: Both *iwa-enogu* (mineral pigment) and *sumi* (black) ink have very beautiful colors of their own. Therefore, I do not mix colors so much. I enjoy the depth of the colors created by layering the colors of the paints themselves.

Q: Your works were represented by galleries from Tokyo, Portland, and Los Angeles. Have you had different experiences in those various collaborations?

SY: It is a strange feeling to have my works accepted in a place I have never visited. Western artists have a sense of color and composition that I don't have. By standing side by side with these artists, I discover new good points about my works. The most moving thing about exhibiting my works overseas is that I am reminded that the sense of beauty in painting is the same all over the world.

Q: Which artist inspired you most?

SY: I entered the world of Japanese-style painting because of my admiration for Gyosyu Hayam. More recently, I rediscovered the greatness of Kaburaki Kiyokata. And my eternal charisma, modern illustrators Yoshitaka Amano and Takato Yamamoto.

Q: Many of your works are named after emotional and poetic titles. What is the basis for these titles?

SY: The titles of my works are words I would like to say to the girl in my paintings: acceptance, cuddling, and a quiet push on the back. Those are also the words I want.

Q: In your works, you depict "a girl who descends with the hope of the near future." What is the inspiration behind this theme? What message or emotion do you hope to convey to the people through this concept?

SY: I had always painted on the theme of negative emotions. But that all changed after the COVID-19 pandemic. I realized that paintings need to be a source of hope in an uncertain world. I do not aim to create works that emit strong energy. If I can bring a feeling

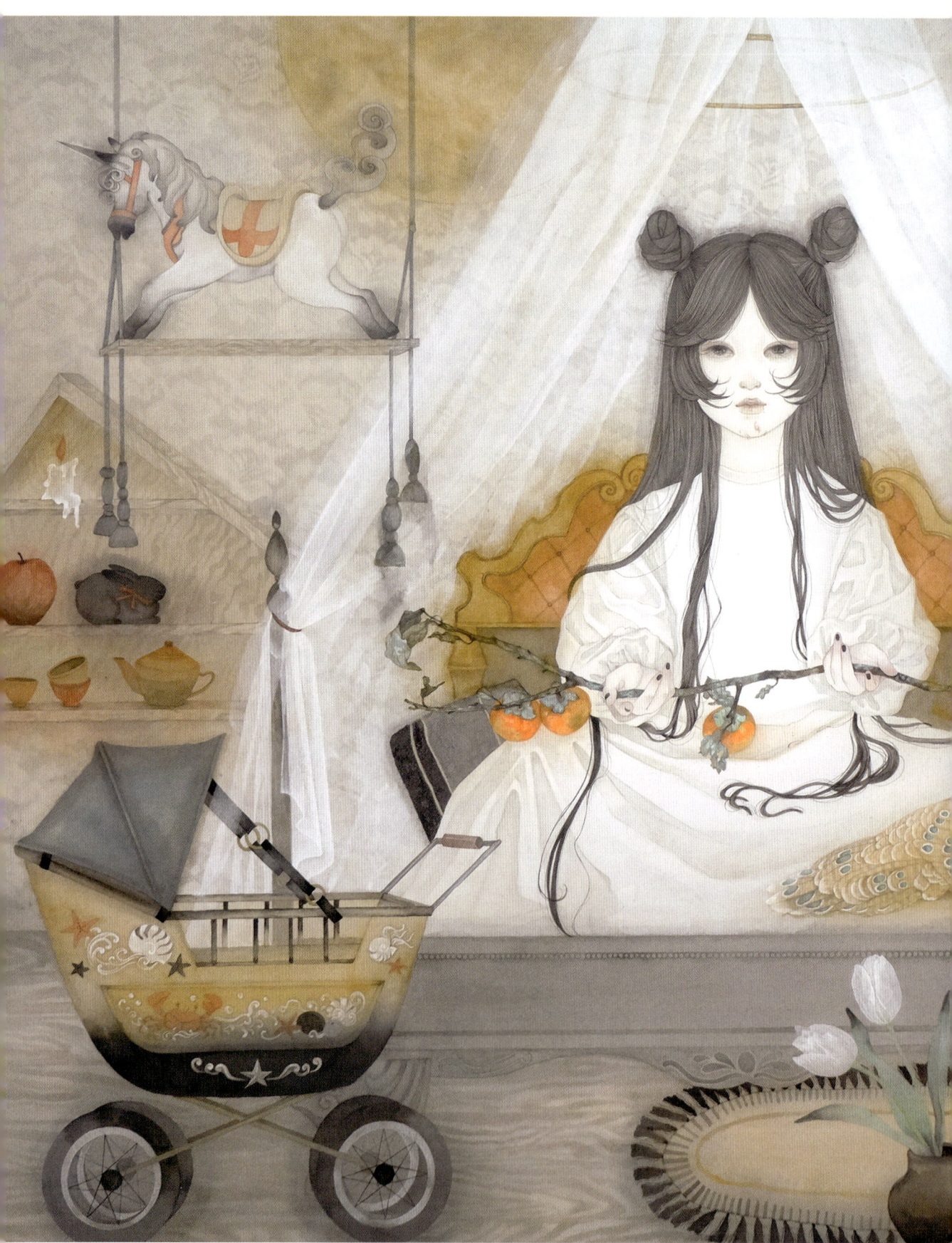

• DREAM THAT IS UNDERMINED •

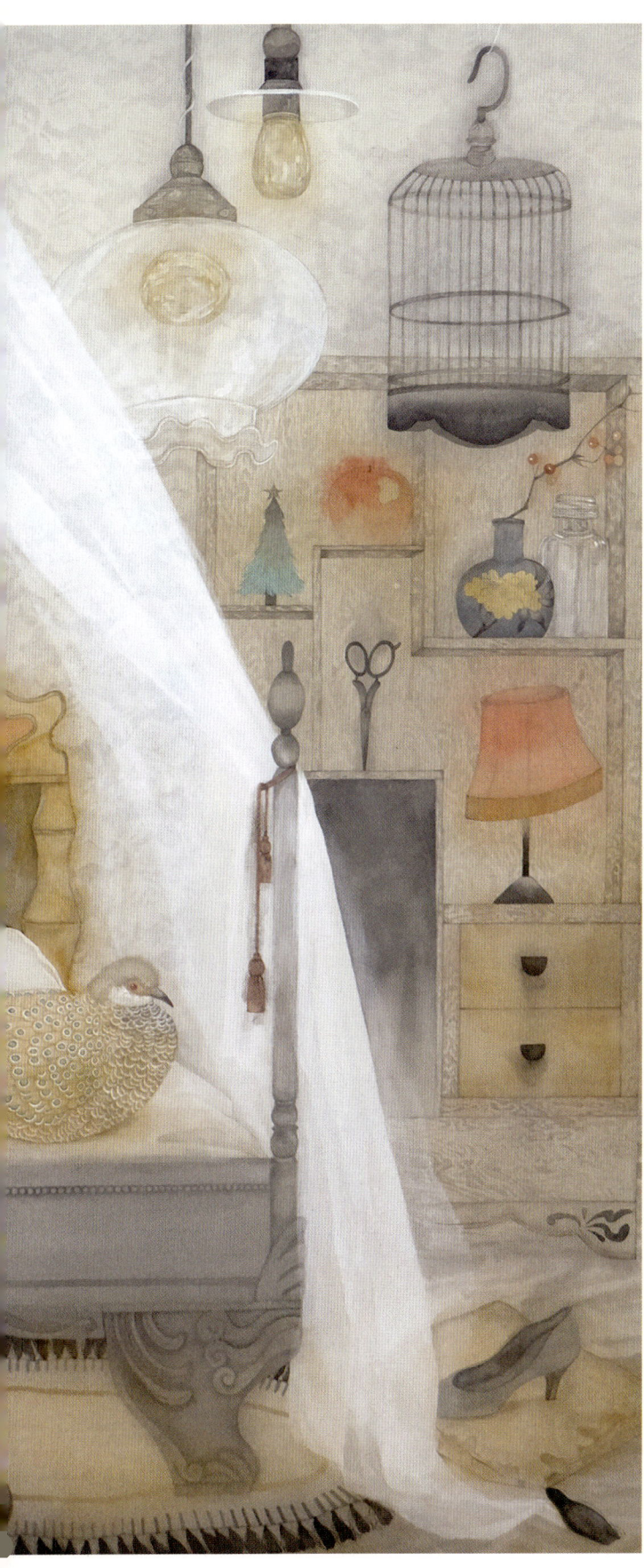

of closeness and a little bit of forward motion, my goal is achieved.

Q: You have a large following on social media. What do you think is the significance of artists showcasing their works on social media? How do you engage with your audience through social media?

SY: As long as you are creating a work of art, the desire to have many people see it is very natural. I do not actively interact on social networking sites. It is enough if the social networking site is a place to see my works, not to get to know me.

Q: What are your plans or expectations for future creations? What concepts do you hope to explore or express in your upcoming works?

SY: The genre of my work is what I call Japanese-style painting. It is a wonderful culture with a context that symbolizes Japan. However, the image that people outside of Japan have of Japanese painting as ukiyo-e has not yet been dispelled. Even after ukiyo-e, there have been many wonderful Japanese paintings created in Japan. I hope that my works will be an opportunity for people to learn about them.

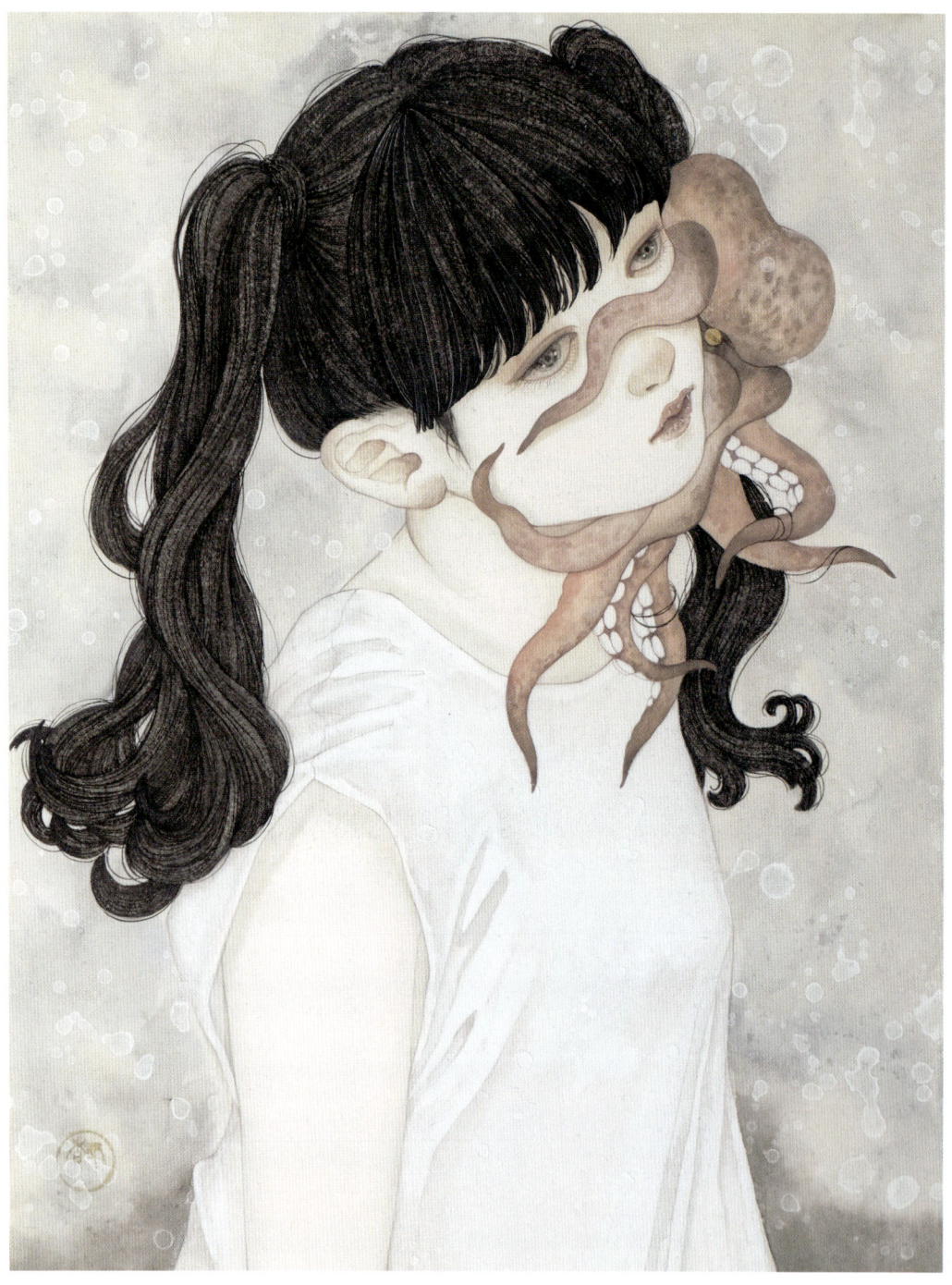

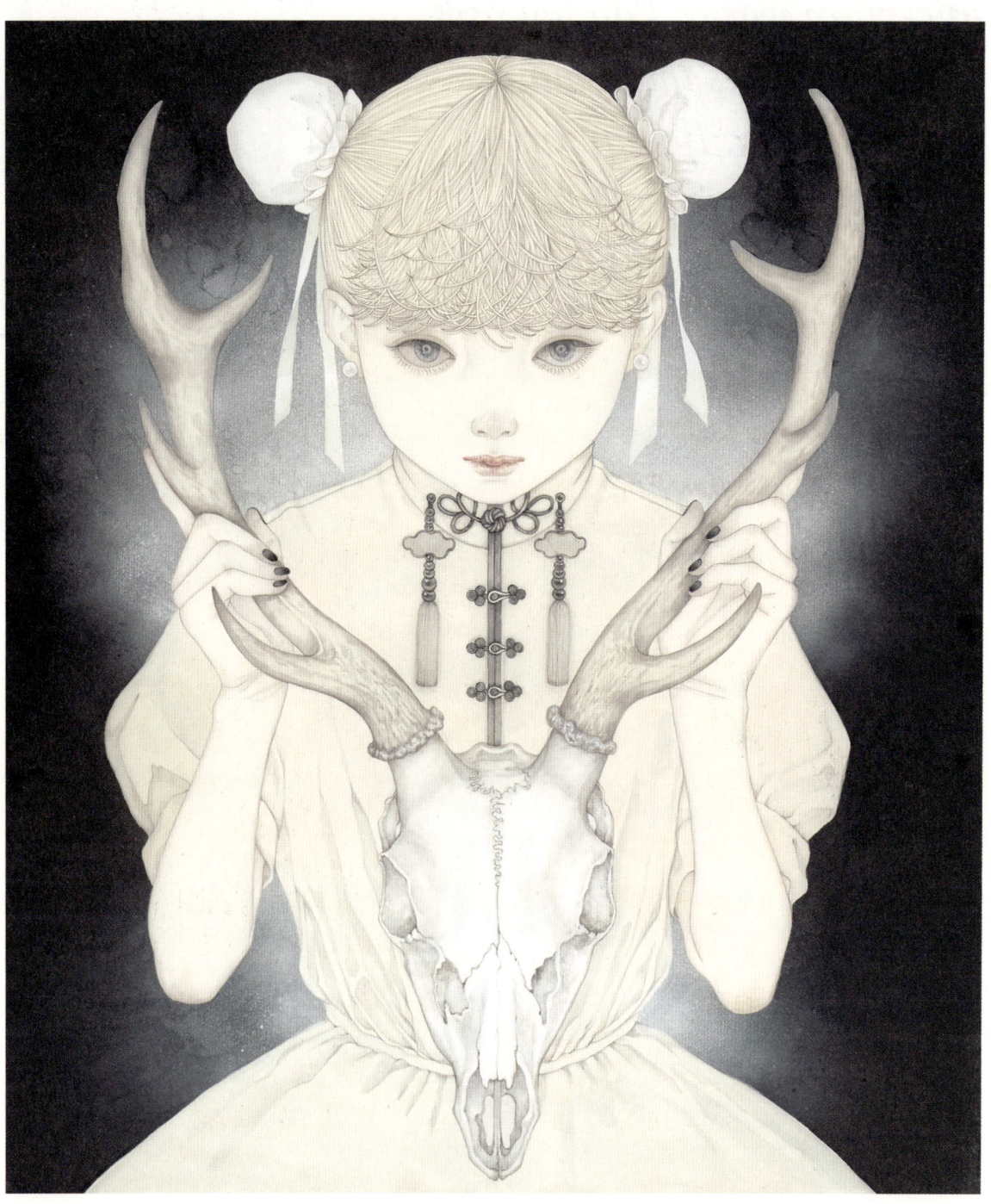

" *I realized that paintings
need to be a source of hope in an
uncertain world. I do not aim
to create works that emit
strong energy. If I can bring
a feeling of closeness and a
little bit of forward motion,
my goal is achieved.* "

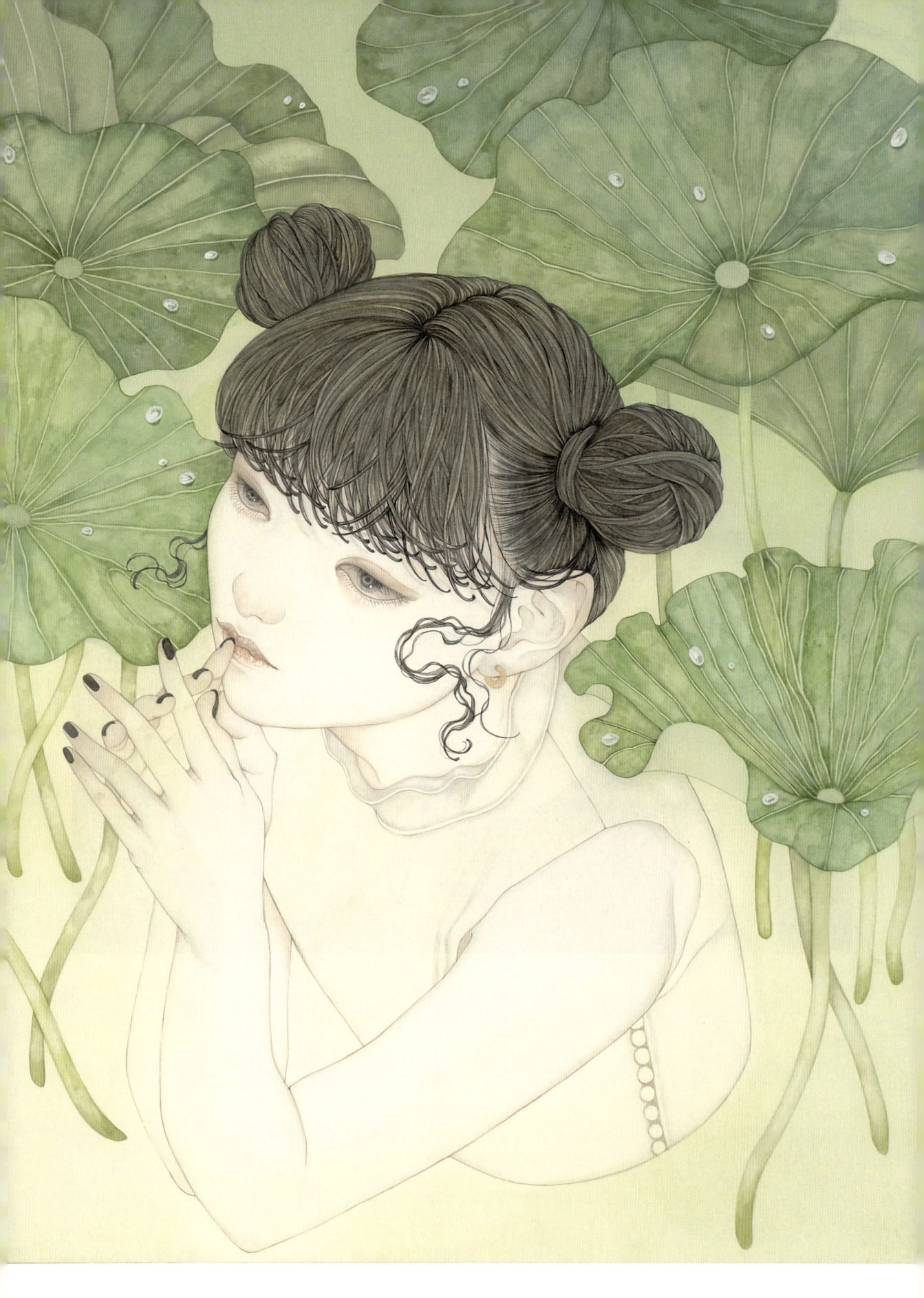

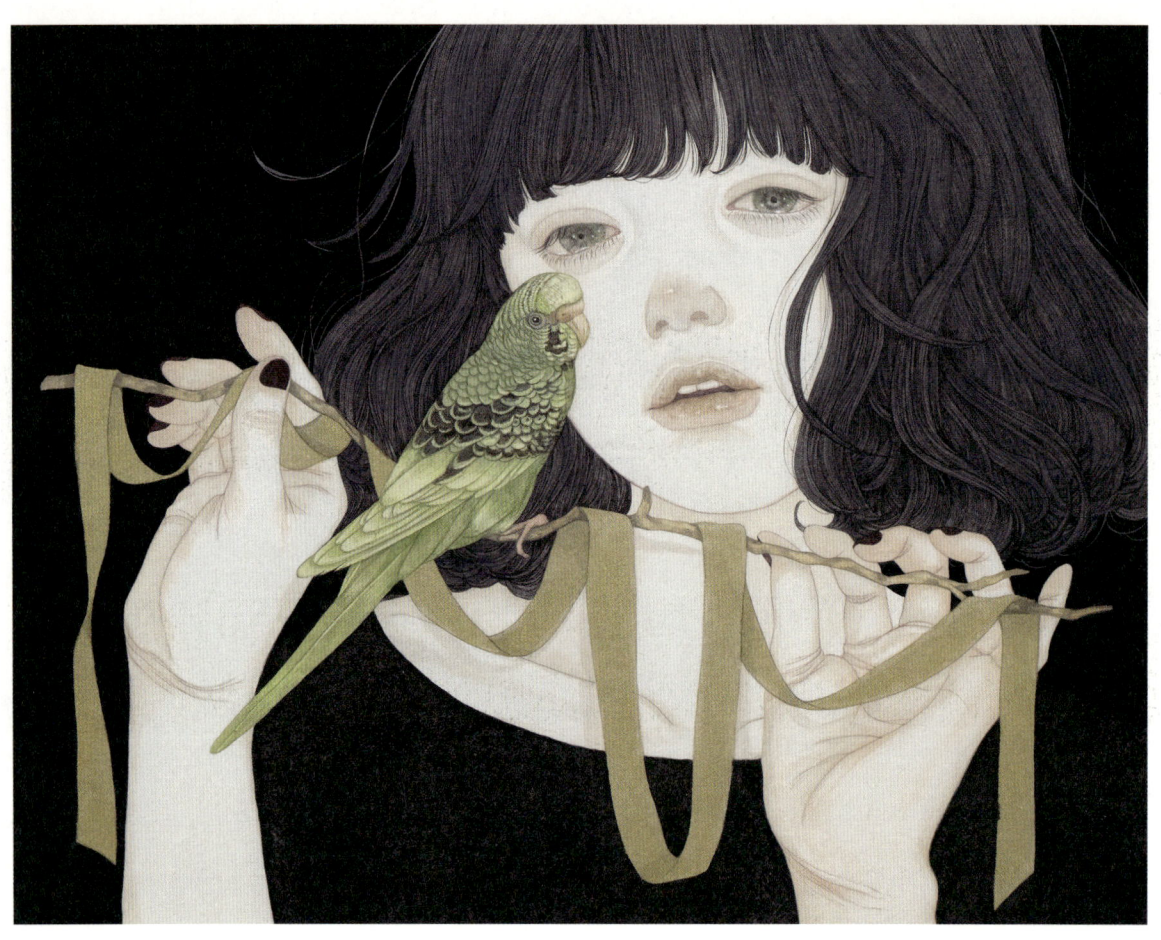

• LAST FLIGHT •

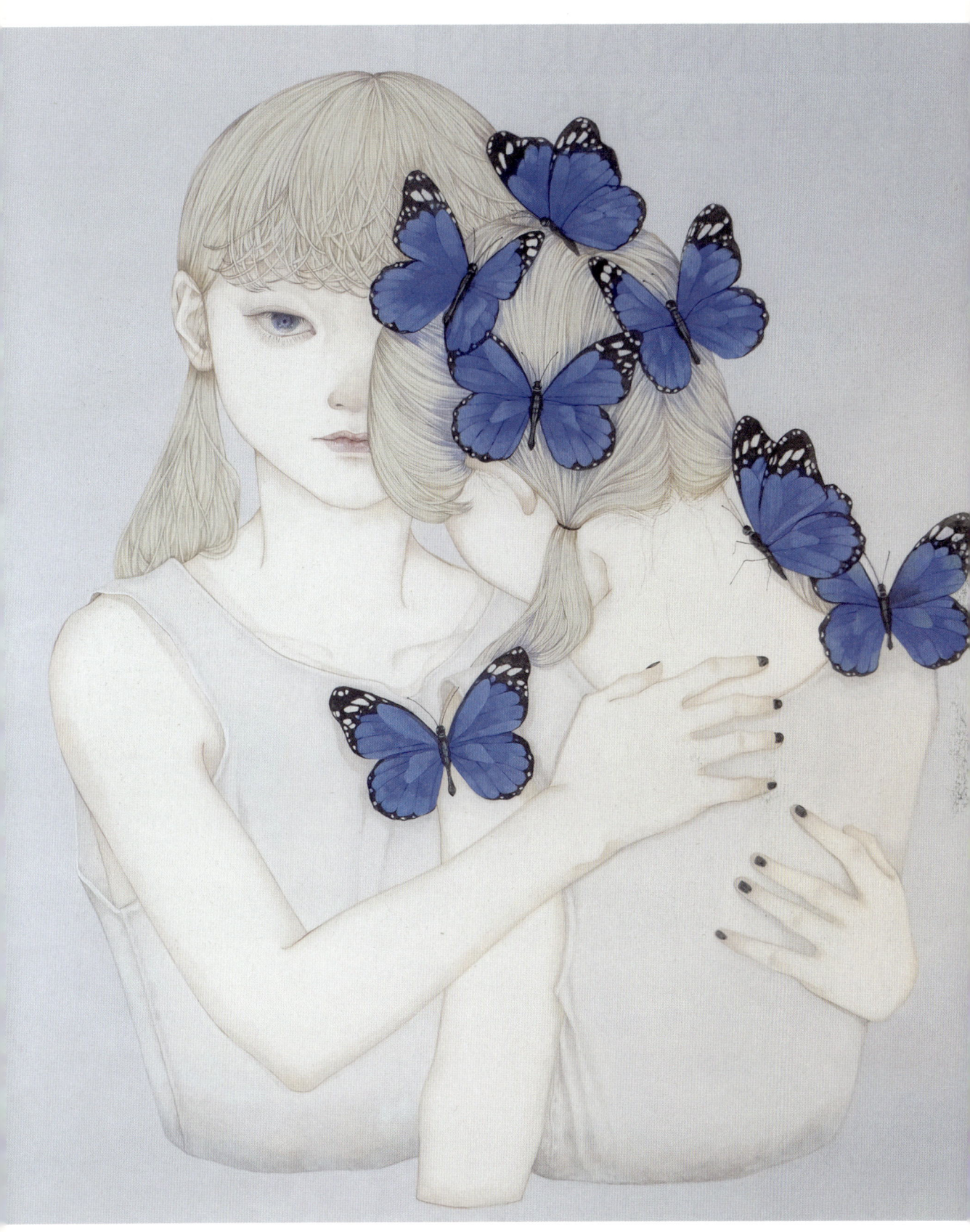

TRANSPARENT FANTASIES

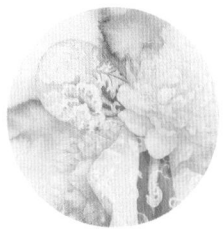

Syuka

As an illustrator and painter, she started
activities around 2010. Using watercolors, she
depicts a world between reality and fiction.

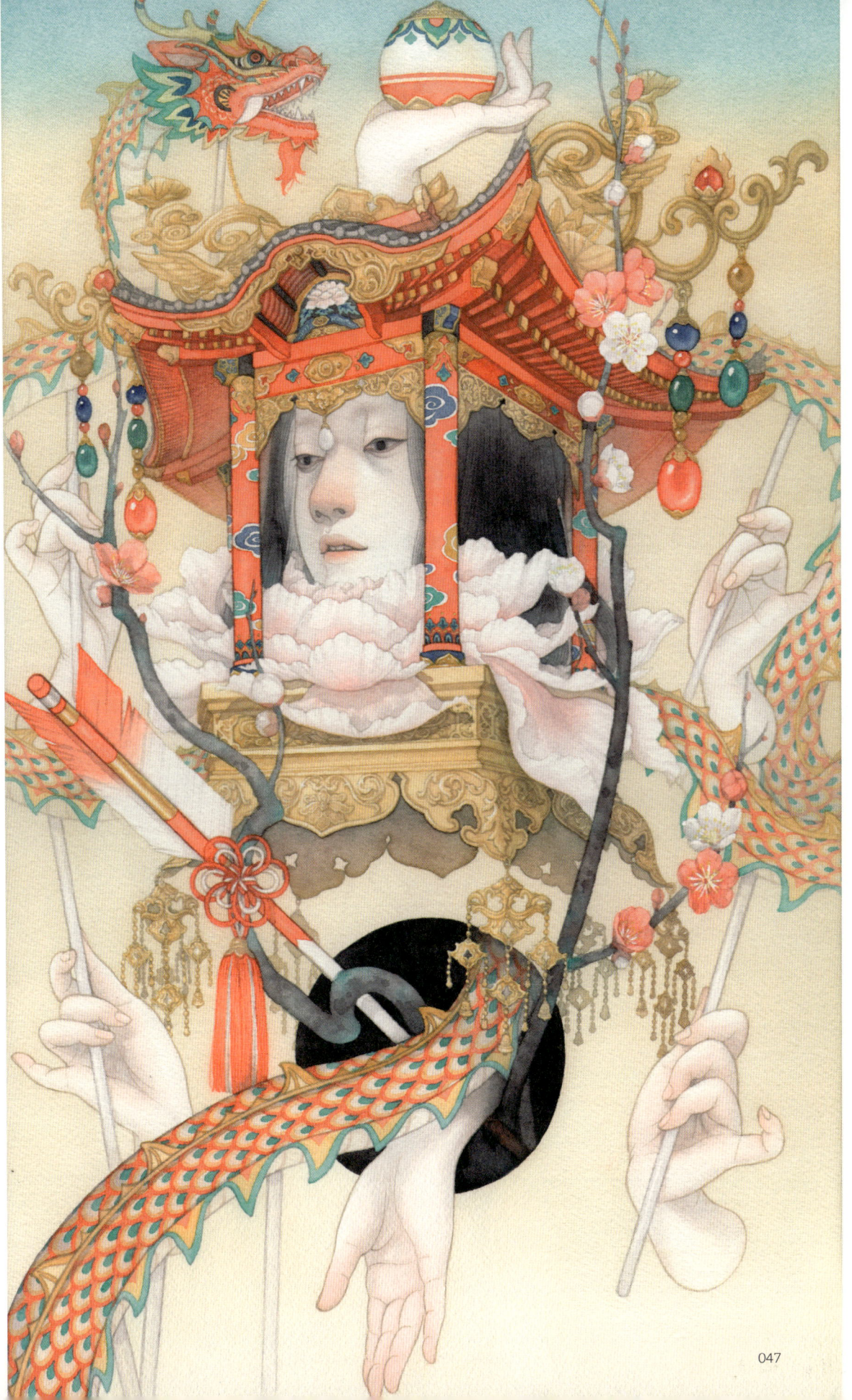

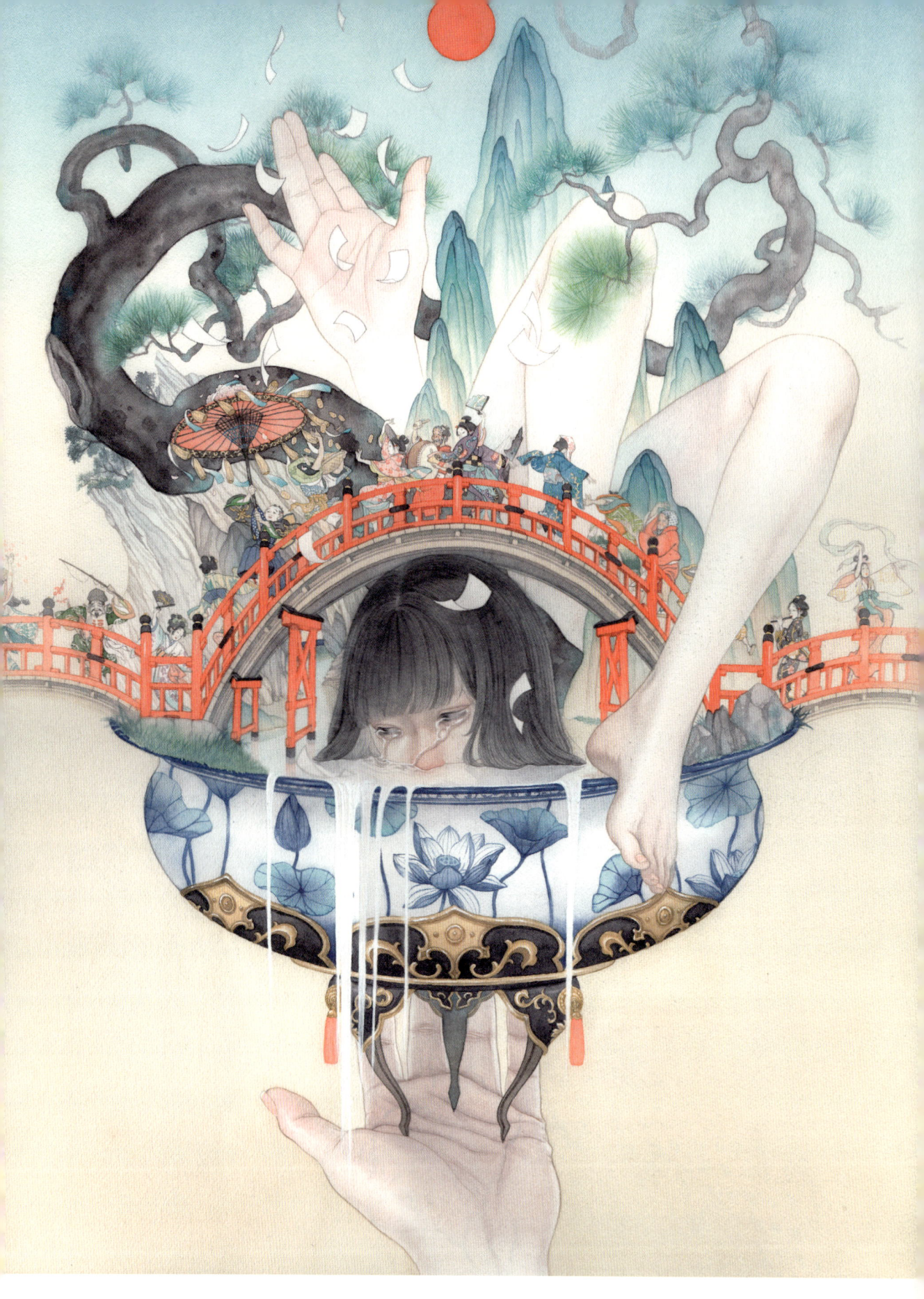

• DREAMING GARDEN-THIS TRANSITORY WORLD •

Q: How did you get started in art? What inspired you to start working with transparent watercolors?

SYUKA: I have loved drawing since I was a child, and I continue to draw as an extension of that.

I originally started with CG, but I started drawing in analog because I was worried about my eyes getting tired.

I started using transparent watercolors after my sister gave me one that she no longer used.

Q: Your works often depict worlds and characters between fiction and reality. Is there any special meaning or story behind the choice of this theme?

SYUKA: I developed a love for fantasy through manga and games and began drawing pictures that expressed my longing for a world far away from reality, somewhere other than here.

Afterwards, as I continued to exhibit, I began to draw pictures that not only contained fantasy, but also included more personal details, and I think my current style has developed.

Q: How do you utilize the unique rendering effects of watercolor in your works? What do you think this technique brings to your work that is special?

SYUKA: I like the transparency of watercolors and often use soft gradations. The patterns created by the bleeding of the paint are also very beautiful and create a fantastic atmosphere.

Lately, I've been intentionally using gouache to maintain different textures. And I've been using glittery colors to make it more enjoyable to look at an actual painting.

Q: How do you find inspiration for your creations? Are there specific environments or mindsets that best stimulate your creative inspiration?

SYUKA: I draw while incorporating my own emotions and experiences, incorporating places I want to go to and things I find beautiful.

I sometimes get inspiration from novels and movies. It is also very stimulating to see the works of various people in museums and galleries.

Q: Your paintings incorporate many elements of Japanese tradition. Could you share how Japanese culture influences your work?

SYUKA: I don't really think about it, but I think the things I've seen since I was a child have a big influence on me. I love Japanese paintings, and depending on the work, I am influenced by the use of space and deformation. Lately, I've been interested in *karesansui* (Japanese dry garden), *bonsai* (tray planting), and *ikebana* (way of flowers), and I'd like to incorporate them into my work.

Q: Your extensive experience with solo and group exhibitions hold importance in your artistic journey. How do you perceive these exhibitions shaping your career? What are your thoughts about the importance of exhibitions and other showcases for artists in general?

SYUKA: I want to deliver my work to as many people as possible, so I hold exhibitions.

A group exhibition opens up a new world with a different theme than usual, and a solo exhibition is an opportunity to reconsider the world I want to depict, and at the same time, I think it is a place where I can explore the world of my work more deeply.

Q: What kind of reactions have your works received from audiences during exhibitions? Have there been any particularly profound exchanges or feedback that influenced your creative process?

SYUKA: I'm very happy to be able to go to the place where my work is exhibited and have people intuitively look at the original drawings, and it's also encouraging to hear people's impressions directly.

Q: Apart from painting, what are your other daily interests and hobbies?

SYUKA: Since I usually draw women, I have started looking at fashion photos a lot because I want to incorporate various fashions. I also draw patterns a lot, so I'm also interested in textiles.

Recently, I like sewing and knitting, and I enjoy working with my hands without thinking about anything.

Q: Could you give some advice or encouragement to those who want to try watercolor?

SYUKA: I think watercolor is an art medium that is easy to get started with even for beginners, so I think you can enjoy painting without worries. I would be happy if more people would experience the beauty of paint spreading in water and start taking watercolor painting seriously.

Q: Are there any upcoming projects or plans? What are your expectations for your future creations?

SYUKA: While continuing to hold exhibitions, I would like to expand the range of my activities so that my works can reach more people.

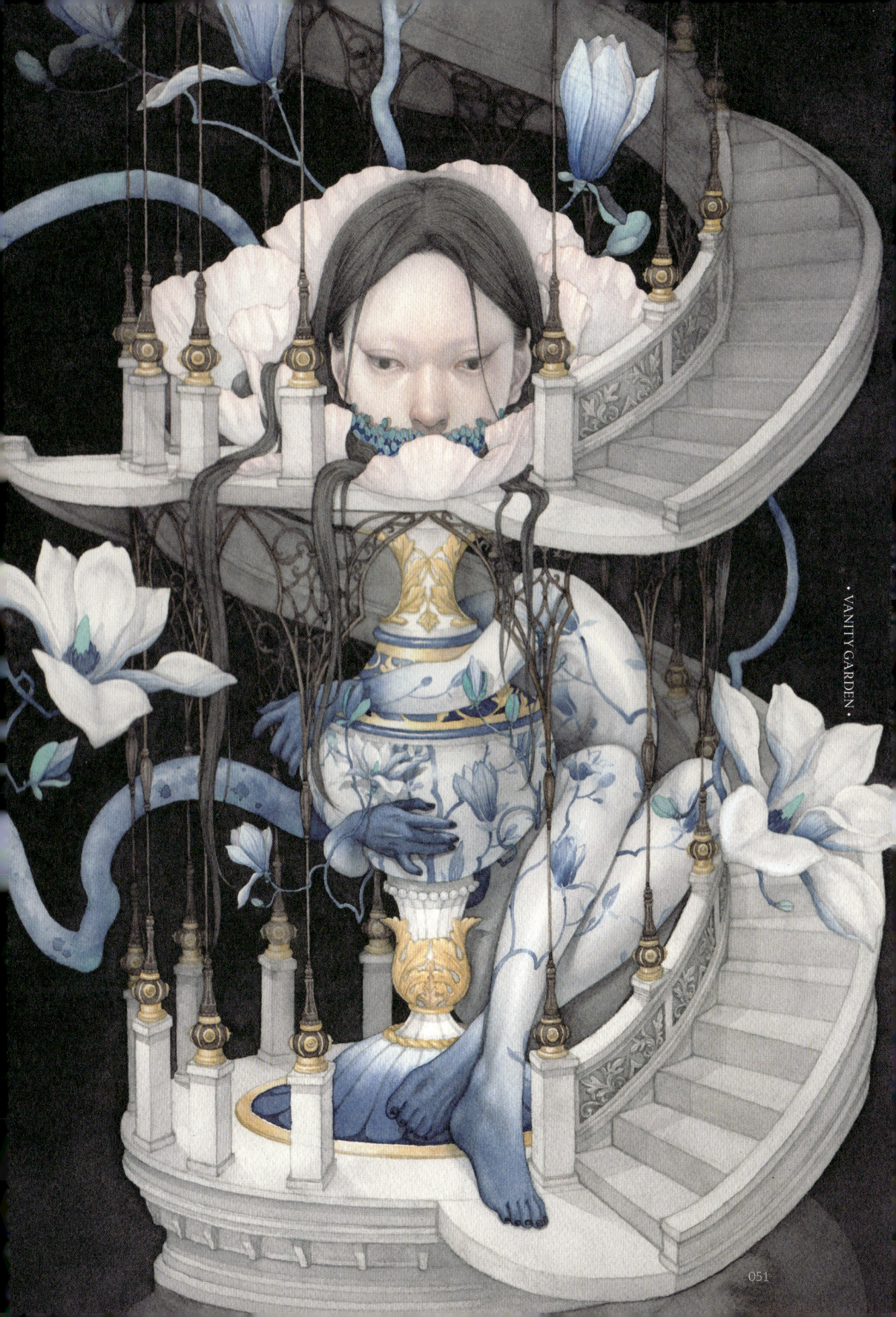

· VANITY GARDEN ·

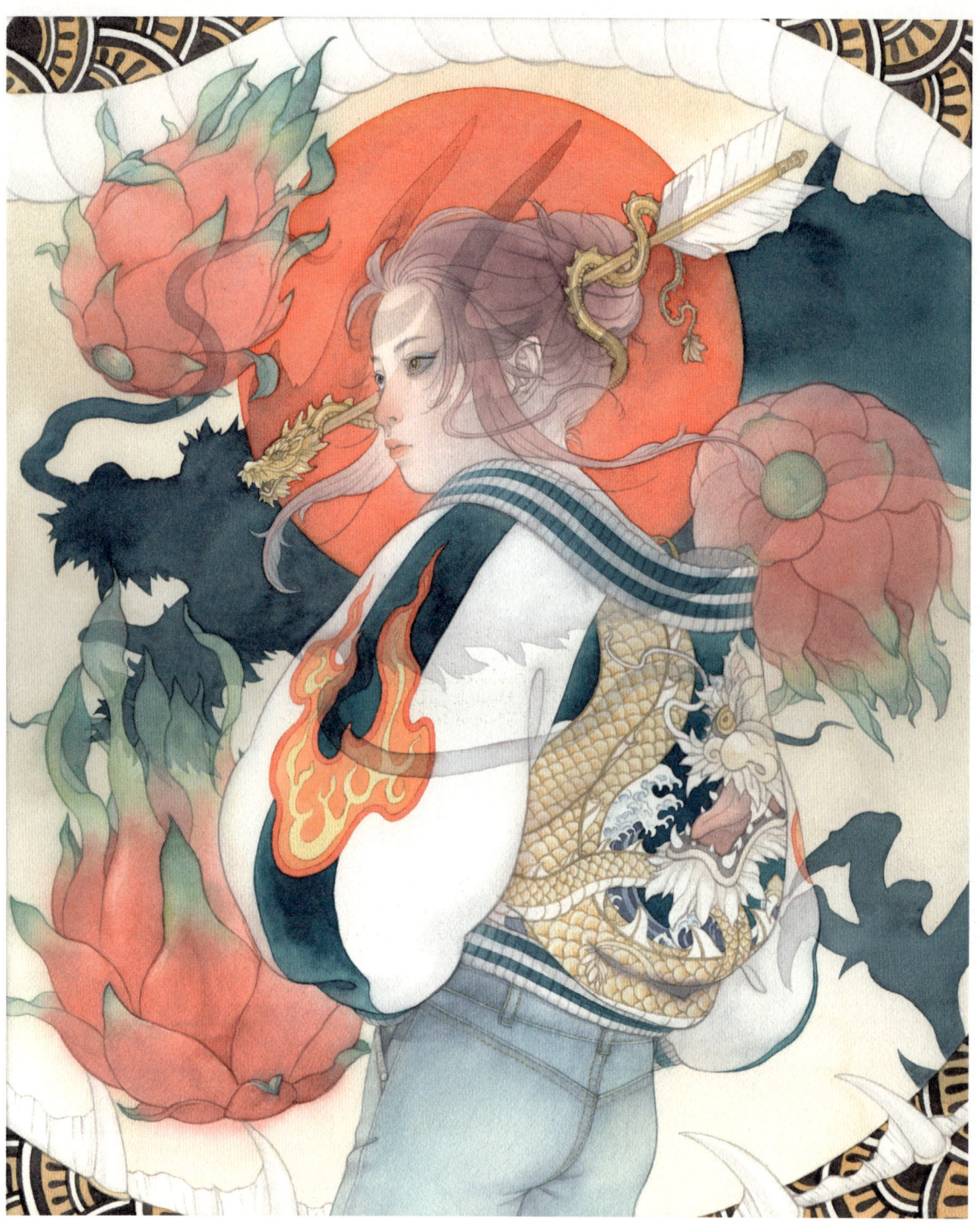

• DRAGON GIRL •

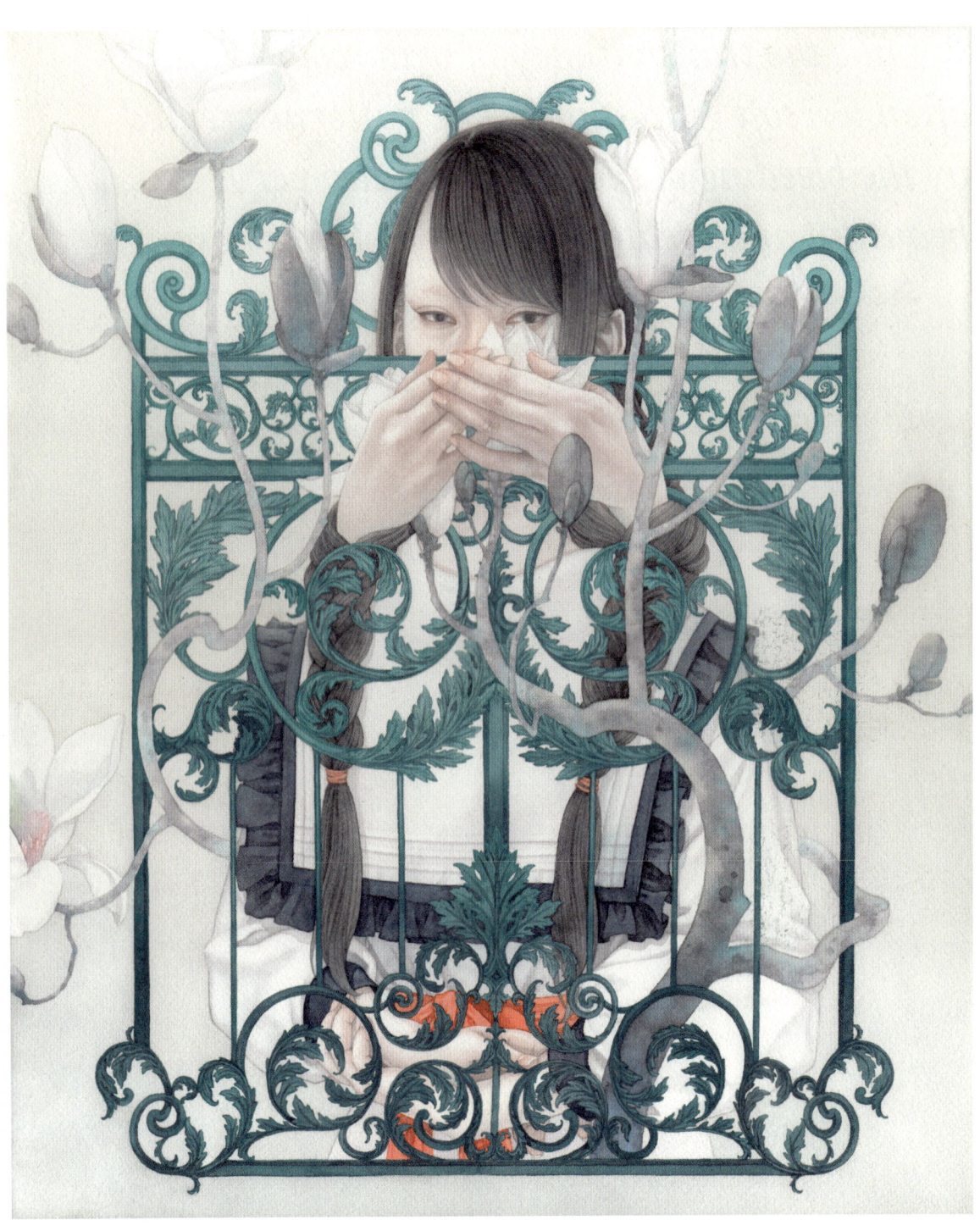

" *I like the transparency of watercolors and often use soft gradations. The patterns created by the bleeding of the paint are also very beautiful and create a fantastic atmosphere.* "

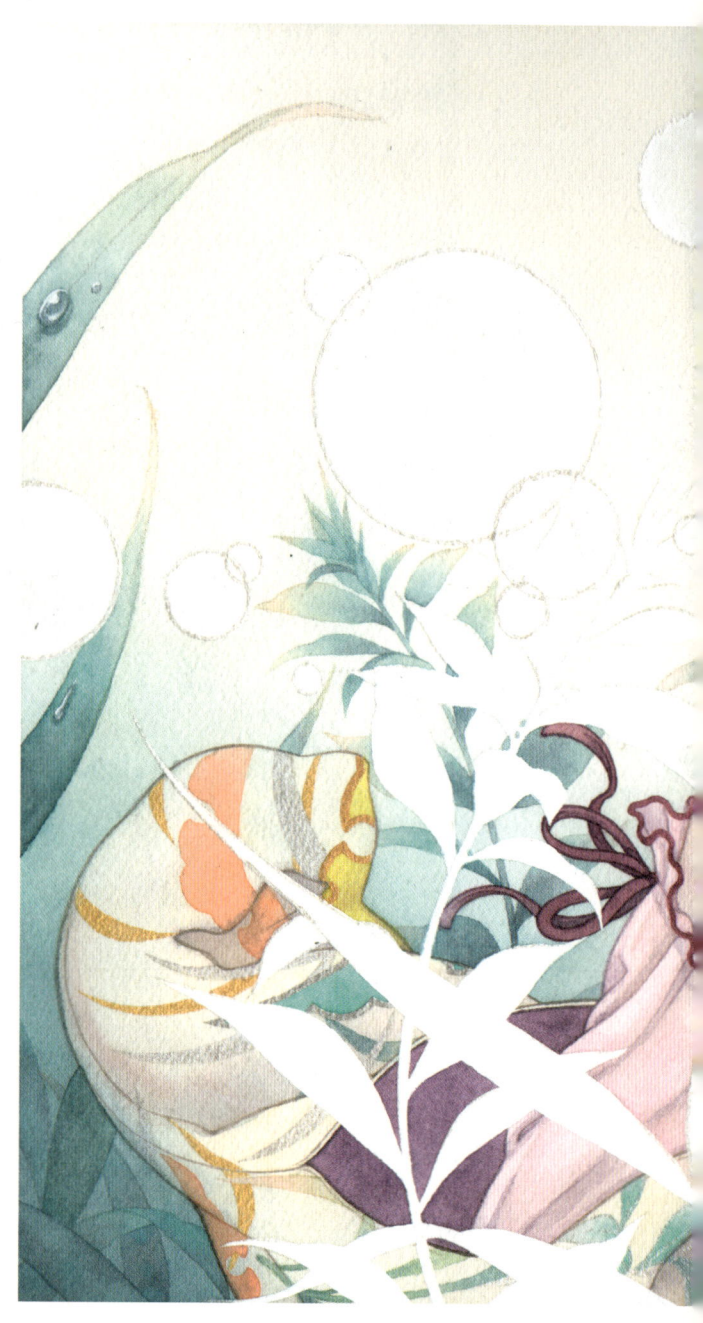

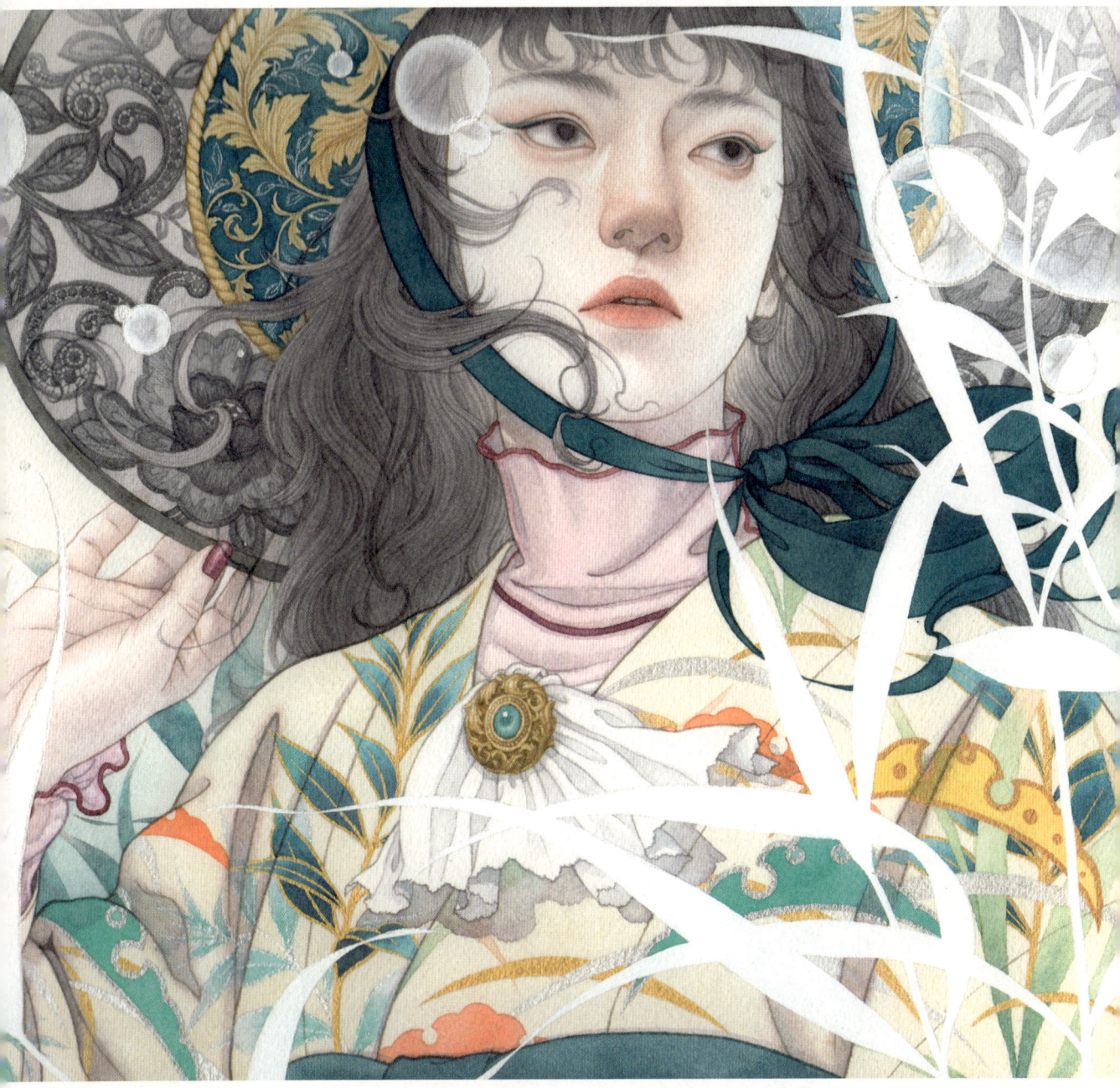

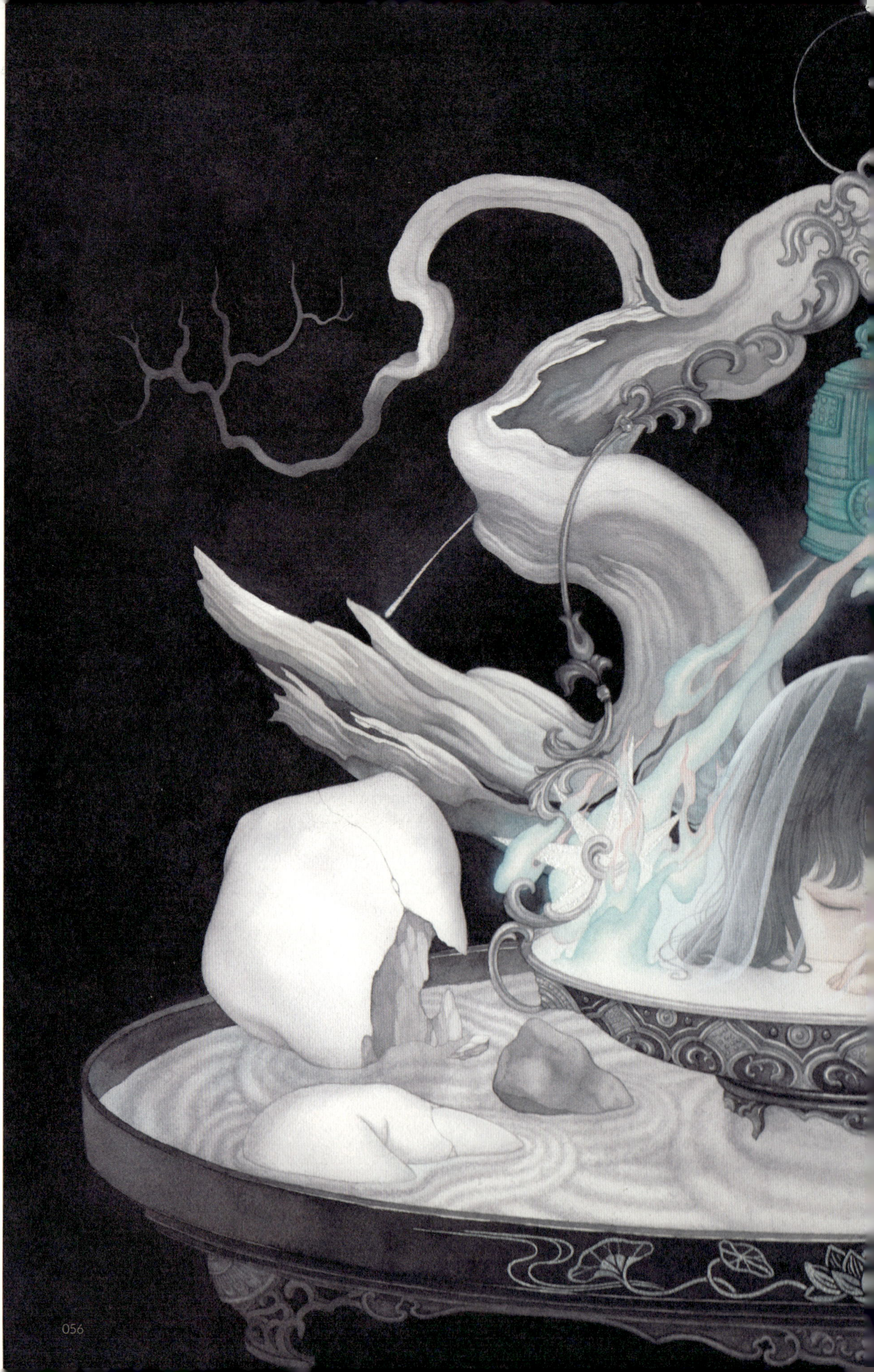

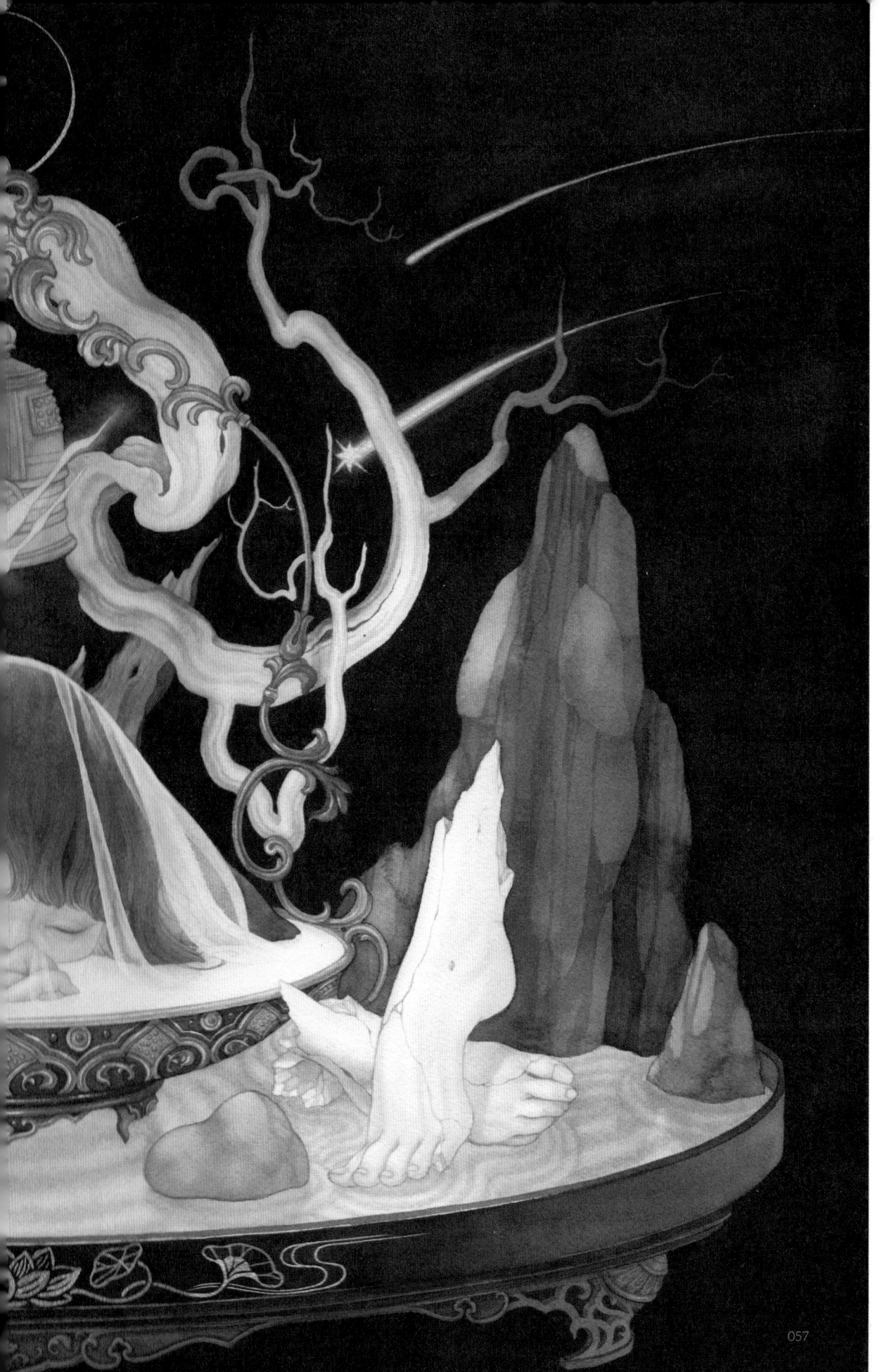

FORBIDDEN AESTHETICISM

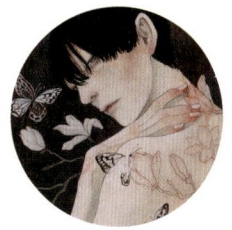

Mari Shimazaki

A painter based in Japan. Through the motif of
a young man, Mari Shimazaki depicts things,
landscapes, and words that she is strongly
attracted to.

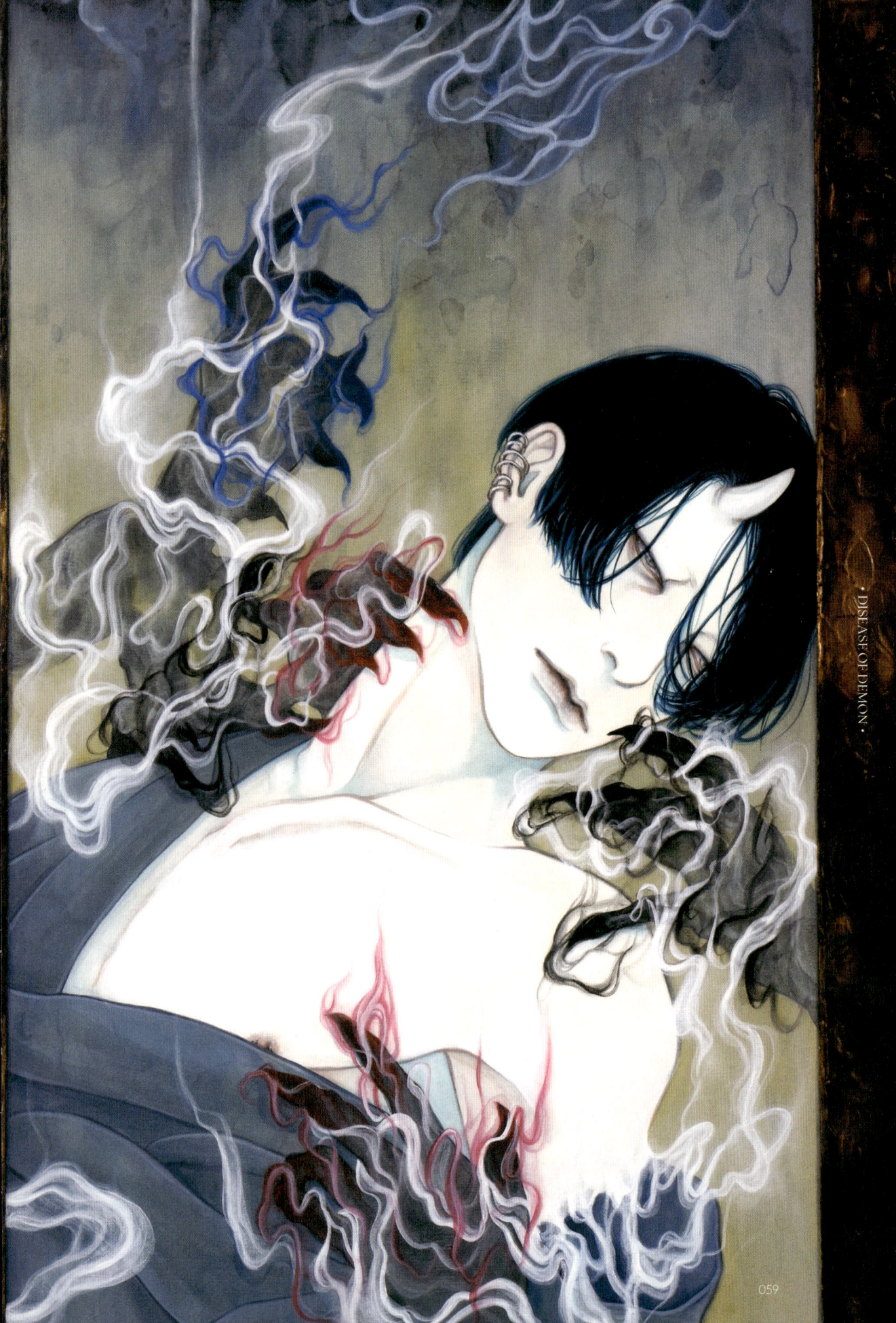

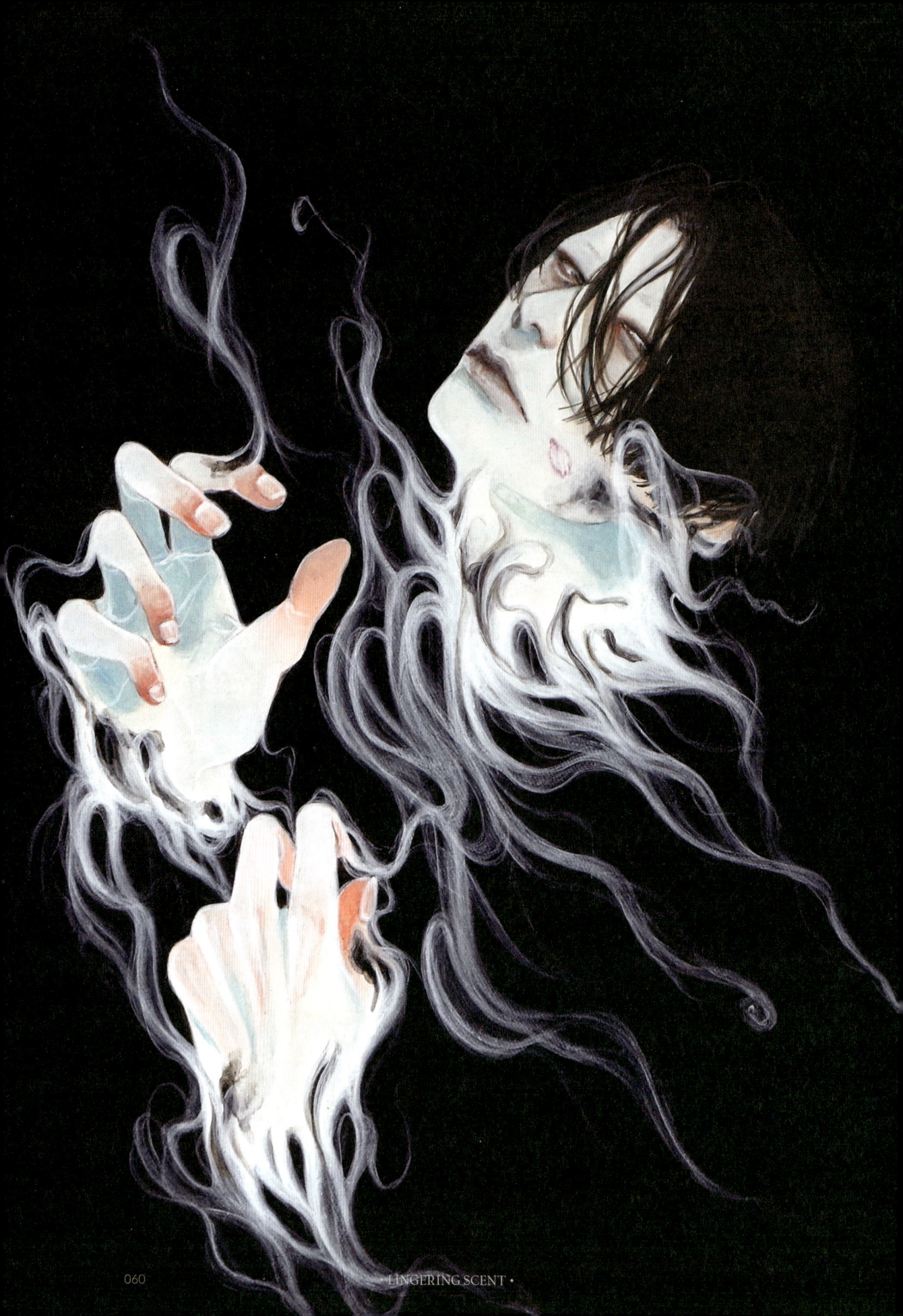

LINGERING SCENT •

Q: Could you tell us about your artistic background? How did you get interested in art?

MS: I've loved drawing since I was a child.

When I was a student, a friend invited me to visit an art museum, which gradually sparked my interest in art.

Q: Your artworks predominantly feature pale skin males with dark hair. Do they hold any particular symbolic or emotional significance? When depicting male illustrations, what emotions do you primarily aim to convey?

MS: The elements of pale skin and dark hair lend themselves to expressing coldness and mystery for me.

I also chose the male motif because I find beauty in the linear form of the skeleton and muscles.

Each work has its own theme or story, but I want the viewer to freely imagine and interpret it from the perspective of the characters, their gestures, and the motifs I have placed in the work.

Q: Acrylic painting serves as your primary medium. Could you elaborate on what makes this medium special for your creative process? Do you typically spend a significant amount of time on each creation?

MS: Since I do not decide on a finished form from the beginning, but rather add or subtract motifs along the way, acrylic paints, which can be easily layered, are the right painting medium for me.

The work depends on the size and other details but is usually completed in about three weeks.

Q: You utilize multiple social media accounts to promote and share updates about your artworks across different platforms. How does interaction and feedback from your audience influence or inspire your creations?

MS: By utilizing multiple social media accounts, you can get a better idea of how your work looks from various perspectives. The interaction with and feedback from the audience is a great motivator for continuing to create.

Q: How do you perceive the impact of AI technology on traditional painting?

MS: I feel that there are still many issues that need to be resolved before AI technology can become one of the catalysts for exploring new forms of expression, but I do not believe that this will diminish the value of painting.

Q: Many of your illustrations are made into products such as postcards, tote bags, and multipurpose cases. How do you manage or coordinate the works with the products?

MS: Except for the artwork collection, the artwork and products are coordinated based on audience requests.

Q: Your artworks evoke a sense of darkness and coldness. Do you have specific color preferences? How do you select colors to convey your thematic elements?

MS: Depending on the theme, light or neutral colors are often chosen so that the artwork does not look too graphic. Blue is a particular favorite color, especially the phthalo turquoise, which is important for expressing the coldness of figures and other objects.

Q: Do you follow a specific workflow or habits during your creative process? Could you share some of your secrets to successful creation?

MS: I always start drawing from the most important part. In my case, I often start painting from the eyes and facial expressions of the person. By completing the most important part, I can keep myself motivated until the end.

Q: How significant do you consider the influence of Japanese culture on your work?

What aspects of Japanese culture do you particularly enjoy?

MS: There are many aspects of Japanese culture that I like, such as kimonos and customs, but I especially like old words and expressions unique to the Japanese language.

It is interesting to note that the same word gives a different impression depending on whether it is written in *kanji* or *hiragana*. I feel that the fact that most of the titles of recent works are in Japanese is also a strong reflection of this influence.

Q: Lastly, what are your future creative plans? Do you intend to continue exploring the themes and styles present in your current works, or do you have new directions and challenges in mind?

MS: I would like to explore in depth the themes and styles in my current work while introducing new things and working with people from different fields to change for the better.

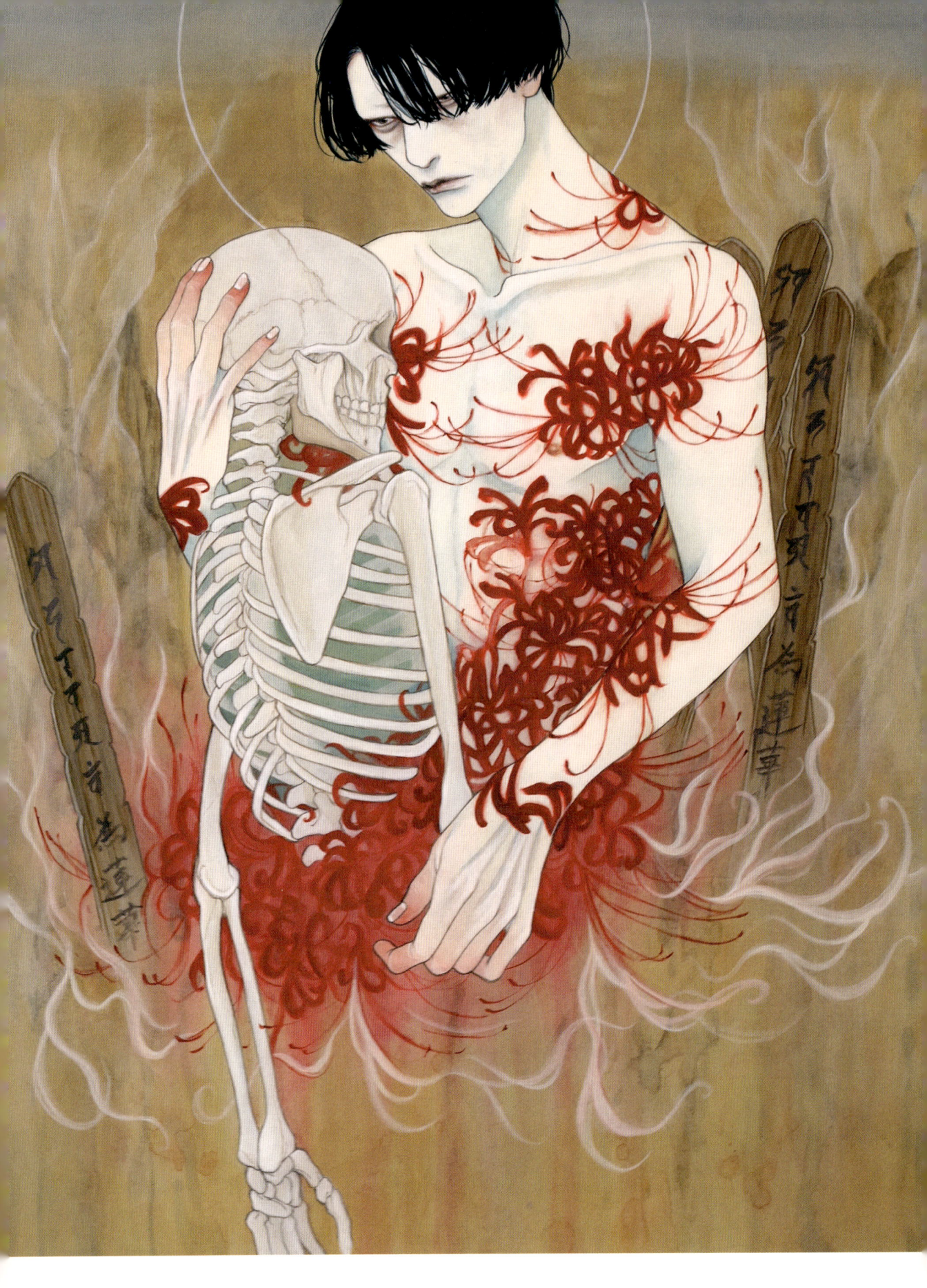

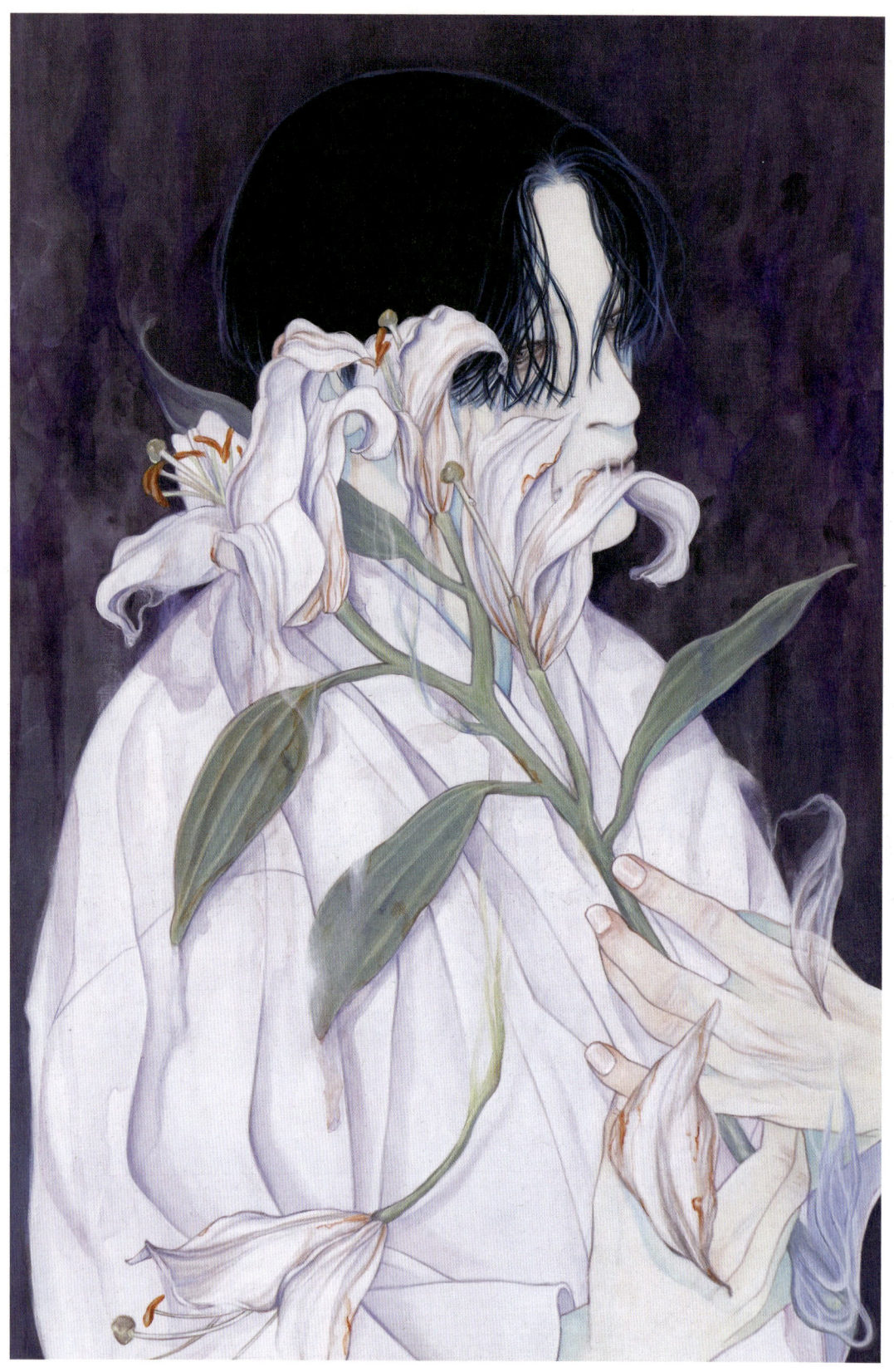

· VOICE ·

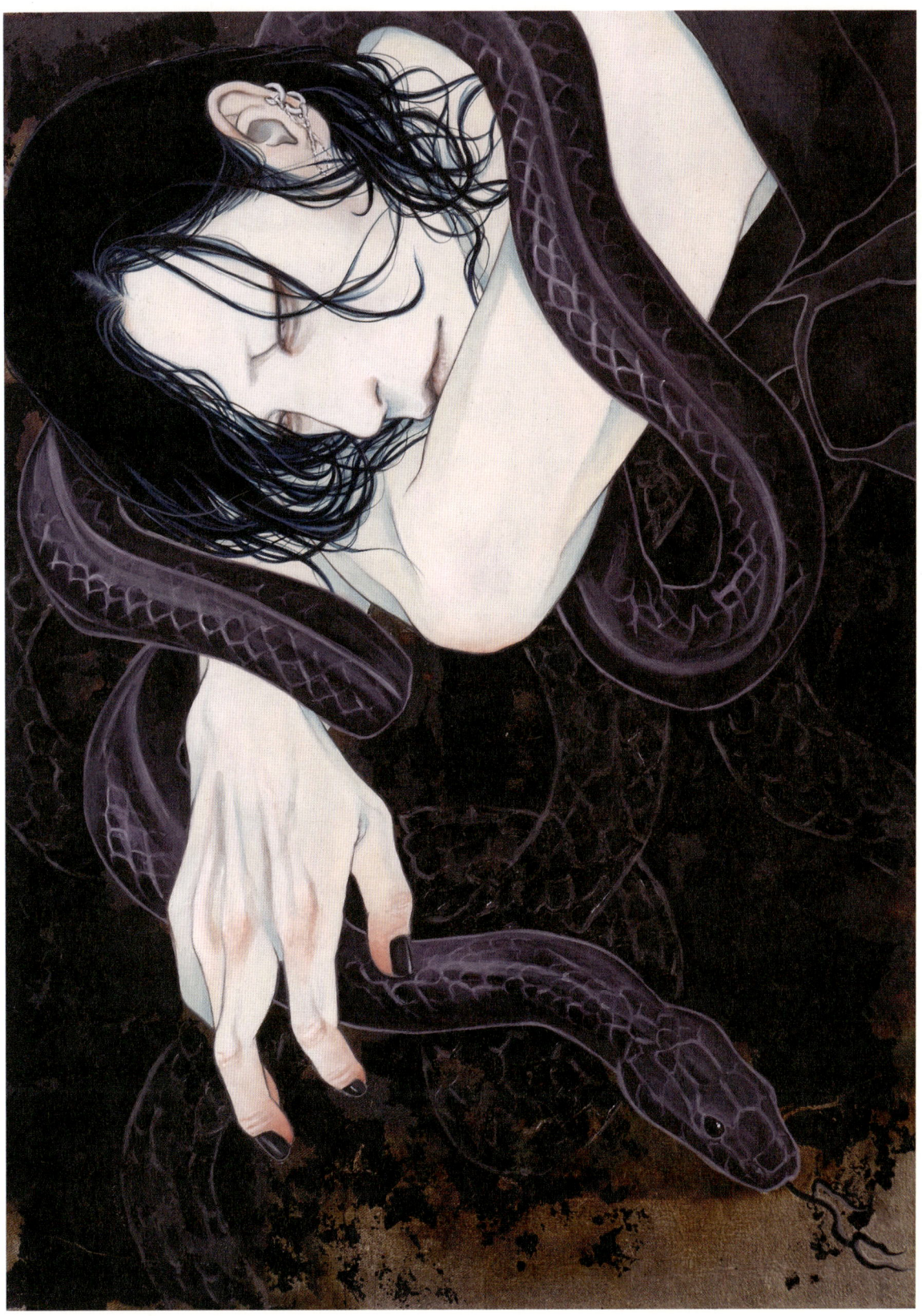

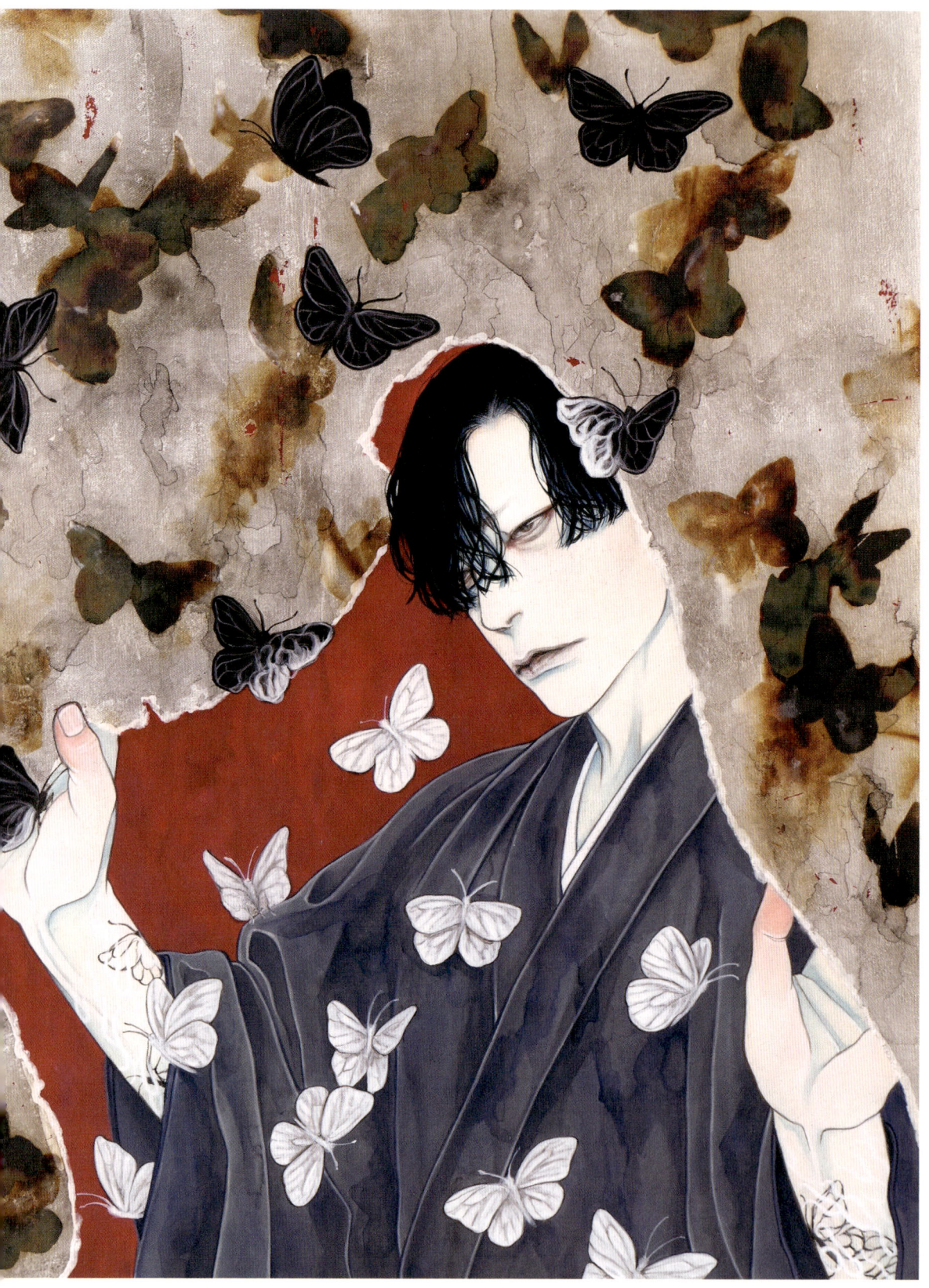

• DANCE IN THE DREAM •

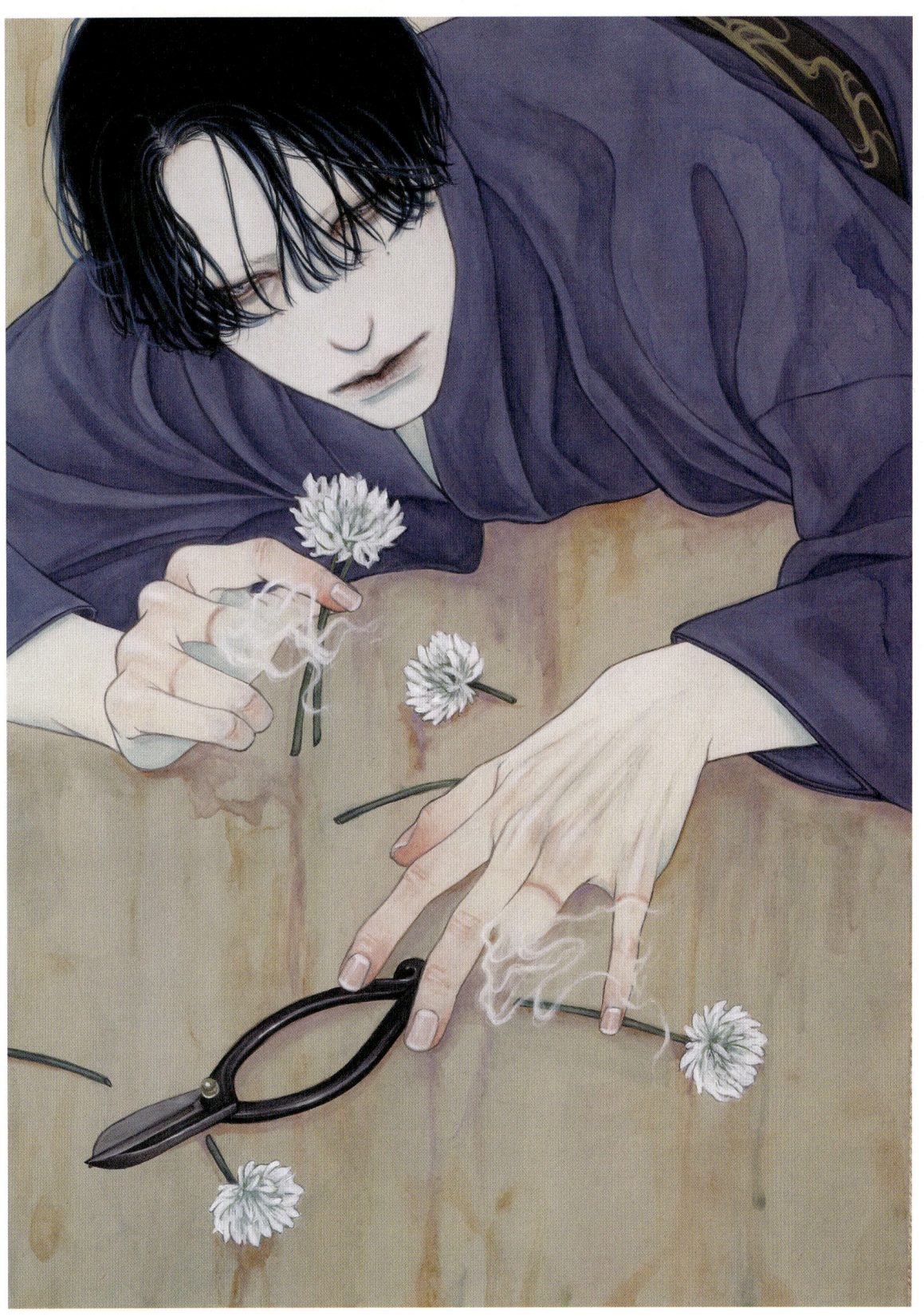

" *The elements of pale skin and dark hair lend themselves to expressing coldness and mystery for me.* "

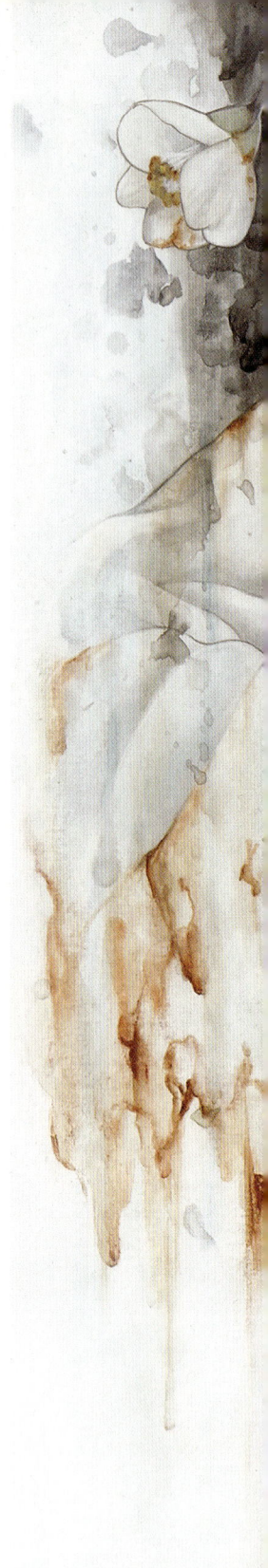

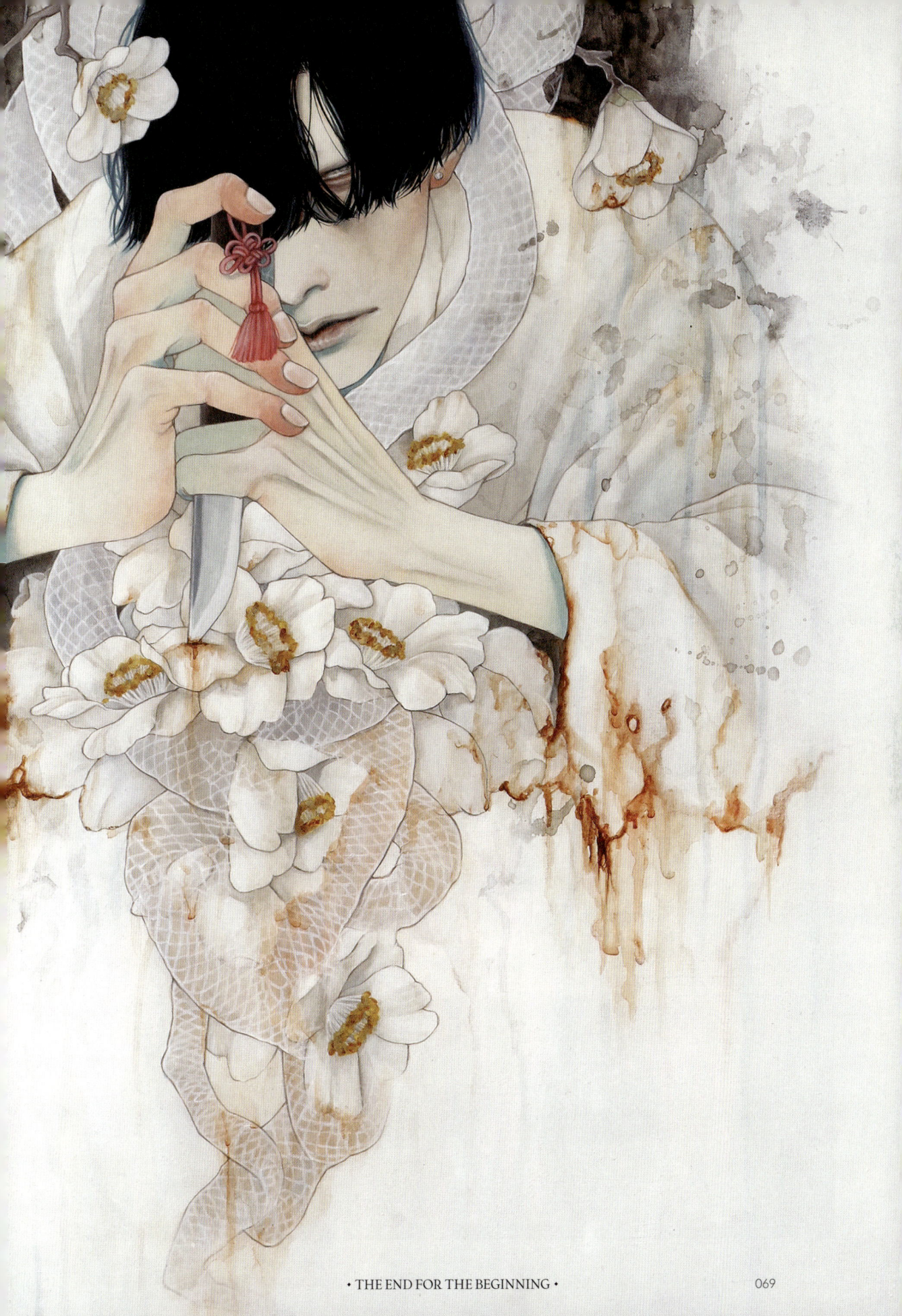

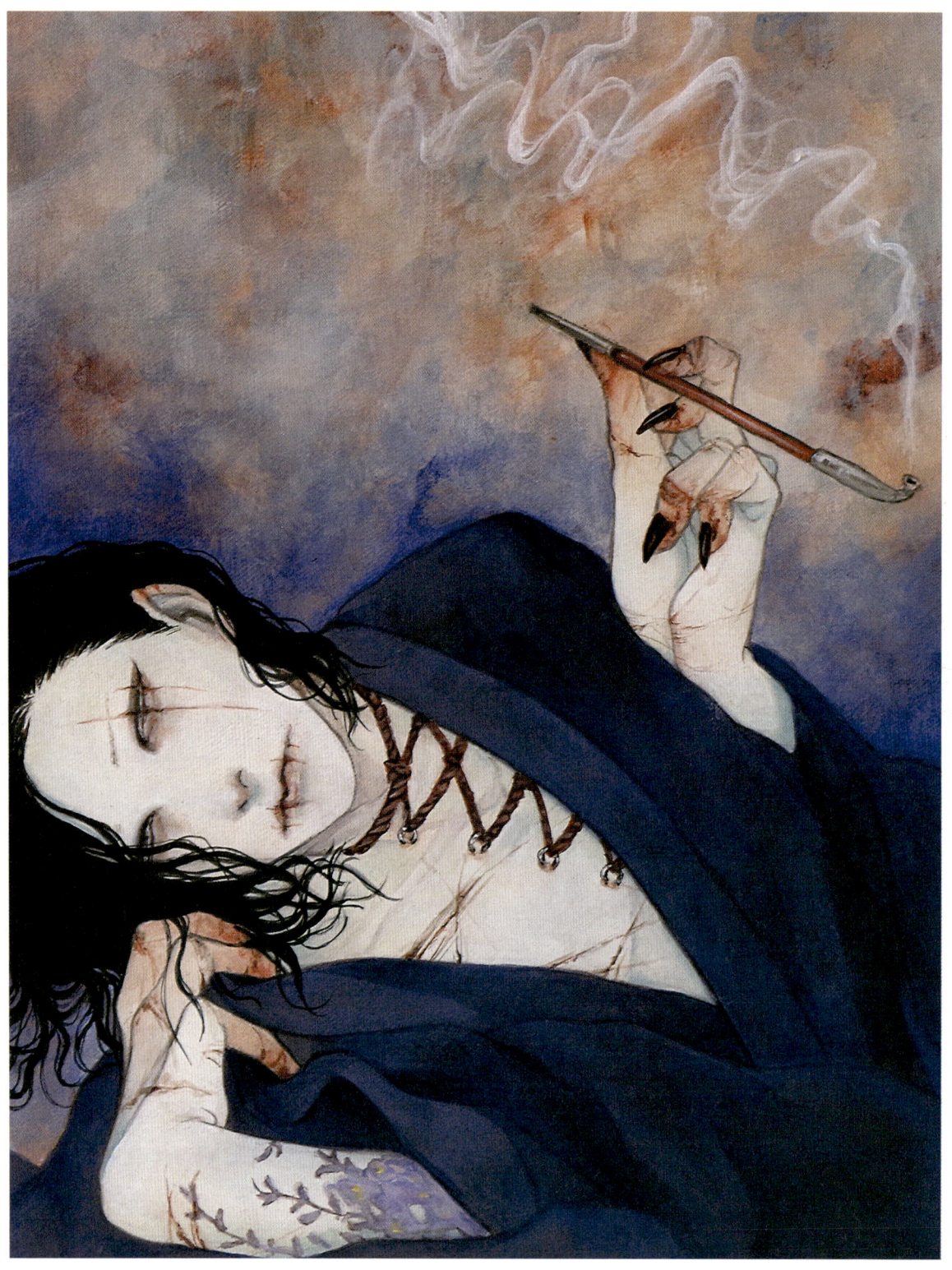

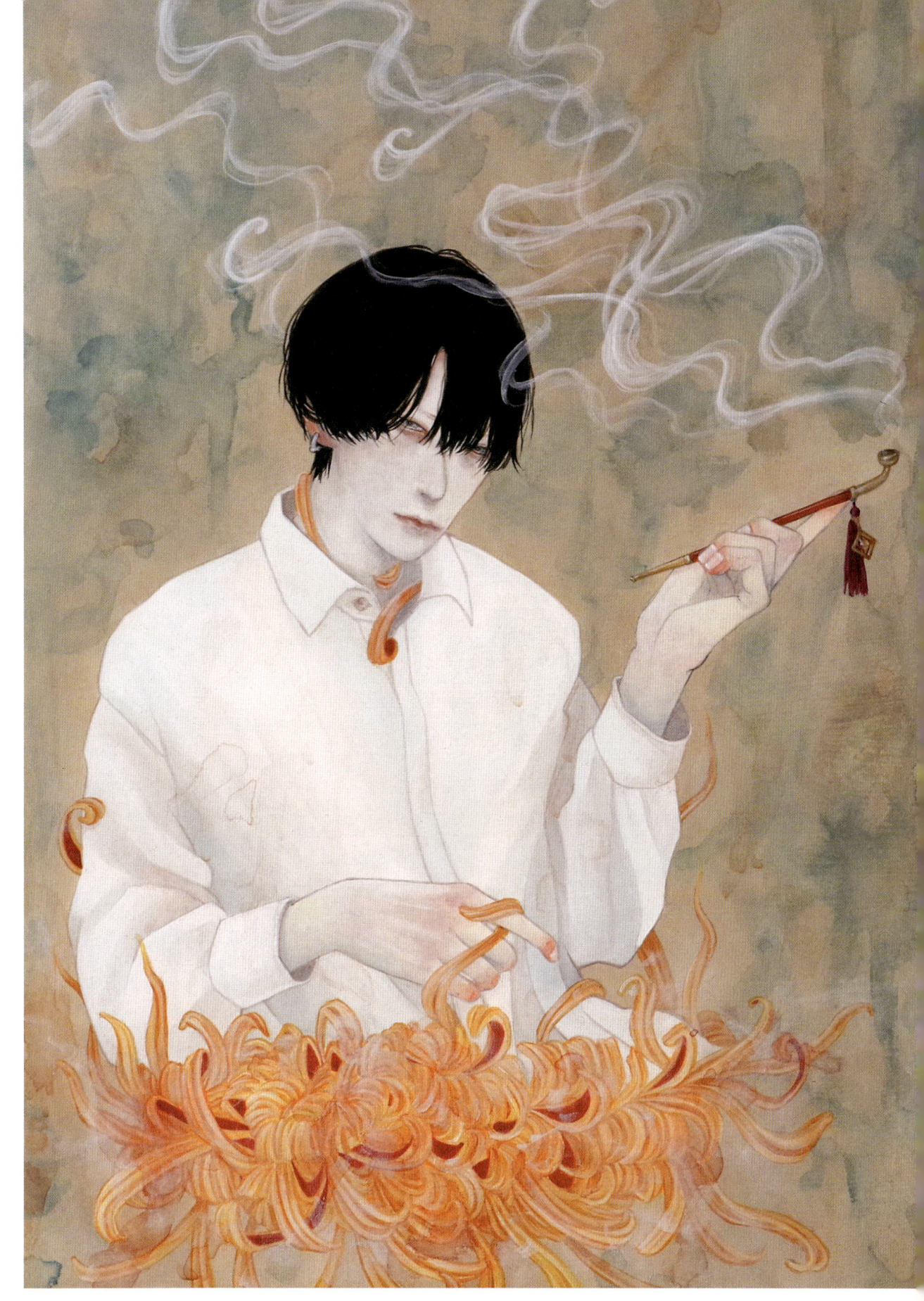

RENEWAL OF LEGENDS AND MYTHS

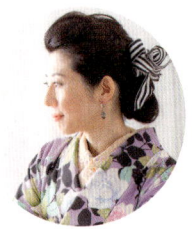

Miki Katoh

Born in 1973, she is a Japanese artist and one of the members of the contemporary art movement. Katoh's primary subject is the beautiful woman wearing a kimono, and her works are marked by the viewpoint of aestheticism. Amongst her figurative works which include mythologies and allegories, she mainly paints themes to do with reincarnation and natural cycles.

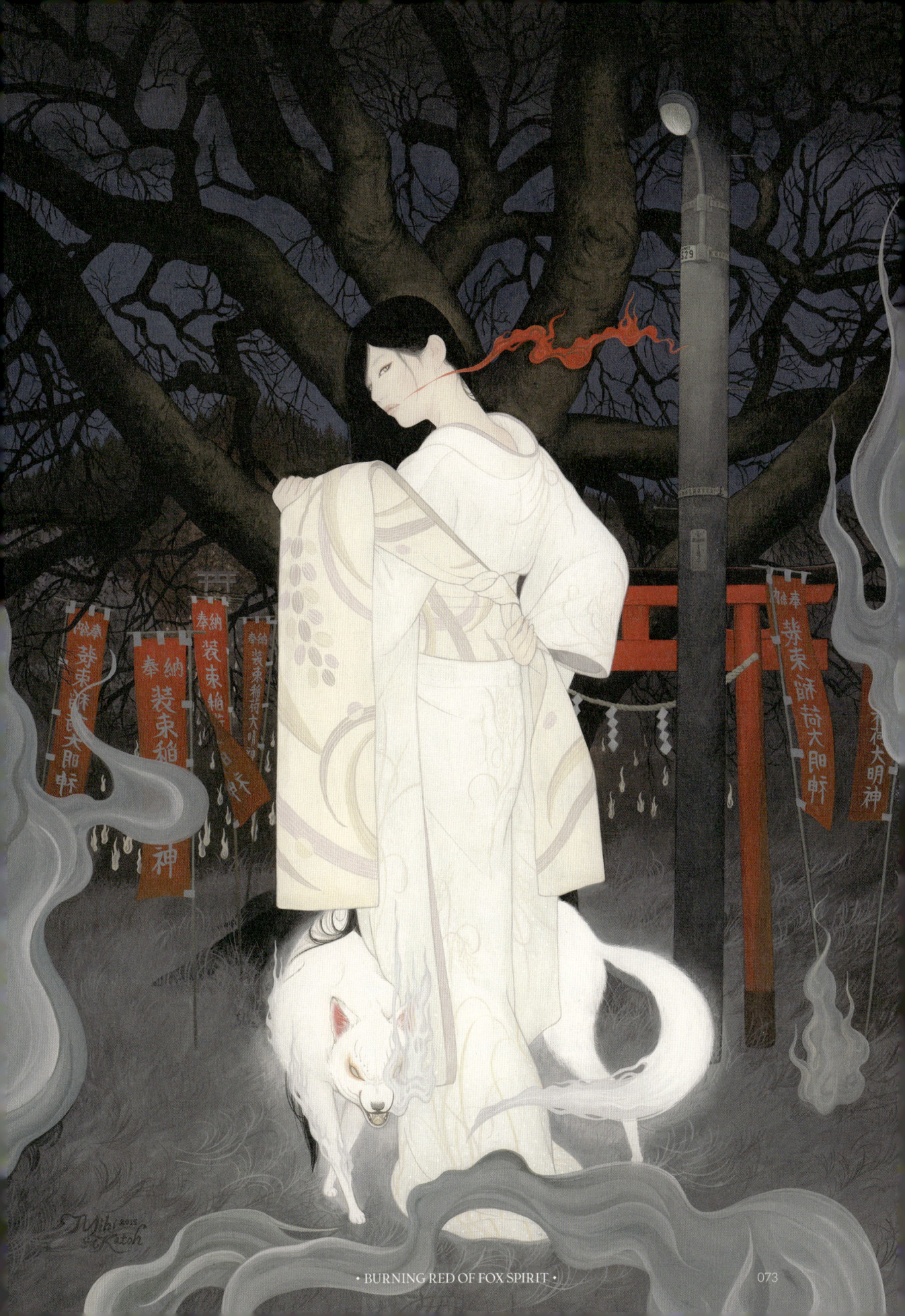

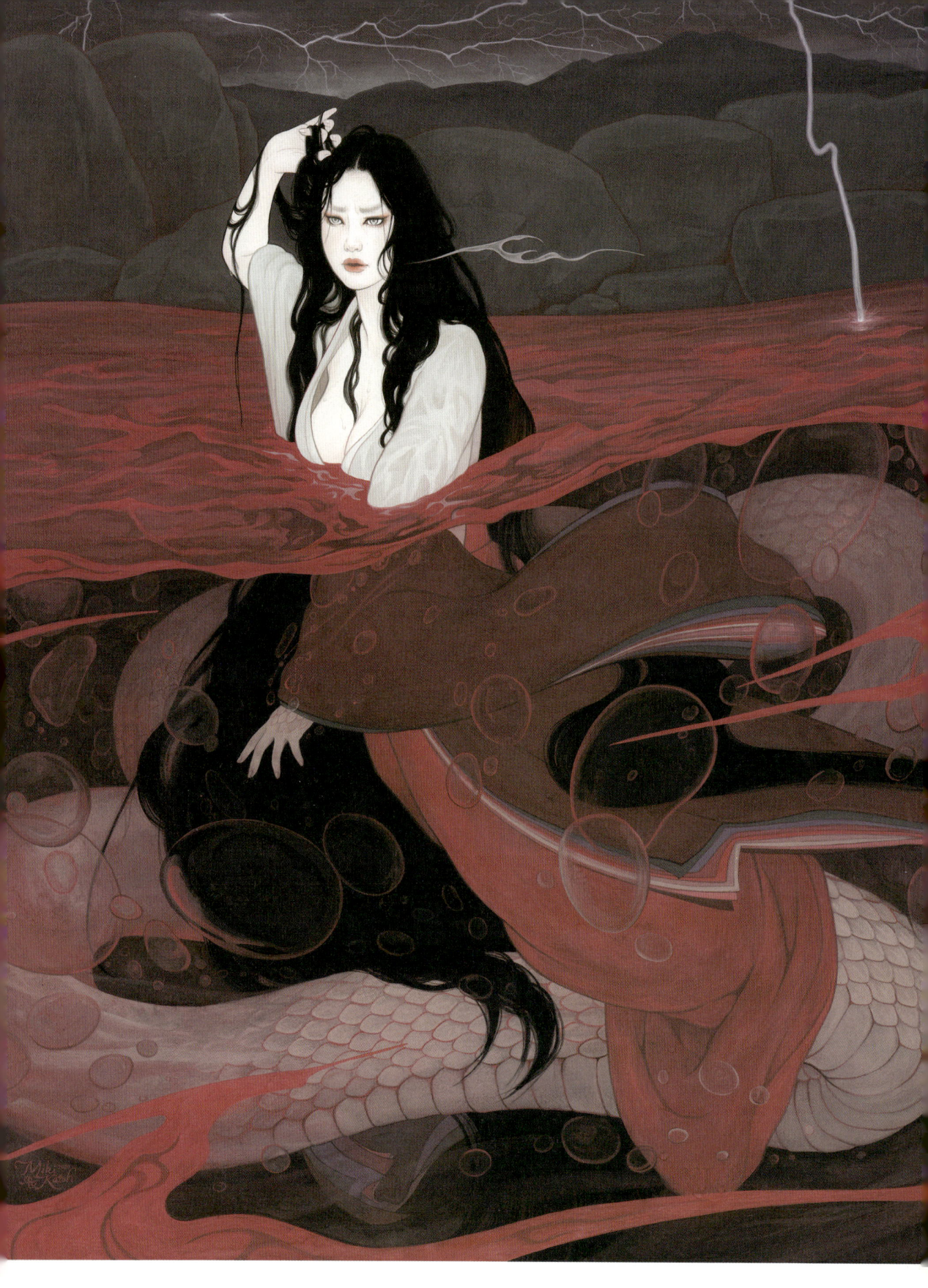

• HIDAKA RIVER •

Q: When did you start becoming interested in art? What initially led you in artistic creation?

MK: As far back as I can remember, my world was filled with art. The reason is that my father is a famous sculptor, and the studio in our house was crowded with his sculptures. In addition, many paintings by his friends were decorated on the walls. Deciphering the meaning of artworks in this wonderland became part of my daily routine. It was exciting, like playing magnificent games. As a result, by the time I was in kindergarten, my future dream was to become a painter unconditionally.

Q: How has traditional Japanese culture, like kimonos, shrines, streets, and cherry blossoms, influenced your way of observing and creating? How do you integrate these traditional elements into contemporary artistic creation?

MK: Traditional Japanese culture has given birth to many epic stories and is one of the sources of artistic creativity. As a Japanese, it is not an exaggeration to say that my aesthetic sense, sensibilities, and considerations are a part of modern Japanese culture. I use traditional culture as a subject to create works that can only be created now. Then, I believe that in 100 years, these works will be interesting works that reveal the differences between the eras. Therefore, my works which are rooted in traditional Japanese culture are so unique in the world.

Q: Which artists or artworks have had the greatest influence on your and why?

MK: Alphonse Mucha and Paul Delvaux had great influences on my life. Mucha's graphic beauty and Delvaux's nostalgic worldview have guided my creations. During the Meiji and Taishō eras in Japan, Art Nouveau had a major influence on Japanese culture, including book-binding and kimono patterns. I really think that Art Nouveau and Japanese culture have a good chemistry.

Q: The female figures in your works often wear kimonos, and you are frequently seen wearing kimonos as well. What special significance does kimono hold in your creations? Do you collect kimonos as a source of inspiration for your artwork?

MK: My favorite kimonos are called "antique kimonos." They were made in Japan 150~180 years ago. After Japan ended its national isolation, modern culture flooded into Japan from Western countries. The patterns of kimono became a combination of Japanese and Western styles and became flashier and more colorful with novel dyes imported from overseas. Antique kimonos look new and modern even today, and they inspire artistic creation. The kimono was also a symbol of women at the time who sought female liberation and rebelled against feudal Japanese society. In contrast to the traditional kimono, the way they dressed was flashy and free-spirited, and they were in the minority. By depicting such distinctive kimonos, I would like to express the visual beauty and independent attitude of women towards life.

Q: What drives your preference for using gouache and Watson paper as your mediums? How do these mediums showcase your ideas and emotions?

MK: When painting methods with gouache, the pigment color can be felt directly and the surface has a beautiful matte finish. Watson paper and gouache are a perfect match. Gouache is a paint that allows me to express my images more precisely. However, gouache is also a difficult paint to work with. It is because the surface crumbles depending on how it is dissolved in water, and it has strong hiding power. I always use gouache from Turner Color Works Ltd. and Watson paper from Muse Company Ltd. Both of them are Japanese manufacturers.

Q: Could you share any memorable experiences from your exhibition journeys? Many exhibitions were canceled during the pandemic, and your artwork *Baku's Dream* (P083) depicts a mythical creature devouring nightmares, symbolizing impending good fortune. Could you discuss how the pandemic has influenced your creativity or altered any of your thoughts?

MK: During the COVID-19 pandemic, human interaction was severely restricted. The tourism and restaurant industries were severely damaged and downtown areas became the target of social criticism and prejudices. It was precisely for times like these that I

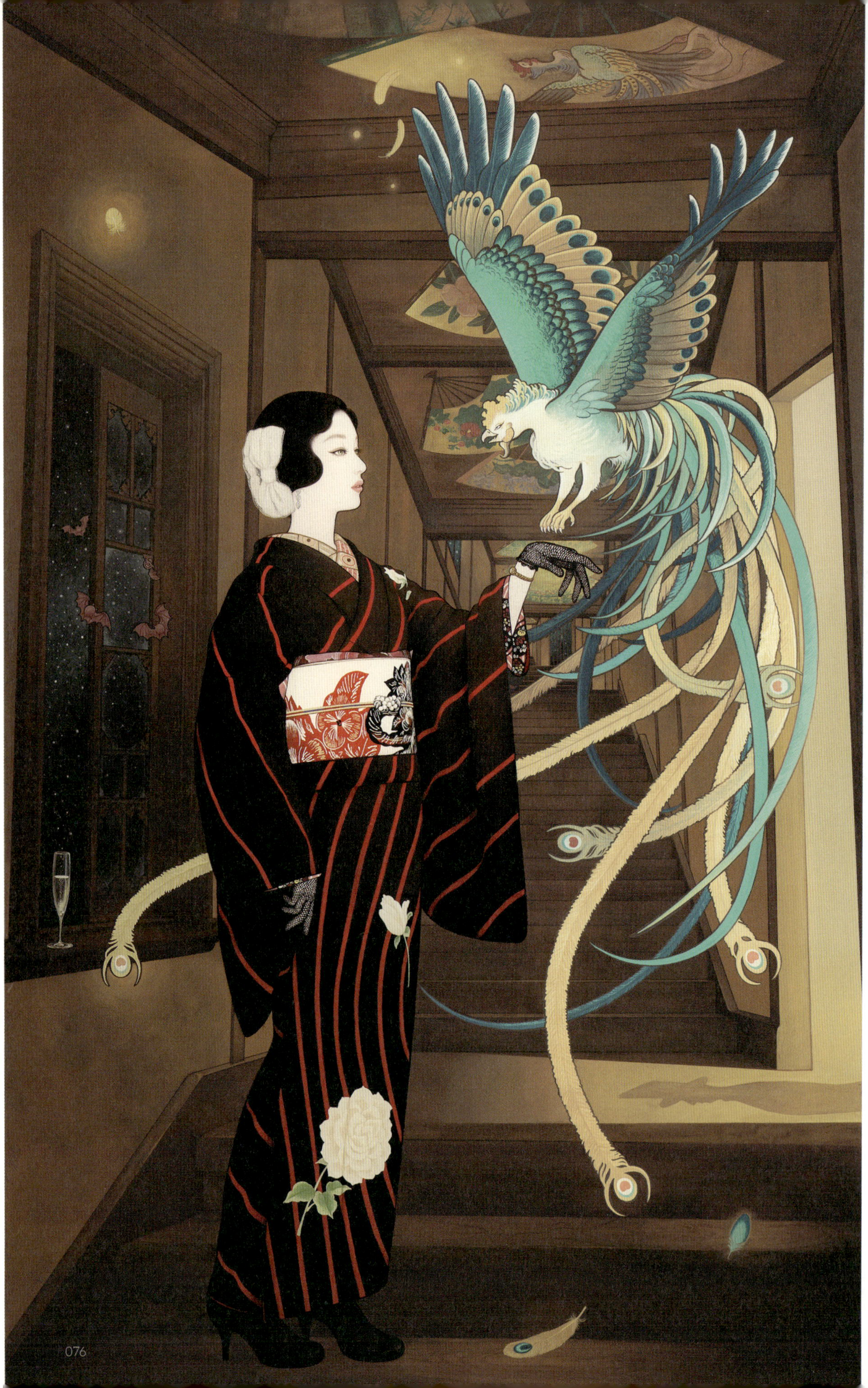

created *Baku's Dream* set in Shibuya, Tokyo's downtown. I have depicted this painting with the theme of the *baku*, a mythical creature that eats nightmares, and fervently prays for happiness to come to a dark world. The COVID-19 pandemic has highlighted various problems facing human society. However, it is also true that it has revealed humanity's tireless efforts and hope.

Q: Your works include many myths and fables, such as *Burning Red of Fox Spirit* (P073) based on *One Hundred Famous Views of Edo: Kitsunebi on New Year's Night under the Enoki Tree near Ōji*, and *Hidaka River* (P074) based on the "Anchin-Kiyohime" legend. Which mythological fables do you feel the deepest or like the most?

MK: The ancient Japanese belief in spirits "animism" has had a major influence on my creative career. Animism is the concept that everything regardless of a living thing or a non-living object has a spirit or a soul. Therefore, we can naturally accept stories about animals and flowering trees that transformed into humans and fell in love. That is why there are so many stories including mythologies and allegories of interspecies marriages in Japan. The ability to think of such unrealistic things as "maybe it's possible" is the source of stories and what makes them so interesting.

Q: How do you intertwine themes of reincarnation and natural cycles with Japanese culture in your artworks? What is so special about this theme for you?

MK: The cycle of life, in which we are reincarnated and reborn into various creatures, is a Buddhist doctrine called "reincarnation." Nature that surrounds us is also constantly cycling and never stays in the same state. Nature is an object of worship all over the world, and many mythologies and allegories feature deities that are personified or deified natural objects and phenomena. This idea of nature worship, "physiolatry" is also closely related to "animism" which worships the souls and spirits that reside in all things. All of these things are fundamentally connected. Therefore, my goal is to work on creating something that will embody and transfer the information from this dynamic and magnificent spiritual world into the real world. As an artist, it is an honor and a joy to create works that incorporate uniquely Japanese culture such as kimonos and the four seasons with the central theme of "the cycle of life and nature" and invite the viewers to another world that transcends time and space.

Q: As a member of the contemporary art movement, what do you think the art world needs most right now? What are your views or expectations on the role of artists in today's society?

MK: I strongly believe the "power of art" lies in its ability to awaken joy, anger, sorrow, and happiness, to discover new perspectives and values, and to convey sensations that cannot be put into words. Art's mission is not just to achieve superficial beauty or originality, but also to wish for and realize happiness and peace for people across borders in the chaotic world of today.

Q: Do you have any new projects or plans? What are your expectations for future artistic endeavors?

MK: In the future, I would like to take on the challenge of creating works in a larger scale and further deepen my worldview. I would also like to have more people view my work and continue to promote the "power of art" in a way that leaves a lasting impression.

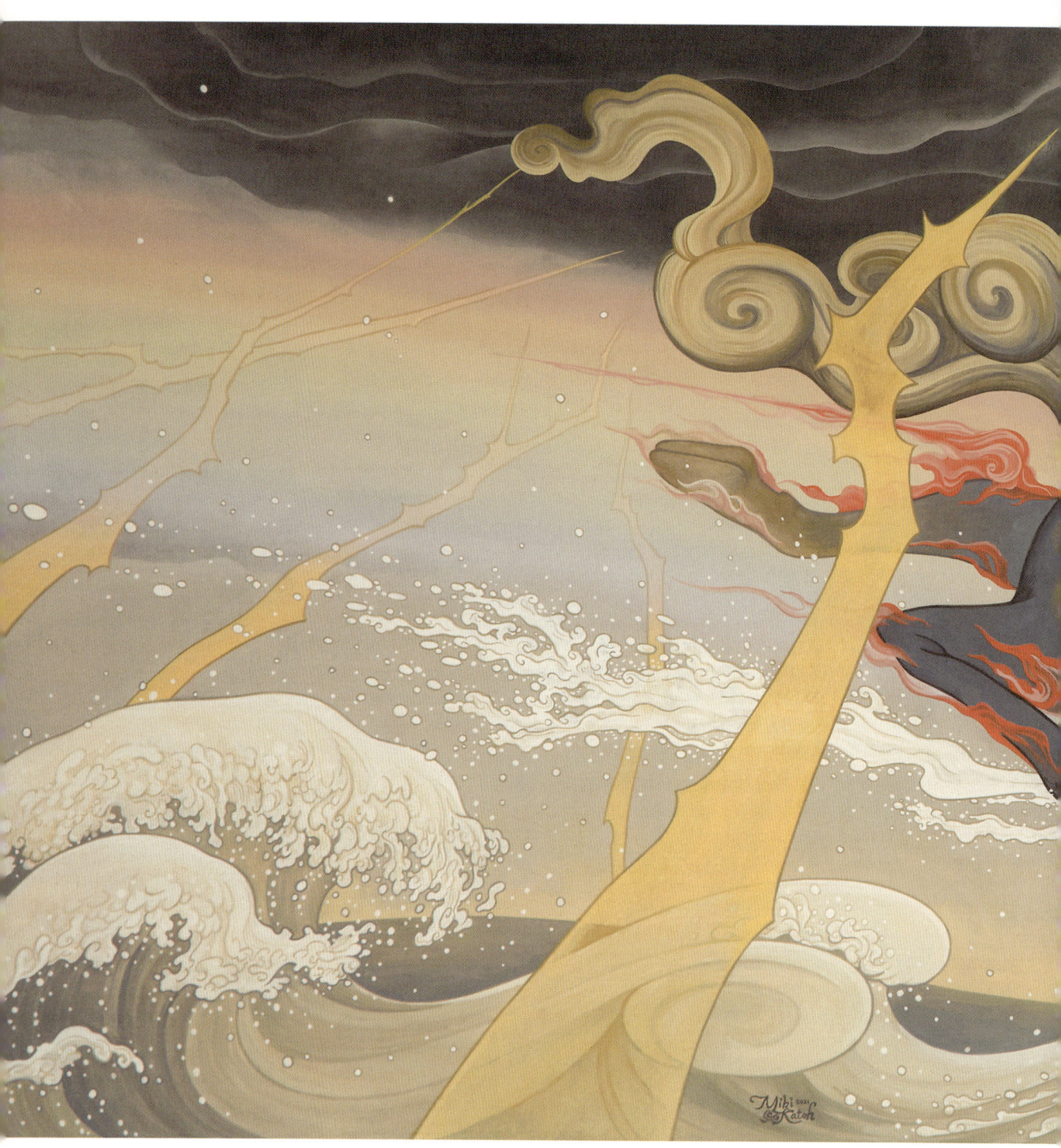

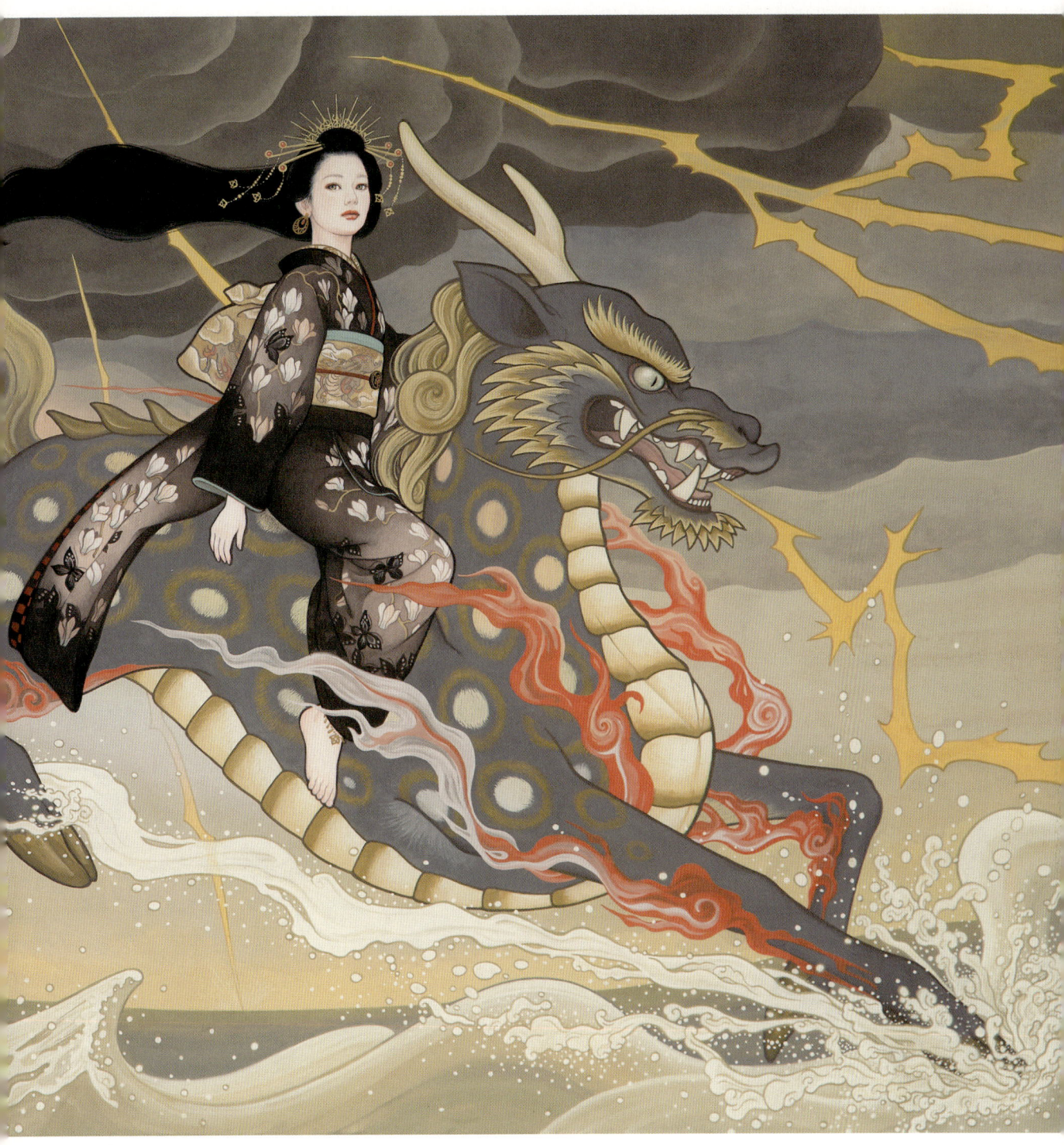

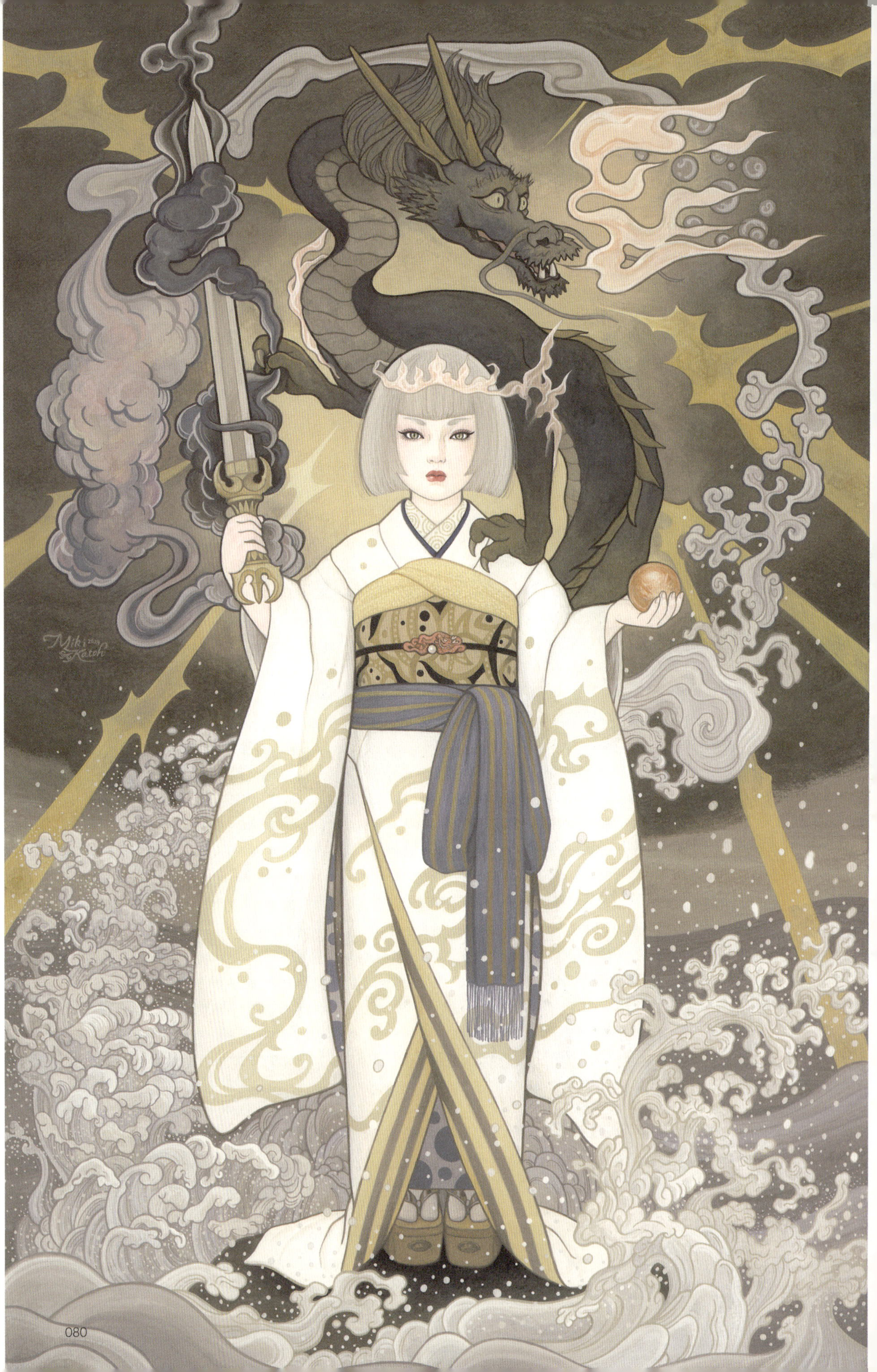

• RAINMAKER •

" I strongly believe the 'power of art' lies in its ability to awaken joy, anger, sorrow, and happiness, to discover new perspectives and values, and to convey sensations that cannot be put into words. "

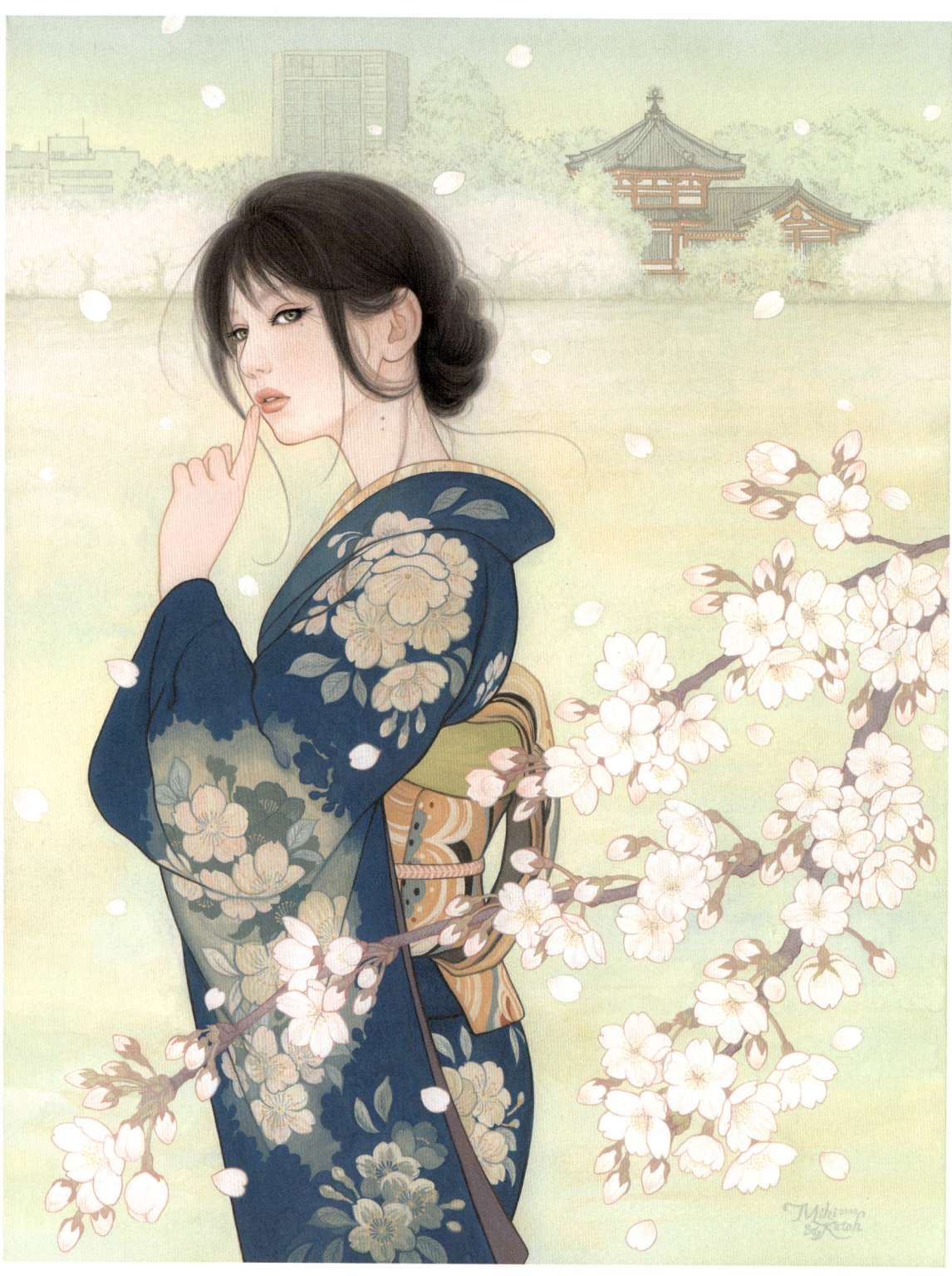

• CHERRY BLOSSOM STORM FOR SECRET LOVERS •

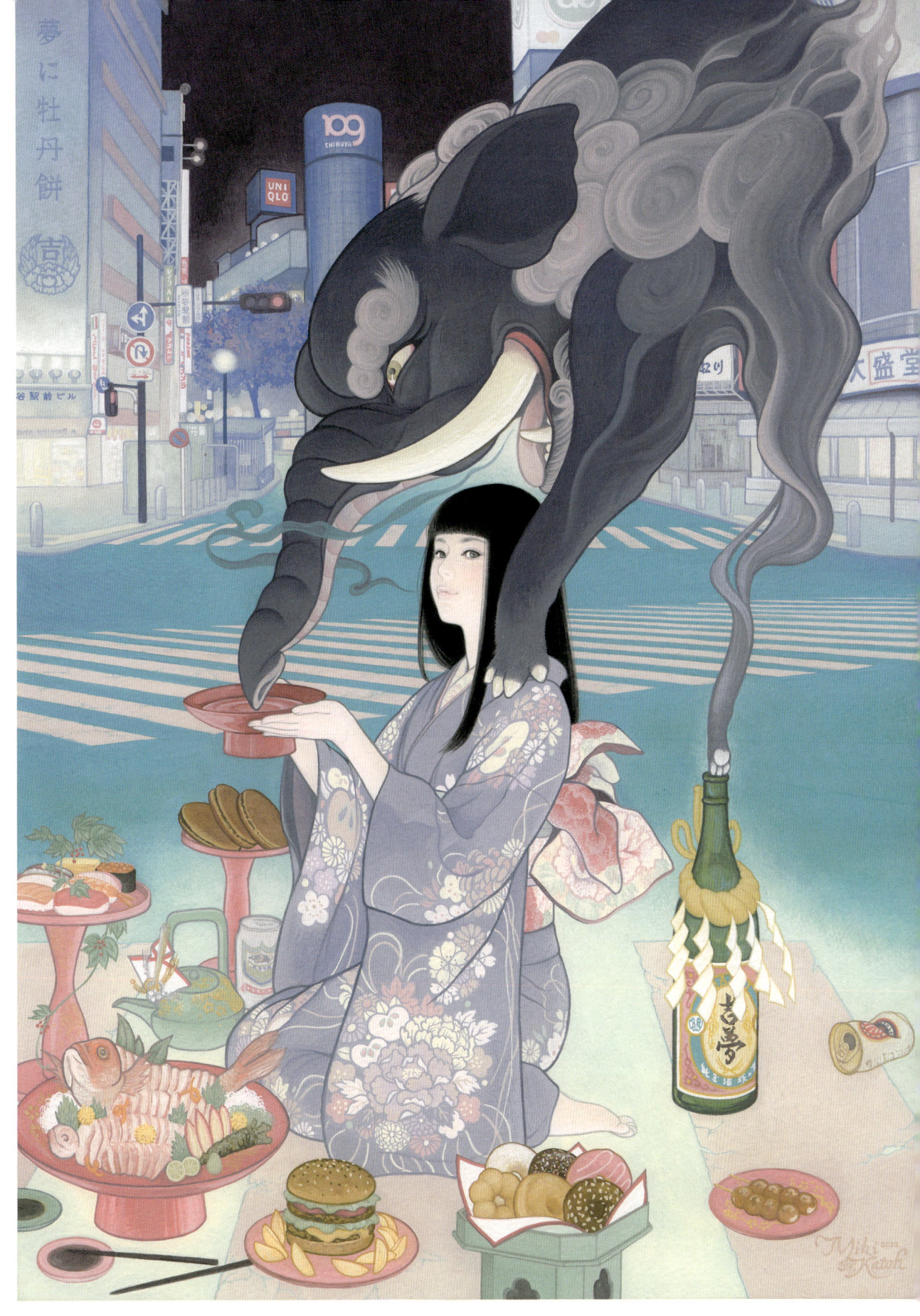

THE REAPPEARANCE
OF BEAUTIES

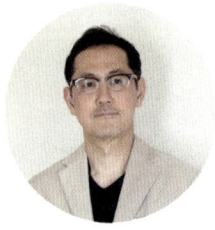

Takahito Izumi

He is an artist born in Tokyo, Japan. He is very good at drawing
Japanese traditional beauty and *bijin-ga* (beautiful women pictures).
He is currently focusing on illustration work for advertising,
publishing, and the websites. He held a solo exhibition in 2012 at
Tambourine Gallery in Omotesando, Tokyo. He is a member of the
Tokyo Illustrators Society (TIS).

085

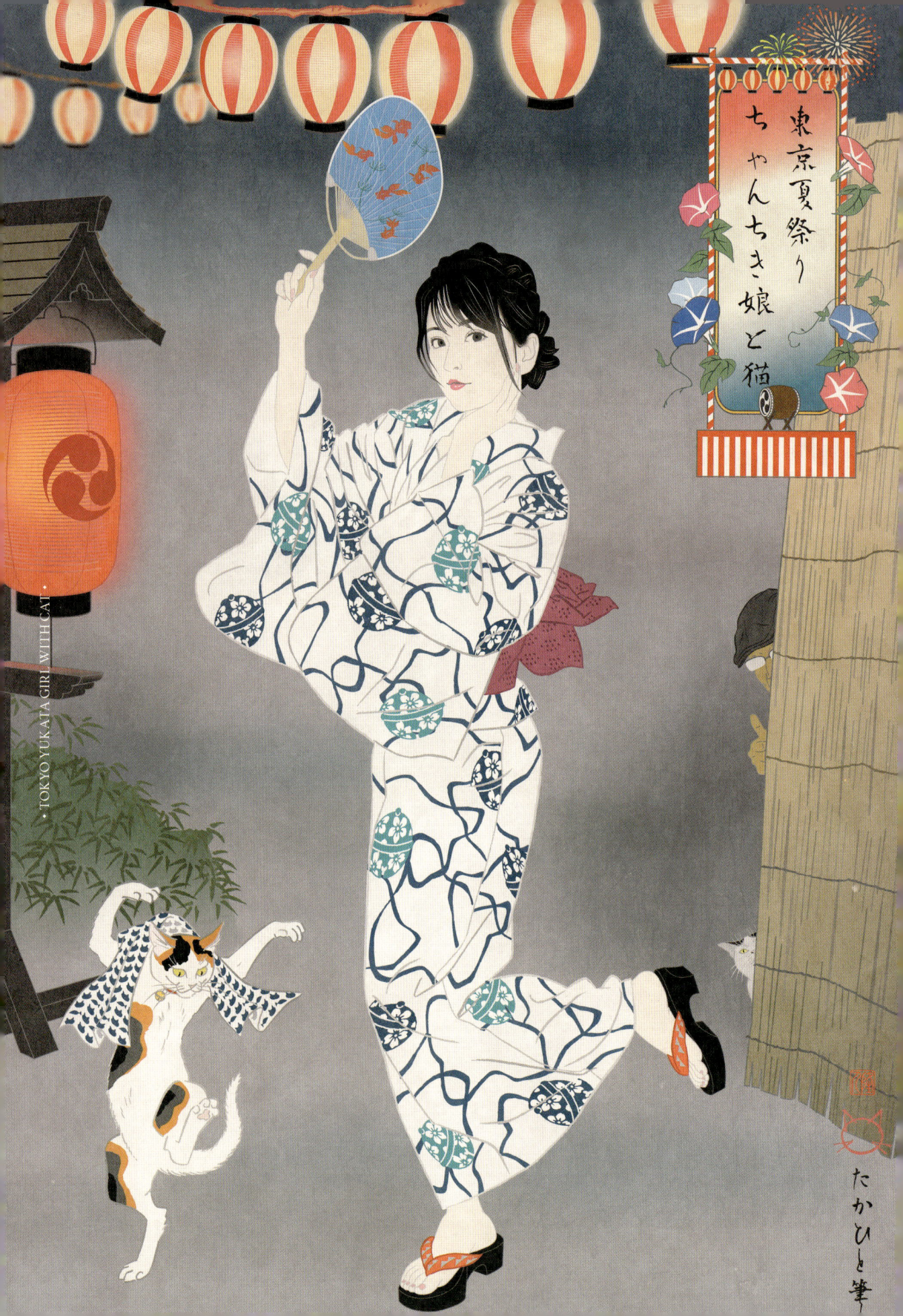

東京夏祭り
ちゃんちき娘と猫

TOKYO YUKATA GIRL WITH CAT

たかひと筆

Q: How did you start your artistic career? And what made you focus on depicting traditional Japanese beauty in your artwork?

TI: I began my career as a salaried illustrator employed at a company. Then, around 2010, I went independent as a freelance illustrator. I've always loved Italian Renaissance art and oil paintings. But I began to think that rather than simply imitating Western paintings like those made by Italians, there must be something more unique to me as a Japanese that I could create. So I decided to find my own style in the direction of traditional Japanese painting and ukiyo-e. Japanese paintings are traditionally flat, so I felt that suited me better than the three-dimensional Western style.

Q: Could you share your experience of holding a solo exhibition at Tambourine Gallery in Omotesando, Tokyo in 2012. How did that exhibition impact your career?

TI: The title of the solo exhibition was "WABIJINZU." It means an exhibition of Japanese-style beauties. It was around that time that I started to paint pictures with themes of traditional Japanese painting and ukiyo-e. This solo exhibition marked the starting point of my career as an artist.

Q: As a freelance illustrator, how do you find inspiration and ideas? Where do you usually seek creative inspiration from?

TI: To put it simply, I think a lot of items from my own hobbies and interests. I think I'm also influenced by the historical stories I read as a child and robot manga. Ukiyo-e artists I like include Utamaro and Hokusai. For Japanese painting, I like Kaburagi Kiyokata, Ito Shinsui, and Uemura Shōen. Basically, I like drawing beautiful women, so my motifs are mainly women.

Q: As a member of the Tokyo Illustrators Society, how do you perceive the development trends in the Japanese illustration industry? What do you think will be the future direction of illustration?

TI: Recently, I feel that there has been an increase in illustrations inspired by the style of Japanese animation. As the era has changed to digital, I think there are more and more highly refined images than analog hand-drawn works. I think that in the future, images in areas where AI excels will be naturally selected out. Conversely, I think that artists will need to compete with images that AI cannot draw.

Q: Your work *Ward Off Pandemic* (P094) conveys your aspirations and hopes for a better outcome. Can you talk about the changes and impacts of the epidemic on your creation?

TI: Something that the whole world never expected actually happened. Until then, I often had to go to publishers and design production companies for work meetings, but since the COVID-19 pandemic, most meetings have been done by phone and email. However, considering the travel expenses and the effort it takes to go to meetings, I personally feel that the current style is easier.

Q: Your artworks often feature elements of Japanese culture, such as *yukata* and ukiyo-e. What special meaning or emotional connection do these elements have for you? How do you think Japanese culture affects your way of observation? What culture are you most proud of?

TI: I think it's because of my identity as a Japanese. When you look at ukiyo-e prints from the Edo period, you can see that the compositions are very designed and the figures

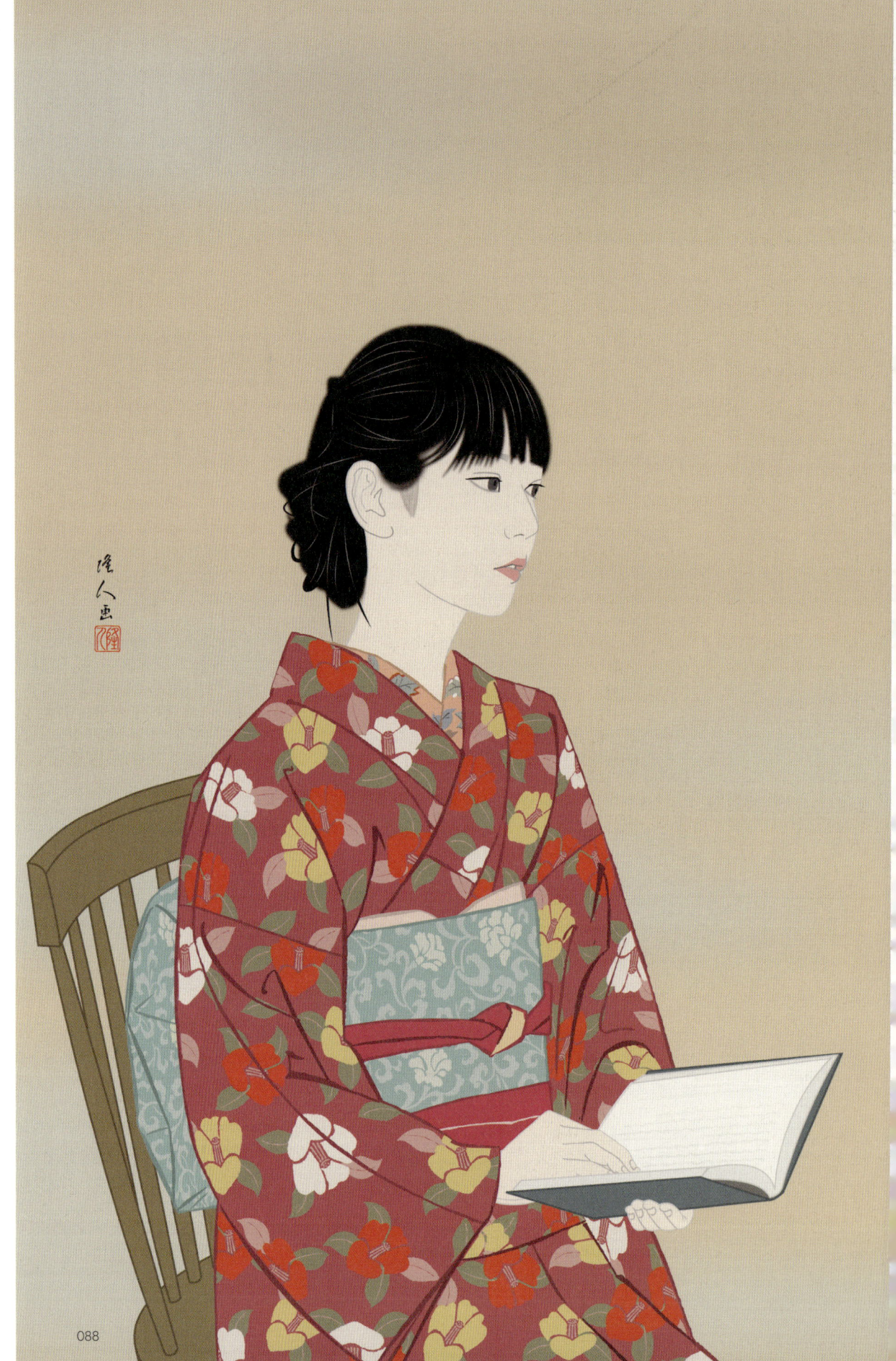

are tastefully arranged. I never draw the subject as it is, I always draw it through my own filter and design it. In my case, there is a lot to learn from ukiyo-e prints of Edo culture, and I think it is meaningful.

Q: Having graduated from the Business Administration Department at Meiji University, how has this business background influenced your artistic creation? How do you integrate business concepts with your artistic creation?

TI: I don't think there is much of a direct impact. However, unlike people who studied at art schools, I don't have any standards or concepts imposed on me. So, I think there is a part of me that perceives art from my own unique perspective based on what I see and feel. We live in an age of information overload, so if there are too many options, it's hard to know what to choose. I think it's important to collect a certain amount of information and then isolate yourself and shut yourself in.

Q: Your works are often captivating and offer viewers aesthetic enjoyment. What emotions and reflections do you hope viewers can experience when appreciating your artworks?

TI: I would be happy if you could feel the Japanese sense of beauty and the beauty of the postures and mannerisms of Japanese women. My paintings are in the style of Japanese painting and ukiyo-e, but I have arranged the women's faces to be modern Japanese beauties rather than the beauties that were popular in the Edo period. I am also particular about the female form. I do not use lines that are traced from photographs to outline actual people. I idealize the form according to my own sensibility.

Q: What are your plans and visions for future creations? Do you plan to continue exploring traditional aesthetics and *bijin-ga*, or do you intend to experiment with other artistic styles?

TI: I've always wanted to portray beautiful Japanese women. Japanese faces are flatter than Western faces, so it's easier to capture their shape with lines. Conversely, it's easier to draw Western faces using surfaces (shadows) rather than lines. That's why I think the flat style of Japanese painting and ukiyo-e is the best way to express the beauty of Japanese women. I think I'll continue with this style, but if I find a better art style, I might move in that direction.

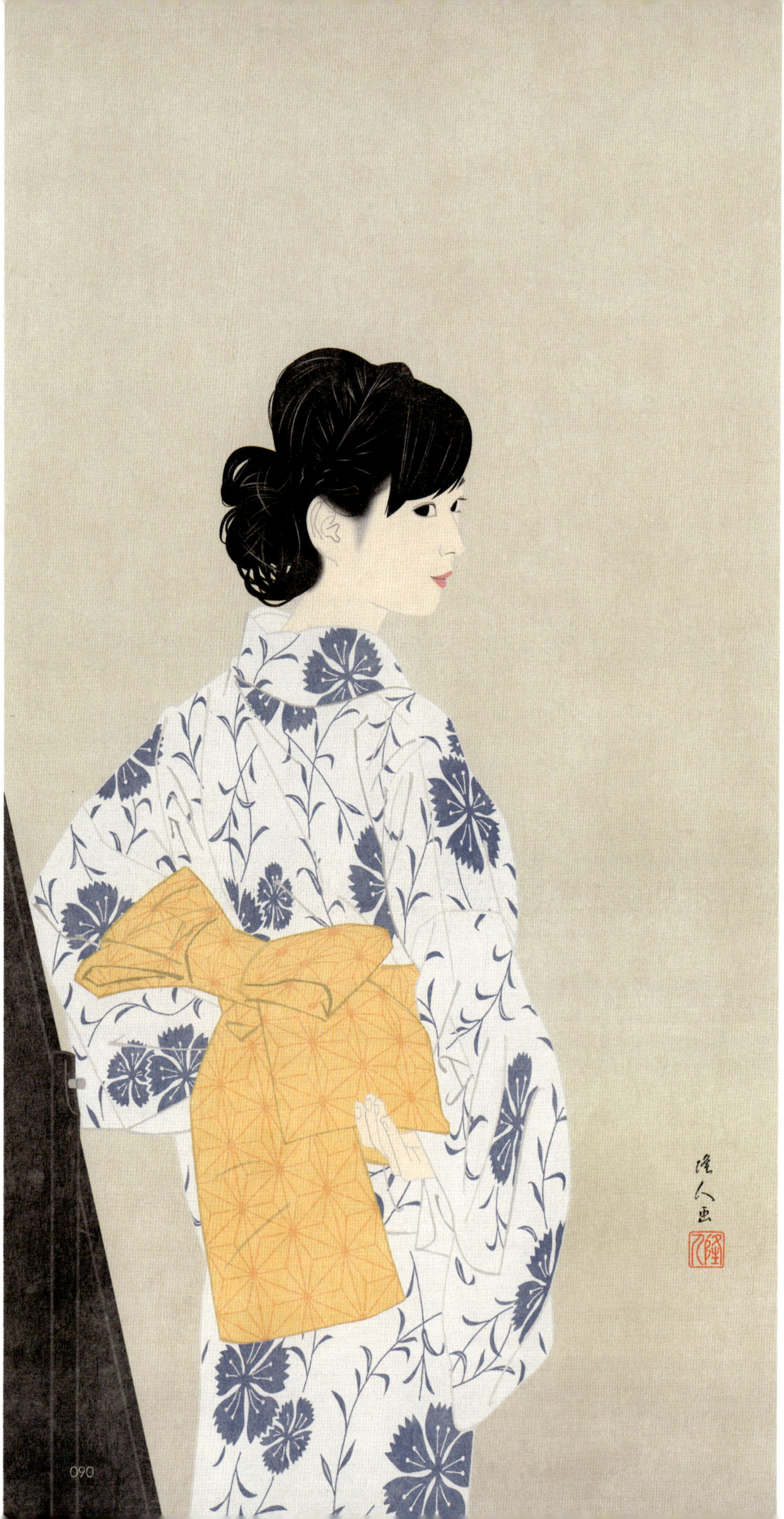
隆人画

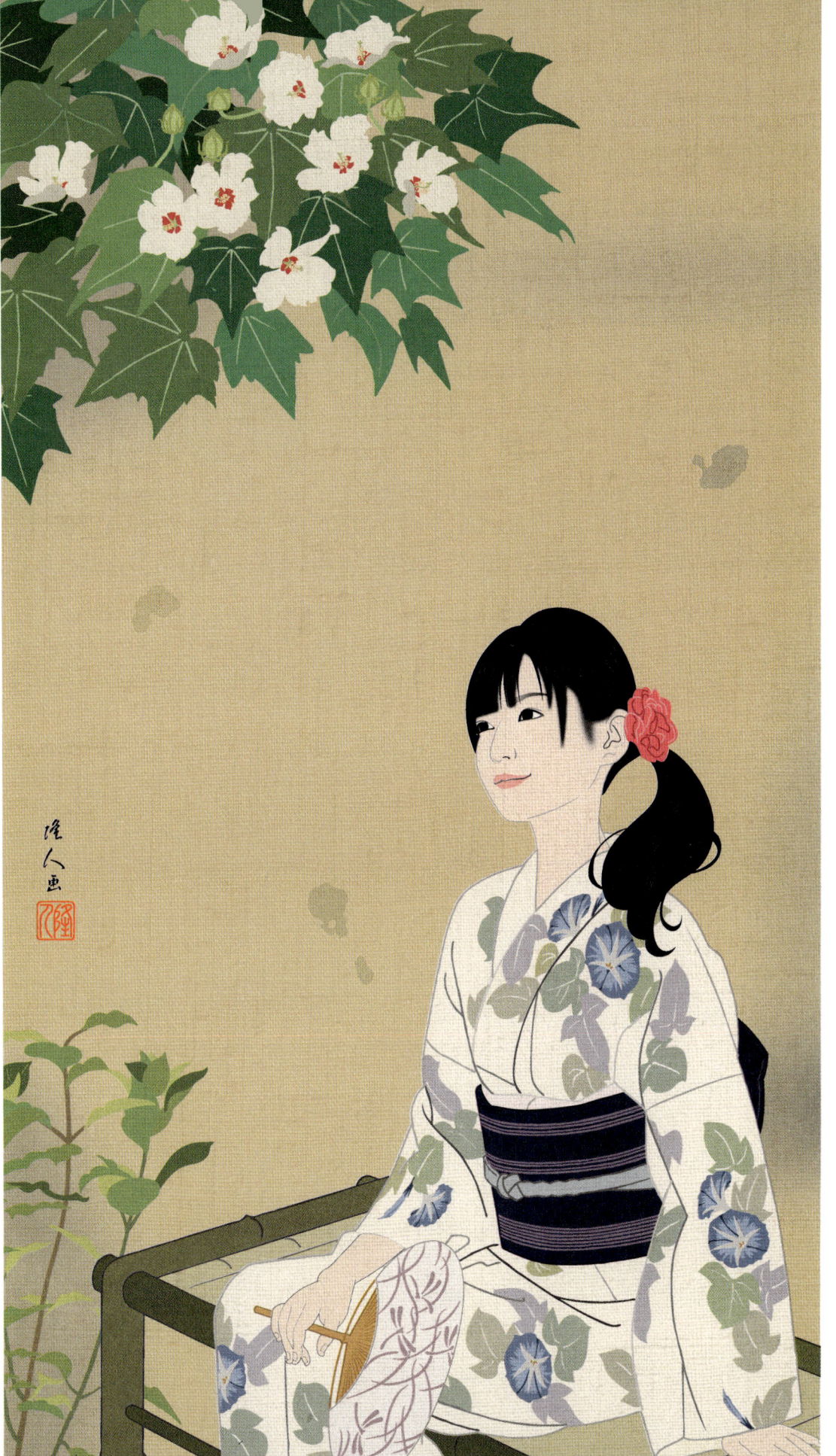

" My paintings are in the style of Japanese painting and ukiyo-e, but I have arranged the women's faces to be modern Japanese beauties rather than the beauties that were popular in the Edo era. "

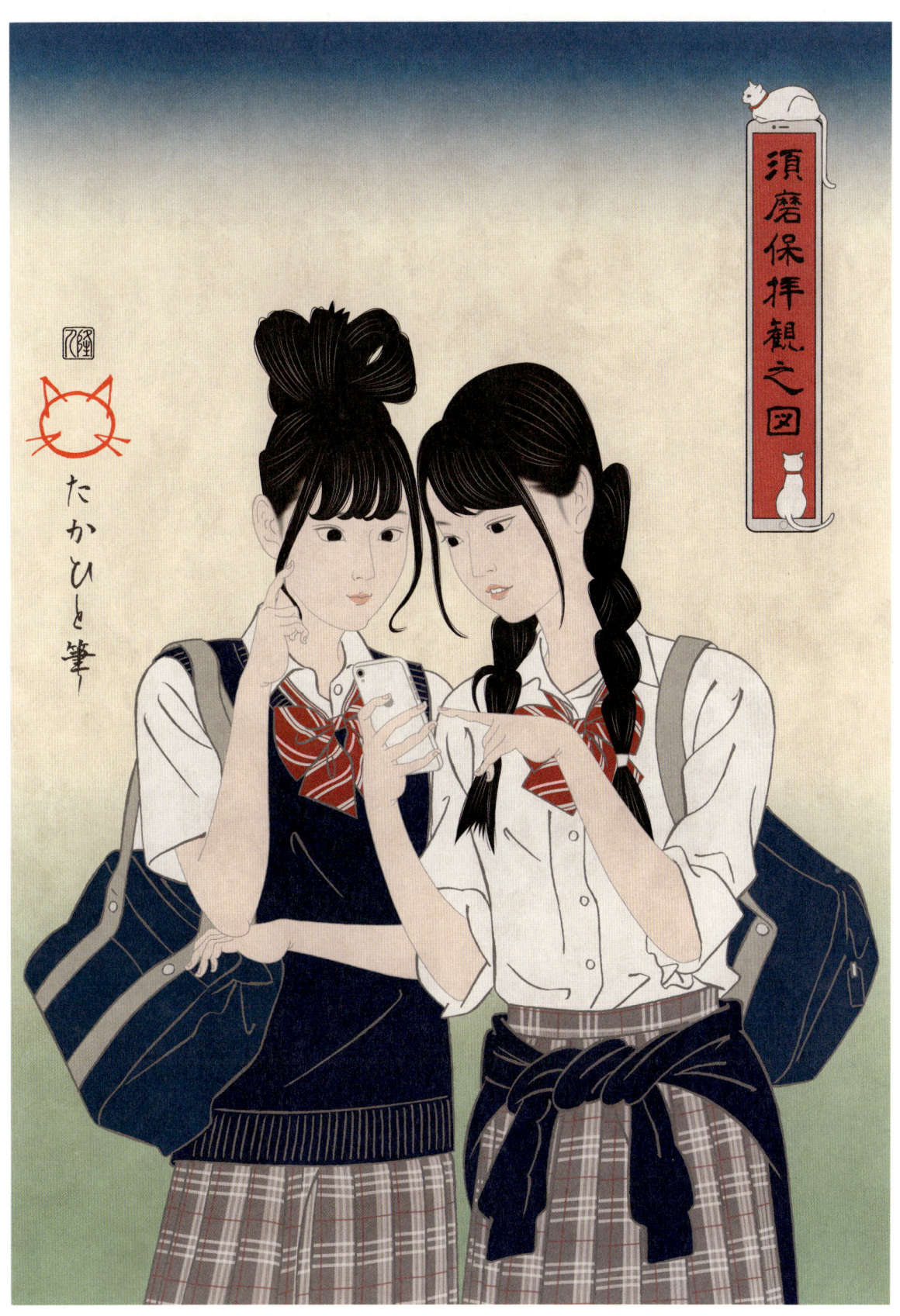

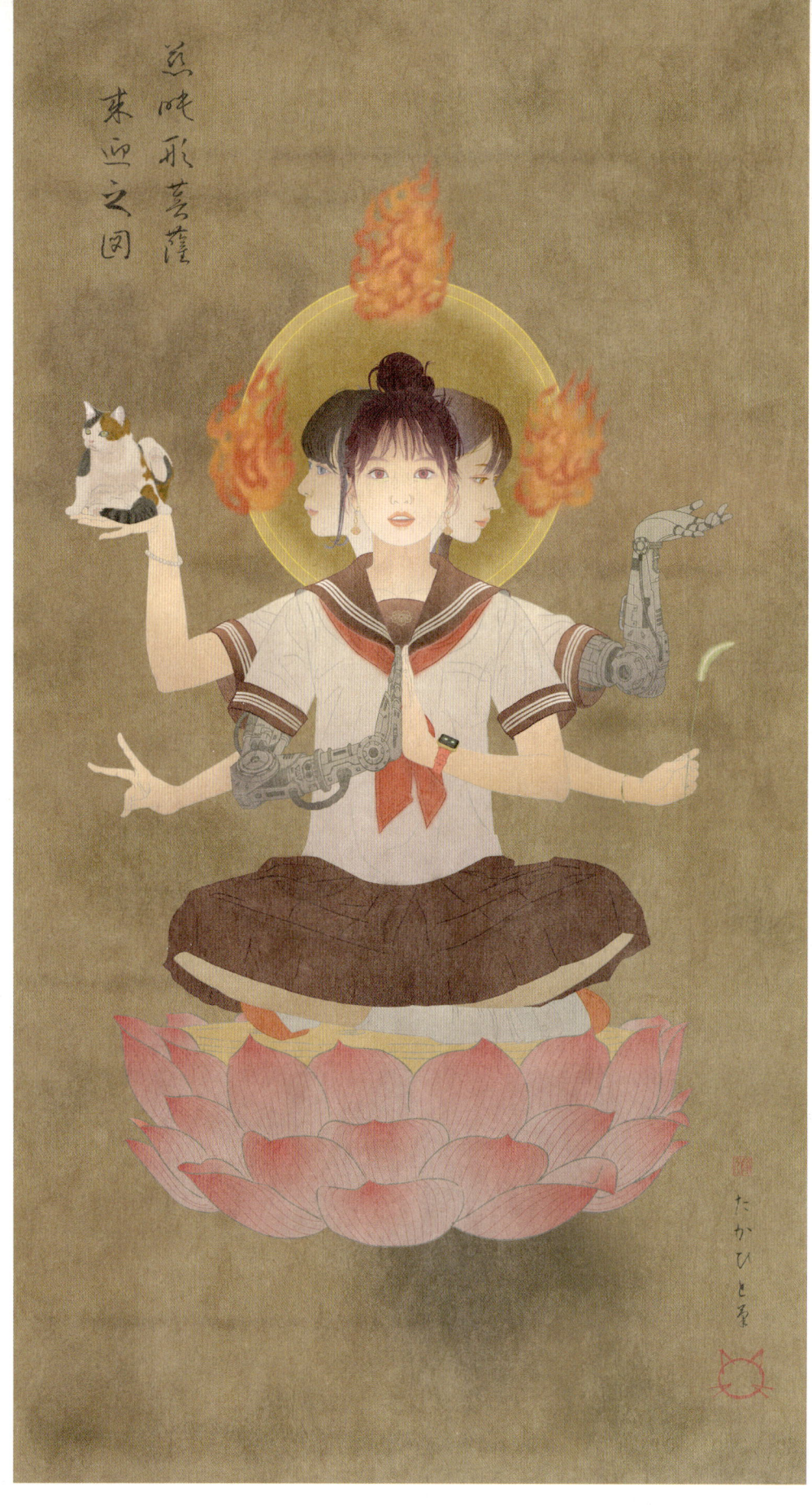

たかひと 京

BEAUTIES AS CENTRAL AESTHETICS

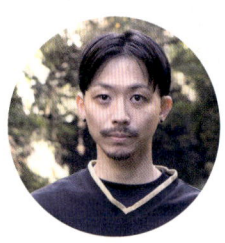

Ryohei Shimazaki

Born and living in 1986 at Hinohara Village (the last remaining village in the non-insular area of Tokyo). Ryohei Shimazaki studies under the influence of the Rinpa school, ukiyo-e, Japanese art from the Edo and Meiji periods, and Chinese painting. He mainly draws women, monsters, *Yaoyorozu no Kami* (Eight Million Gods), beasts, *okame* (traditional masks), and living creatures.

While learning the traditional techniques, compositions, and motifs of ukiyo-e from history, he also expresses the world seen from a private perspective, what he actually feels and notices in his daily life, and sometimes his passions by incorporating his unique humor and metaphor.

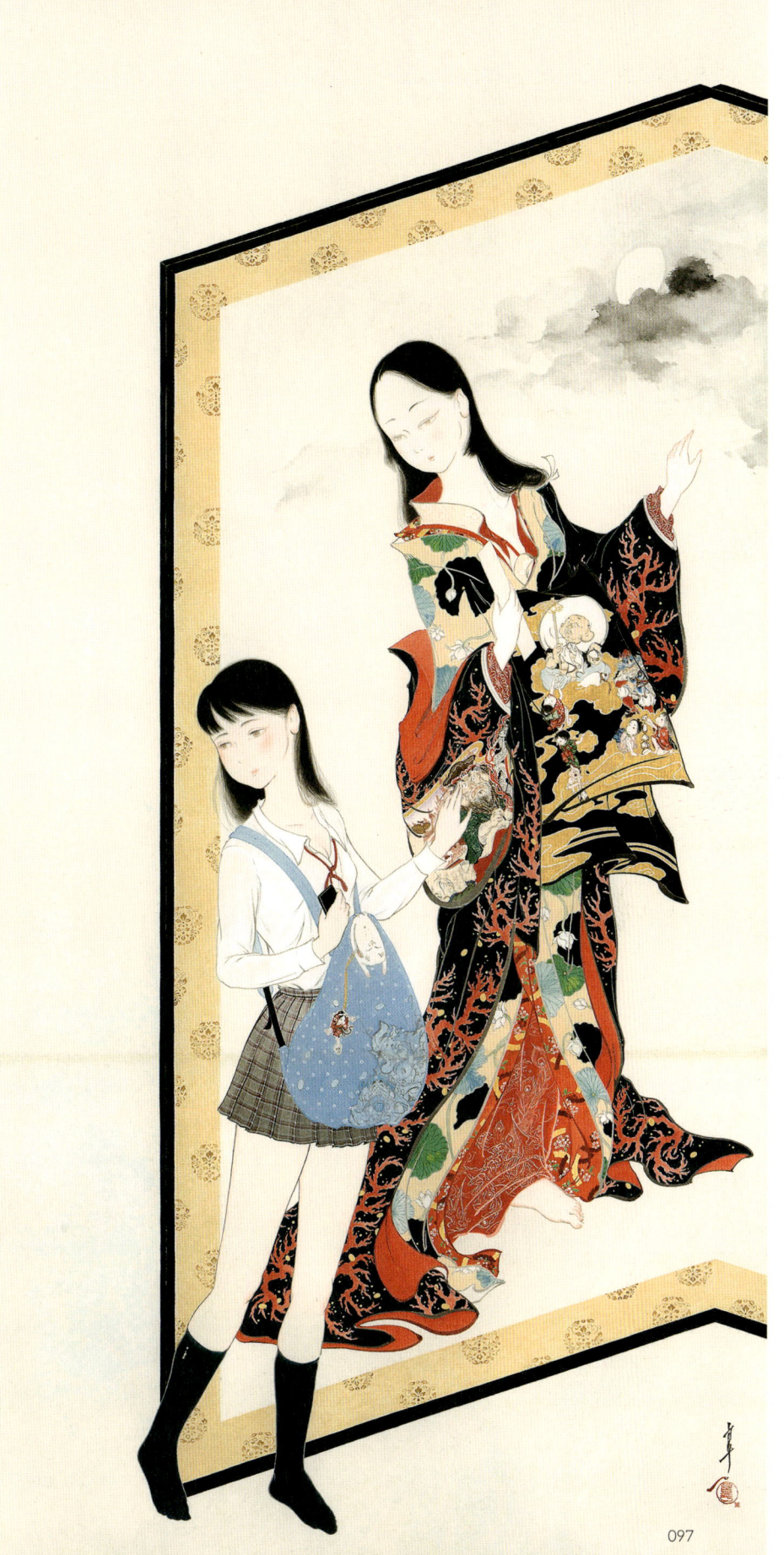

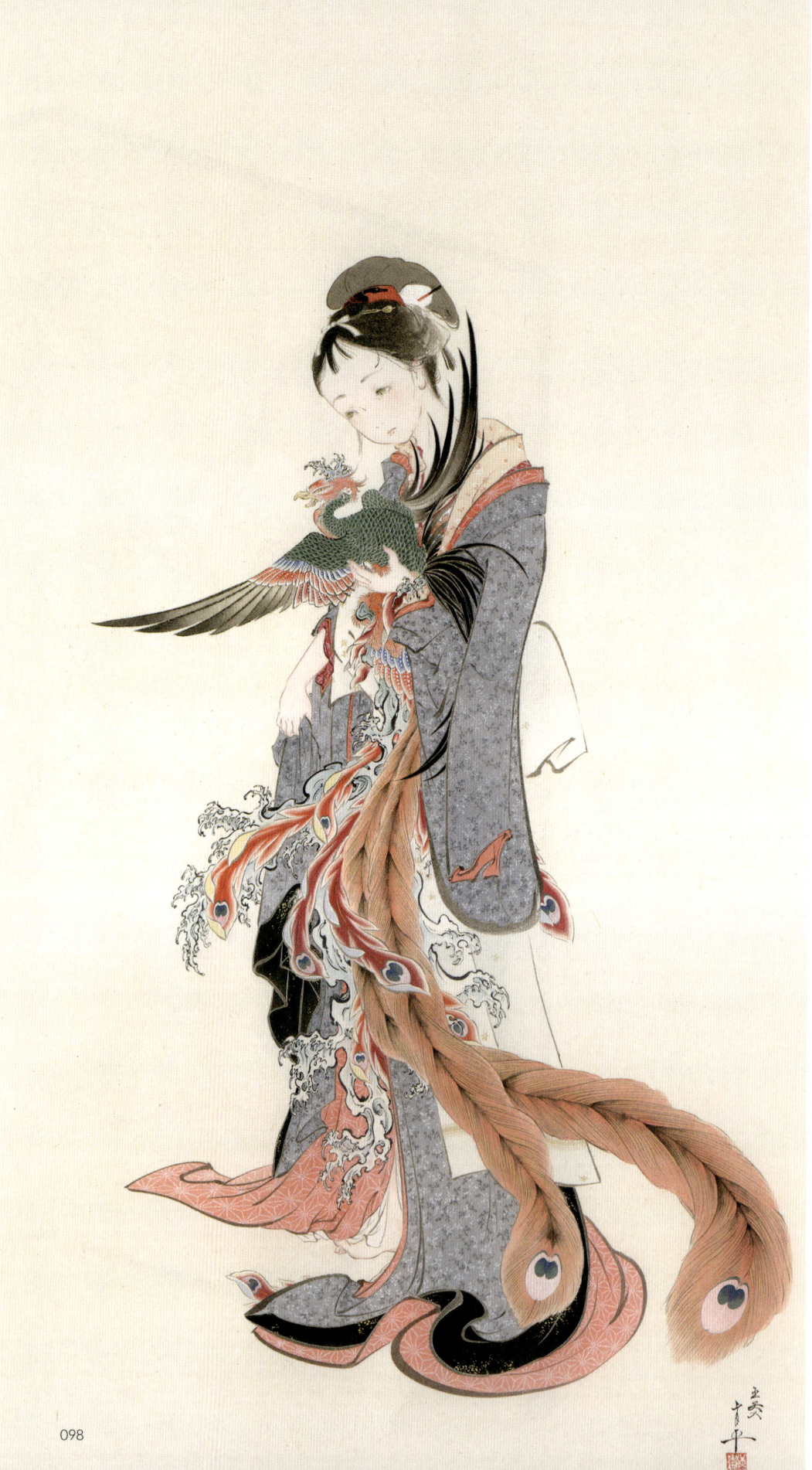

Q: How did you begin your artistic journey? What led you to become an artist?

RS: It all started when I met my master, Hakuro, a Chinese ink painter living in Japan. By witnessing my master's skills, I learned compositional skills, drawing skills, ways of thinking that I lacked, and the approach to working with passion and calmness. After that, I feel like my paintings suddenly became freer and expanded.

Before I met him, I was creating works while working at another job. I think meeting and learning from him and winning the Foreign Minister's Award for the genre of ink painting was a big reason why I decided to live with the art for my works.

Q: How has living in Hinohara Village influenced your art? How has this place shaped your artistic style and inspiration?

RS: When I create work, some parts are based on what I feel in my own life and what I feel in my daily life. Hinohara Village is a place with a lot of nature, so when I take a walk or climb a mountain, I can feel the life and death of plants, insects, and animals daily. When I witness such things, there are times when my mind and body are shaken. I think this is the fundamental motivation for me to create works. I create works based on themes, such as the fragility of life, the sense of impermanence, and memories of people and places.

Q: Your work is influenced by the Rinpa school, ukiyo-e, as well as Japanese art from the Edo and Meiji periods, and Chinese painting. How do you integrate these traditional elements into your works? What role do these traditions play in your creation?

RS: Seeing the transcendental skill of the ancient *maki-e* (sprinkled picture) craftsmen, considered the pinnacle of beauty, and seeing the laughter, humor, and fragility of ukiyo-e, I thought I might be able to do the same thing through painting. I create works through trial and error, trying to learn from them in my own way, and incorporate and turn them into works. I think that traditional techniques give the work a sense of depth, so that's what I want to do.

Regarding the incorporation of traditional motifs into my works, I believe that the traditional subjects and motifs that still exist today have some kind of universal aspect and I think the universal aspect includes the interesting shapes or characters that contain generalities that people can relate to even today.

Q: You mainly depict women, monsters, *Yaoyorozu no Kami* (Eight Million Gods), beasts, and surrounding creatures. Is there a deeper meaning or symbolism behind these themes?

RS: Monsters and Eight Million Gods are themes that have been familiar to me since I was a child through manga, Japanese folktales, and anime.

So, I naturally incorporated those subjects into my work. The monsters are often depicted as beings between life and death, or as beings that transcend them.

When I draw demons and dragons, I feel like I often draw elements that are like projections of myself. About women appearing in almost all of my works, I simply want to depict the beautiful bodies of women, as well as their innocent beauty and motherhood.

Q: You have extensive exhibition experience, including at The Artcomplex Center of Tokyo, Naguri Forest, Ginza Mitsukoshi, and Gallery MUMON. Is there a particular exhibition that stands out as especially memorable or influential for you?

RS: I feel that each gallery has a really different way of thinking, passion, and sense of distance from the artists. Experiencing such things is interesting, stimulating, and educational. When I held a solo exhibition at Naguri Forest, Toshio Yoshikawa, the owner of Naguri Forest and a sculptor, told me something like "26-years-old is not young," when I was 26 years old and just starting out as an artist. Those words left a strong impression on me. From then on, I may have started trying to draw things that could only be drawn at that time, regardless of age.

Q: Many of your inspirations come from Katsushika Hokusai. How do you typically learn from the works of the distinguished Japanese artists? Are there any other artists you particularly admire?

RS: I see works in person at exhibitions, and I collect old books and catalogs from past exhibitions, which often give me ideas. I not

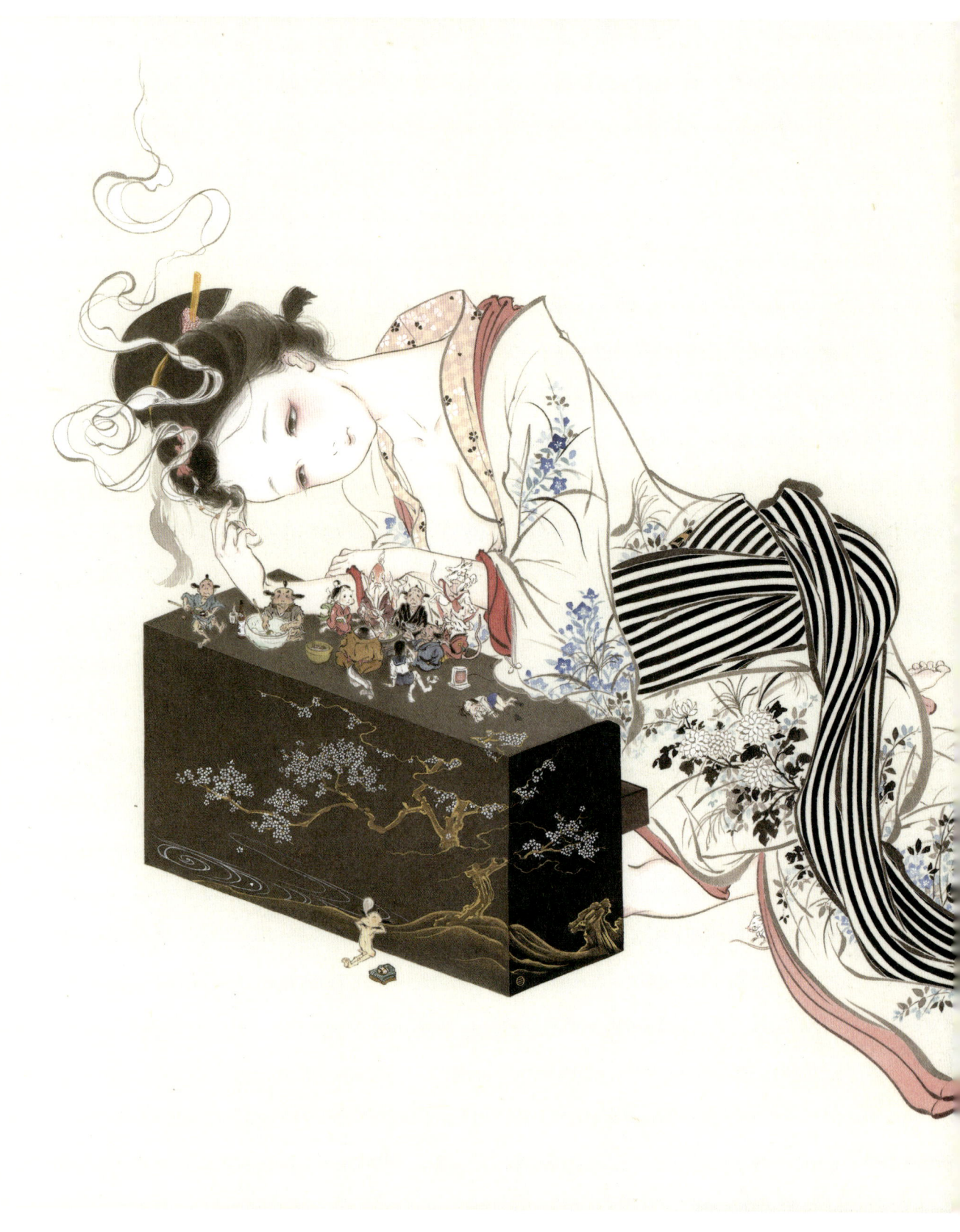

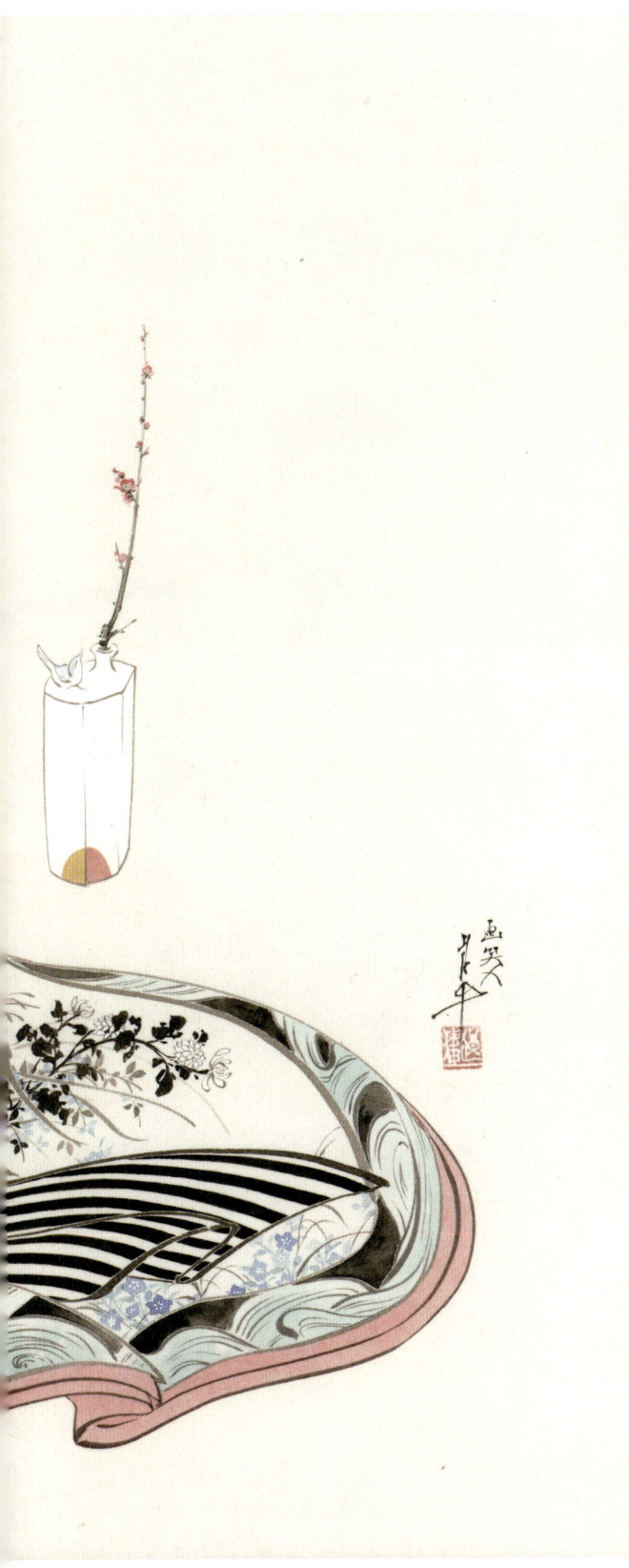

only learn about techniques and composition, but also learn about ideas, and I use them as references. In recent years, I have been shocked by the works of the Chinese artist Luo Hanlei, and I have a lot of respect for her secretly.

I knew about Luo Hanlei when my master Hakuro sent me some of her works' images online, telling me that there is such an artist and that she is similar to me. I got this artist's guidebook and saw it with an influence.

Q: Your work uses ink, acrylic, gold leaf, and Japanese paper. How did you start using these media as your primary tools for painting? Have you tried other media?

RS: I like *washi* (traditional Japanese paper) because it has a unique texture and taste, and unlike a stable and uniform medium like silk, it has an unstable fluctuation in a sense. *Sumi* (black ink) and acrylic are things that are familiar to me, and I have been using them naturally without any particular reason. Maybe acrylic paints suit my nature because I can draw pictures right away. Other mediums include pencil drawings and Adobe Illustrator software.

Q: You have received several awards, including the All Japan Exhibition and the Asian Digital Award, among others. How have these awards impacted your art career?

RS: When I think about it now, I realize that receiving those awards led to new connections and relationships with people. I met Yuji Yamashita, a Japanese art historian and art critic, at the 7th Adachi Contemporary Ukiyo-e Grand Award, and that led to my encounter with Gallery MUMON, where I am currently based. I think the change in environment helped me realize what I was lacking in, which helped me step up.

Q: What are your future artistic plans?

RS: One of my major goals is to draw a work like Soga Shohaku's *Immortals* with my own interpretation and creativity. This work has detailed drawings of the people, the vibrancy of the background, flora and fauna, and the overwhelming energy of the work itself. Now, I lack almost all of them, but I would like to steadily learn the techniques and draw my own *Immortals* someday.

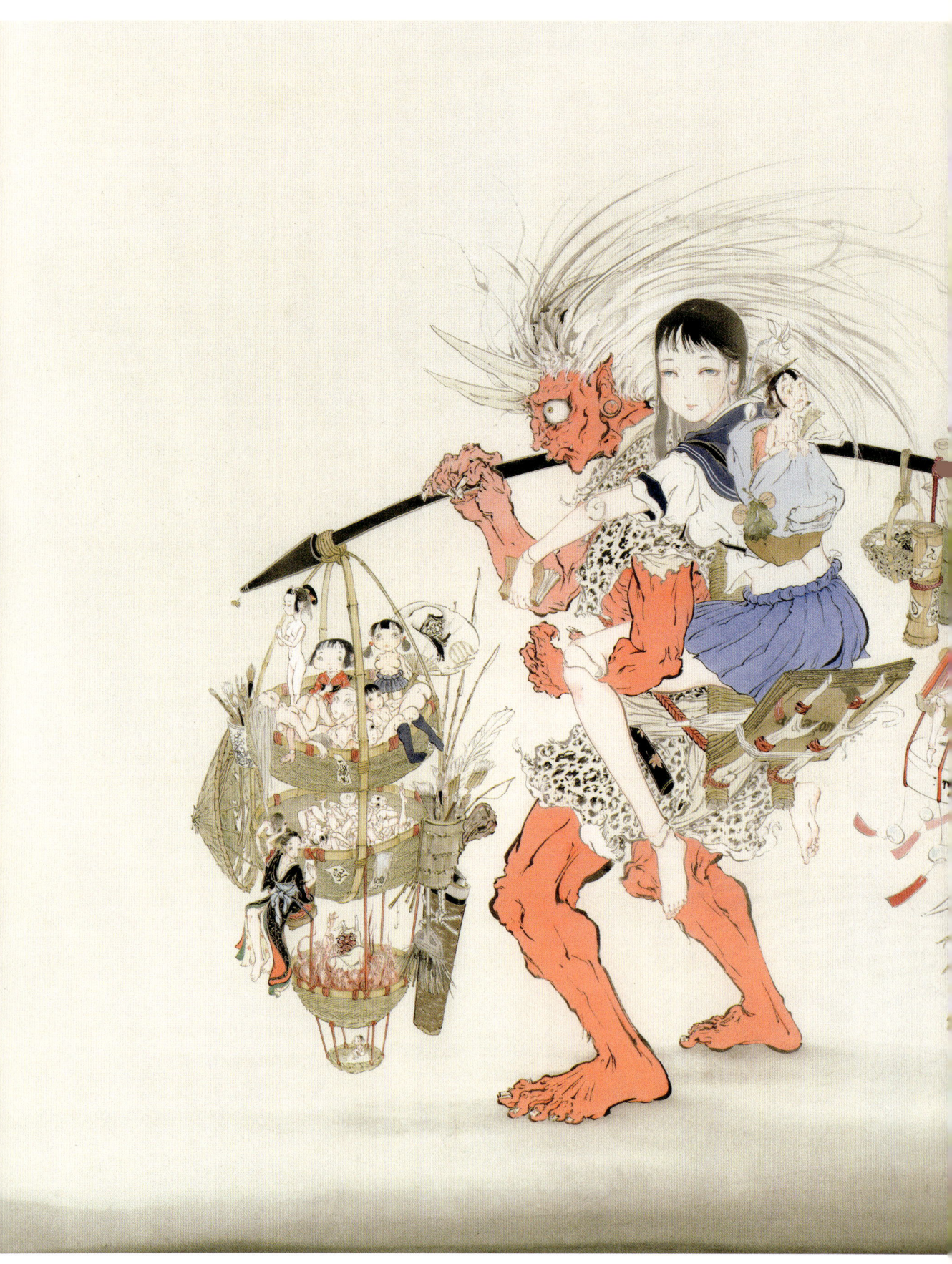

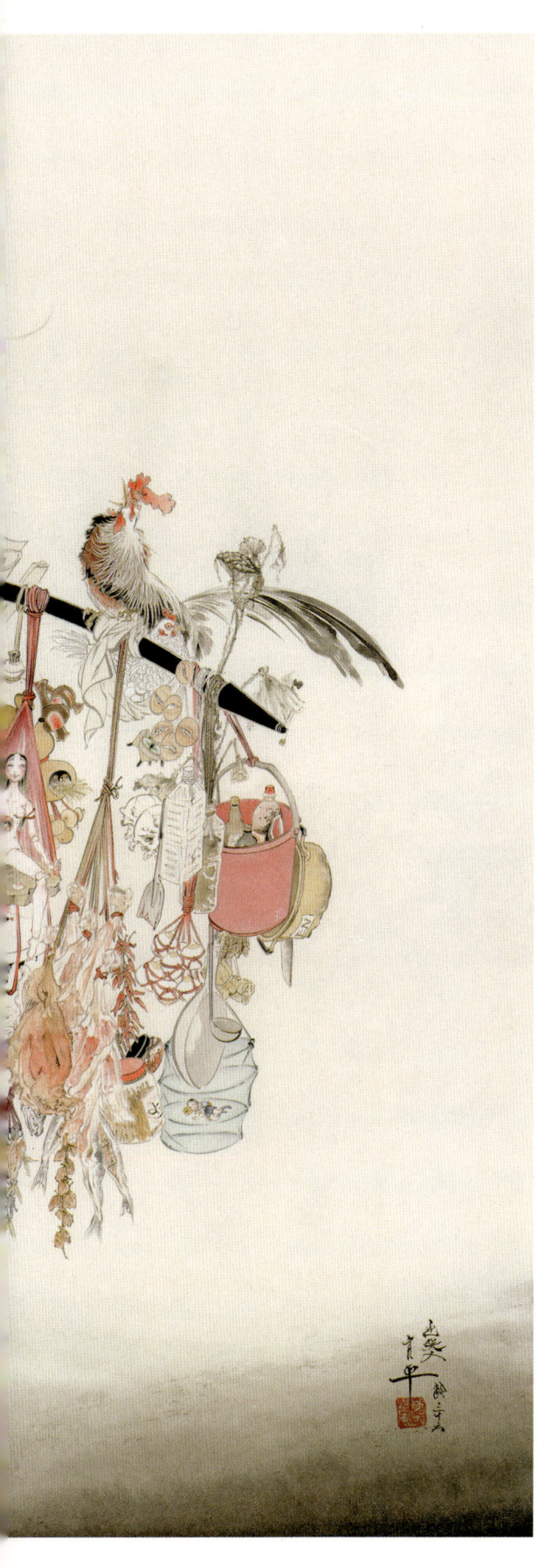

" *When I draw demons and dragons, I feel like I often draw elements that are like projections of myself. About women appearing in almost all of my works, I simply want to depict the beautiful bodies of women, as well as their innocent beauty and motherhood.* "

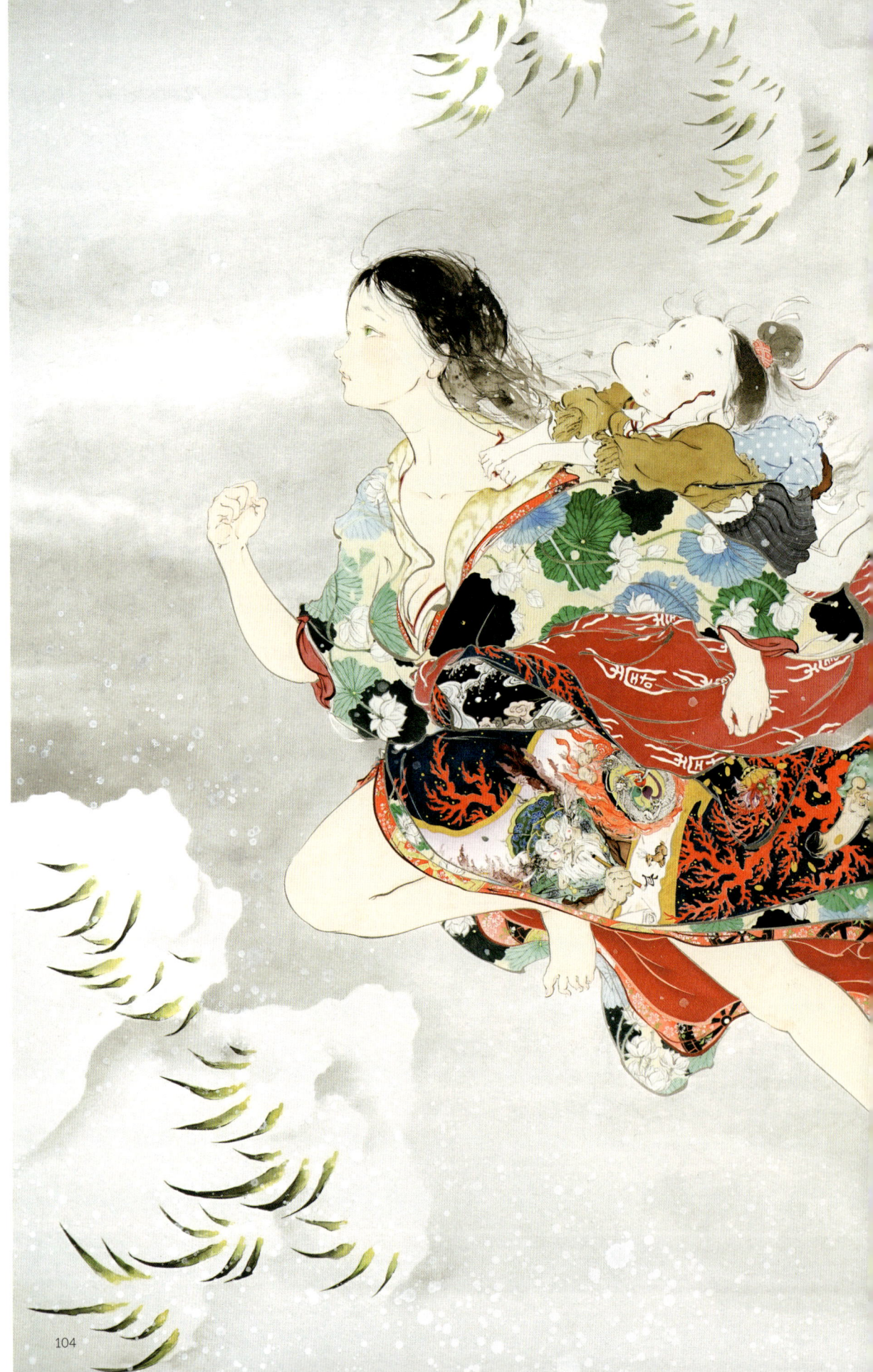

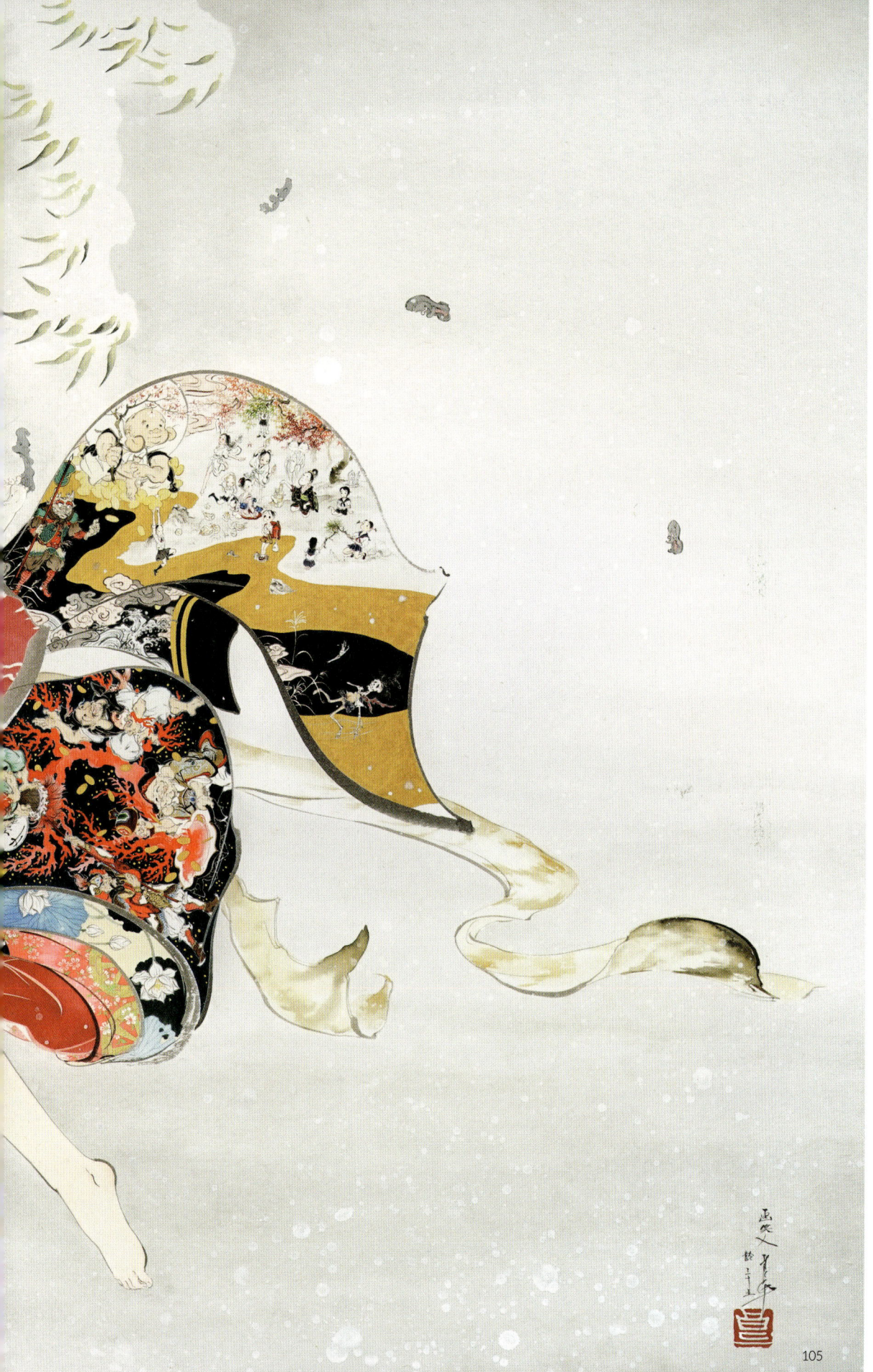

NINJA STYLE

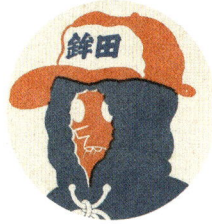

Ichiraku Studio

He is passionately dedicated to the creation of ukiyo-e prints, skillfully blending traditional brushwork with modern silkscreen techniques. Through such harmonious fusion, his works embody depth, vibrancy, and timeless allure.

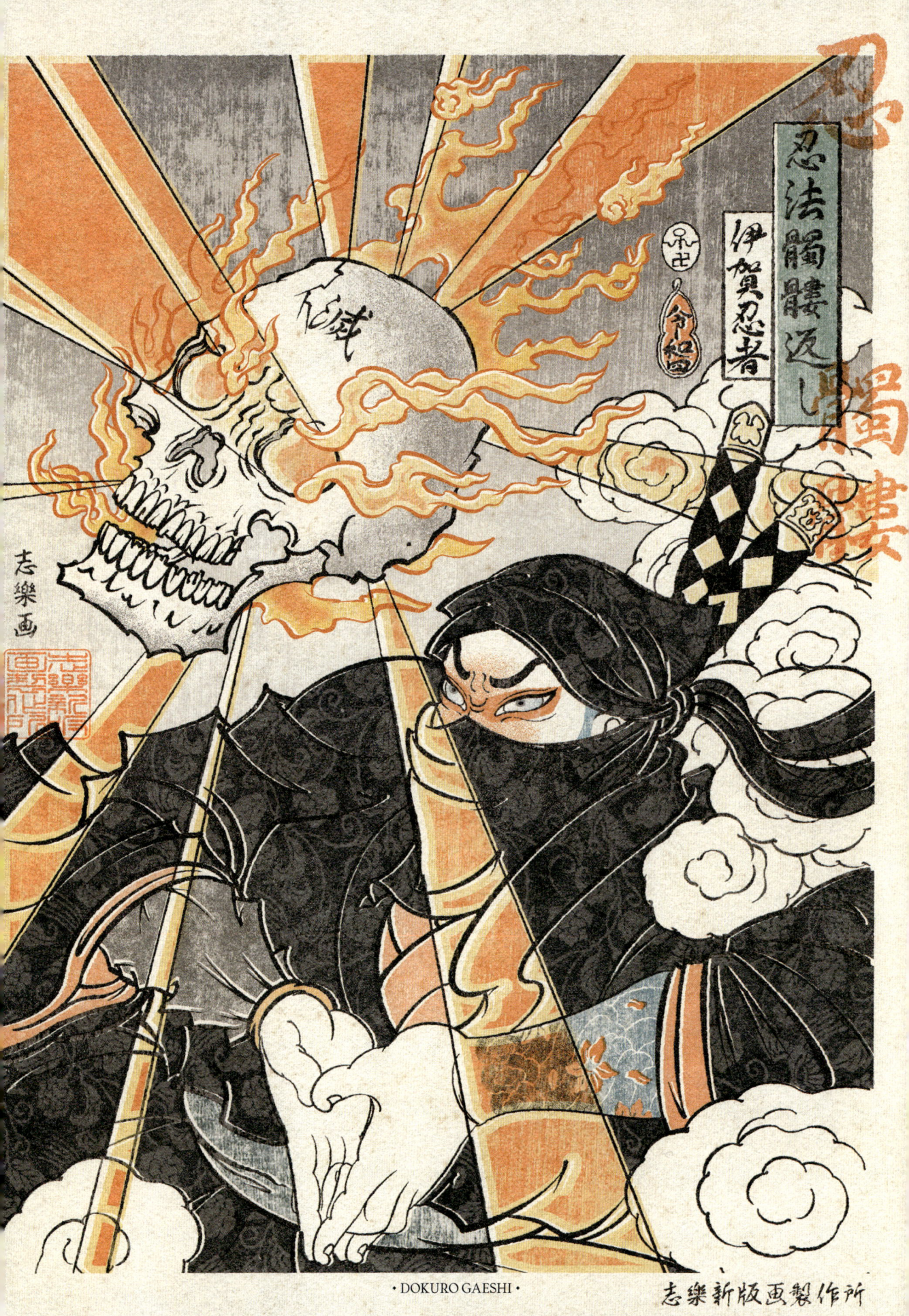

· DOKURO GAESHI ·

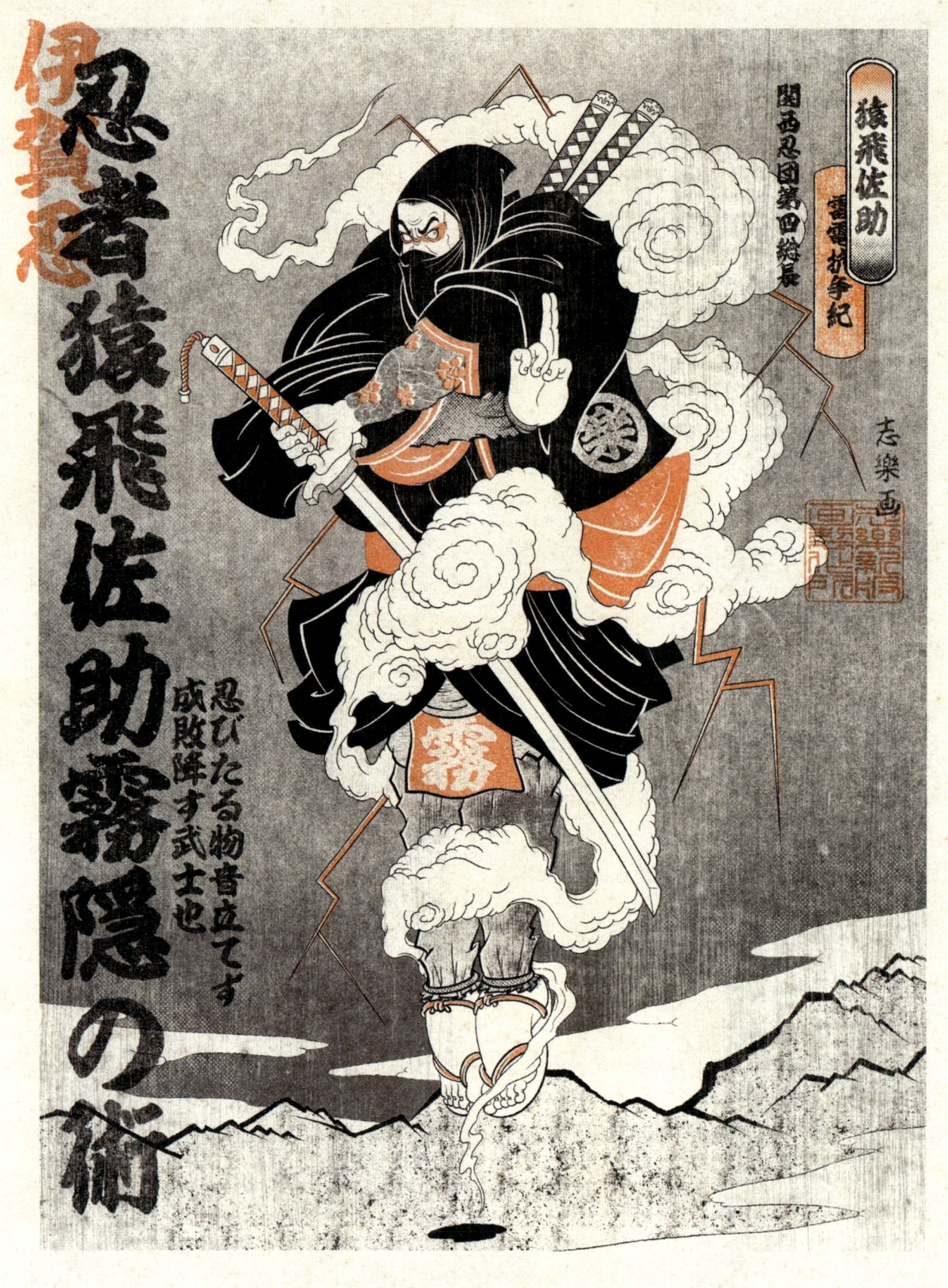

Q: Could you tell us your artistic background? When did you begin to be interested in art?

IS: I have loved drawing since childhood and have been drawing consistently ever since. Over time, it naturally led me to develop a deep interest in art.

Q: How has ukiyo-e influenced you? Which aspects have had the deepest impact on your creative work? Are there any particular ukiyo-e artists who have had a significant influence on you?

IS: The first ukiyo-e artist who influenced me was Tōshūsai Sharaku, whose works I encountered in textbooks during my school days. His bold and striking compositions left a lasting impression on me, and I often imitated his style when I was younger. I also admire Tsukioka Yoshitoshi and Kawanabe Kyosai.

Q: Is there any special significance or reason behind your choice involving samurais and ninjas in your paintings?

IS: There isn't any particular reason. Simply put, I find them cool. I don't have much historical knowledge or scholarly background, and my paintings don't carry deep meanings. I create my work based on the intuitive sense of "coolness" I felt when watching anime and robots as a child.

Q: Traditional ukiyo-e and screen print have a significant influence on your creative process. Could you tell us how these two techniques have played a role in your work?

IS: Besides the intuitive sense of "coolness" in my works, I also value the expressions of aging such as wear, blurring, and smudging. Screen printing is a very suitable tool for reproducing these elements of aging.

Q: Is it challenging for you to transition between different styles in your artworks, such as ukiyo-e, comic style, and abstract style? How do you balance these shifts between different styles?

IS: It's not that difficult. However, it requires continuous practice and dedication, which has taken up lots of my time. Before I knew it, I was already 38 years old. To move forward, I plan to focus solely on ukiyo-e.

Q: You have set up your YouTube channel to share the creative process. Could you tell us any challenges or something interesting during your creation? How has the sharing impacted your creative process?

IS: I use brushes for my paintings, and they are very delicate tools. Even slight mental disturbances or changes in my physical condition can affect the lines I draw. As a result, I have become more conscious of basic life habits, such as my lifestyle and diet.

Q: You have opened an online shop. How do you balance your role between a business operator and a creator?

IS: I'm still figuring it out!

Q: Do you have any new plans or projects for your future creations? Are you considering exploring other styles?

IS: I don't plan to pursue many styles anymore. I intend to delve deeper into creating new ukiyo-e. My immediate goal is to hold a solo exhibition.

Q: Can you give some advice for illustrators who want to try the ukiyo-e style?

IS: I'm still exploring it myself, so I don't have enough experience to advise others. However, I believe that if you continue at your own pace without giving up, the results will follow naturally.

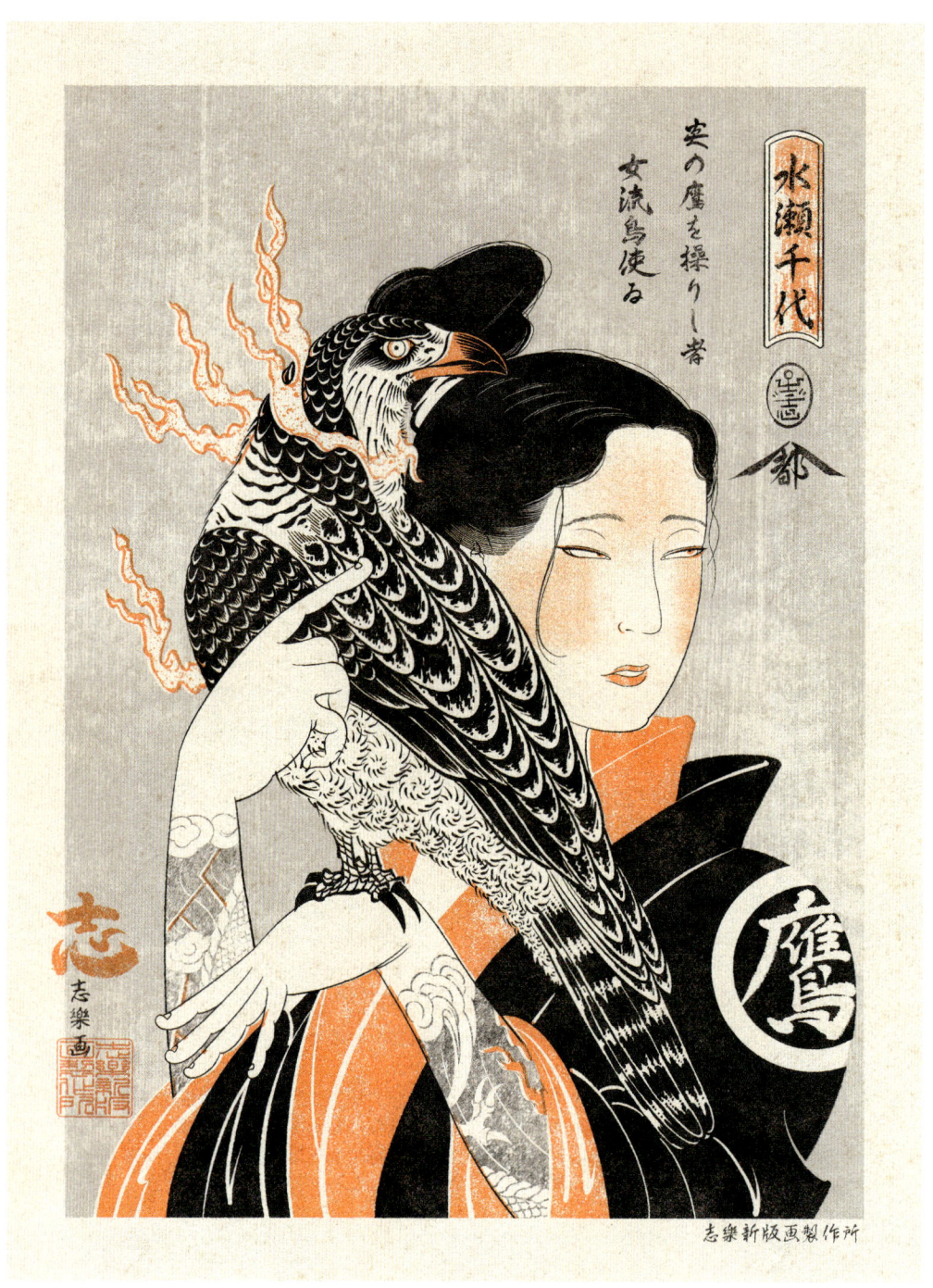

• FALCON AND WOMAN •

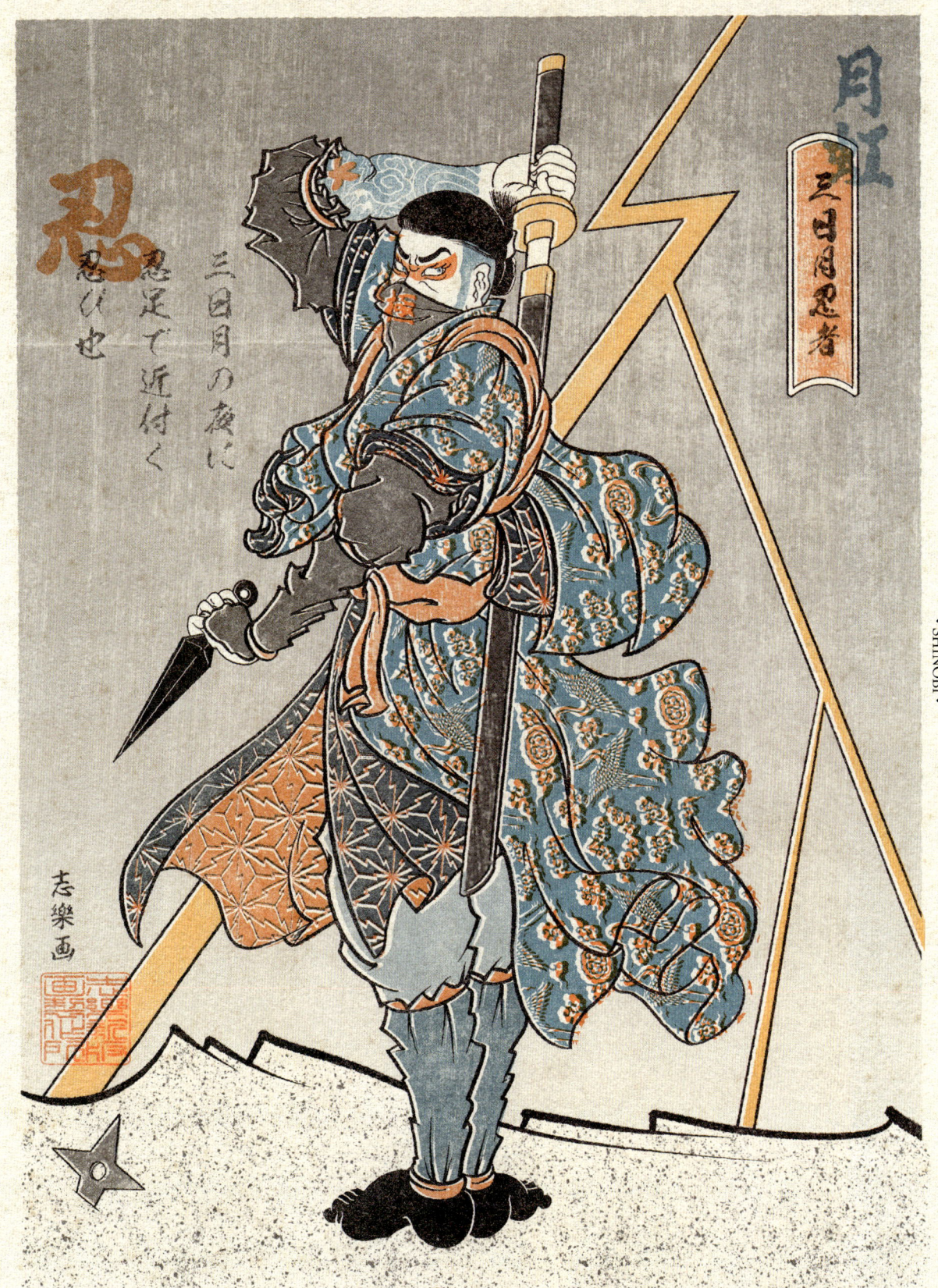

月姫
三日月忍者

忍
忍び也

三日月の夜に
忍足で近付く

志樂画

・SHINOBI・

志樂新版画製作所
111

" *I create my work based
on the intuitive sense of 'coolness'
I felt when watching anime
and robots as a child.* "

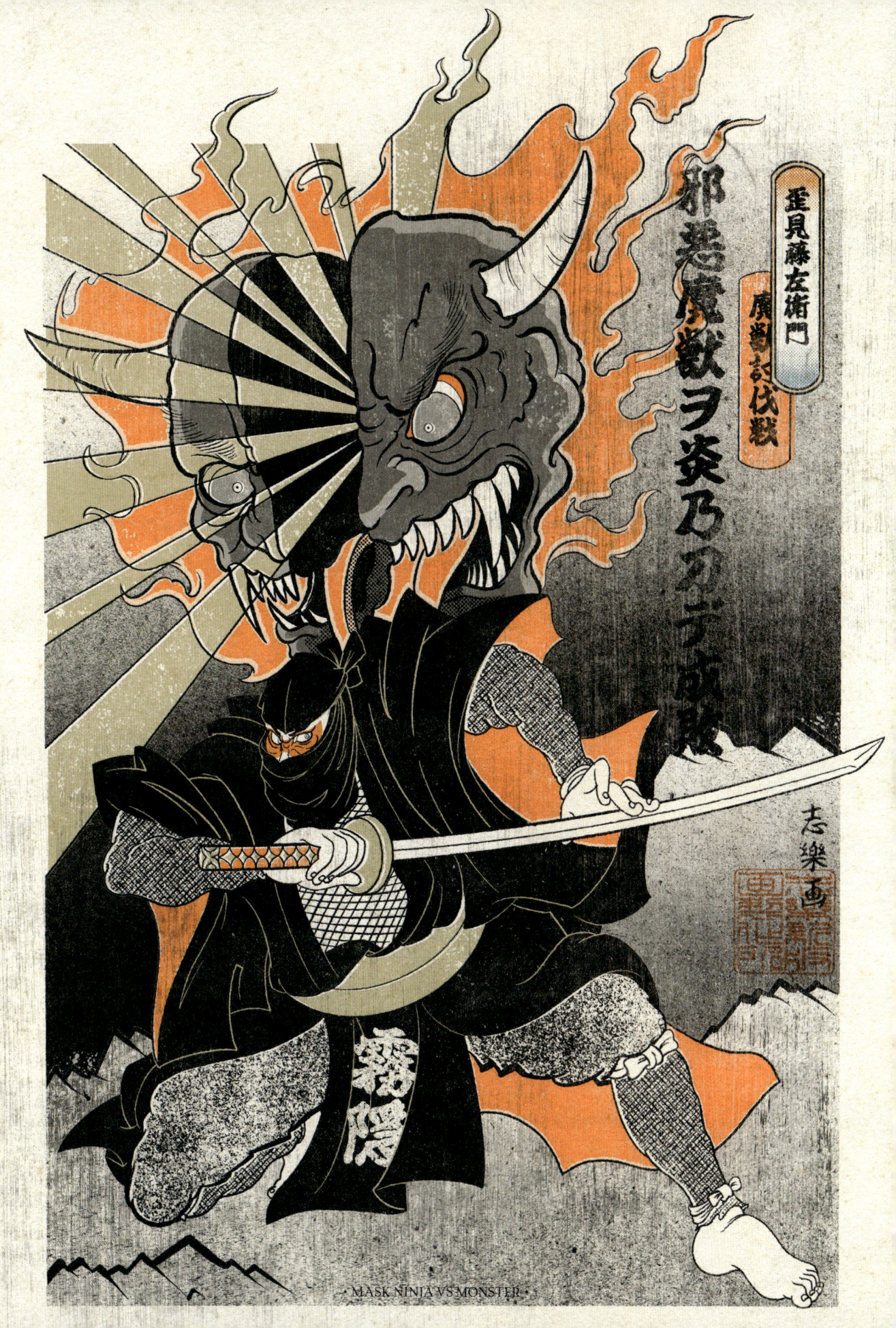

MASK NINJA VS MONSTER

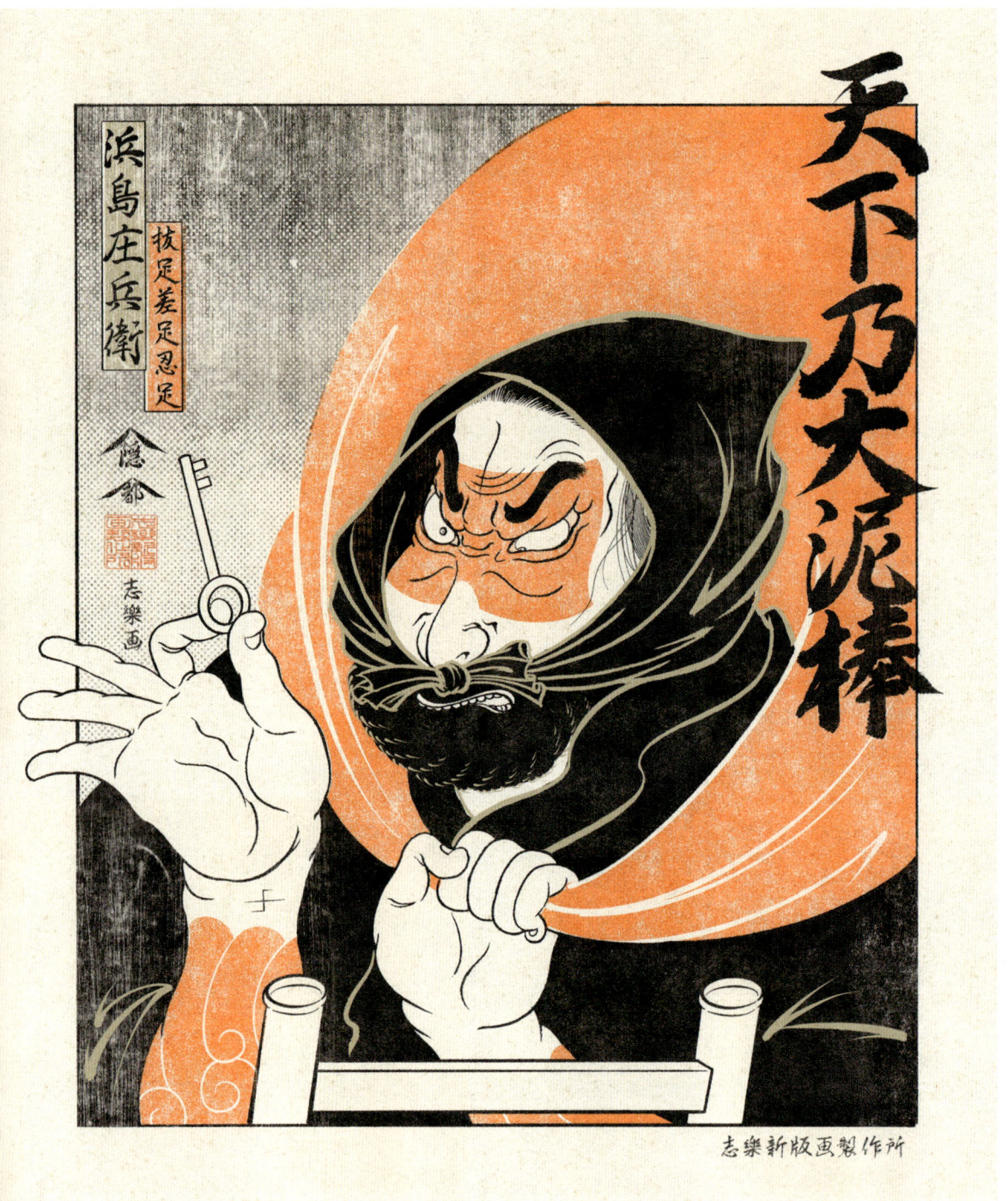

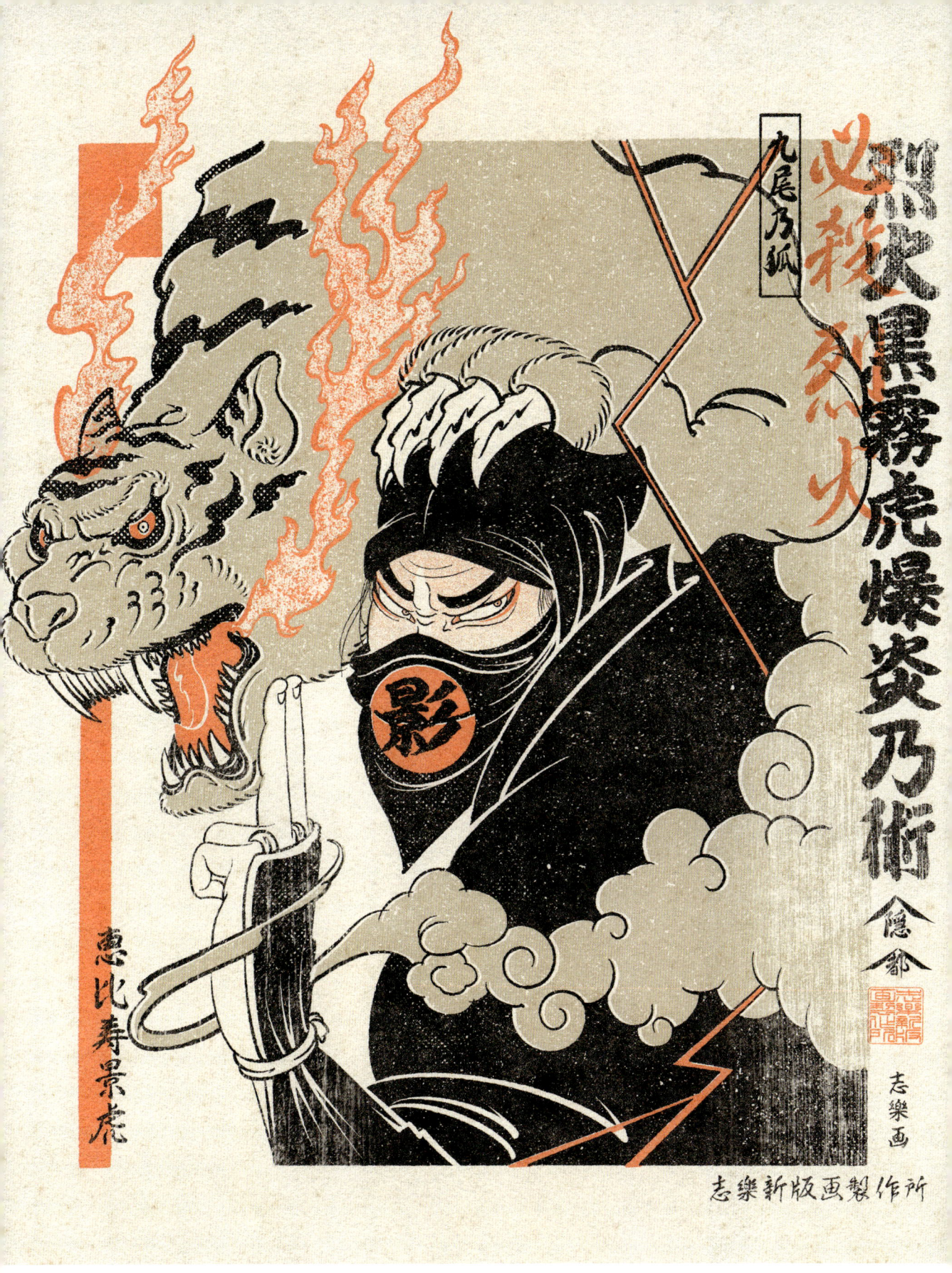

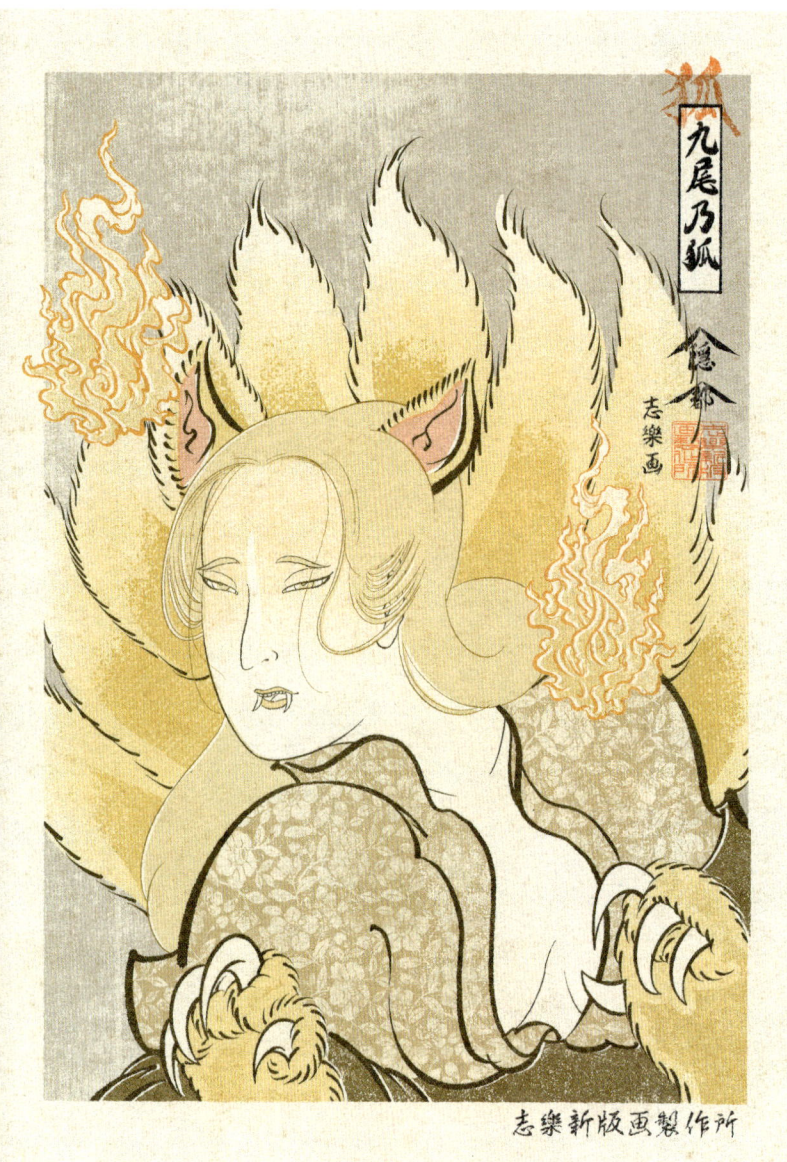

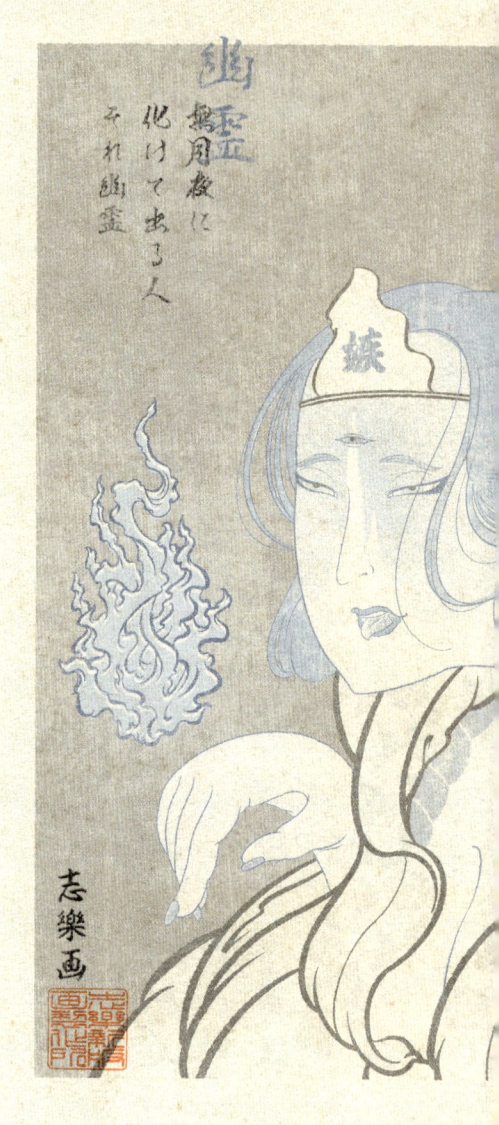

　• OBAKE (LEFT), KYŪBINOKITSUNE (MIDDLE), BAKE NEKO (RIGHT) •

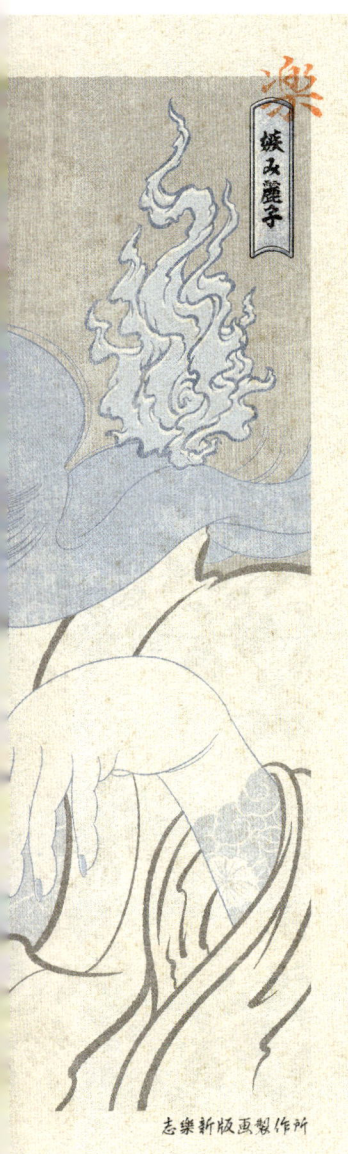

吉沼乃化け猫

志樂画

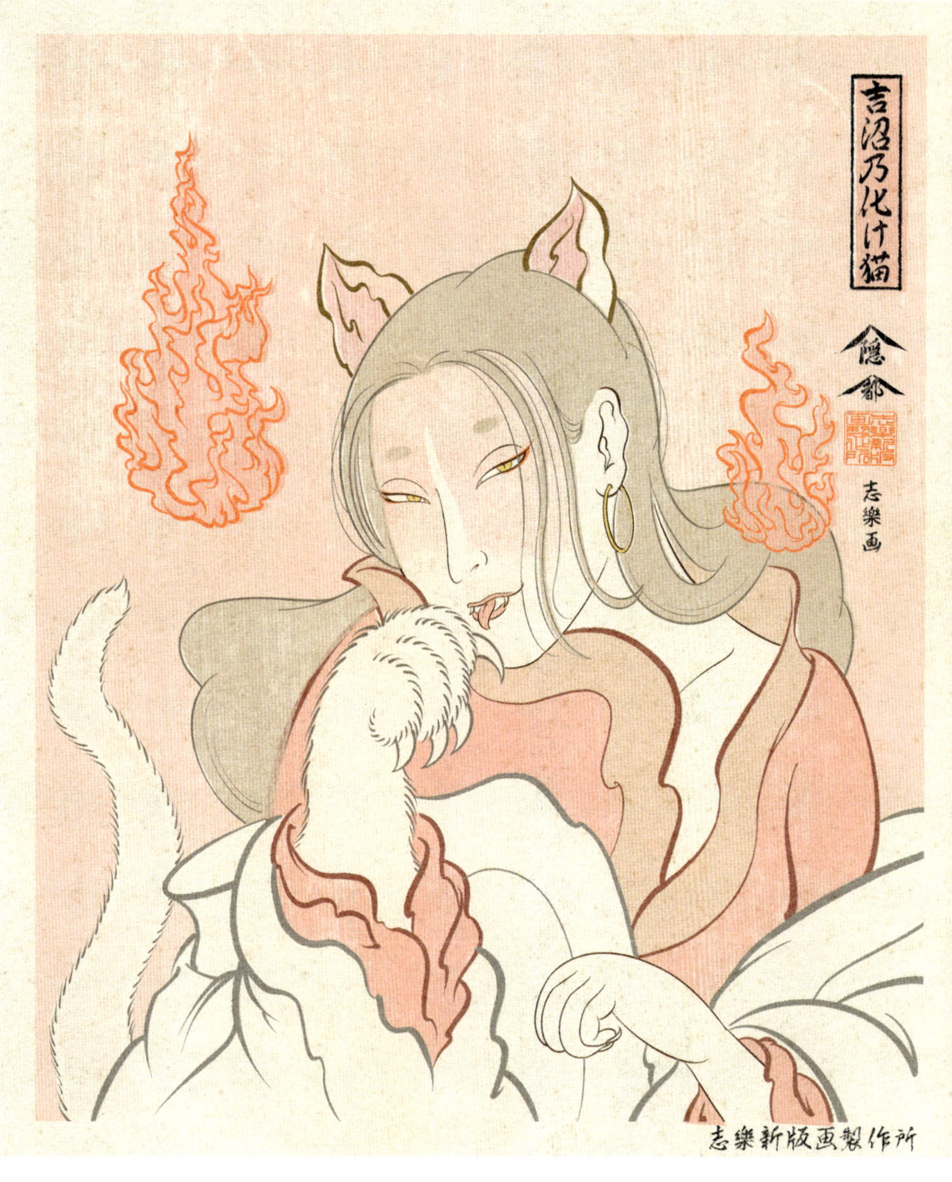

志樂新版画製作所

GAZE TO GAZE

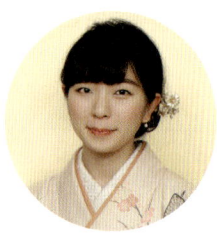

Shihori Hattori

Born in Kyoto, Japan in 1988. Shihori completed a master's course in Japanese painting, at Kyoto City University of Arts, Graduate School of Fine Arts in 2013. Unraveling the haze within herself, she expresses the Japanese beauty cultivated in her daily life and the fashionable state of people through *ossan* (middle-aged man), which is often depicted as a symbol of the humor that emerges from human life—elegant humor, the spirit of an ordinary person, and a bird's eye view of human weaknesses. She prefers using light ink colors in her paintings and aims to create Japanese artworks that emphasize the ink lines she has mastered since childhood.

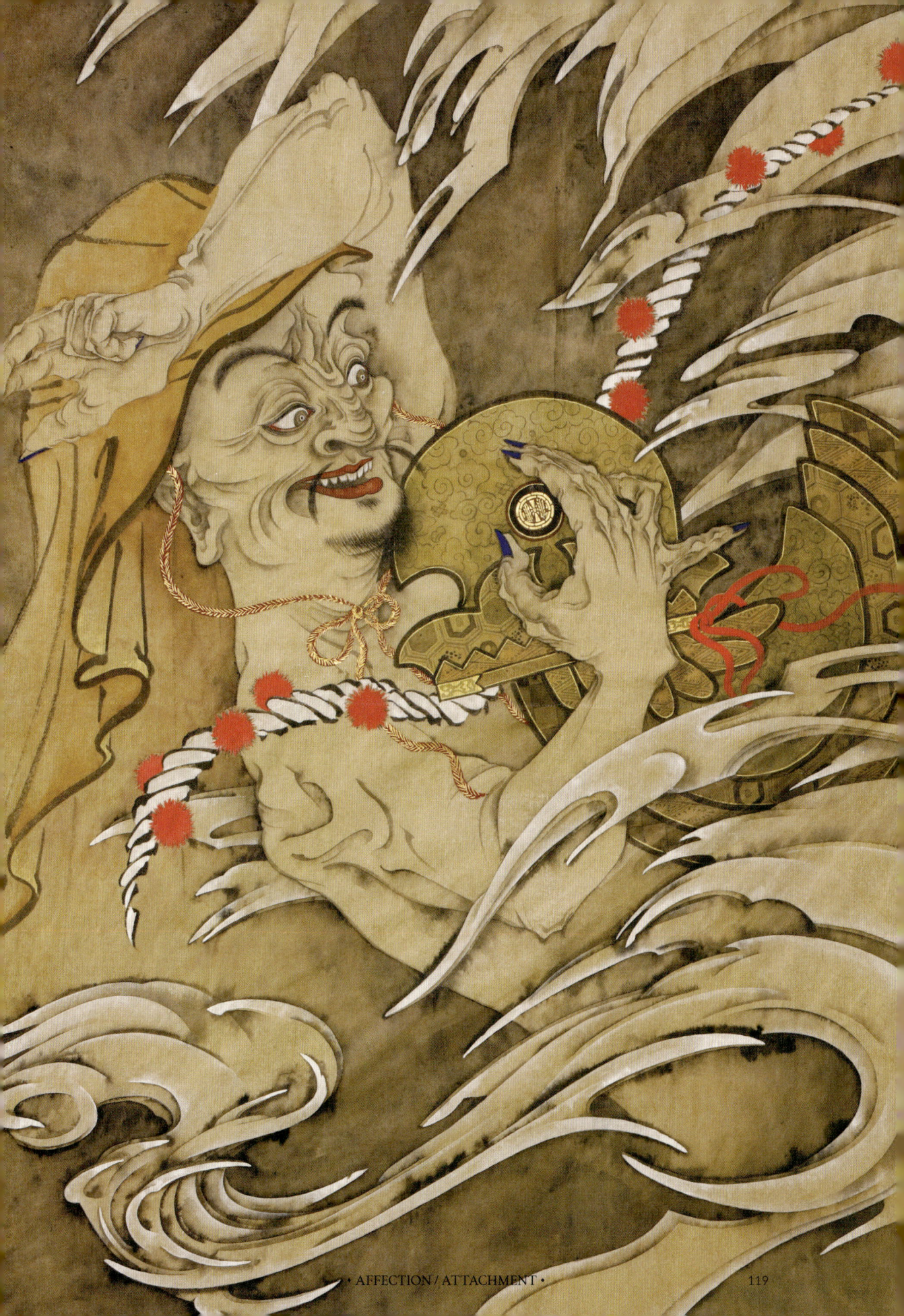

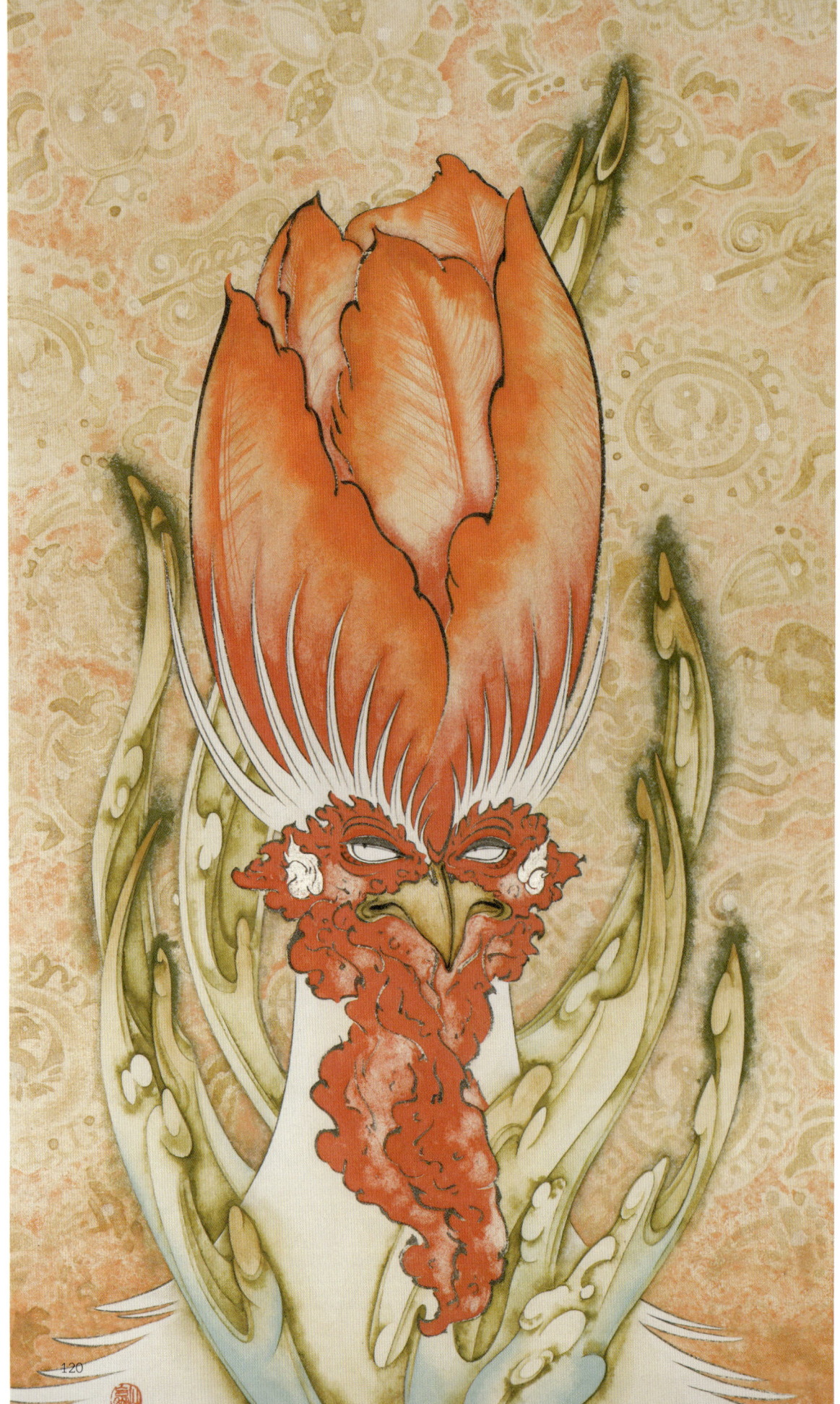

120

Q: When did your interest in painting begin? You have been studying Japanese painting at Kyoto City University of Arts. What help and influence does this experience bring you?

SH: Drawing came very naturally to me, even before I was old enough to remember. Watching my 6-year-old daughter now, I can imagine how I must have drawn just as naturally at her age. At Kyoto City University of Arts, I learned Japanese painting from scratch, something I had no prior experience with. My existing aesthetic sense and the line techniques I developed through calligraphy since childhood gradually merged with these newly learned methods. In particular, the university's tradition of observing and depicting the true essence of objects with sincerity has become the foundation of my current artistic practice.

Q: How do you use Japanese-style elements to interpret "Japanese beauty"? Which artists or works have influenced and inspired your creation?

SH: While it's difficult to define Japanese beauty in a single phrase, I'm drawn to aspects of our culture that might seem a bit mysterious to modern eyes—from traditional culture and crafts to performing arts like Noh and popular culture rooted in Shinto rituals like sumo wrestling. I've been particularly influenced by the Kanō school, which created a Japanese-Chinese hybrid style based on Chinese painting that later became a major foundation for Japanese painting. I also draw significant inspiration from ukiyo-e.

Q: You mentioned that "the essence of Japanese painting is the line." Can you reference your daily work to illustrate the core of this concept?

SH: The way lines transform into objects and landscapes—it's like the magical essence of painting itself. Particularly central to my work is the distinctly East Asian sensibility of finding rich landscapes within lines.

Q: You mentioned "Hattori Universe" on your official website. Is this a worldview built in your artistic creation? Can you talk about the meaning and source of this concept?

SH: "Hattori Universe" is a phrase I started using as a website title during my student days. It doesn't have any grandiose meaning. I just wanted to express the simple fact that everyone has their own universe and unique worldview inside them.

Q: You look at life and art with a humorous attitude of "ossan (middle-aged man)." How does this attitude affect your painting creation?

SH: The *ossan* is my self-portrait. I've packed it with my ideals of how I'd like to live. While the *ossan* might appear ugly or strange at first glance, I'm drawn to his easygoing and free-spirited way of life.

Q: In your works, the eyes of characters and animals are impressive. What kind of emotions or meanings do you want to reveal with these expressions?

SH: While I hadn't consciously focused on the expression of eyes, the depiction of faces and eyes is indeed crucial. Eyes don't just convey expression; they create a mutual gaze between the viewer and the viewed. When a painted face looks back at you, it adds depth to the artwork beyond a one-sided relationship, emphasizing the connection between the observer and the observed. This reciprocal exchange of gazes is a vital element for me.

Q: You have only begun to depict female characters in the work in recent years. What is the reason for you to avoid female images previously? What does today's change mean for your creation?

SH: Gender has been a significant issue for me, and for a long time, I struggled to come to terms with being female. However, through marriage, pregnancy, and childbirth, I gradually began to accept my "female self." With that acceptance, I naturally became able to depict women in my work.

Q: You have painted covers for multiple books, and also present your own works on paper fans and other products. What do you think of the commercialization of painting art?

SH: Japanese painting often seems intimidating, doesn't it? But that's such a shame. Japanese painting is fundamental to our culture and is one of the roots of manga. That's why I want people to feel closer to it. Commercial projects like book covers and folding fans are important opportunities to realize this goal.

Q: You often record diaries and share your life on the official website and Instagram. In view of the need for painting creation to be highly focused and introspective, what impact does this record have on your artistic creation? How did you find a balance between family life and creation?

SH: Actually, I'm not very good with social media, and finding time for it has become even more challenging since I started raising children. However, sharing information on social media provides good opportunities for self-reflection, so I continue within my capabilities. While balancing family life and artistic creation is challenging, my artwork is inseparable from

daily life, so I approach each day with the mindset of elevating everyday experiences into art.

Q: What are the new projects or plans you have in mind, or in progress? What are the expectations of the future creative direction?

SH: I will hold a solo exhibition in Kyoto in June 2025. In 2026, I'm scheduled to exhibit at my alma mater, Kyoto City University of Arts, alongside educational materials and works by senior alumni currently archived at the university. This will be a very significant exhibition for me.

Recently, I collaborated with woodblock print artisans to create woodblock prints. Japan has a highly developed woodblock print tradition, as seen in ukiyo-e, and I've always been fascinated by how accessible and easily distributed these prints were historically. Thanks to the cooperation of various people, I could create original woodblock prints.

While woodblock printing is very labor-intensive and might seem to go against current trends, I want to continue this project to spread the appeal of this technique and culture through my work.

As for future works, I'd like to challenge myself with larger-scale pieces and actively explore subjects beyond human figures I haven't depicted before.

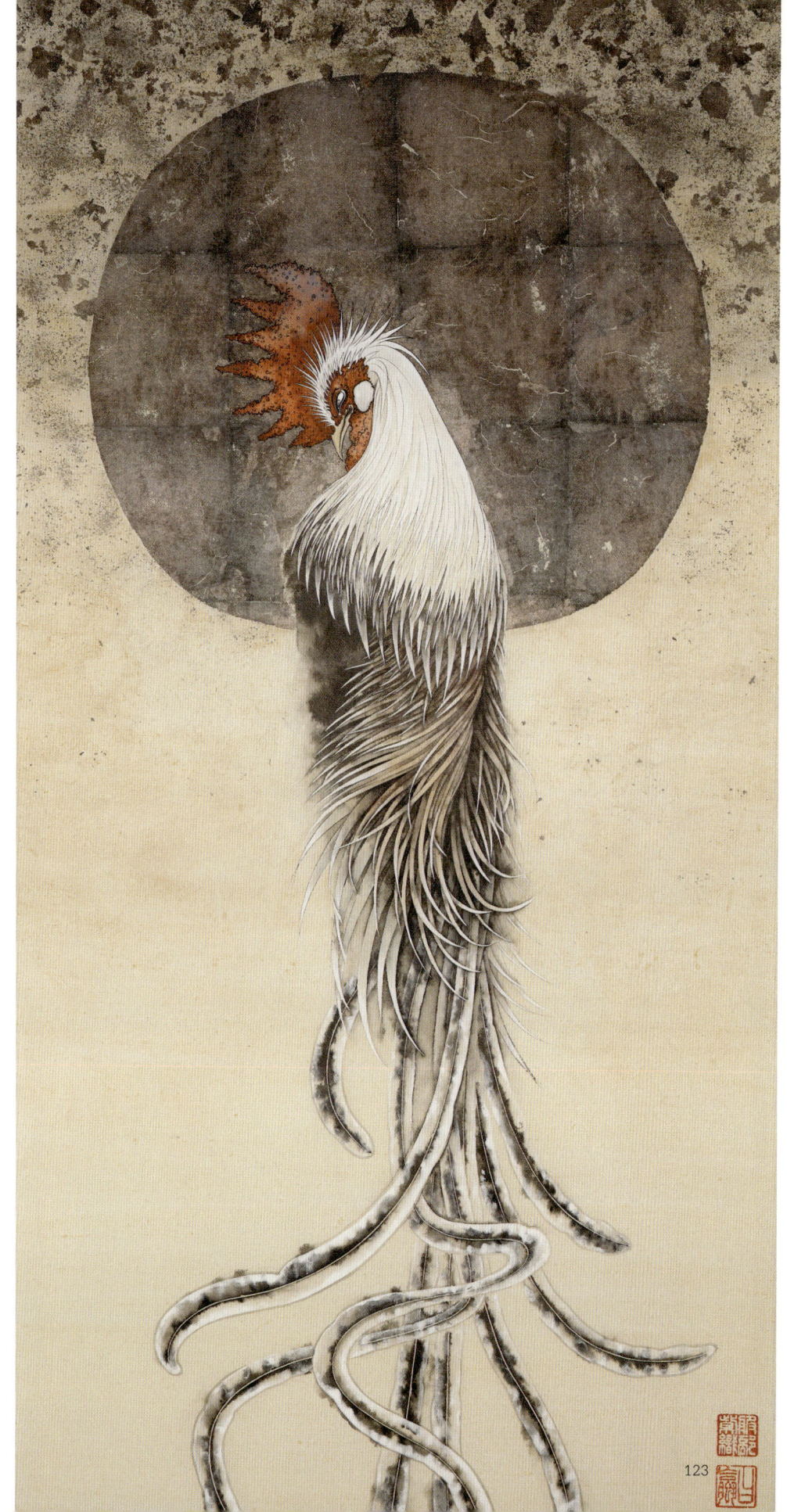

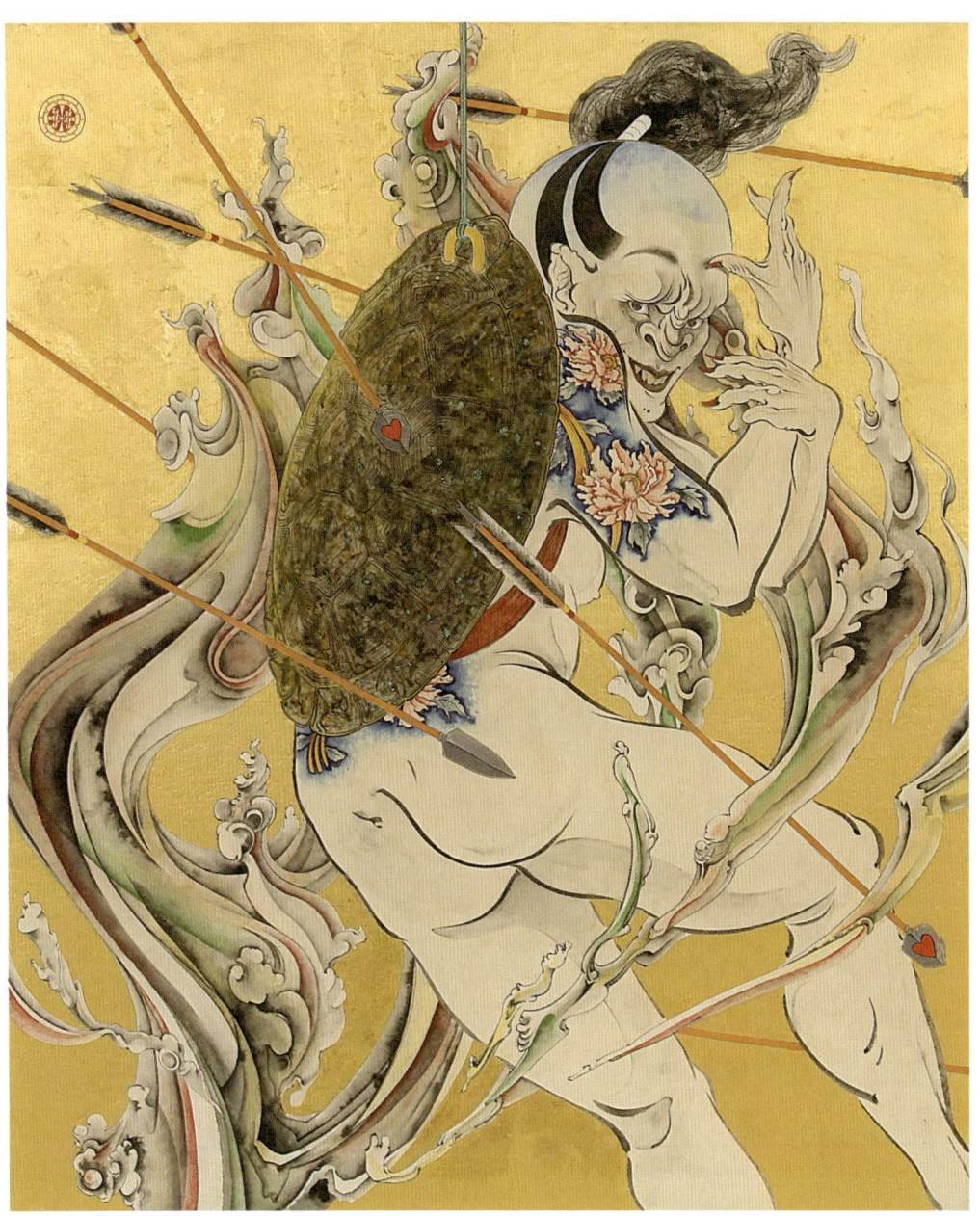

• TURTLE MAN •

" *When a painted face looks back at you, it adds depth to the artwork beyond a one-sided relationship, emphasizing the connection between the observer and the observed. This reciprocal exchange of gazes is a vital element for me.* "

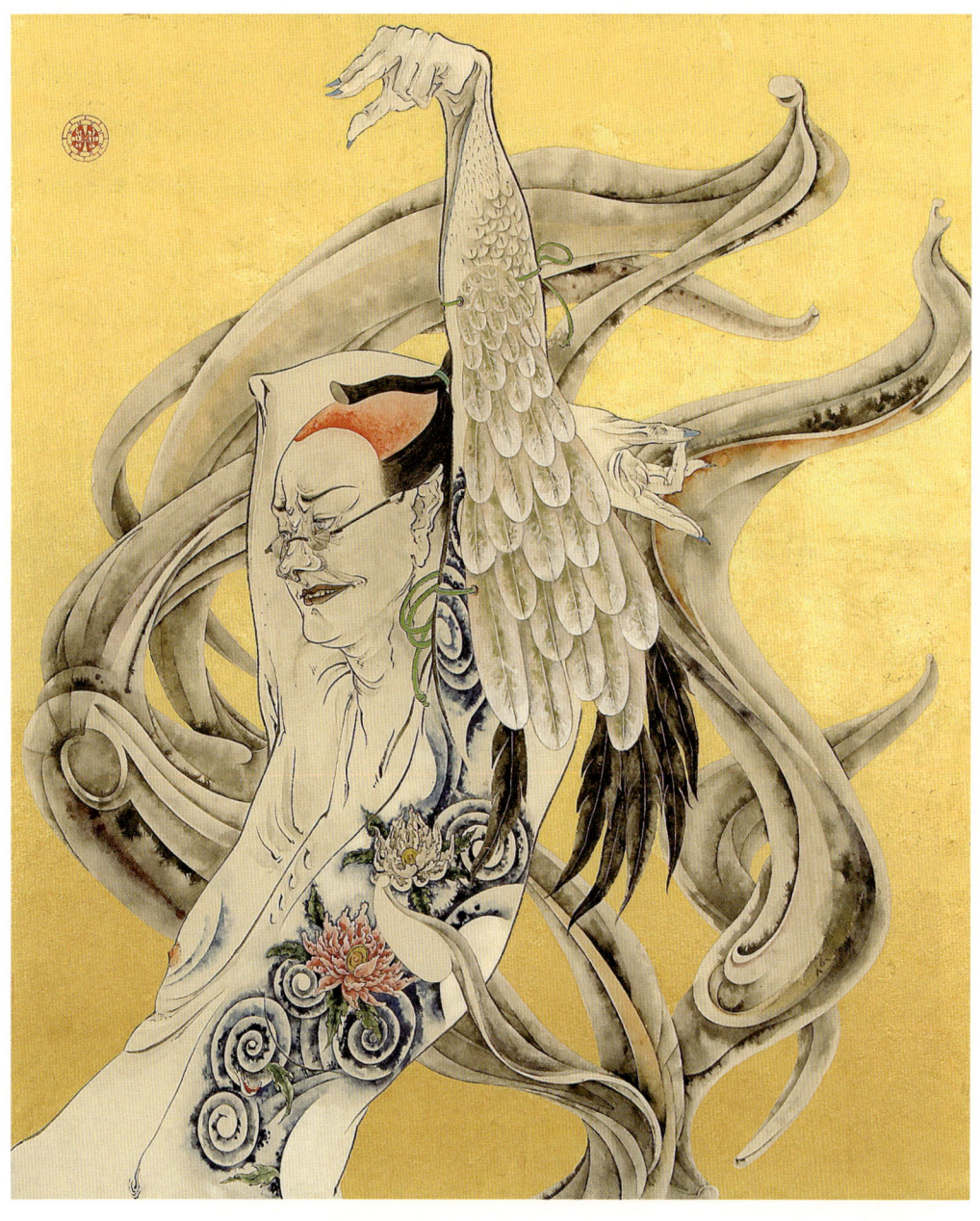

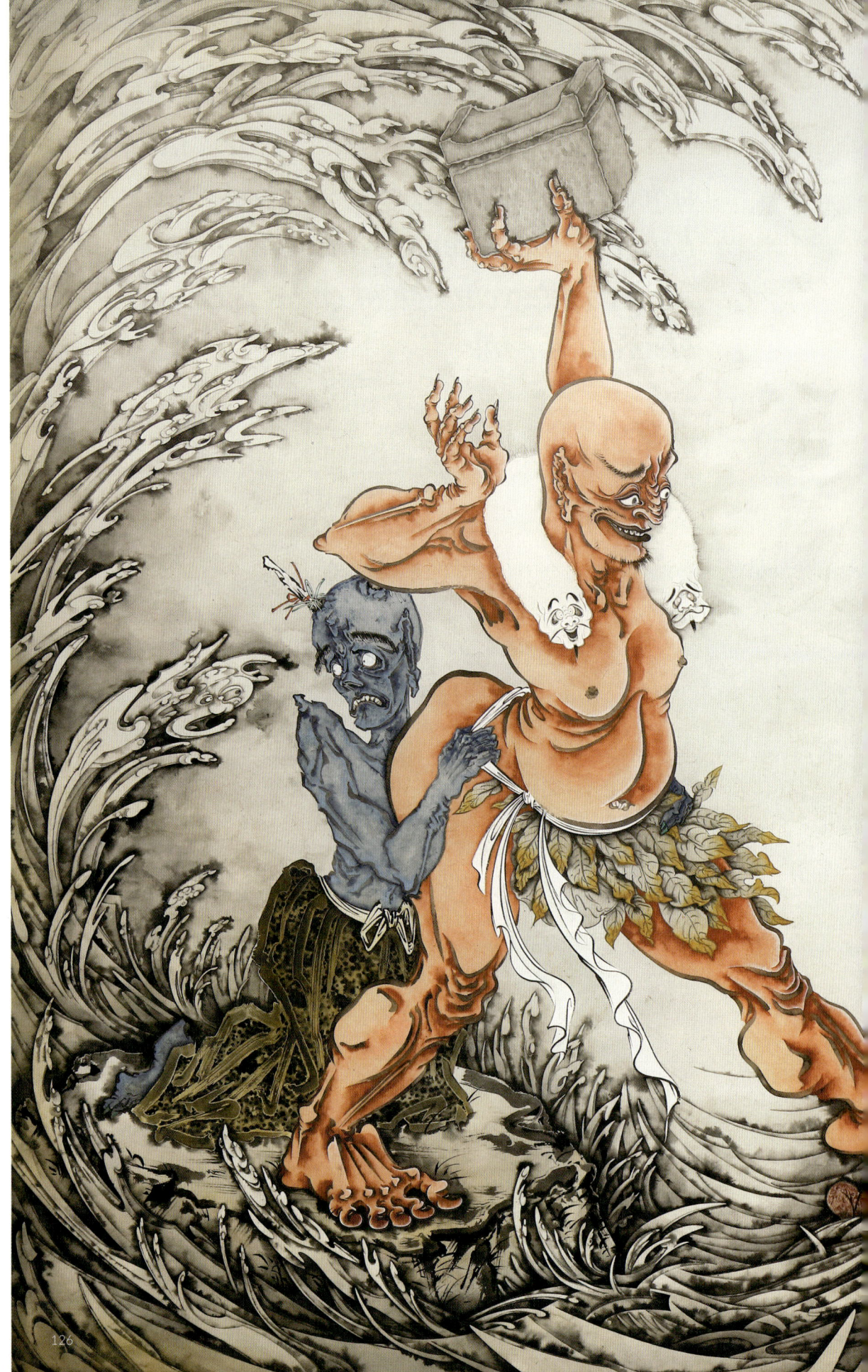

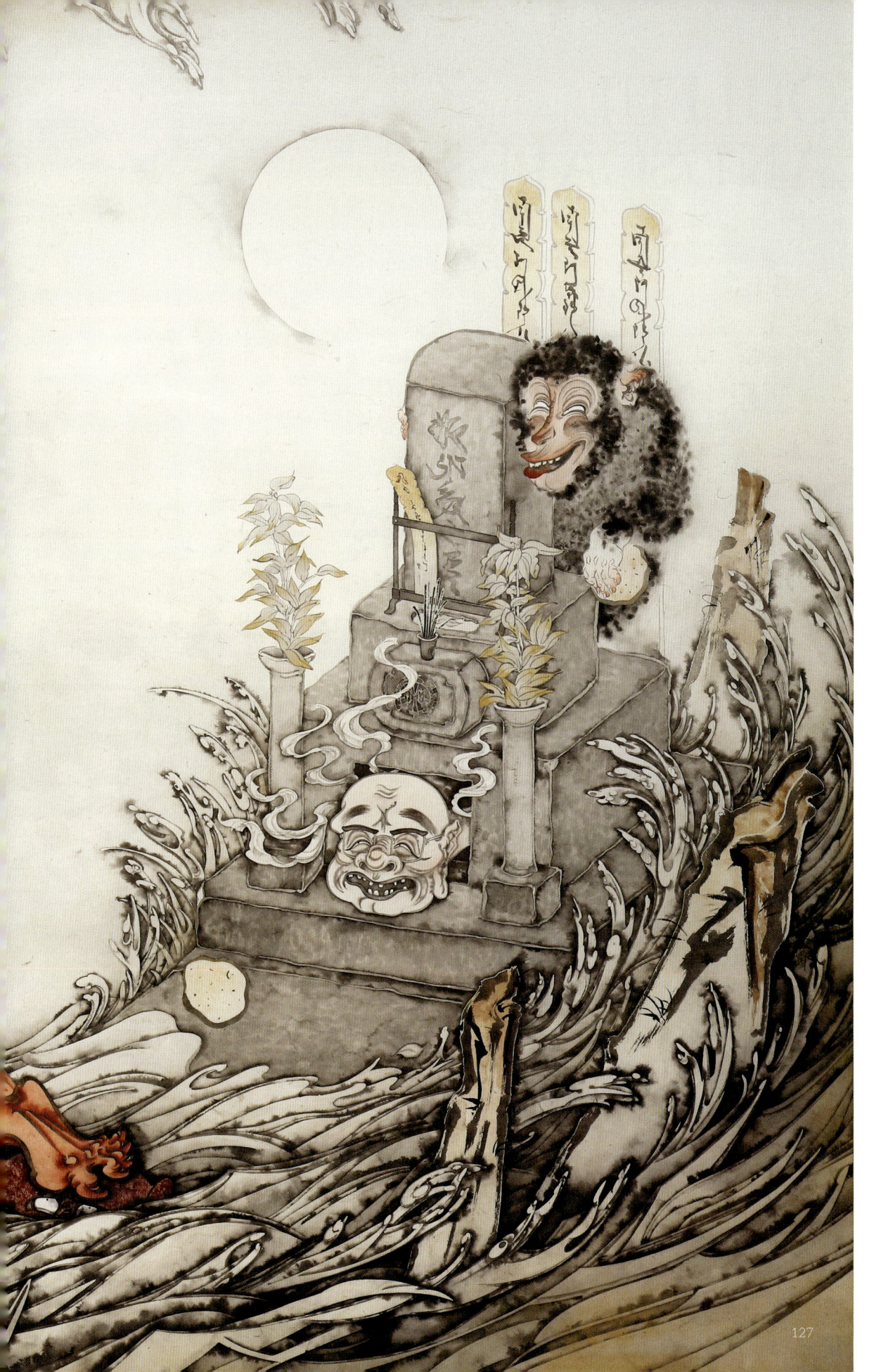

SOULFUL
LANDSCAPES

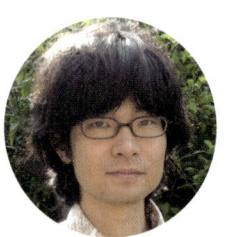

Natsuki Urushihara

Born in 1977 in Kanagawa, Japan, Natsuki Urushihara has been experimenting with painting the souls and spiritual forms of the things that exist around him that attract his awareness, as a symbolic landscape of those beings. He draws on traditional Japanese iconography while adding new stories and symbolism to it by integrating the surrounding landscape of the subject, mainly depicting natural phenomena such as mountains, forests, clouds, and flowing water as the sole forms of the subject's existence.

• HER SCENERY (2018) •

Q: Could you share what initially inspired your interest in art? What sparked your passion for painting?

NU: I know this is a common story, but I have been drawing pictures whenever I had time since I was a child. I was born and raised in the suburbs, where there was a mixture of inhabited towns and nature, so I had many opportunities to come into contact with insects and small animals, which attracted my gaze as a young child and made them very attractive subjects for drawing. I was also fascinated by the various anime and manga in Japan, and as a young child, I admired the characters in those stories and copied them in large quantities. The act of drawing what fascinated me and creating something on paper that could never exist fascinated me as a child. Those childhood memories guided my thought and action principles and greatly influenced my decision to become a painter. I want to savor every bit of the world in front of me, and painting is my way of doing so.

Q: Your works often combine figures with landscape scenery. What thoughts and meanings lie behind this artistic expression?

NU: The subjects of my paintings are people near and dear to me. They are irreplaceable to me, and I fuse them with magnificent landscapes to express them as greater and more precious beings. I believe that by depicting people as landscapes, I can entrust their personalities and thoughts to the topography and phenomena. For example, when I come in contact with a certain person, I sometimes feel that person is like a majestic mountain, or that his or her emotional ups and downs are like a waterfall or a stream of water. I try to depict the essence of a person by entrusting such sensations to various elements that appear in the landscape.

In addition, the natural landscapes around us seem universal, but they have undergone unexpected changes over the years due to tectonic movements. I believe that by depicting the cyclical structure of such seemingly universal things that encompass magnificent changes by applying them to the relationship between human existence and nature, we can further touch upon the essence of human existence.

Q: Your paintings are often quite large in scale. Does the creation process require lots of time? Could you share some interesting things during the creative process?

NU: Indeed, the production process requires a great deal of time. For example, it takes about two to three months for a painting that is about 200 cm on a side. I believe that the process can be shortened a little more, but it requires a lot of preparation to make it a fulfilling painting.

I would like to focus on the unique aspects of my work. First of all, when I paint a person as a landscape, I start with the person's memorable pose, words, and behaviors. I draw the subject and try to capture as many interesting facial expressions and forms as possible. The main characters in my paintings are my family members, and I associate landscapes with the expressions and gestures of these familiar people through a large number of sketches. The process of exploring such unseen landscapes makes me feel like an adventurer exploring uncharted territory.

In the actual painting process, I use traditional Japanese painting materials. I draw lines on Japanese paper with *sumi* (ink), color with pigments made from minerals and soil kneaded with glue, and paint people and backgrounds with gold leaf. Using these materials, I draw on the idea of *sansui-ga* (landscape painting), which is to depict the scenery within the mind and use the spatial expression and brush techniques of historical *sansui-ga* to paint the landscape portions, which represent the figure of the soul of the person being depicted. For the human part, the technique of painting the skin in gold used in Buddhist paintings is cited. This technique allows the skin to be seen as a space like a gold folding screen along with the form of the human body, depicting a luminous presence and the existence itself as a soul that transcends substance.

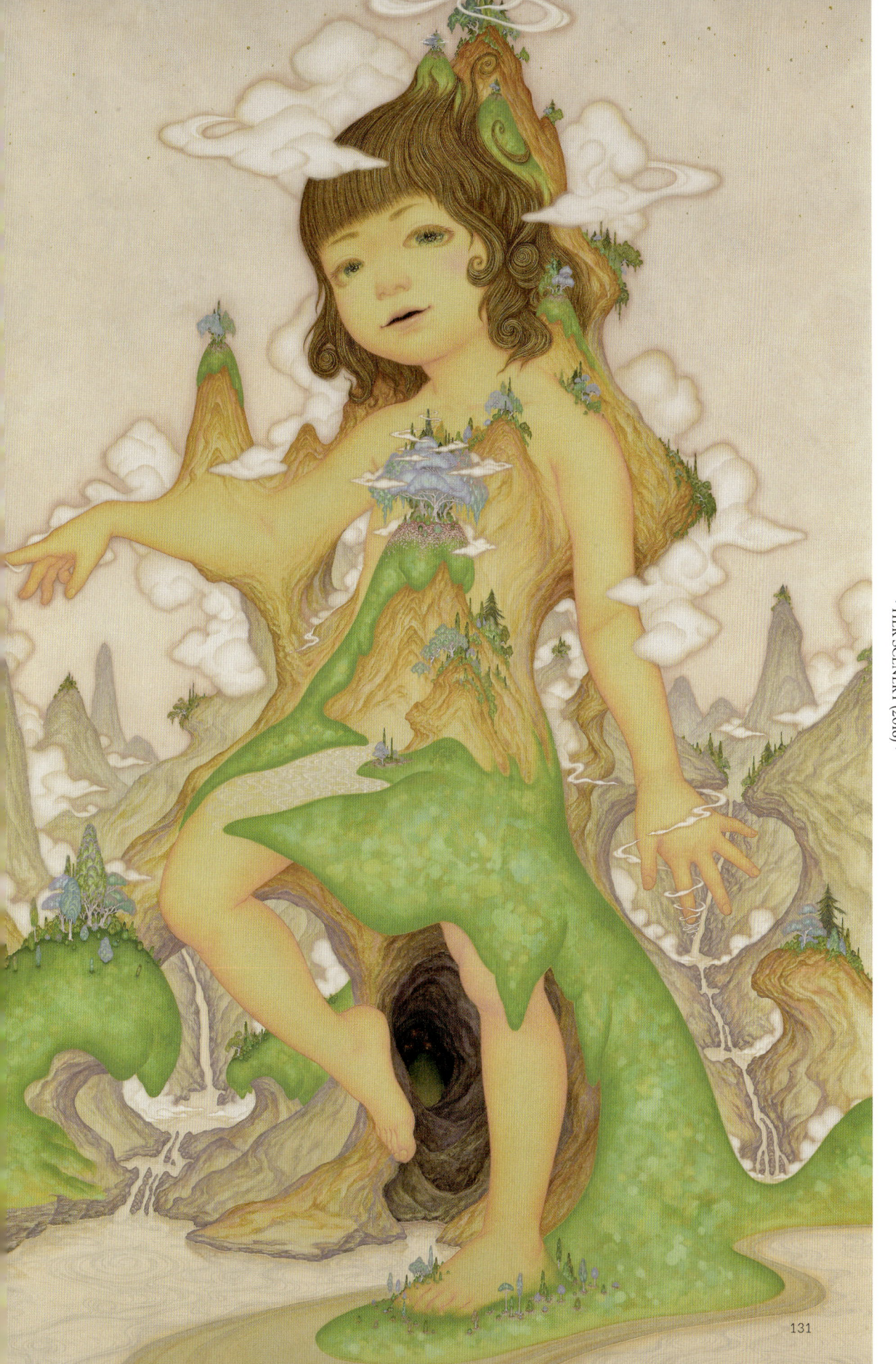

131

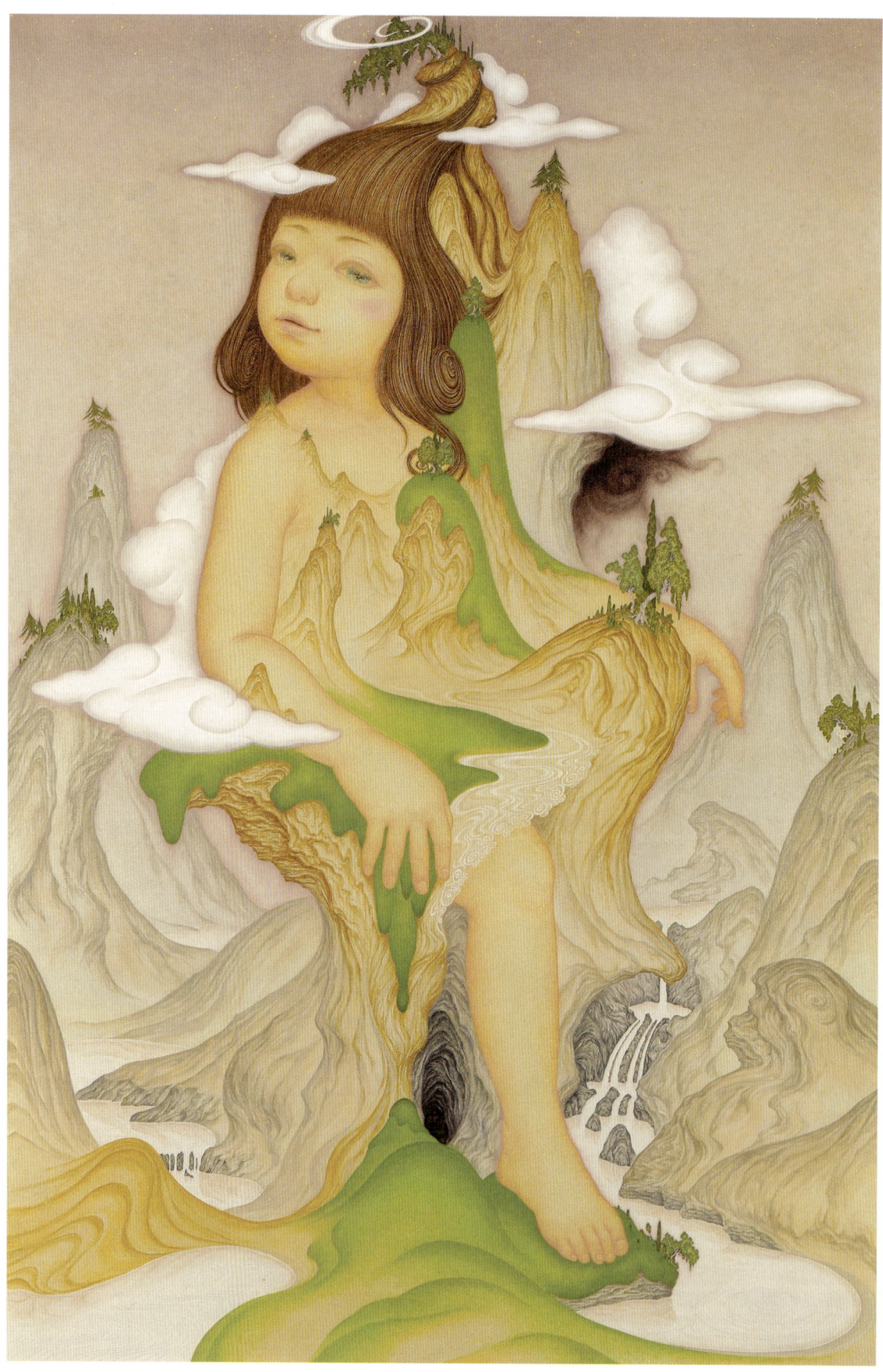

• HER SCENERY (2017) •

Q: What do you believe is the responsibility of an artist? What main message do you hope to convey to the audience through your work?

NU: There are various positions regarding the responsibility of an artist, but I believe that an artist should create artwork that gives us a sense of the beauty and positive aspects of the world in which we live, even if we feel that the world we live in today is unreasonable and inadequate, so that we may find hope for the future. Although there are many different ways for artists to approach this, I believe that artists must express themselves with sincerity, without being trendy, and based on their own solid experience and feelings, and not on borrowed ideas. To achieve this, I believe artists must be in constant communication with the world around them, be alert to the smallest changes and events in their daily lives, and be diligent in their daily studies.

What I hope to convey through my works is that by viewing them, viewers will discover that they, like the beloved characters in my works, exist and are blessed in the cycle of the world and that they will discover the preciousness and greatness of their own existence and have a little hope for the future in which they will live. For those who have not yet encountered my work, I would like to paint a picture that emits a saving light.

Q: Finally, do you have any new plans or visions for future creations? Are there any new artistic directions or themes you would like to explore?

NU: Up to now, I have focused on familiar people and beings, but to have a wider sympathetic audience, I envision a painting that combines people and landscapes that represent a more universal existence. I believe that focusing on animals and plants as objects to be painted will also enable a more universal development. I also had the opportunity to paint the water goddess enshrined at "Ubusuna Hydrology," an art festival held in 2023 at Kisobosui Shrine in Izu city, which is rich in water resources, and I am interested in painting the various gods that exist in Japan. In connection with the fact that I have been painting statues of deities, I am also attracted to simple Japanese Buddhist statues and deities that have been the object of prayers for salvation, and I have been creating 3D wood sculptures in parallel with my paintings.

As a theme for the future, I would like to consider how people should be in the world's cycles based on the relationship between people and nature, and explore what viewers can find some kind of hope or salvation. As one of the clues to this, I believe the technique of *shasei* (painting from nature) in Japanese painting and haiku is important. Sketching is the most basic method of creating traditional Japanese art. It is the act of observing the world around you as if you were capturing the life force of the things that exist there, and discovering the seeds of a work of art from the world. However, I believe that the method of *shasei* in which the world is observed inevitably involves subjectivity and misinterpretation on the part of the observer, and I believe that this may open up new perceptions of the world. For example, just as one accidentally sees the shape of a person in a thicket of trees, or the shape of a cloud appears to be an animal, a world out of phase with the real world may appear there, and a view may unfold in which the soul essence of existence is visible. I would like to create works of art that connect my senses to such perceptions and allow the viewer to be saved by projecting himself or herself onto them.

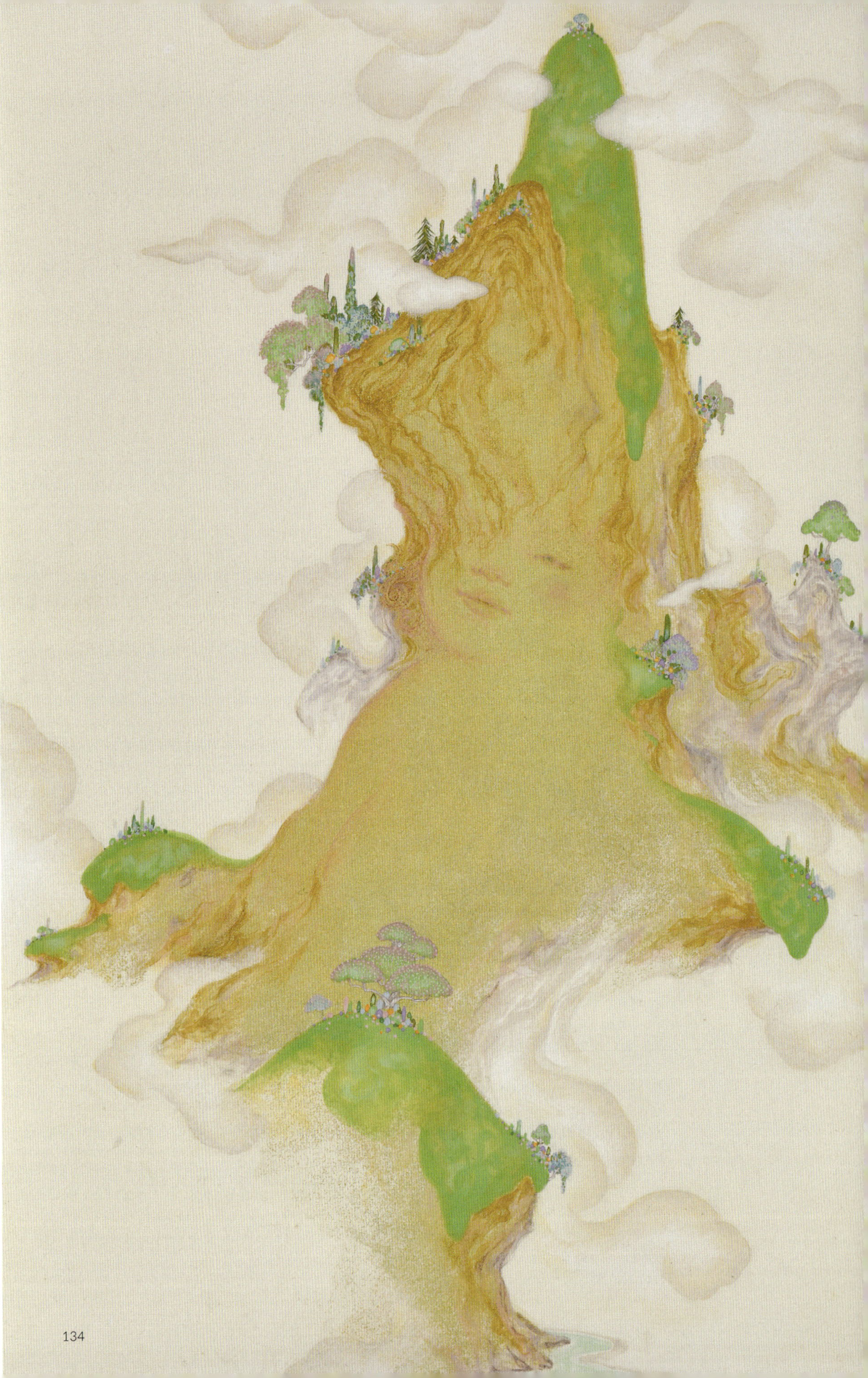

" *I believe that by depicting people as landscapes, I can entrust their personalities and thoughts to the topography and phenomena.* "

IMAGINARY
NEVERLAND

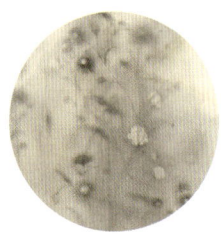

Mika Nitta

Mika Nitta is a Japanese drawing artist. Her works are based on the theme of nature and human beings. She offers a fantastic world in which various plants and animals appear. She continues to question herself about life and death, to search for answers in her creative activities and considers drawing to be "praying."

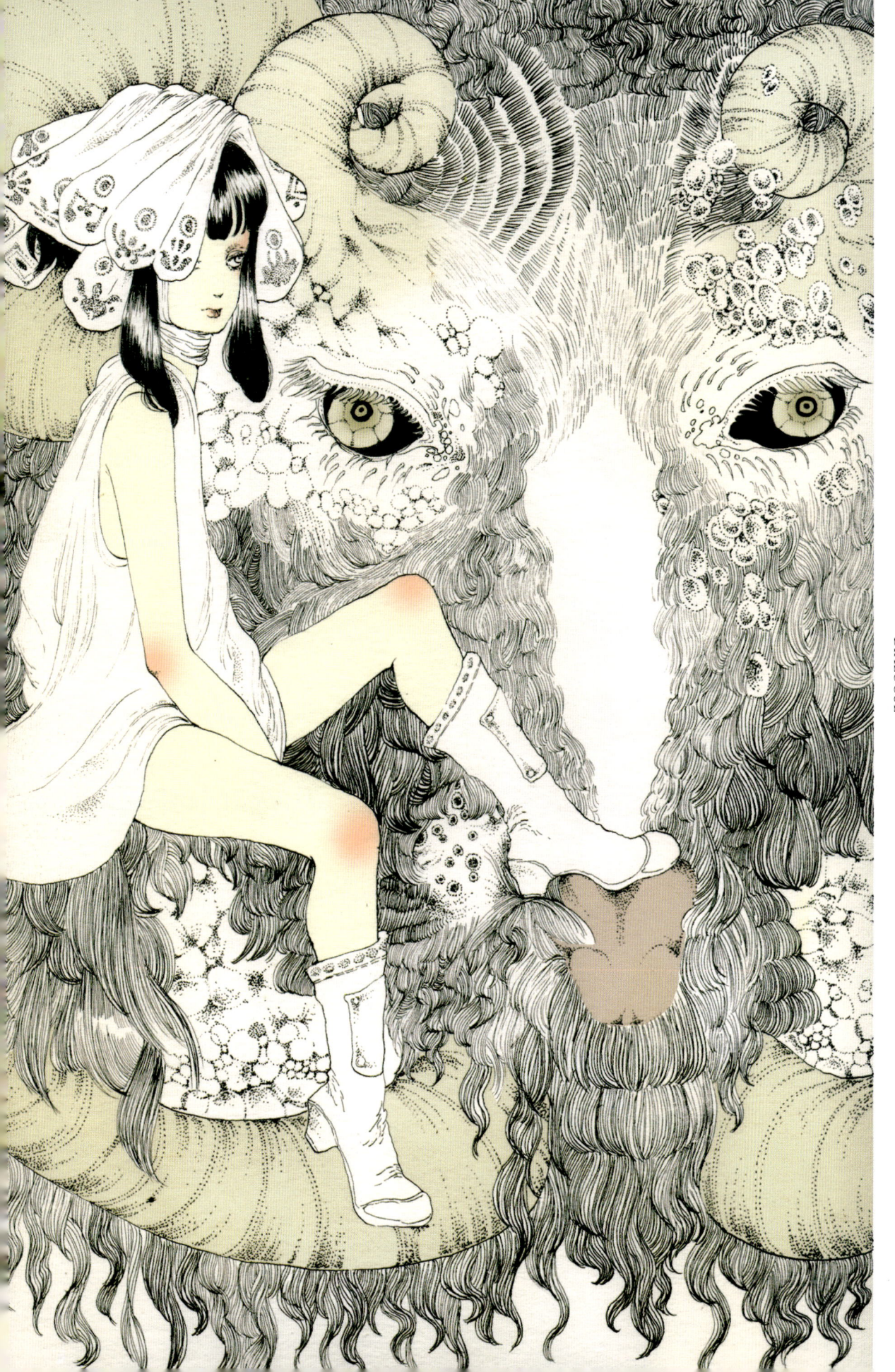

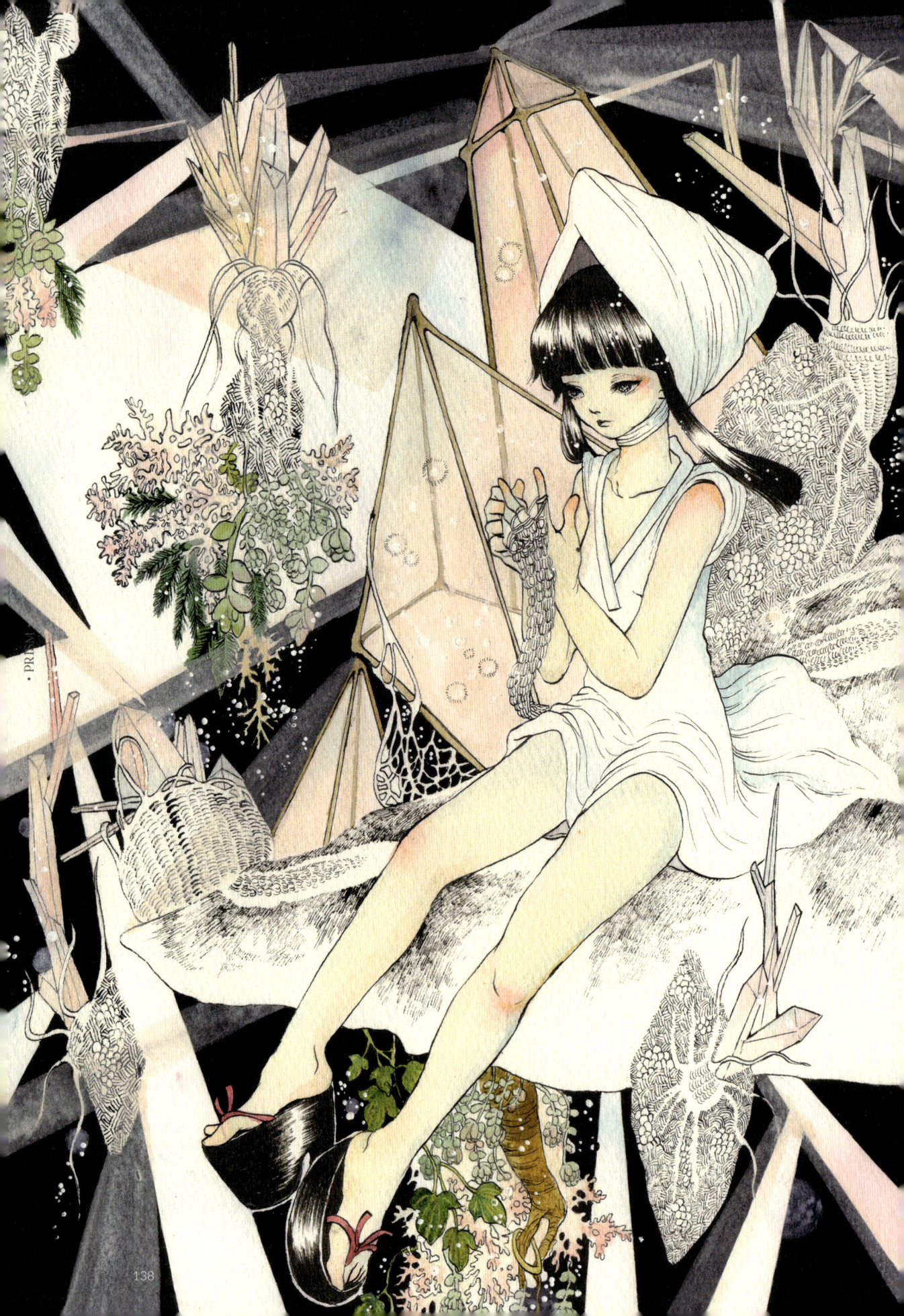

• PRISM

Q: Could you tell us your artistic background? How did you get interested in art?

MN: I have loved manga since I was a child. I was a child who read manga all the time if I had time. For example, *Sailor Moon* and other manga featuring girls. As I imitated the manga I liked, I grew to love drawing pictures myself. When I was in elementary school, I learned that there was a job called illustrator, and my dream is to be an illustrator. Later, I enrolled in college and studied art. After graduation, I started working as a freelance artist, holding solo exhibitions in Japan and exhibiting my work at art fairs overseas.

Q: Your work revolves around nature, plants, animals, and humanity, with a particular focus on the portrayals of young girls. Could you discuss the specific significance behind this choice?

MN: The appearance of girls in my paintings is a legacy of my childhood. I have been drawing girls since I was a child under the influence of manga, so the girls that appear on the screen have somehow become the alter ego of my heart. I was not very good at talking about my thoughts and feelings, so I think I began to entrust my longings, ideals, and desires to the girls in my drawings. The girl in the work, who coexists with nature, plants, and animals, is an ideal figure for me and symbolically represents human innocence and purity.

Q: Your painting style is inspired by ukiyo-e. How this has influenced your creative process?

MN: I focus on the importance of the line in painting. I think this is also due to the influence of manga, but I have always thought that the variety of expression through lines is interesting. If you look closely at ukiyo-e, you will see that the number of colors used is very small. However, they look very colorful and gorgeous. I think this is because of the diversity of lines and patterns on the screen. Ukiyo-e is a Japanese culture, but its origins can be traced back to Tang-style paintings from China and the Korean peninsula. As I research and study how *Yamato-e* was born there and how it is connected to ukiyo-e and the present day, I realize how important the line has been for Japanese people as a method of expression, and this has had a great influence on my work.

Q: You often use ink for your line drawings, then color them either with watercolors or digitally in Photoshop. What differences in feeling do you experience between coloring by hand and coloring digitally? Do you have any color preferences of your own? What aspect of the creative process do you find most enjoyable?

MN: Some of the early works in the book are digitally painted, but most of them are painted with watercolors. Although it is easy to specify colors digitally, I prefer to work in an analog manner. I continue to study the materials used in my work, including the most recent work not shown in this book, which uses only Japanese paper, *sumi* ink, and brushes. Researching painting materials is also an opportunity to learn about history and the natural environment. As I work on the theme of nature and human beings, there is learning that cannot be obtained through digital work. The most enjoyable part of my work is when I am drawing lines. As I get older, I am not just drawing lines for no reason, but I am paying attention to various things, such as margins and balance.

Q: Fantasy creatures and scenes often feature prominently in your works. How do these imaginative elements integrate into your artistic creations? What inspires them?

MN: In Japan, there is an ancient belief in nature worship that God dwells in all things. This ideology has permeated my own life. For example, I have been watching Hayao Miyazaki's movie, *My Neighbor Totoro* since I was a child, and I am unknowingly learning that humans are not the only main characters living on the earth. We live with a variety of creatures. It is not only the creatures we see, but also those we do not see. When I imagine this invisible world, it appears on my screen as fantasy creatures and scenes. It is a manifestation of my thought. The creatures in my paintings are a bit scary, which I think is due to the influence of my favorite painters, Hieronymus Bosch and Maurice Sendak.

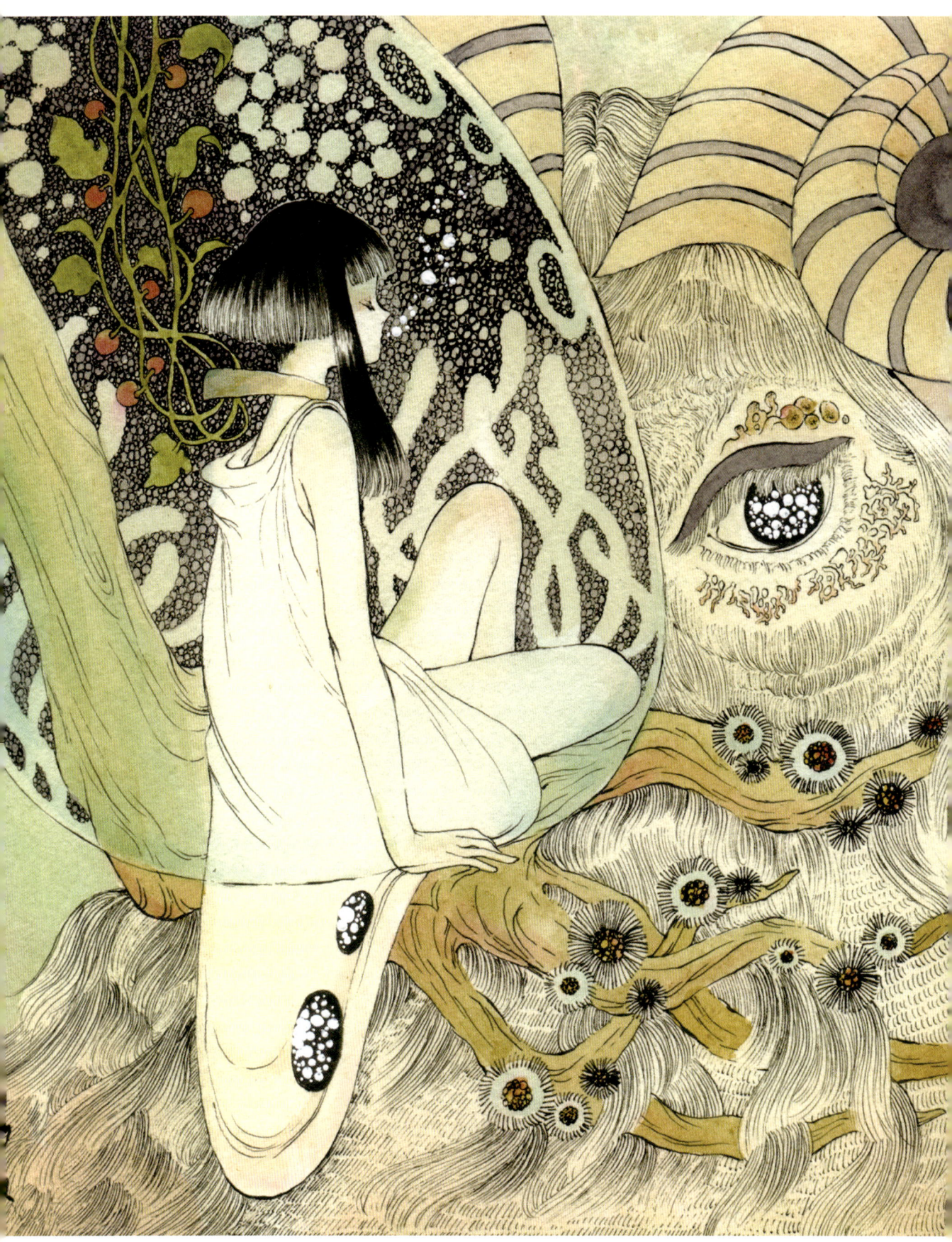

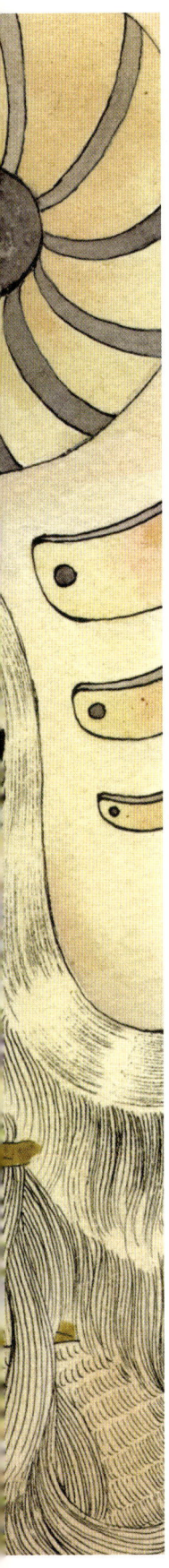

Q: What challenges have you encountered in your creative process? How have these challenges influenced your work?

MN: I believe that my life and my work go on in parallel. I place importance not only on the work itself but also on the spiritual growth that comes from the creation of the work. In thinking about nature and human beings, which has been my theme for many years, I also read many philosophy and natural history books. Among them, I was most impressed by the philosophy of Lao Tzu. His ideas of "letting nature take its course" and "the most wonderful way to live is to live like water" have changed my outlook on life. It has been ten years since I started my career as an artist, and there were times when I was troubled because I could not paint due to childbirth or illness, but Lao Tzu's words saved my life at that time. Of course, as an artist, there is the joy of having your work evaluated and sold, but I believe that the happiness of spiritual enrichment is also something that comes from having continued to be active.

Q: You mentioned seeking answers about life and death through painting, and you view painting as a form of "prayer." What power and insights do you feel art has brought to you?

MN: One of the turning points in my life was the Great East Japan Earthquake that hit Japan in 2011. At that time, I felt close to death, and from there I began to think deeply about life and death. At the same time, I realized that our life and death are deeply connected to nature. Today, we may feel that death is something of a fantasy. Some may feel that death is something in movies, dramas, or cartoons. However, just as a small insect dies or a flower withers, death will eventually come to us. When I accepted this, I felt that nature and the creatures that live with us are very close to us. I believe that "praying" is "hearing voices." Recently, as my life's work, I have been making drawings while carefully observing insects and plants. When I listen carefully to their silent voices, I feel very sacred and peaceful. And I feel that I must live a little more humbly, giving thanks for the reality that I am already alive today.

Q: Your works are depicted very delicately. Among your works, which one is your favorite or holds the deepest meaning for you? Why?

MN: Of all the works featured in the book, *Dialogue* (P137) is my favorite and most memorable. This is because it was one of the first pieces that I started working on as an artist. Until then, I had not established my own style, I had no pictures that I could present with confidence, and I was at a point in my career where I was not sure what kind of themes I should be focusing on in my work. However, when I presented this work on social networking sites, many people liked it, which gave me a lot of confidence. I thought that I should make use of my delicate drawing as one of my strengths.

Q: As a contemporary Japanese artist, how do you believe your works reflect the issues or emotions of modern society?

MN: In Japan, as in the rest of the world, there is much discussion about environmental issues and the negative effects of AI evolution, and I hope that the emergence of AI art will trigger a re-evaluation of beauty.

I am currently working mainly on *sumi* ink painting using Japanese paper and *sumi* ink from before the "Cultural Revolution" in China. While society is moving toward digitalization, I am going the opposite way, and that is the message I want to convey as an artist. The art materials created by the combined efforts of craftsmanship and natural materials are amazingly beautiful. I feel that our five senses have become dull due to our digitalized lifestyles, surrounded by things created by scientific materials. I believe that when we come into contact with natural things and take another look at their beauty and comfort, we will be able to create values that cannot be created by AI, but can only be created by humans. However, modern Japanese society is facing many challenges, such as the need for efficiency and the disappearance of craftspeople who are responsible for traditional crafts. I would like to do my best as an artist to carry on the tradition, even if it is only a small contribution.

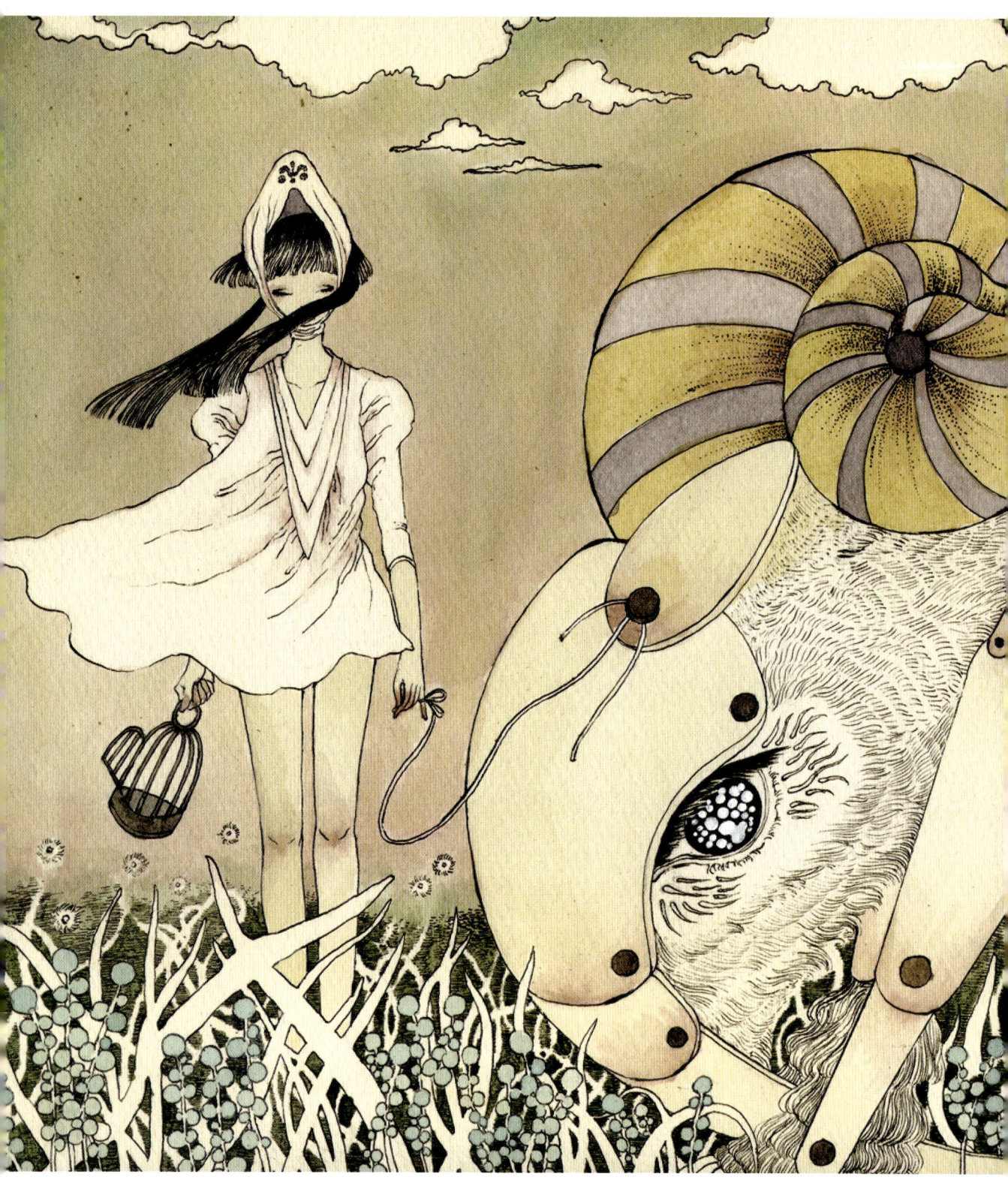

• STAND BY ME •

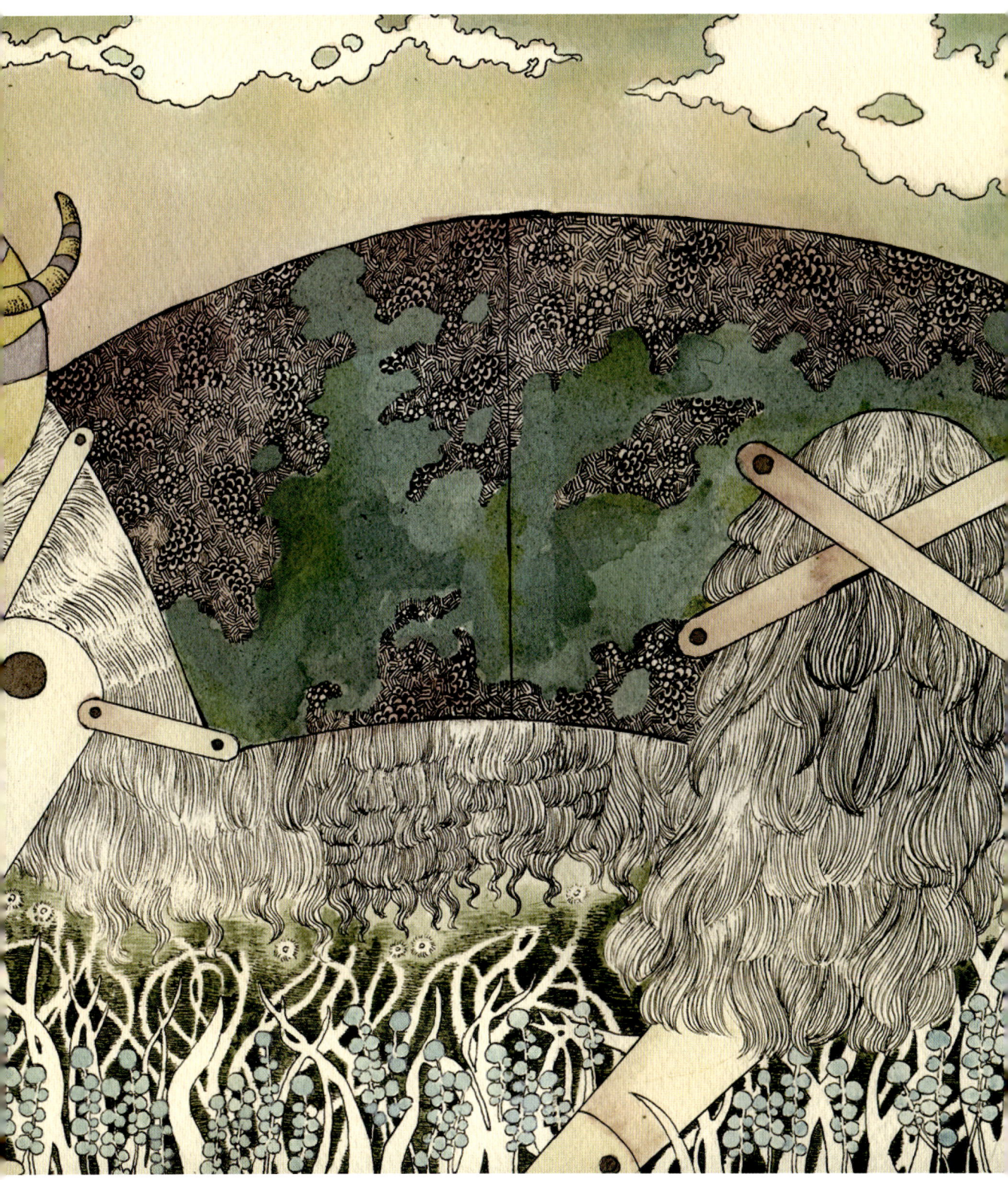

" We live with a variety
of creatures. It is not only
the creatures we see, but
also those we do not see.
When I imagine this
invisible world, it appears
on my screen as fantasy
creatures and scenes.
It is a manifestation
of my thought. "

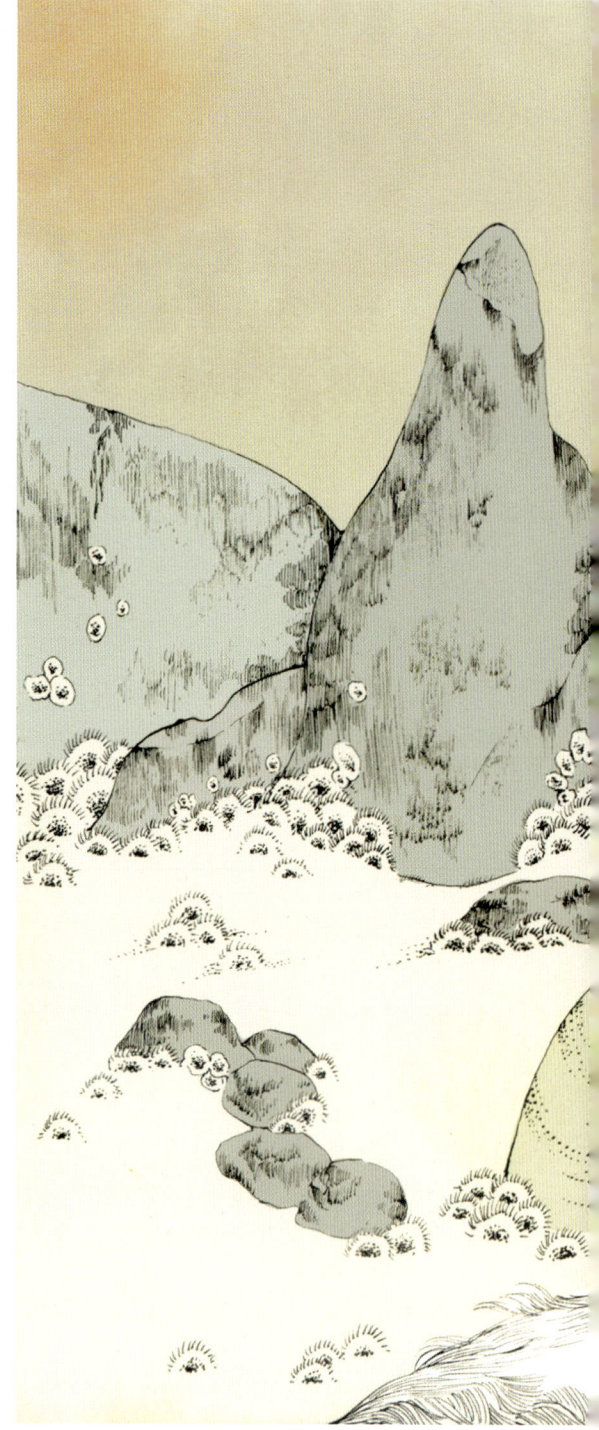

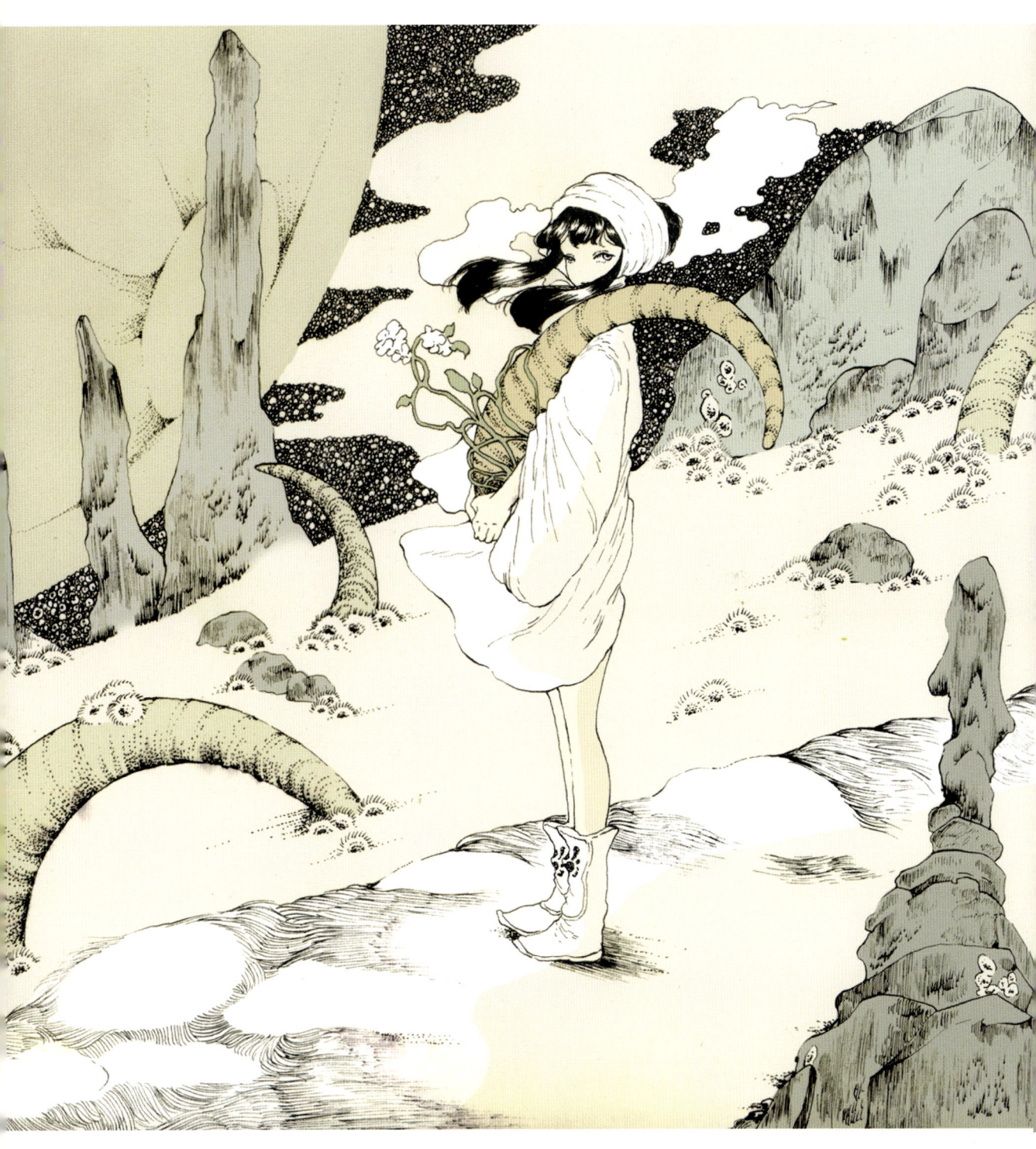

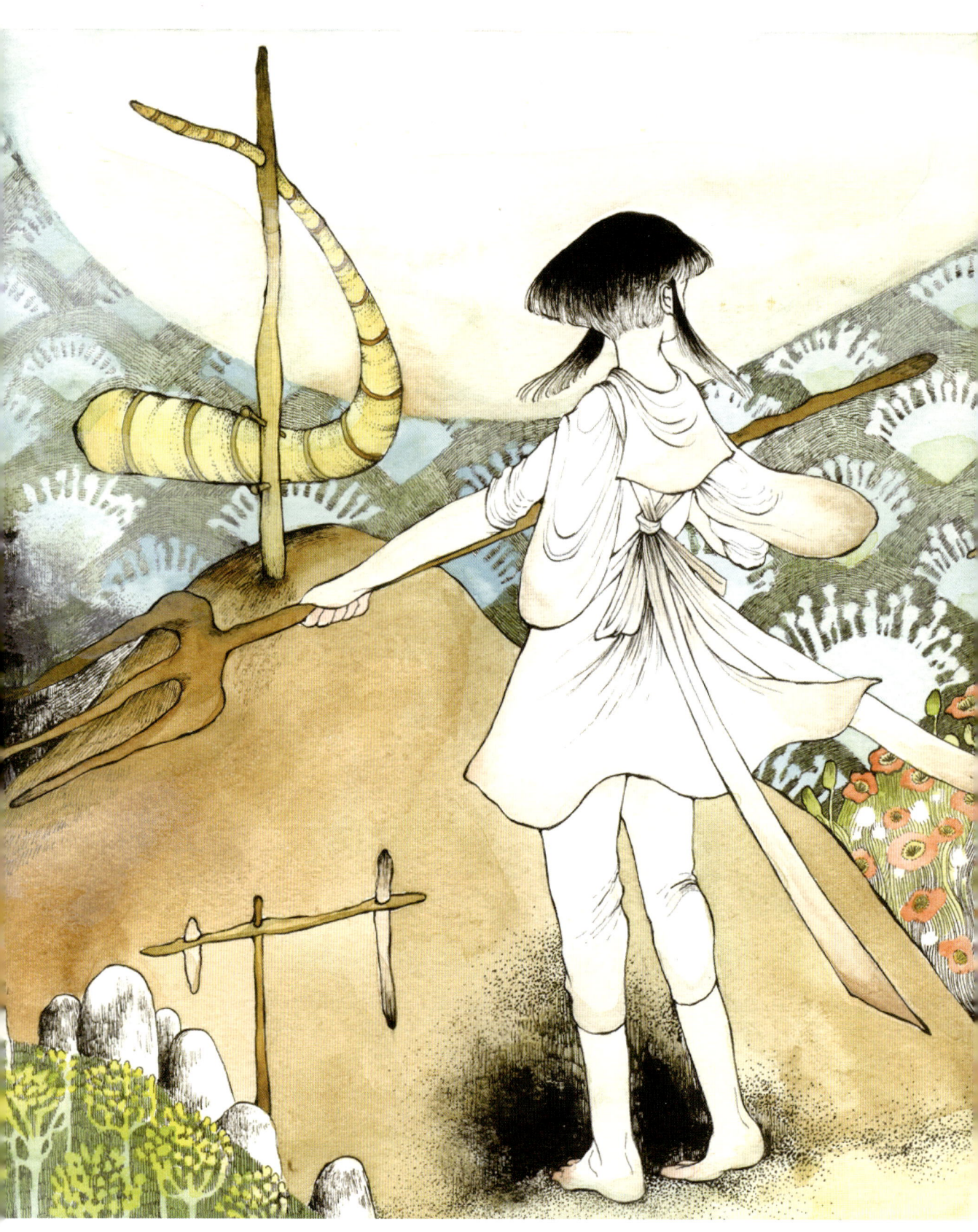

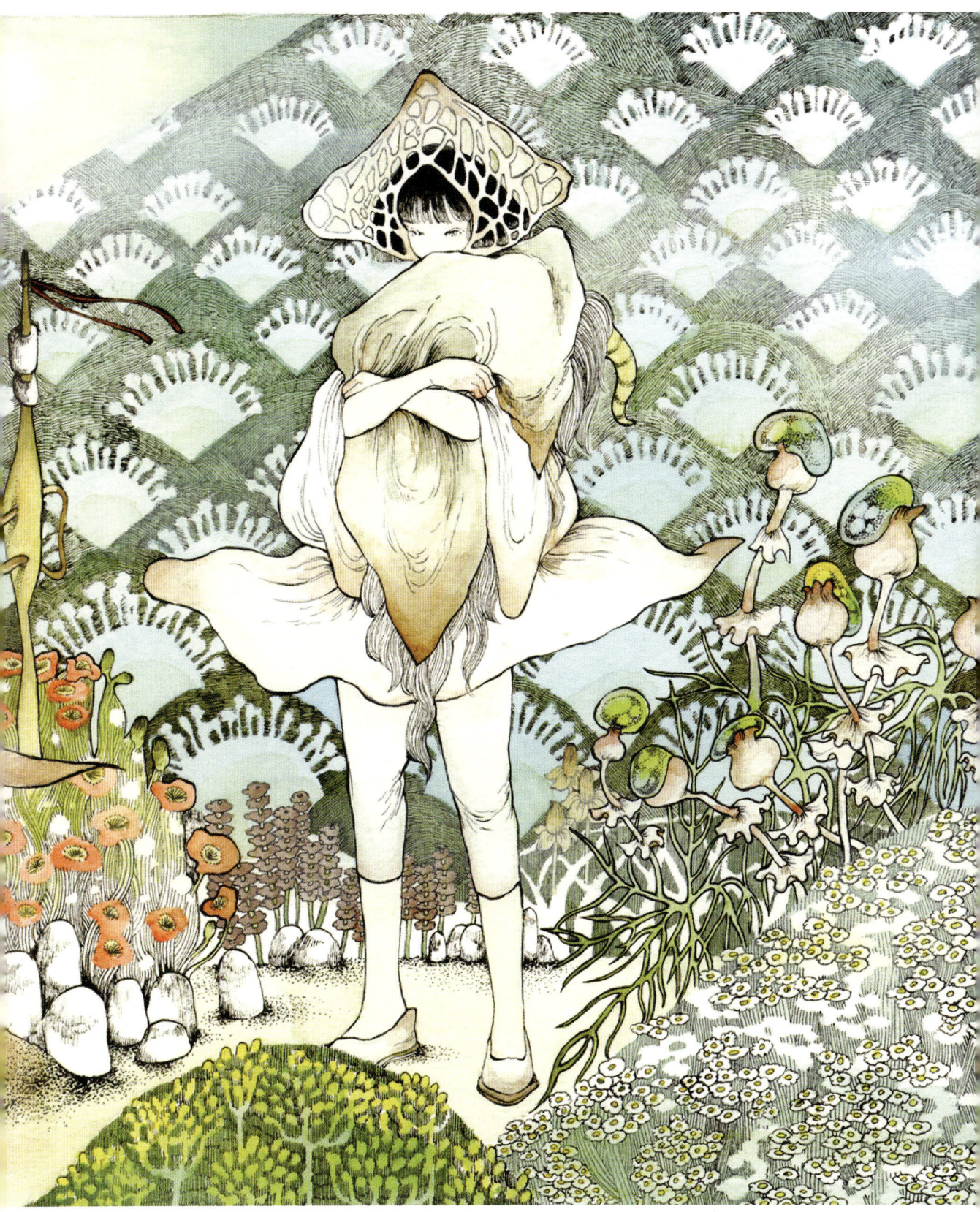

MYSTERIOUS
FANTASY

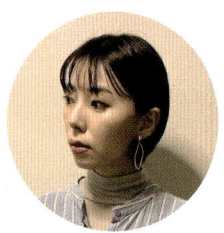

Hanae Nakajima

Hanae Nakajima, born in Tokyo, started working in earnest after participating in an exhibition in 2016. Hanae mainly depicts figures in mysterious costumes that do not seem to belong to any period or country. After graduating from Gakushuin Women's College in 2019, Hanae exhibited at Art Fair Tokyo (Kiyoshi Art Space) and held her first solo exhibition at Ginza. In 2021, Hanae was featured in *Bijin-ga Zukushi-San* (Geijutsu Shinbunsha).

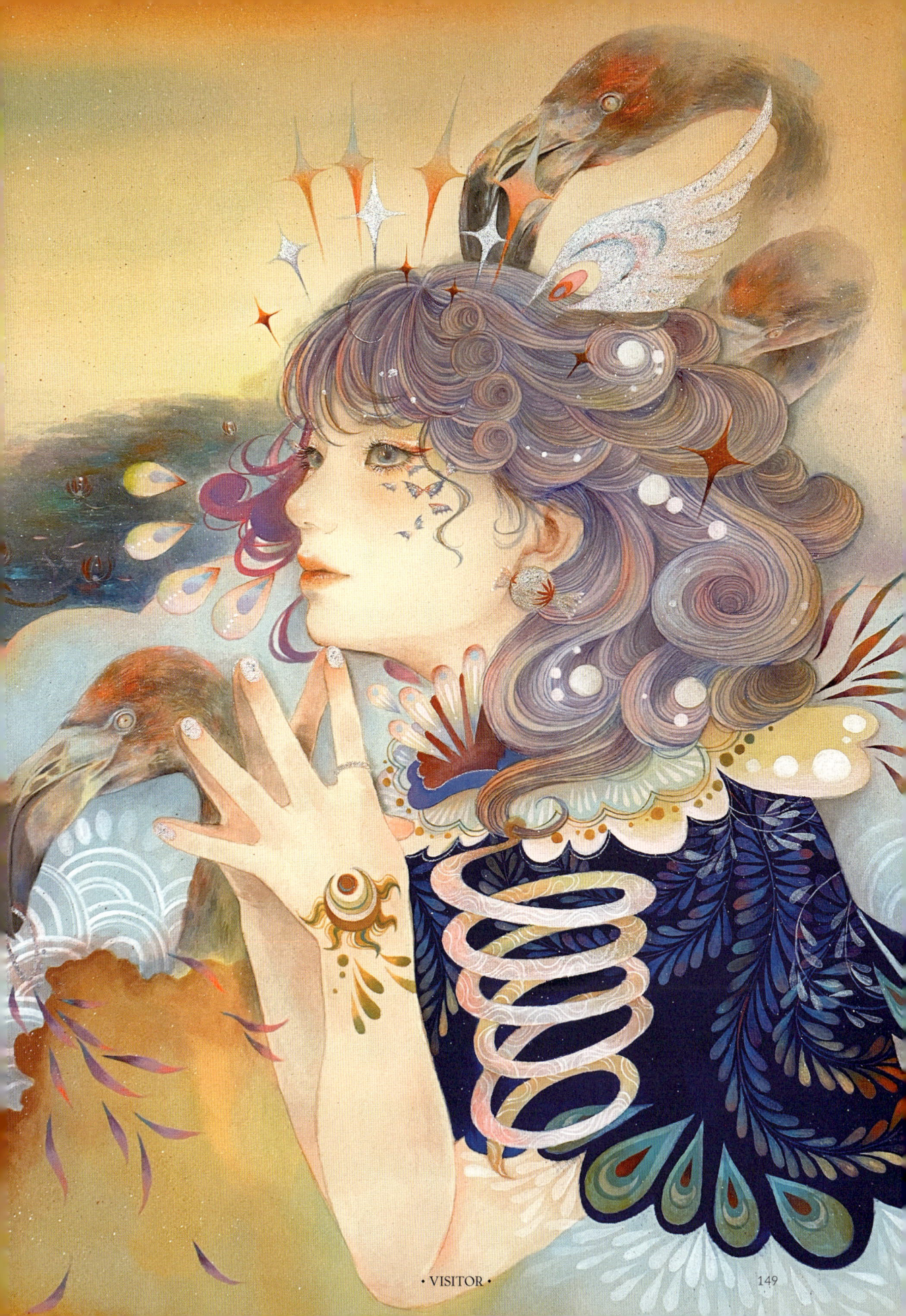

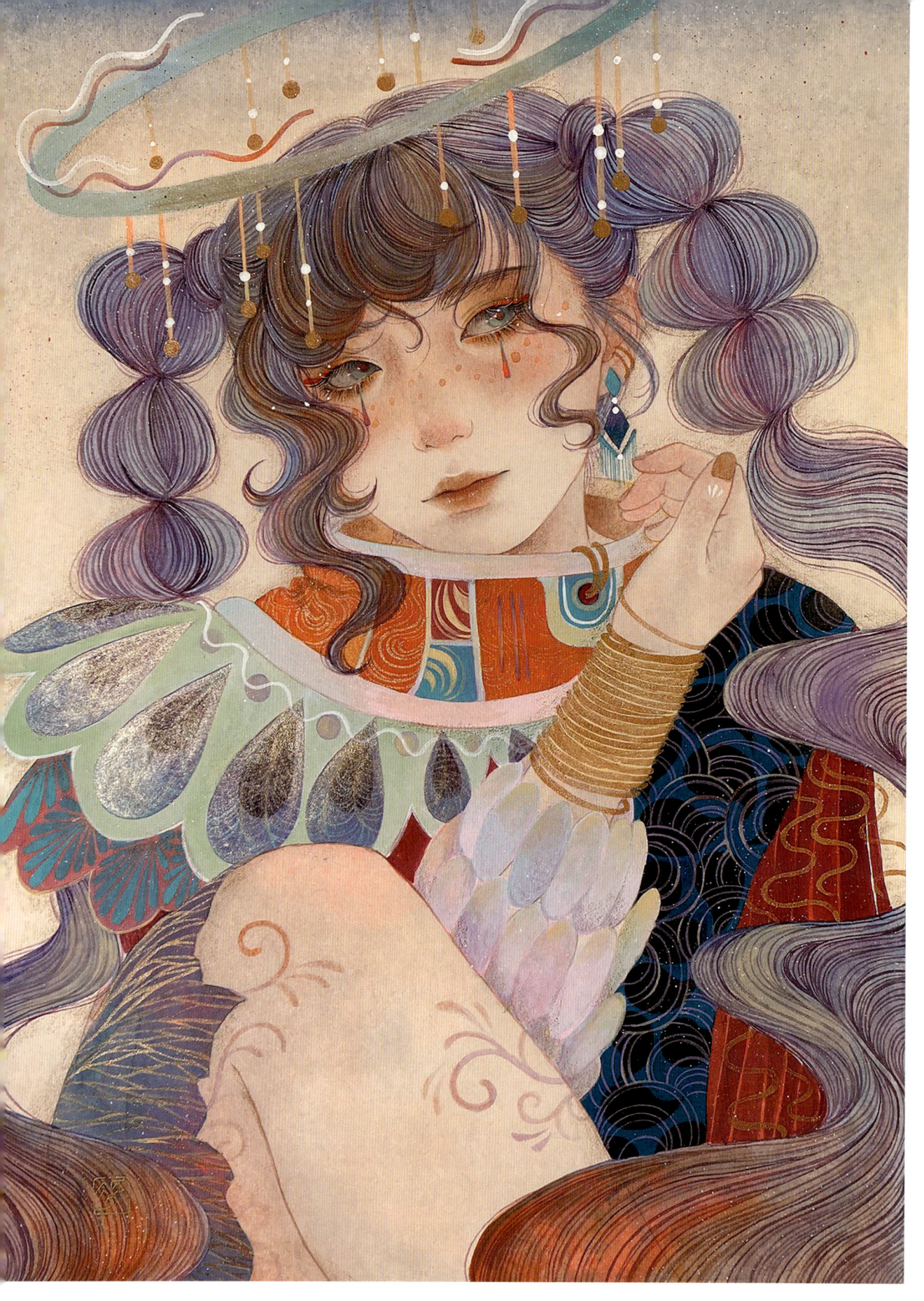

Q: You began to exhibit your works in 2016, can you make a simple description of your art career? What got you started with drawing in the beginning?

HN: I have been drawing pictures ever since I can remember. It was playing with dolls when I was little that got me hooked on painting.

When I participated in an exhibition for the first time in my life, I saw other participants painting on wooden panels with water-stretched paper supports and learned about water-stretching for the first time. From there, I began creating artwork in earnest, asking various people about the brushes and paper they used, using them as references, and doing research on the Internet.

Q: What artists or artistic movements have had the greatest influence on you?

HN: I was influenced by the works of CLAMP, the first manga I ever read.

I especially admired the costume design depicted in *xxxHolic*.

I was not in the habit of reading manga at home, so I borrowed manga from friends and read them.

I was attracted to the slit eyes that leaped up from the corners of the eyes and the gothic costume designs, which I often copied at the time.

Before I started my creative activities in earnest, I was more interested in traditional Japanese culture itself than in drawing, and in high school, I learned about tea ceremonies and flower arrangements as a club activity. I think my experiences from those days have led me to my current work. In particular, I feel that I learned many things from flower arrangement, such as composition, color placement, and a sense of overall balance.

Since I started creation, I have rediscovered the beauty of composition and lines in Japanese painting, and I have begun to incorporate them into my works. I was also inspired by a collection of paintings by Itō Jakuchū that I had at home.

Q: You mention that your work depicts people wearing mysterious costumes that do not seem to belong to any era or country.

How did you decide on this concept of your work?

HN: The concept of my work is rooted in my attraction to ethnic costumes, which was triggered by the Beijing Opera I saw on TV when I was a child. This influence also led me to take courses on Japanese clothing culture and traditional dyeing and weaving at university, and I began to incorporate my admiration for costumes and makeup into my artwork. In the beginning, my works were based on the image of beauty depicted in Japanese paintings, but as I searched for my own unique expression, I gradually began to incorporate my longing for fish swimming underwater, which I had felt since childhood, into the figures in my works. I wanted to depict unique characters who are not bound by anything, just like underwater, where gravity is almost imperceptible, and I reflected this underwater image by adding swirls and wave patterns to the costumes and makeup of the characters in my works.

Q: What was your thinking behind choosing Japanese paper and acrylic as the medium to complete your work? How do you think this medium fits in with the content or theme of your work?

HN: When I started exhibiting, I used acrylic paints on croquis paper or drawing paper. A little later, I began to use Japanese painting techniques when I learned about the water-stretching method, wooden panels, and Japanese paper, so I started to use Japanese paper, which is less uneven and easier to draw lines on. I use thin layers of color and apply color little by little, and I want the lines to flow beautifully, so I think that Japanese paper, which is easy to apply evenly and sturdy, is suited to my painting style.

I have used acrylic paint since my high school art class and it was the only paint I had at home, so I started using it from my first works. After I became accustomed to painting, I started using acrylic gouache as I chose the colors I wanted to use for my work.

In my case, I do not decide on a color in advance and paint it on, but rather I paint in thin layers to find the ideal color on the spot, so I feel that acrylic gouache is the easiest to use when I have an idea for a color.

Q: Most of your works have animal elements such as fish, flamingos, cats, etc. How do they integrate into your works? What is the meaning of animal elements in your works?

HN: When I incorporate living creatures into my works, I choose shapes that I find interesting. I often draw flamingos and shoebills in particular because I think they have unique shapes among birds. Flamingos are unique in both color and shape, so I often use them as a motif when I want to add an unrealistic and somewhat mysterious element. Shoebills are more unique, and the shape of their faces (especially around the eyes) gives them a humorous impression, so I incorporate them into works where I want to make the story clear.

In my case, river fish tend to be more subdued than brightly colored, so I mainly draw fish with simple colors and shapes. I began to incorporate fish into my works because I felt that the sensation I get when I am developing a concept is similar to the sensation I get when I am underwater, and I long to see fish swimming freely underwater.

Q: Could you share some techniques or methods for portrait creation? How do you give life and personality to each character?

HN: When drawing the human face, I am particularly conscious of the shape and placement of facial parts. I refer to various makeup videos and pay particular attention to the shape of eyebrows and eye makeup.

When I want to create a softer impression, I distance the eyebrows from the eyes or draw the eyebrows thicker to create a natural look. Conversely, if I want to create a cool impression, I move the distance between the eyes and eyebrows closer or draw thin eyebrows. The distance between the eyes and eyebrows, the shape of the eyes, and the thickness and angle of the eyebrows can change the impression even if they are slightly different, so I always adjust them down to the very last millimeter.

I also try to avoid drawing in too much shadow to emphasize the lines. I try to draw with an awareness of the overall balance, making sure that there is a balance between areas that are detailed and areas that are not.

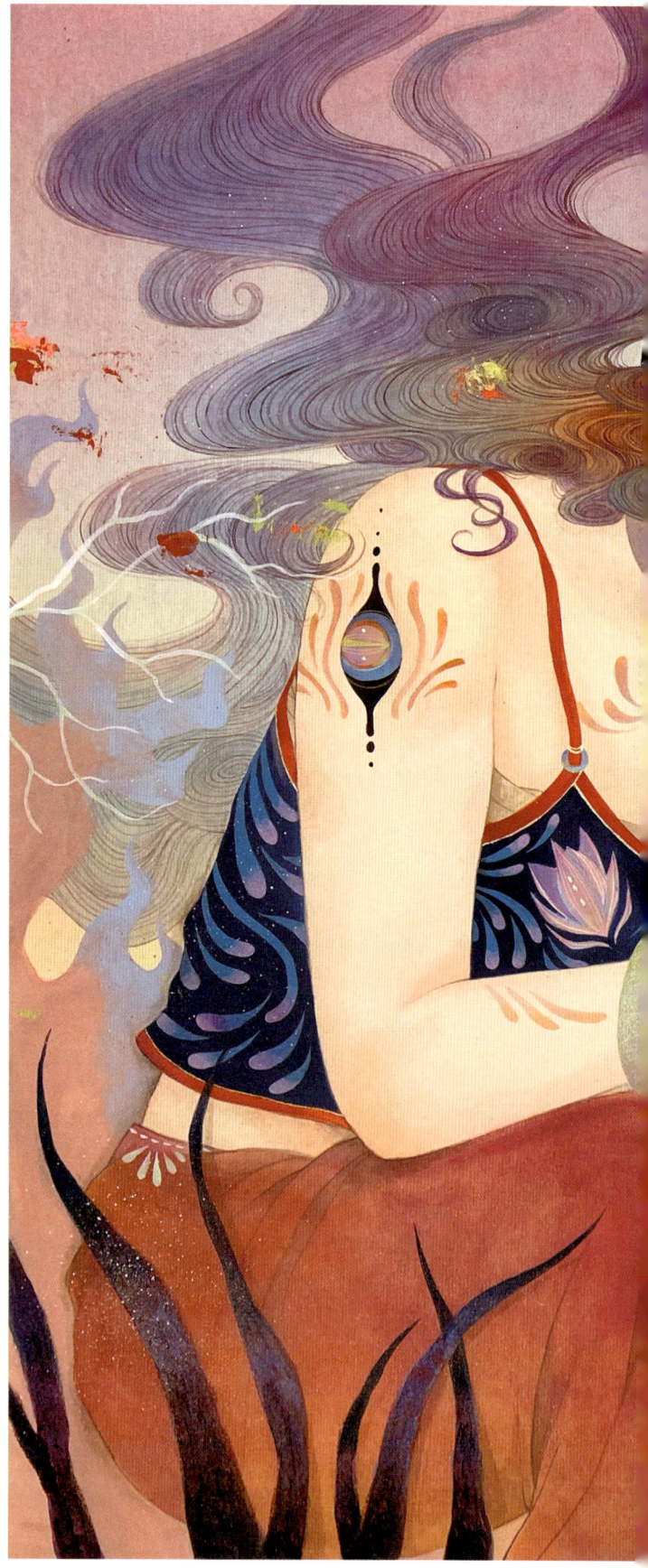

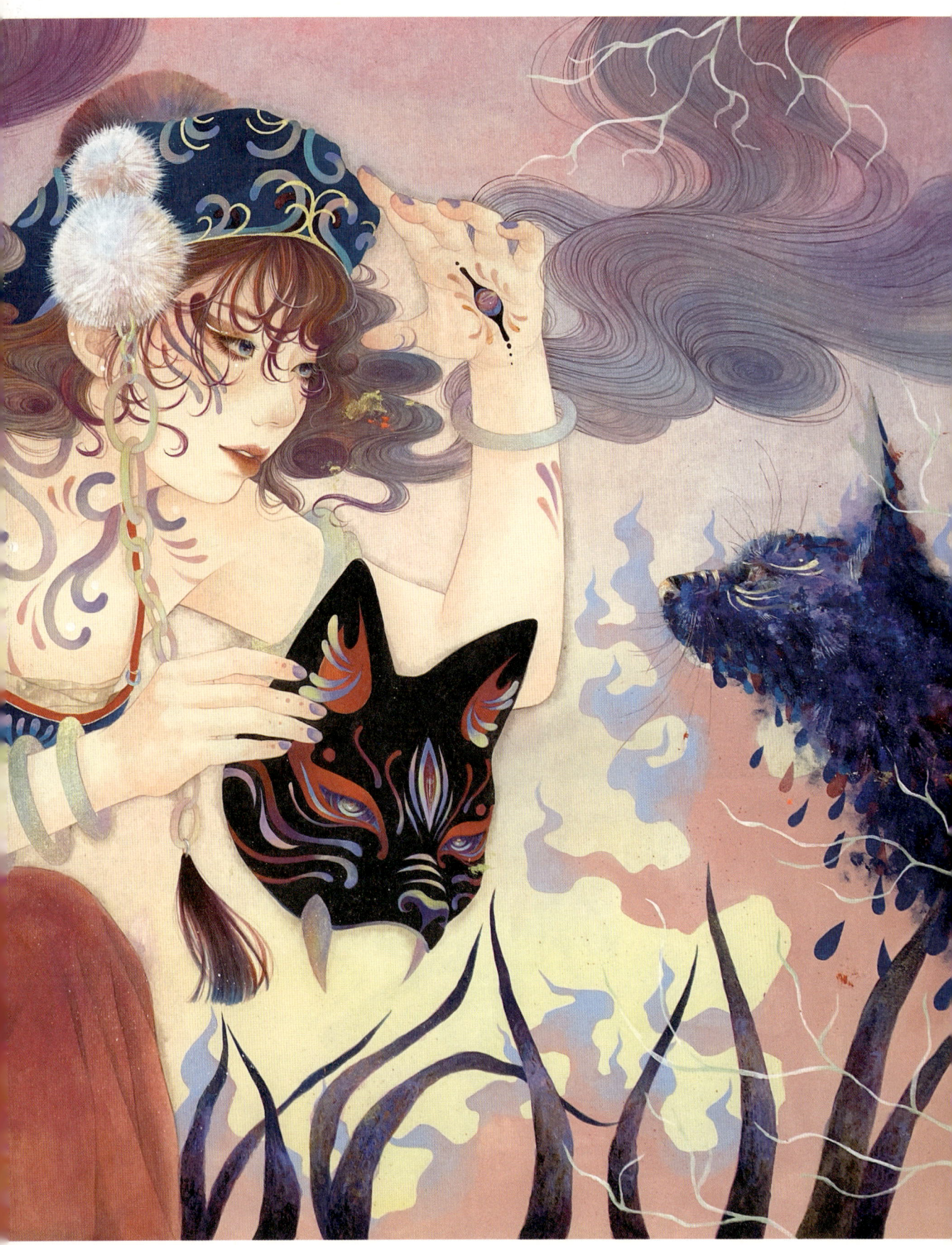

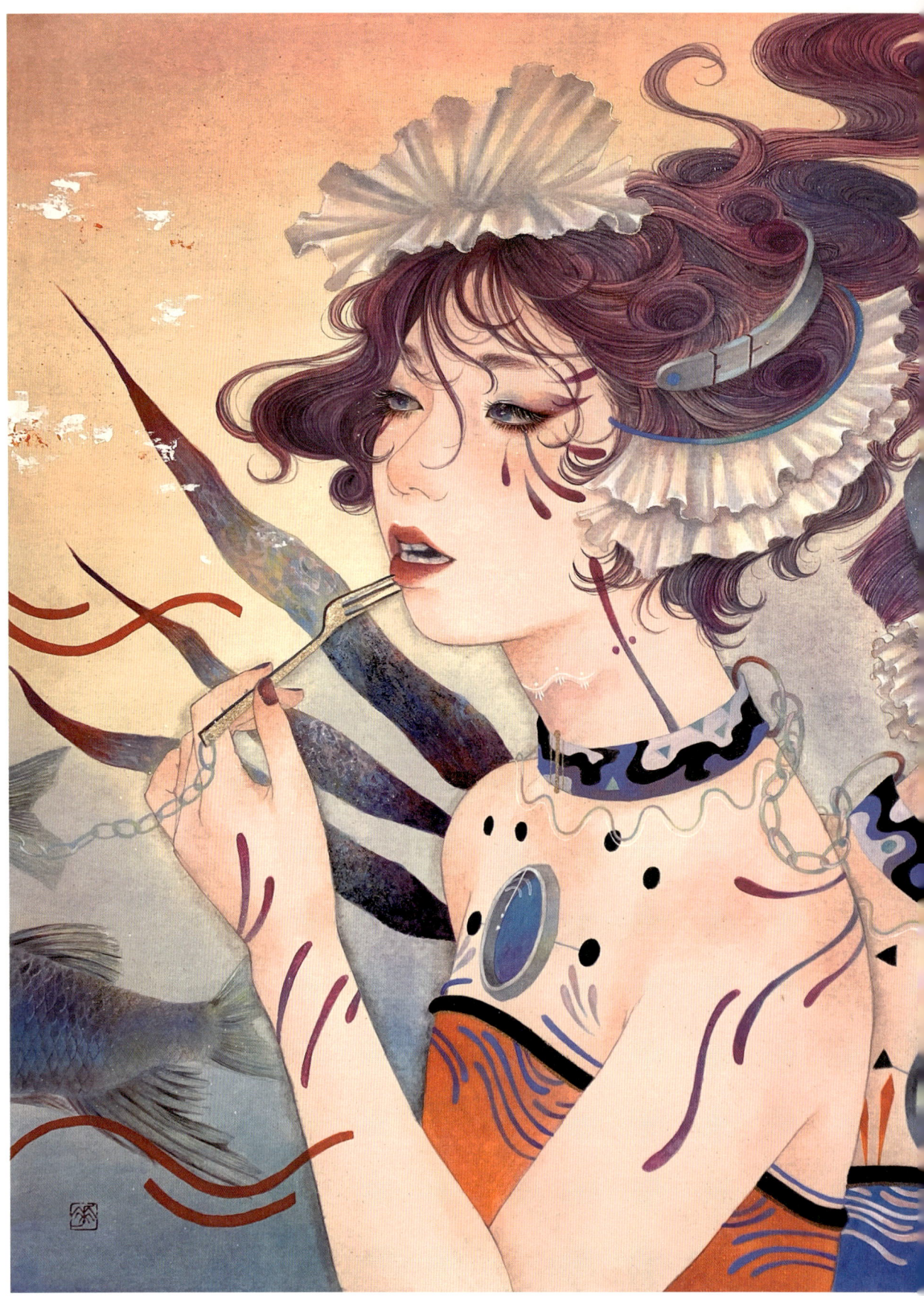

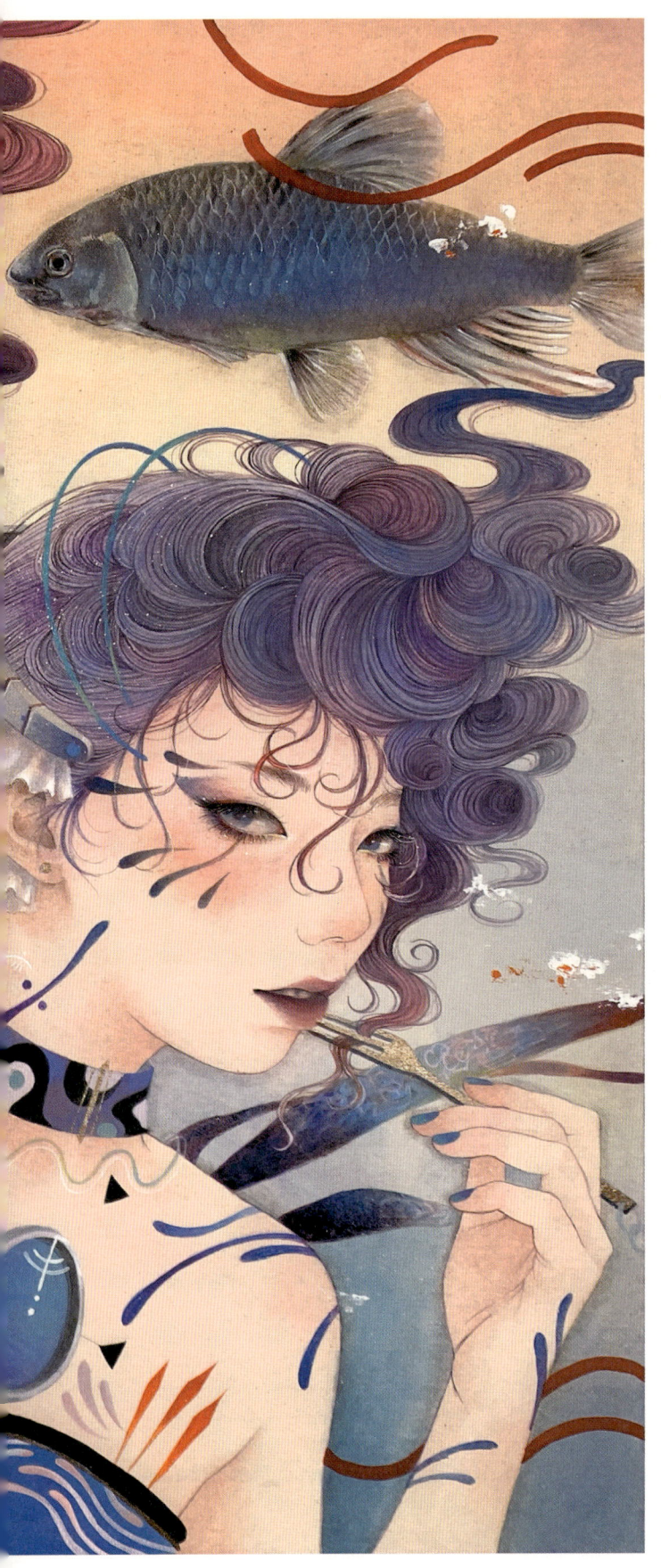

Q: You held your first solo exhibition in Ginza in 2019, how did that experience impact your art career?

HN: When I first started my solo exhibition, I thought I would be happy if I could have a solo exhibition once in my lifetime, so my first solo exhibition was like being in a dream. However, at the same time as creating works for the solo exhibition, I was also creating works for the Tokyo Art Fair and working on my graduation thesis at the same time, so it was the time when I was mentally pushed the hardest. I had never had the opportunity to create a large number of works at once, and I had little experience painting on panels larger than F20 (727×606mm), so this solo exhibition was quite a challenge for me. Through this challenge, I was able to reconfirm the unique elements of my style that I had been searching for, and I think I was able to grasp more clearly what I wanted to paint. It also strengthened my desire to live my life as a painter.

Q: As a young artist of the new generation, can you give some advice to other young artists? What special ideas and plans do you have for your future creations?

HN: I am still painting today because I participated in that first exhibition.

At that time, I had almost no knowledge of painting, but I still gathered the courage to participate, and I believe that this is what led me to where I am today. Looking back, the most important thing for me was that I continued to exhibit my work for the next eight years. I don't know how many times I thought about quitting, but I kept on painting. I always tried to complete the work without worrying too much about the quality and to apply my reflections to the next work. I believe that improving the quality of work is not only a matter of quantity but also a matter of "noticing" the quality of the work. When I was a child, I used to draw people by directly connecting the face to the torso, but one day I realized that there was a neck between the head and the torso, so I started drawing the neck. In the same way, I was conscious of noticing something, no matter how small, with each piece I completed. In the future, I would like to not only draw pictures but also try new things, such as trying to create 3D versions of the people in my works.

" I wanted to depict unique characters who are not bound by anything, just like underwater, where gravity is almost imperceptible... "

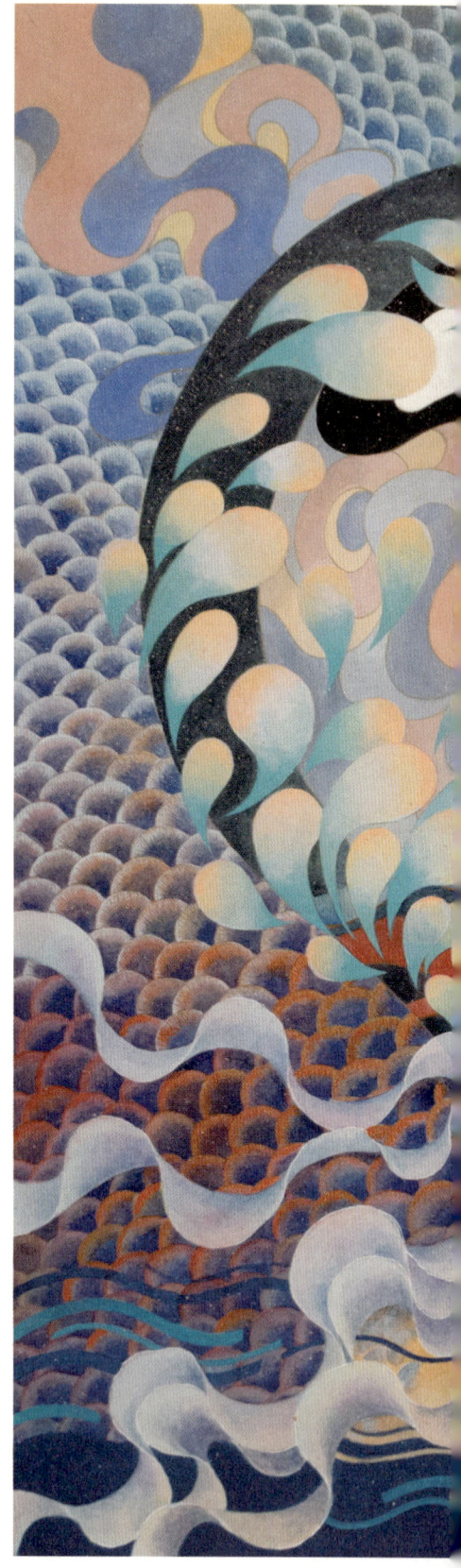

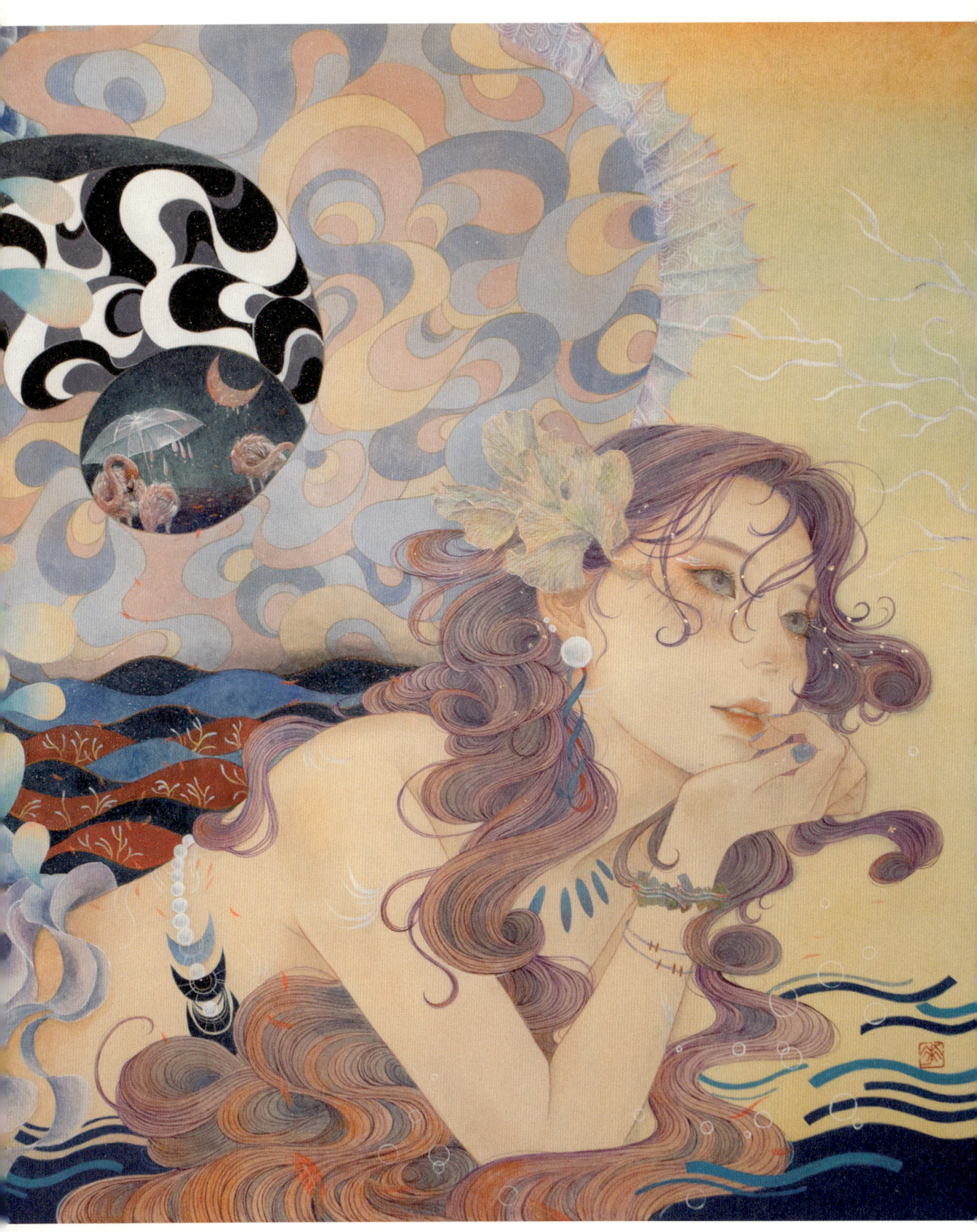

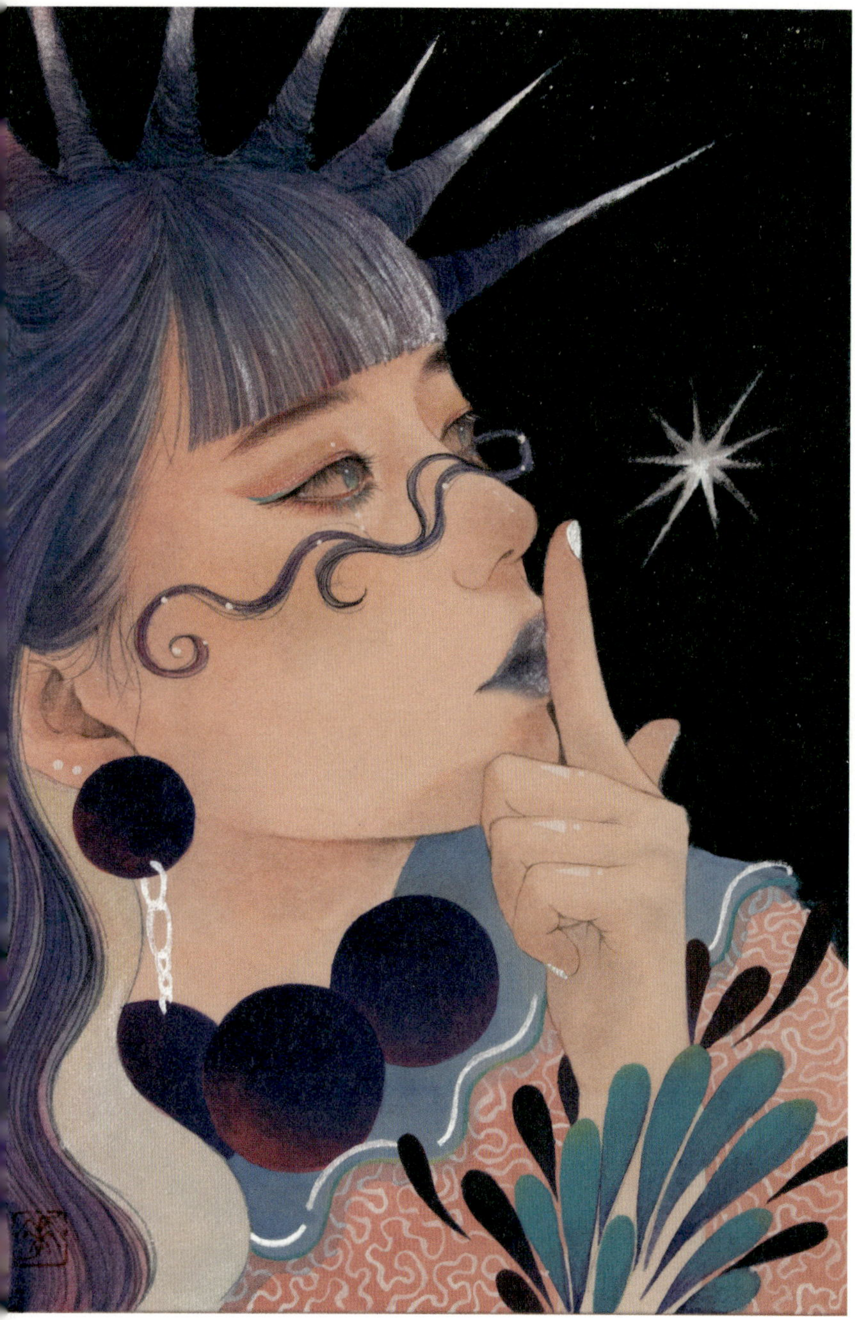

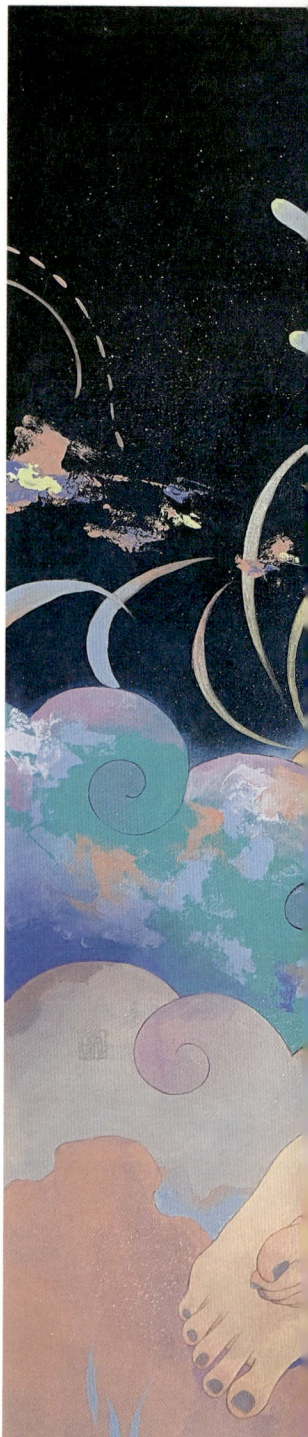

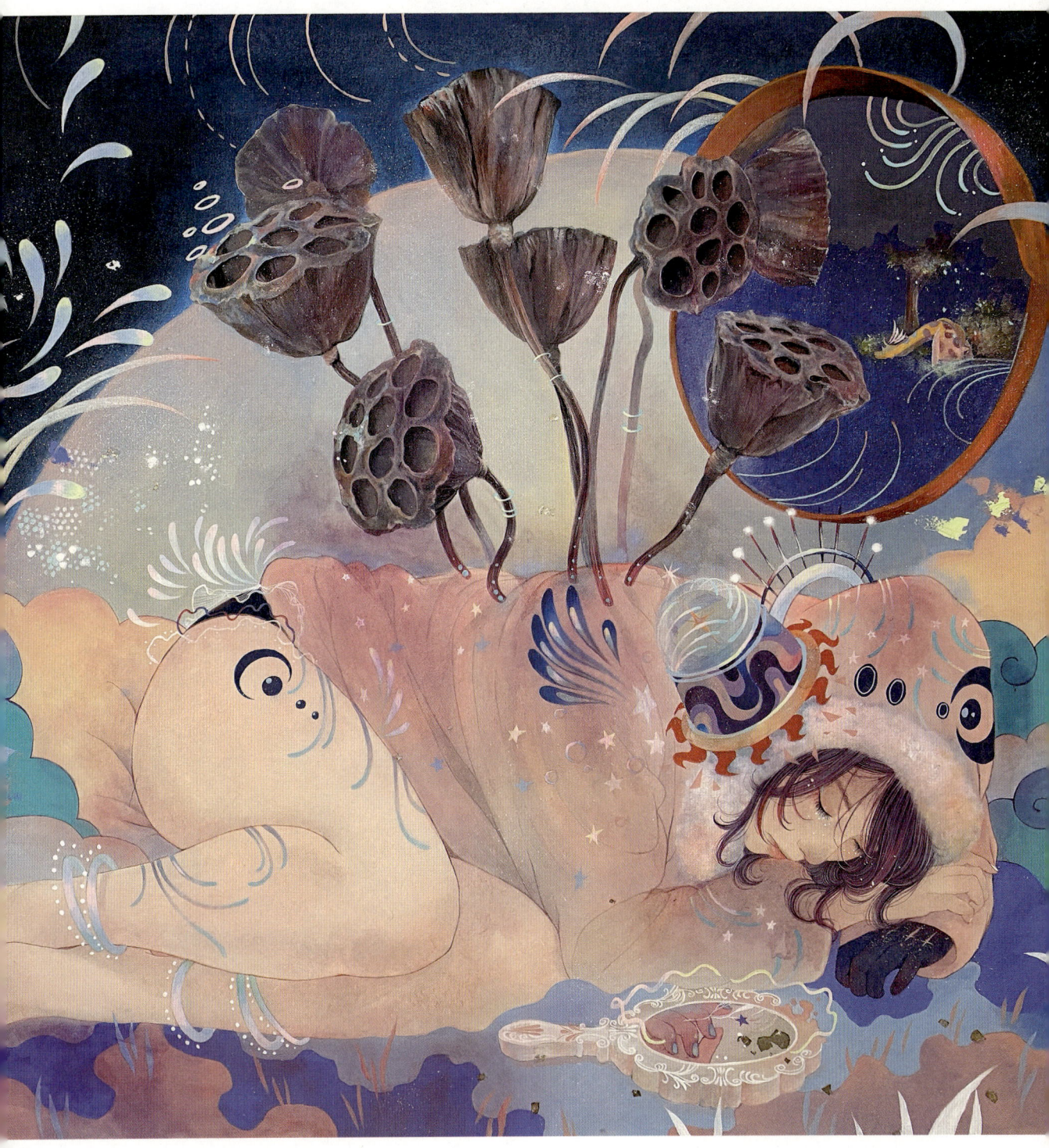

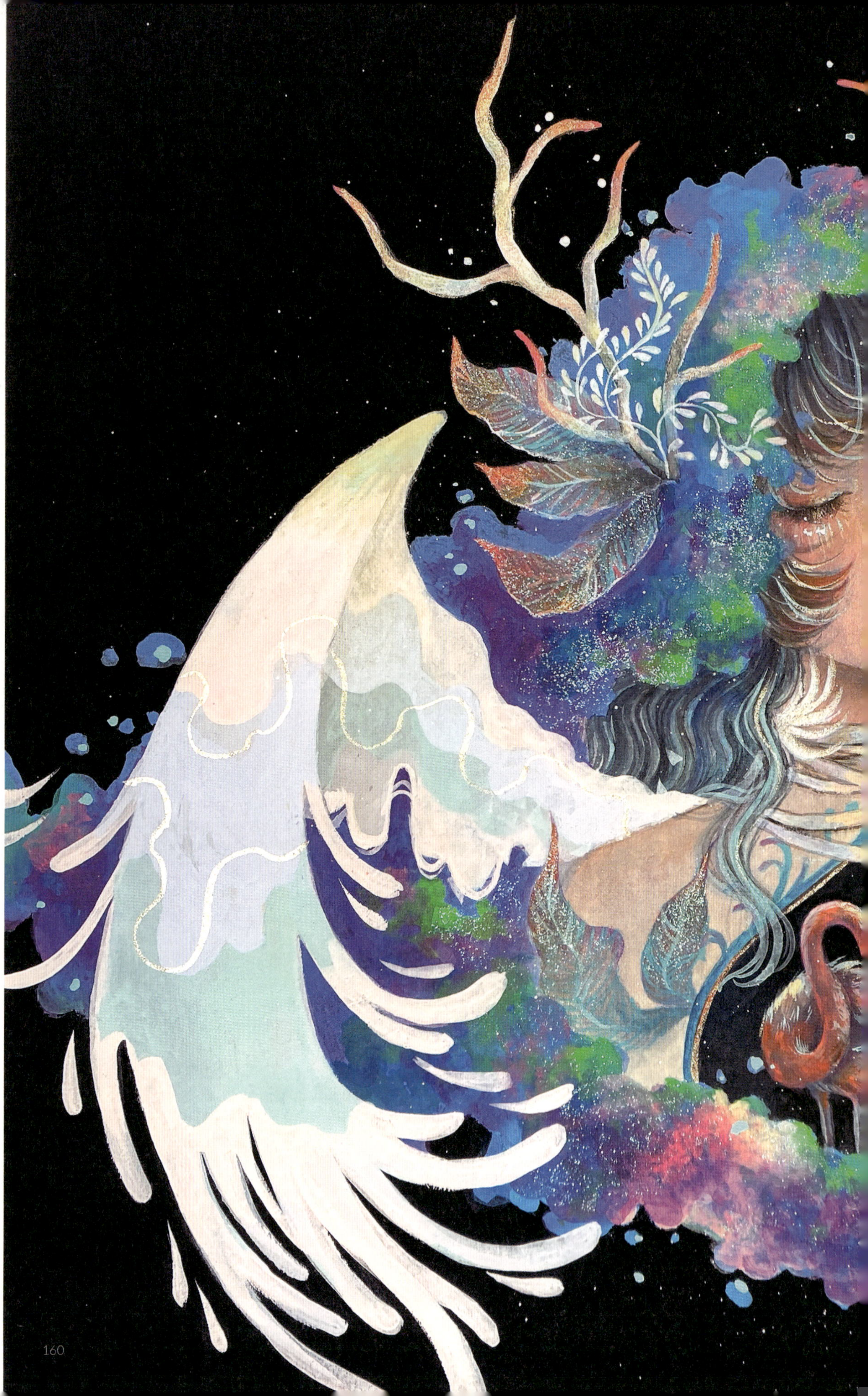

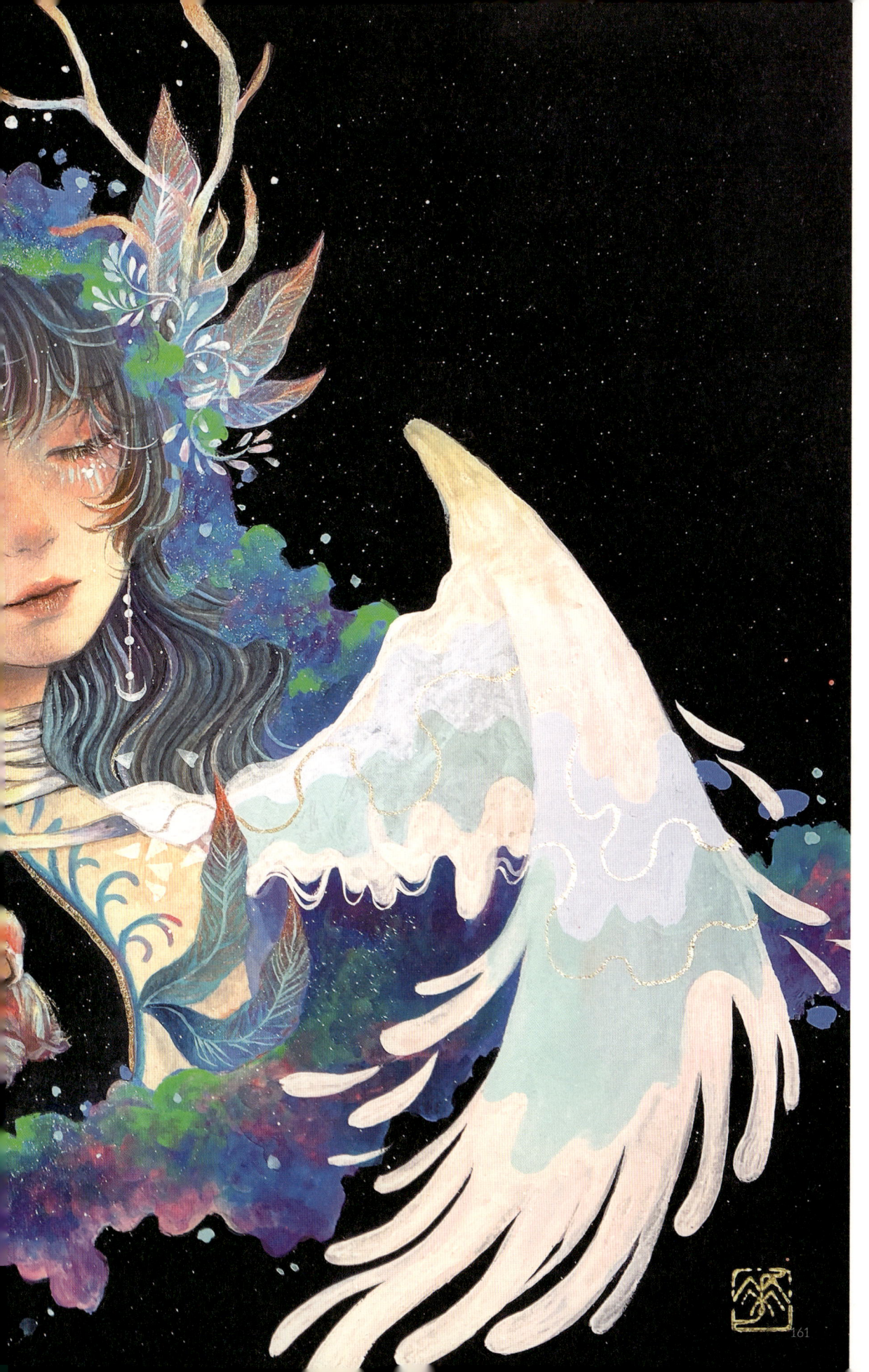

MIDNIGHT UNDERSTREET

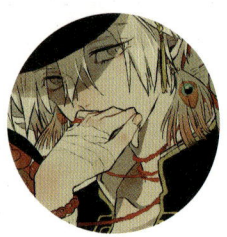

Tsubonari

A manga artist and illustrator known for her unique view of the world. She depicts an aesthetic world by using elements of Japanese and Chinoiserie styles. Her creations are based on the fictional world of *Antengai*. She also published books: *Antengai Gensou* Kiroku (Fantasy Tales of Antengai), *Antengai Kisou Yakyoku* (Strange Nocturne of Antengai), and *Antengai Rasen Souki* (Spiral Legend of Antengai). In addition to her personal creations, she takes part in many works on game illustrations and character designs.

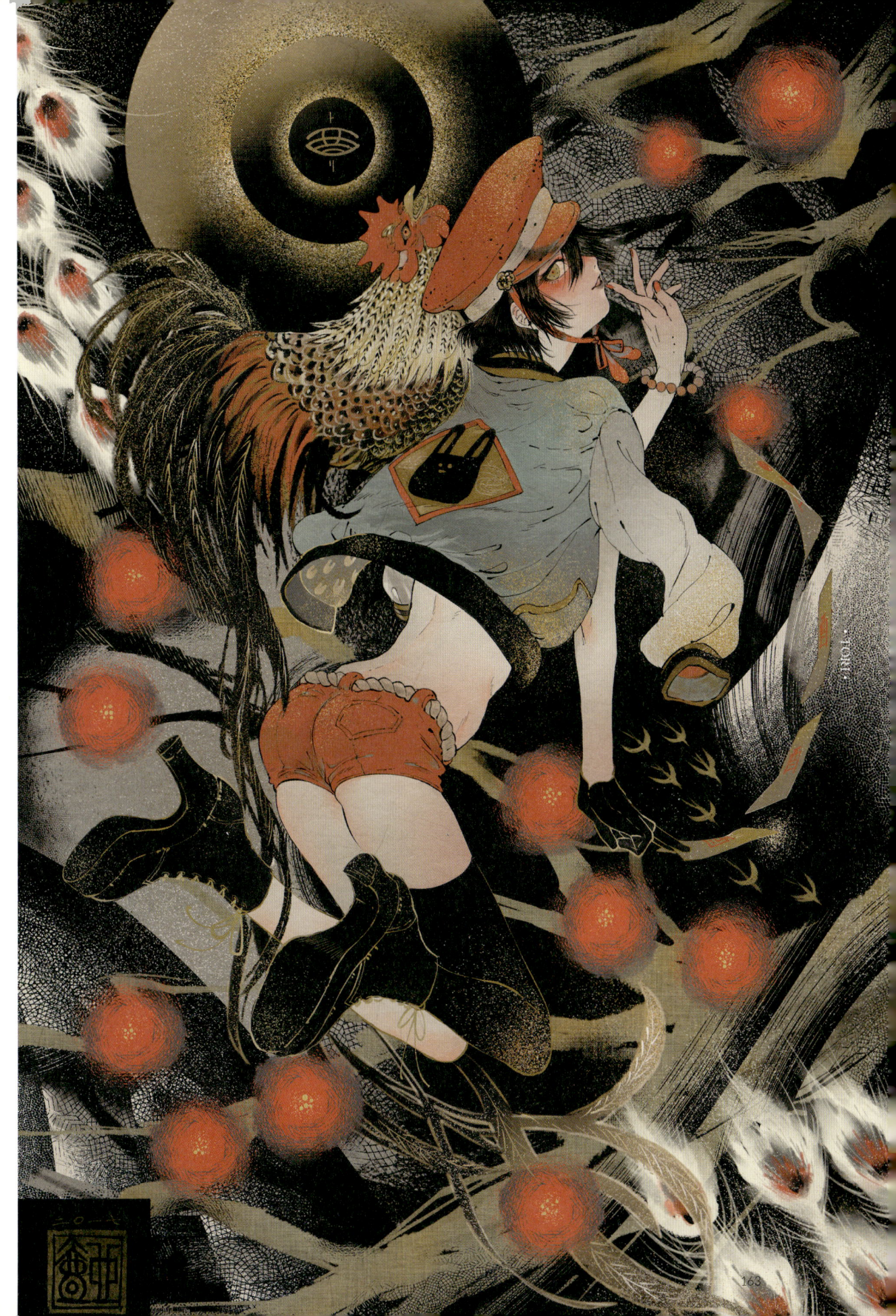

·TORI·

165

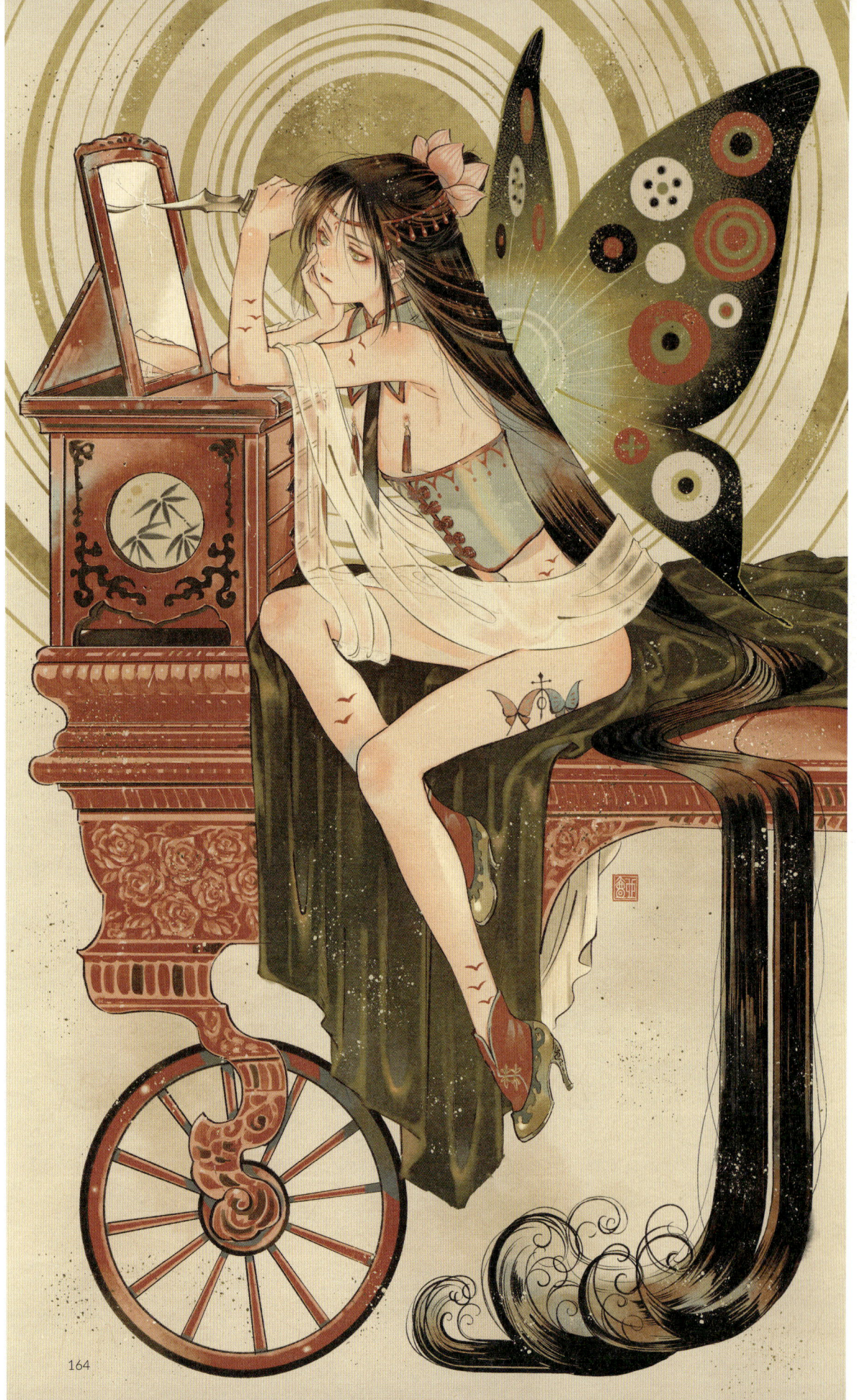

· LUO ·

Q: How did you begin your journey as a manga artist and illustrator? What inspired you to choose this profession?

T: I have loved creating and drawing a great deal more than anything, and started gaining attention from publishing companies and game companies by sharing my work on social media and events during my student days. This naturally brought me into this ballpark. I found that drawing and manga were the quickest ways to express myself and the world I wanted to create with the skills I had at the time.

Q: How do you incorporate elements of Japanese and Chinese styles into your aesthetic world? How do these styles influence your work? Which artists or artworks have had the greatest impact on your creations?

T: I initially studied traditional Japanese crafts. I got interested in interchanging various cultures into my works after learning that Japanese art and crafts are derived from China. After that, I started drawing my works with inspiration from cultures around the world. The influence of Rumiko Takahashi's *Ranma 1/2* was significant as my first exposure to Chinese culture in my manga and anime. Thank you!

Q: Your works are based on the fictional *Antengai* world and you have also published books. What inspired the creation of this world? Could you share some stories behind these?

T: The idea of *Antengai* (Midnight Understreet) was originally created for a manga *Yubikiri Leo* I drew in my teens. When I published my first art collection, I thought it would be good to gather all the stocks of my illustrations in various themes into one art book. It would be interesting to make all residents act in this city together. After that, I have created my works based on this world. I haven't expected this casual idea to lead to such a long-lasting part of my work. I would love to create stories in which the lives and destinies of those characters are gradually intertwined to make various stories. I'm also interested in reinterpreting legends and fairytales to create my fictional religions, believing that the setting of my work *Antengai* can create a mysterious world to condense reality and fantasy. Meanwhile, I'm quite interested in and influenced by Kowloon Walled City in Hong Kong which was often featured in movies and anime but had been distinguished already when I was born.

Q: Apart from your personal creations, you are also involved in game illustrations and character designs. How does this field differ from your personal work? How do you balance the creative demands between these two fields?

T: I like my specialty in Japanese and Chinese styles with underground atmospheres, motifs, and individualistic philosophies. Working on games for the mass market, however, often makes me limit my expression just to popularly conceived ideas and the world. I feel that my creative "force" is completely different from those standardized ones. I'll keep doing my best to meet the demands of those seeking my unique ideas, concepts, individuality, and technical skills to realize them in my manga works!

Q: You have shown some of your early works in the book. Do you think there are any differences or changes compared to your current works?

T: I believe that every aspect directly expressed in my works has changed while the direction I want to convey has not changed. My radical style and technical skills have evolved with my personal growth. The use of colors, touch, atmosphere in way of expression, etc. might have changed along with the expansion of my technical repertoire. Drawing grotesque and explicit images might be, previously, one of the ways to cope with my stress and solace, but it has gradually changed also due to recent trends that images with extreme elements have become less accepted. Changes in my various experiences, knowledge, and perspectives would be reflected in my work.

Q: Your work *Mind's Eye* (P169) combines the traditional Japanese lacquerware technique (*maki-e*) with your own artwork. Besides this, what other traditional crafts interest you?

T: I am interested in various traditional crafts and folk art not only in Japan but also around the world. I am also fascinated by architecture and performing arts. I would like to experience various craftsman activities.

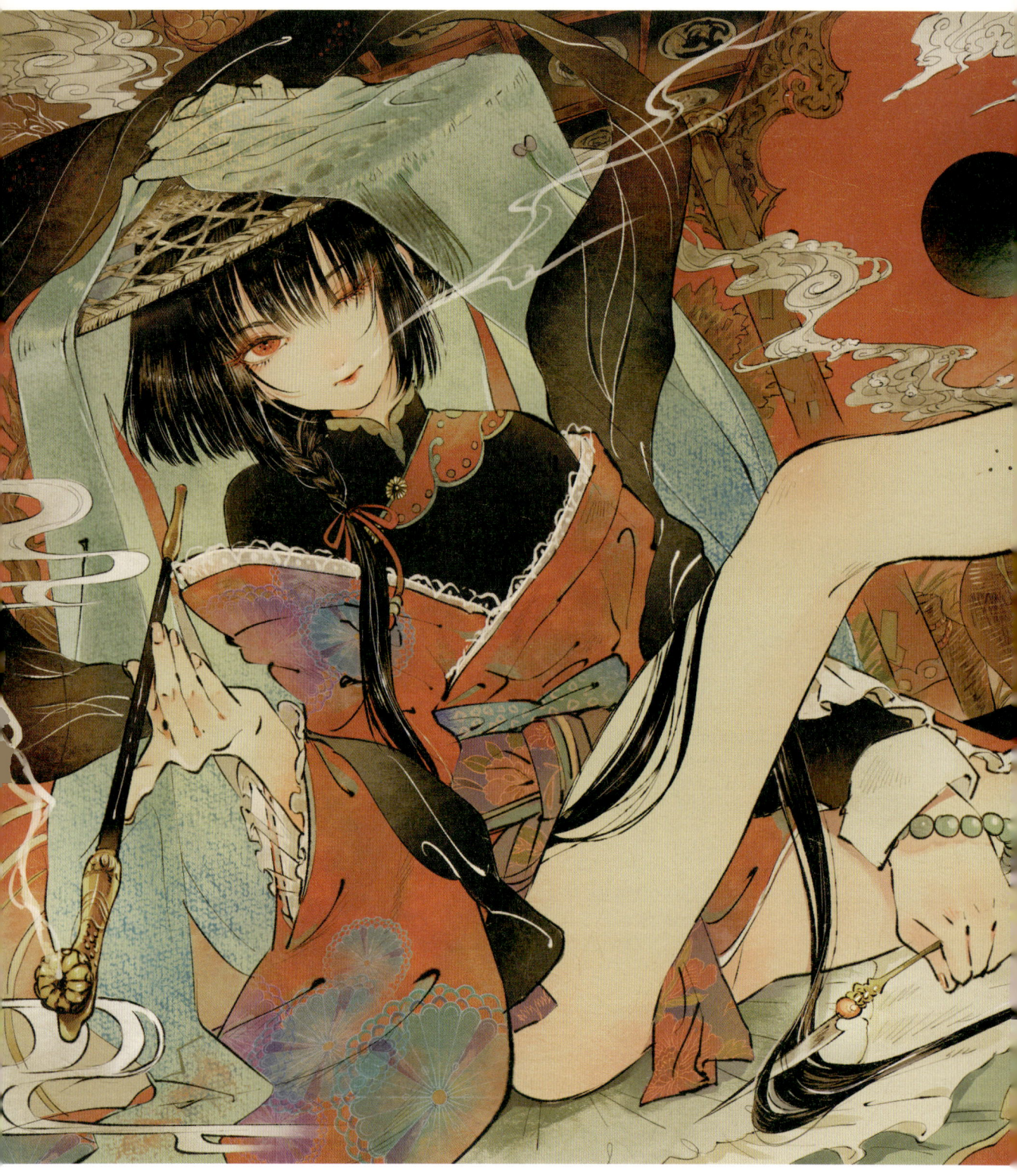

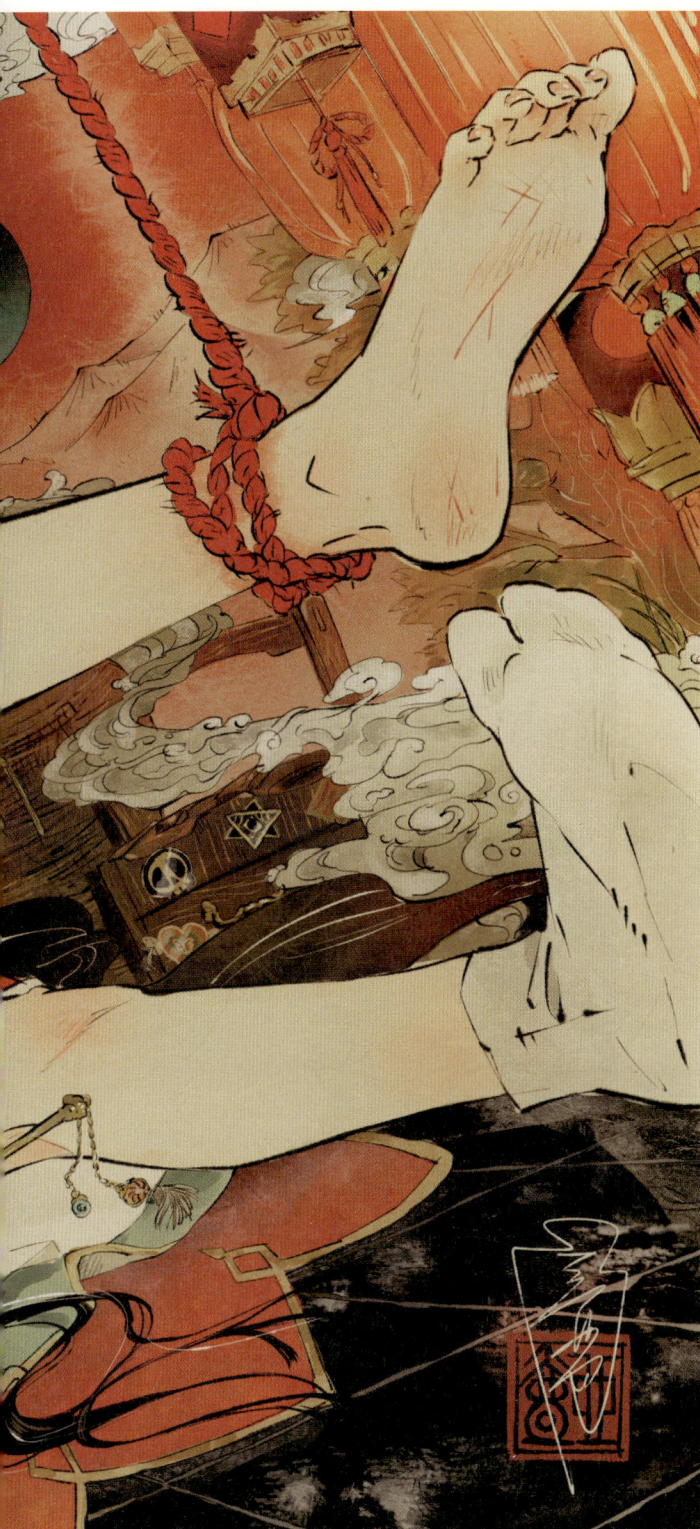

Q: It's noticeable that your works often use red and black colors. Do you have any personal preferences or reasons behind your choices in color?

T: I learned Japanese traditional arts and works, and quite liked the color of black, Japanese vermilion, and gold used in those Japanese lacquer crafts. I was attracted by these simple but relaxing colors and I think I became seeking for less combination of colors with flamboyant images. There were fewer works with low saturation and brightness at that time, so it would be somehow unique.

Q: How do you view the impact of AI technology on traditional painting?

T: I think that AI in art can serve as an excellent assistant to artists, but at this stage, there are many issues regarding its use and legal aspects, and it is not yet in a secure environment for use. I hope that these issues will be resolved in the future. I don't think AI technology should be compared to human-made art. While AI is an amazing technology, it does not have its own will, and for now, I see it as a tool used by humans. I would like to separate the use of AI by humans from works created by AI.

Q: What are your future creative plans? Do you intend to continue exploring themes and styles present in your work, or do you have new directions and challenges in mind?

T: I'm going to keep creating my works in the same direction until I find another new horizon. I want to create works that are fantastical yet somehow realistic, like a mirage. Through manga and illustrations, I would be happy to receive any feedback, as long as there is some new discovery or realization for me. Technically, I want to continue studying new ways to refine the style I have cultivated so far. I always try to integrate traditional techniques into various forms, not just 2D art. It's my long-standing wish!

" *I'm also interested in reinterpreting legends and fairytales to create my fictional religions, believing that the setting of my works Antengai can create a mysterious world to condense reality and fantasy.* "

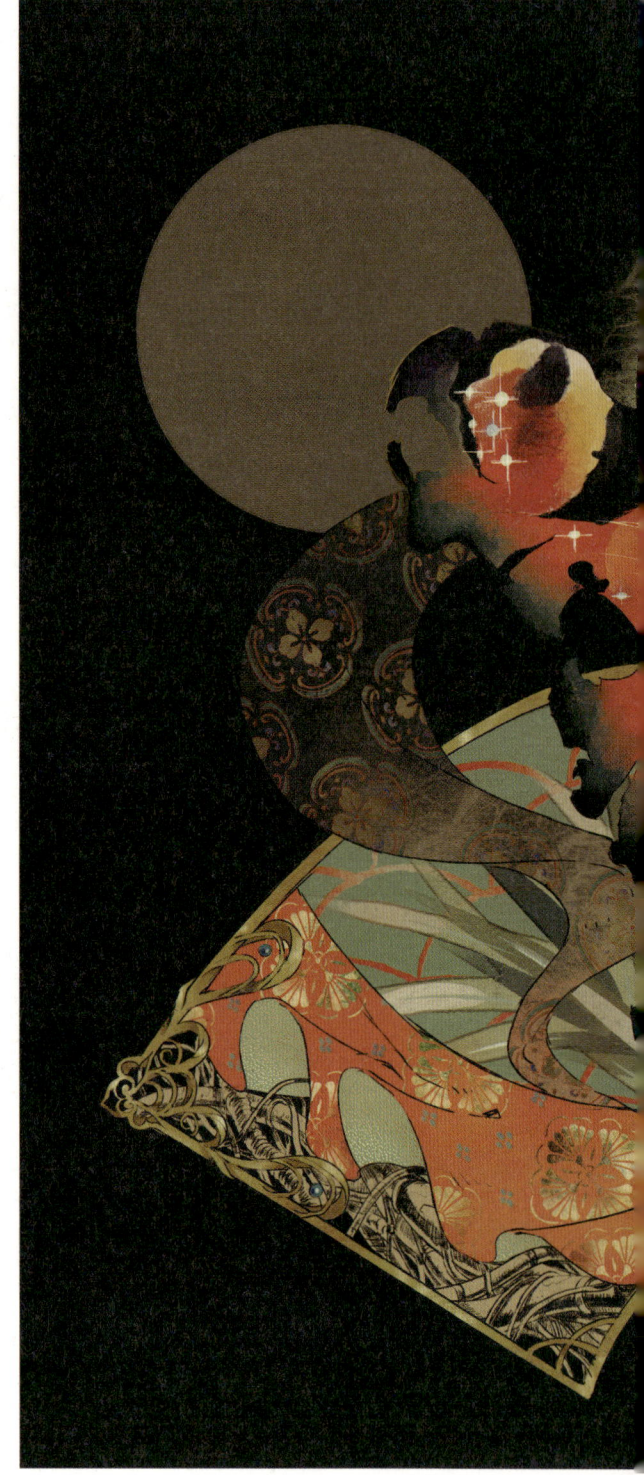

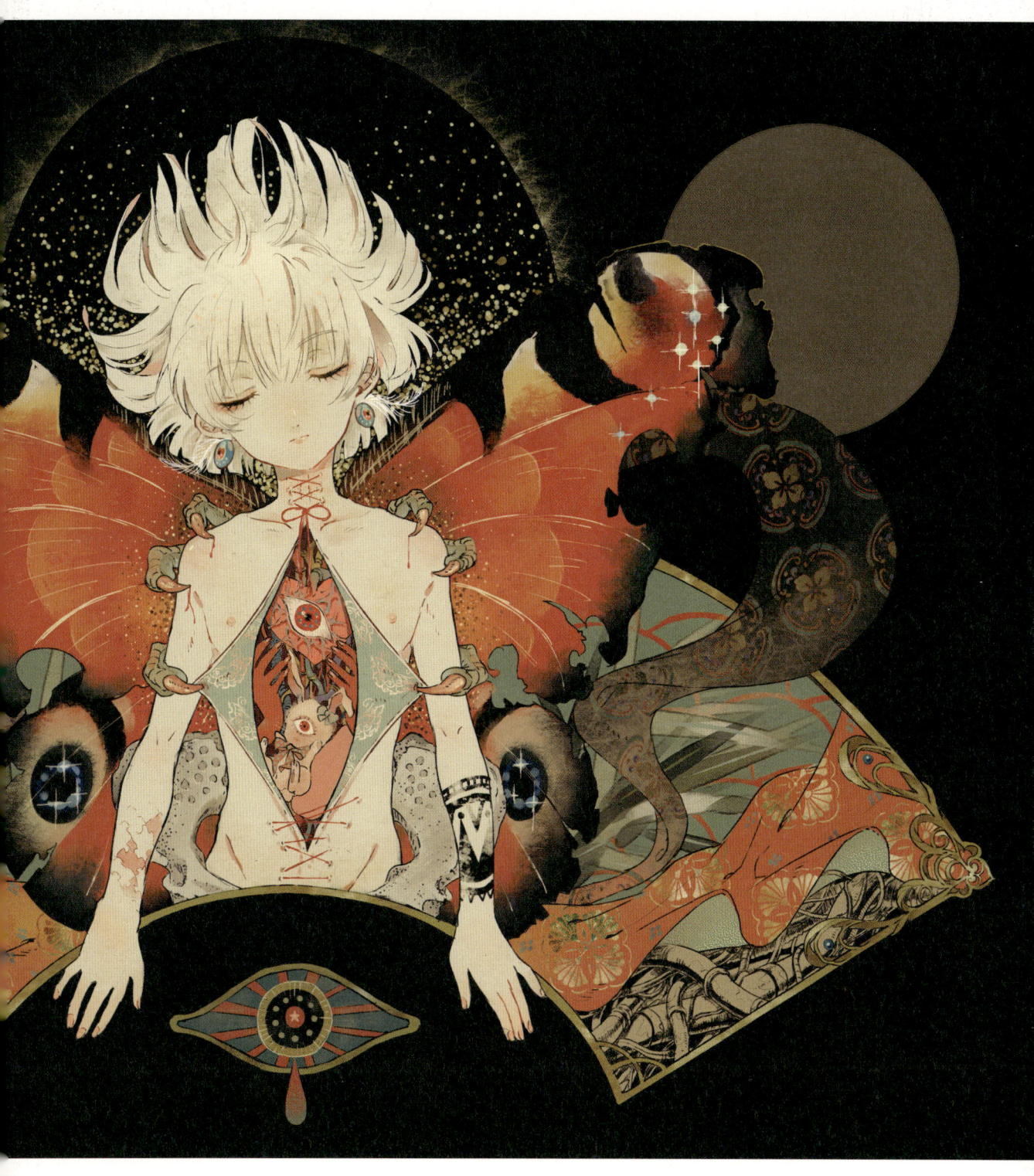

THE SHADOW PLAY

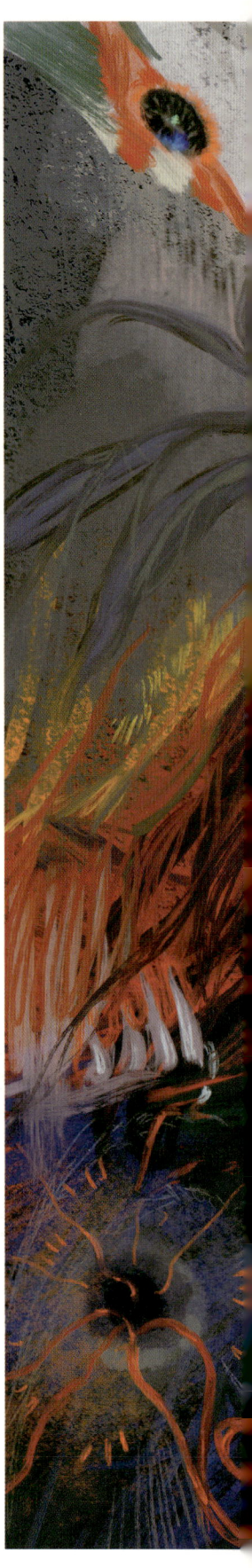

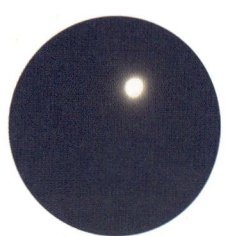

Kaihara

Currently a student at Tama Art University in Japan, majoring in oil painting. He creates works that obscure the roots of living things, and is always considering attempts to question the viewer's roots. In addition to oil paintings, he also creates digital works.

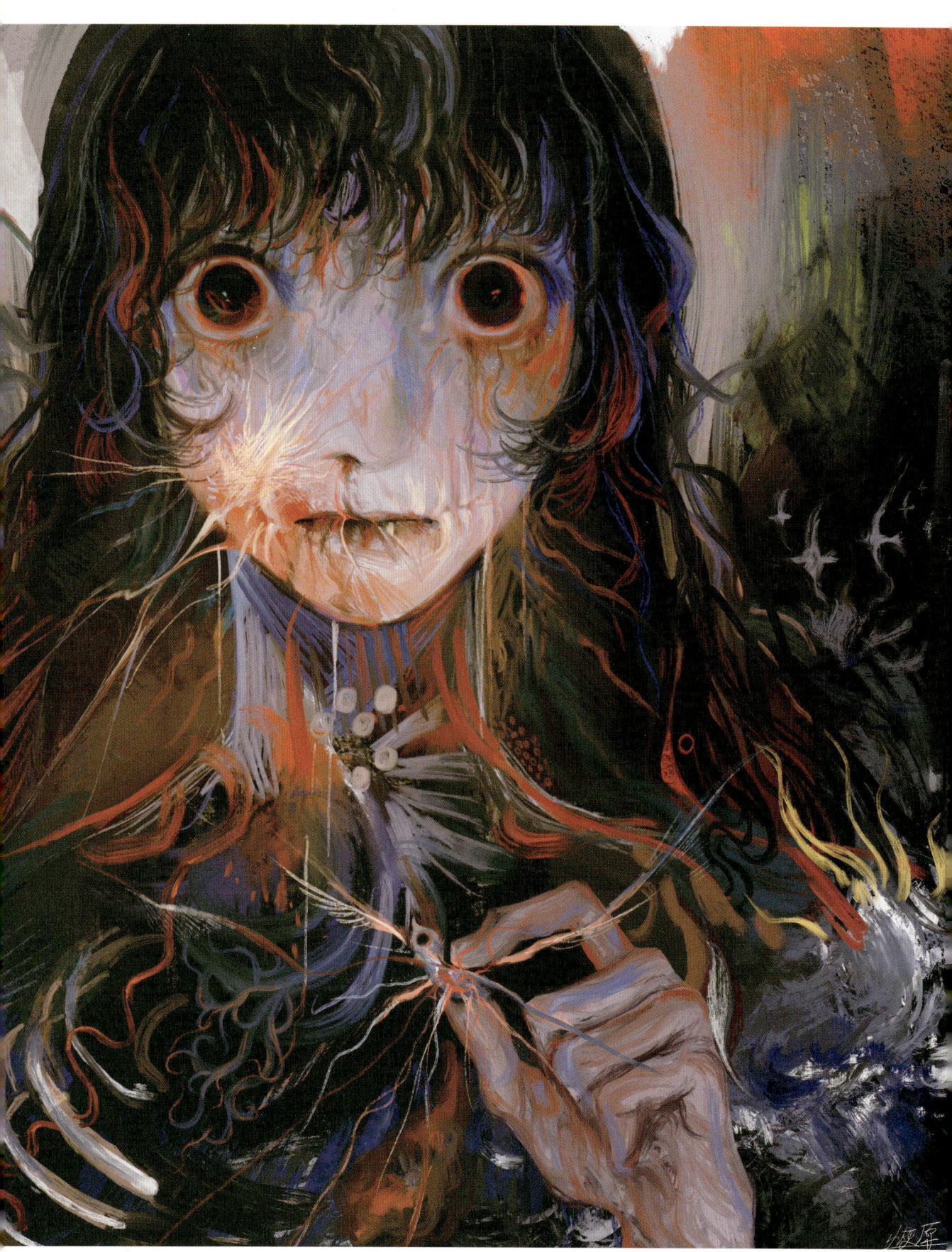

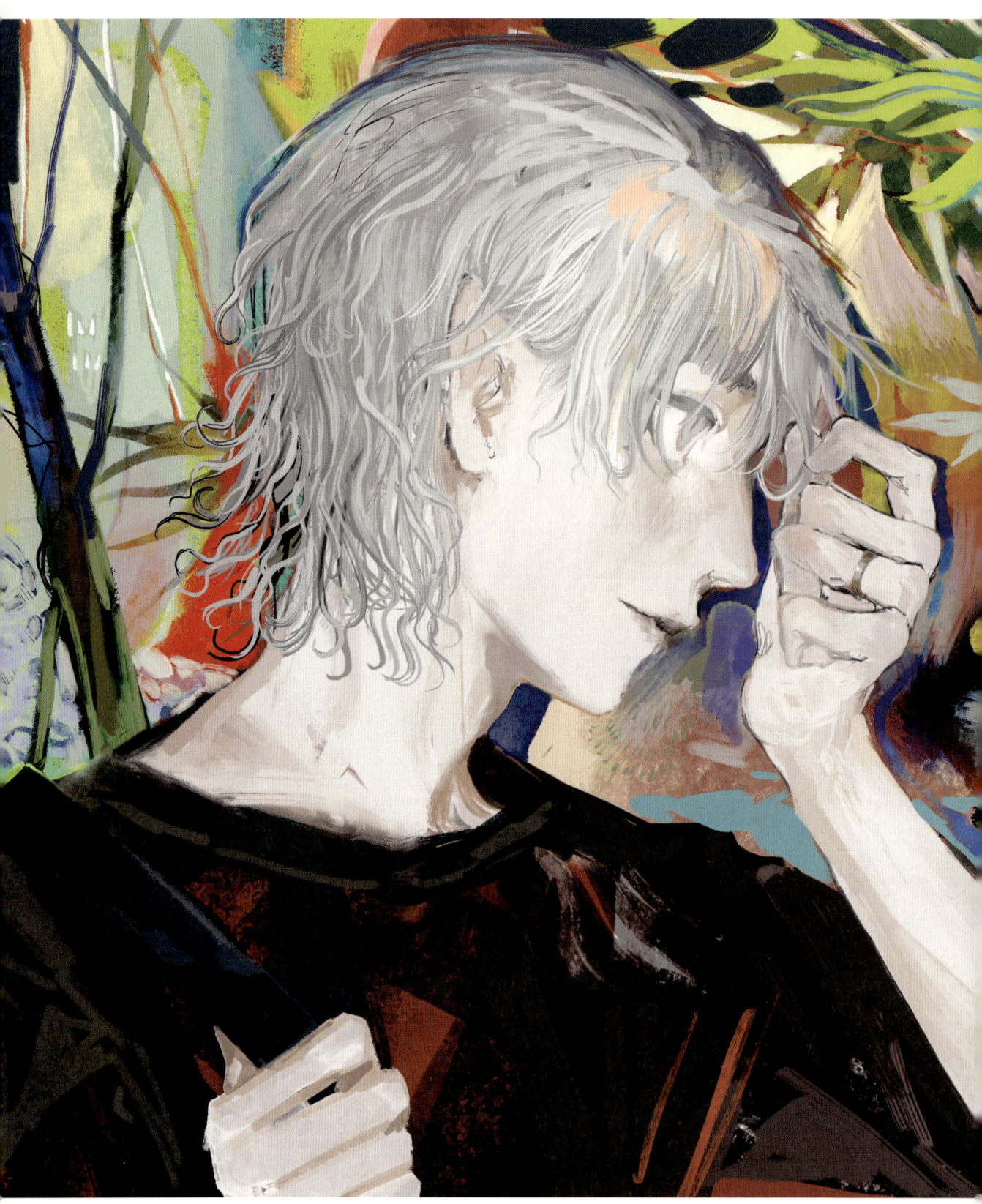

· PORTRAIT ·

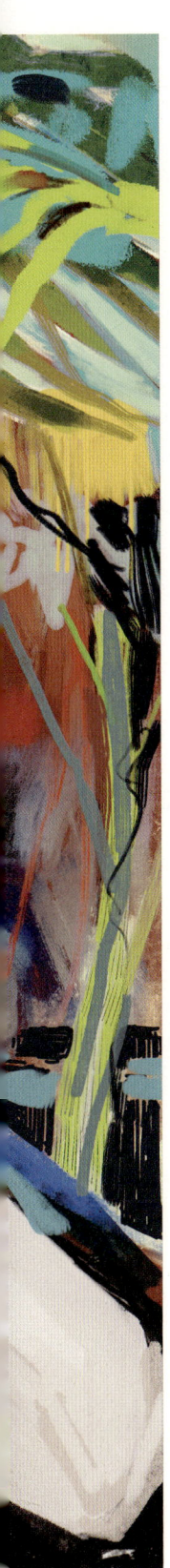

Q: When did you start becoming interested in art? How did studying oil painting in the painting department at Tama Art University help your technique and creativity?

K: When I was a kid, I did more doodles than paintings. I majored in oil painting from high school to university. Oil painting is one of the few things that I was able to continue without giving up, so I think it is closely related to my current creative activities.

Q: With a large following on X, how do you utilize and manage social media to showcase your work? How does this benefit your art career?

K: When I was a child, smartphones were already widespread, and I had many opportunities to think about how to interact with SNS. I try to refrain from posting personal things on SNS, and I want to convey my work to others in the form of words. I think this is also a motivation for my activities.

Q: You mentioned using painting to combat daily pain and explore your emotions. What healing power does painting hold for you?

K: The scenery and words that dwell in a painting can be sensed and experienced by the viewer according to their own rhythm, and as a painter myself, I can feel this as well.

"Healing" is difficult, but I cherish the time I spend gradually uncovering the scenery with my own hands.

Q: Your works have dreamlike colors, shining as if in the dark night. What are your color preferences? Could you share your creative process and whether you use any special techniques or tools?

K: The motif is always the journey of a particular person. I began to carefully and boldly mix colors to express words and feelings that could not be conveyed through motifs alone.

I'm currently experimenting with various things, including inputting the textures of oil paintings into digital art tools.

Q: You've created many character designs that seem like combinations of humans and creatures, full of creativity. Could you share the inspiration behind these designs?

K: It all started when I caught insects and observed them. I studied animal anatomy at university, and while expanding and contracting the straight lines and curves of the human body, I create designs by freely combining them with the skeletons of various living things.

Q: You provided illustrations in Mili's *Between Two Worlds* and CIEL's *Fukuiku no Machi* (Fragrant Street) music videos. How did you collaborate with these music projects? How did these experiences influence your artwork?

K: It's very exciting and fun to see my paintings move and merge with music.

The job of conveying someone's thoughts, voice, sounds, and words to a large number of people was new, a little scary, and a source of pride.

Q: What was the experience like having a solo exhibition "Ignorant Moon" at Anicoremix Gallery? What was your biggest takeaway from this process? Were there any particularly memorable experiences or challenges?

K: The biggest achievement was that the exhibition was a success. It takes ingenuity and effort to objectively view your works and entertain and fascinate people. The exhibition was made possible with the cooperation of many people.

Q: You mentioned paralleling creation with physical activity. What is the relationship between these two? How does exercise influence your creative process?

K: In fact, creative activities not only consume physical strength but can make you feel unwell. When drawing the human body, I sometimes refer to my own body to consider the structure of muscles and bones, so I don't want to be unable to draw due to a lack of physical strength or poor health.

Q: As a young new generation artist, can you give some advice to other young artists?

K: Life is a "long-time killer." There are times when I can't move.

Even so, if you find the little hopes or small joys, I want you to grasp them, express them, and continue to pursue them.

Because it is the light that guides your life.

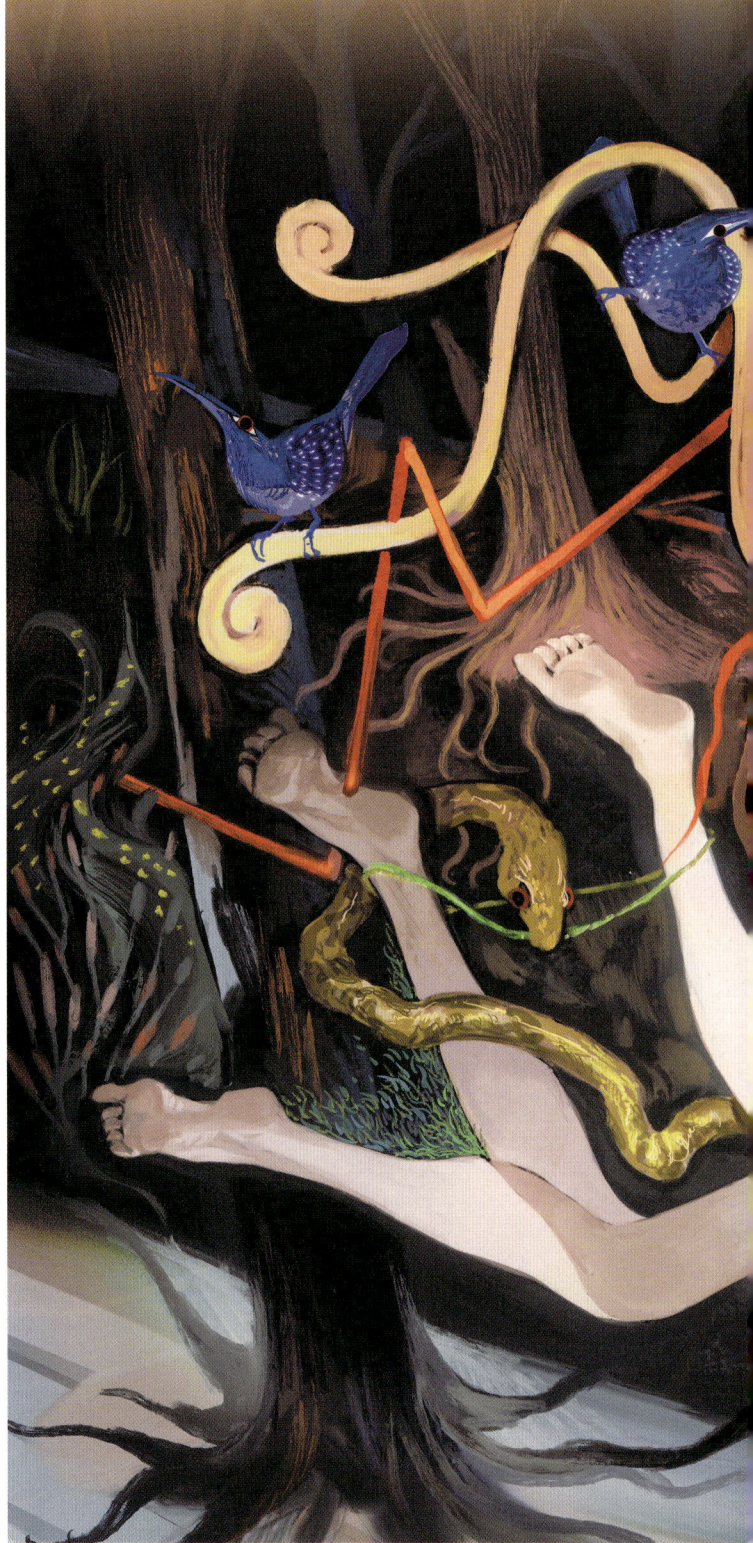

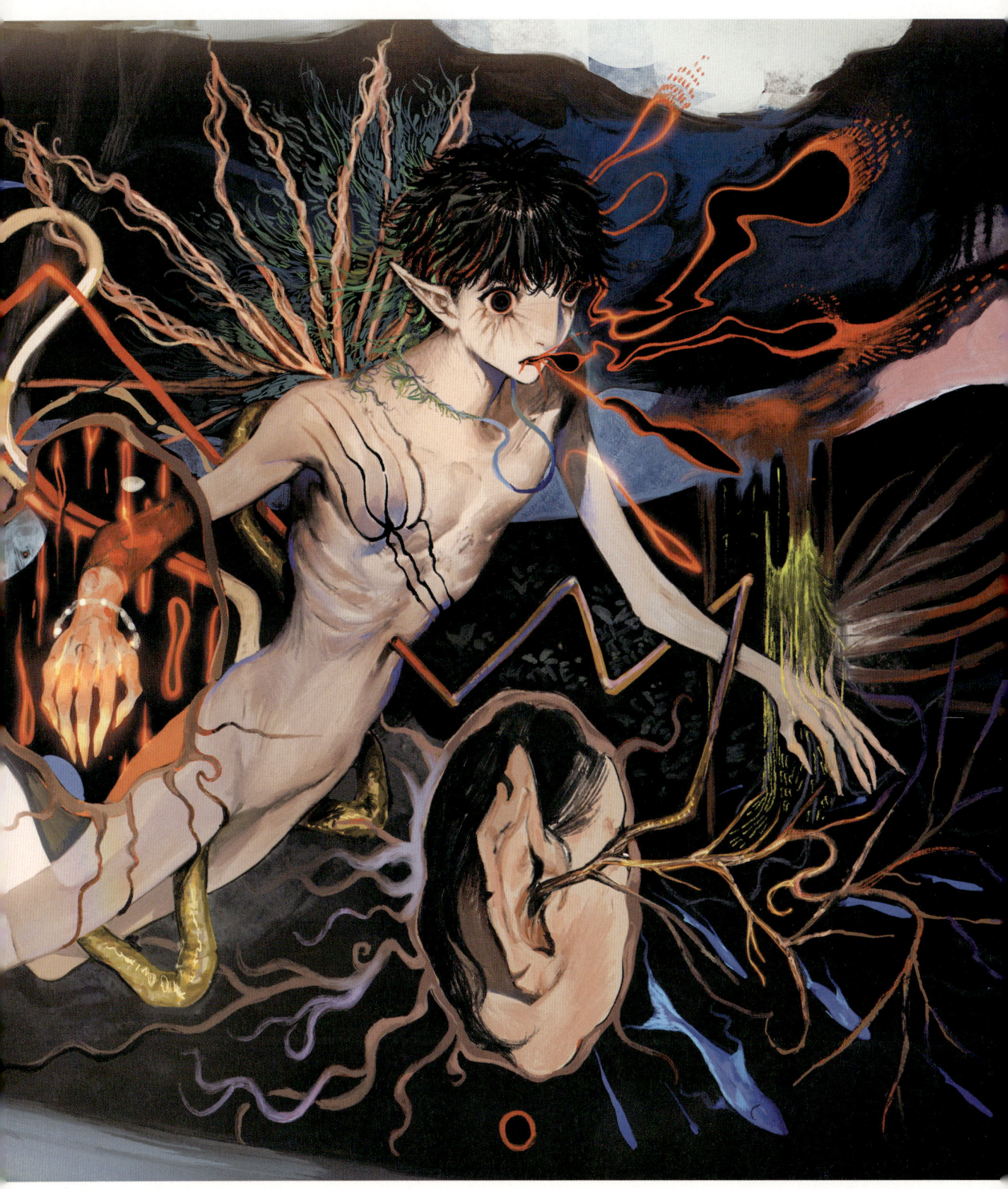

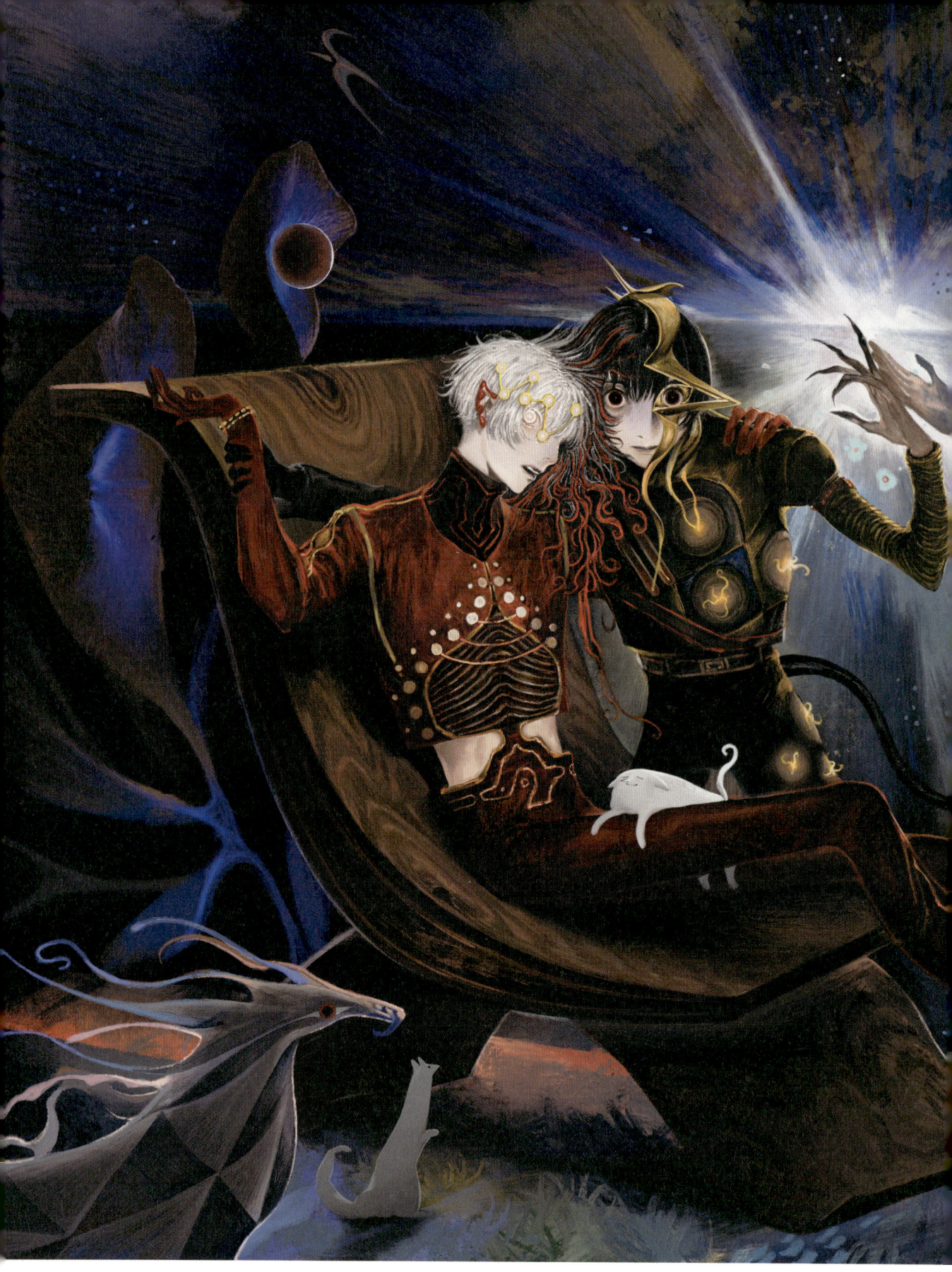

• THE GREAT GOAT OF THE MORNING STAR •

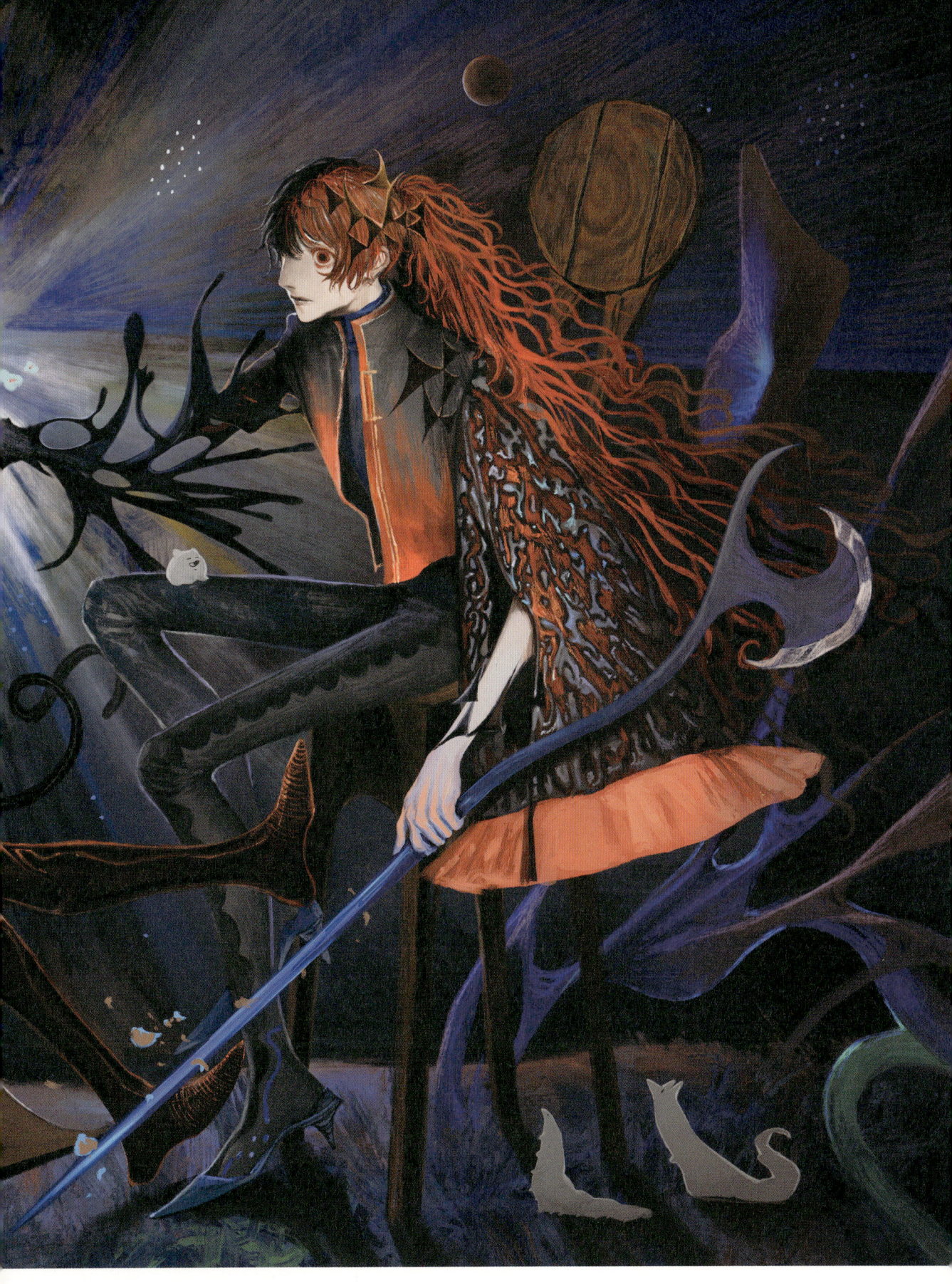

" *I cherish the time I spend gradually uncovering the scenery with my own hands.* "

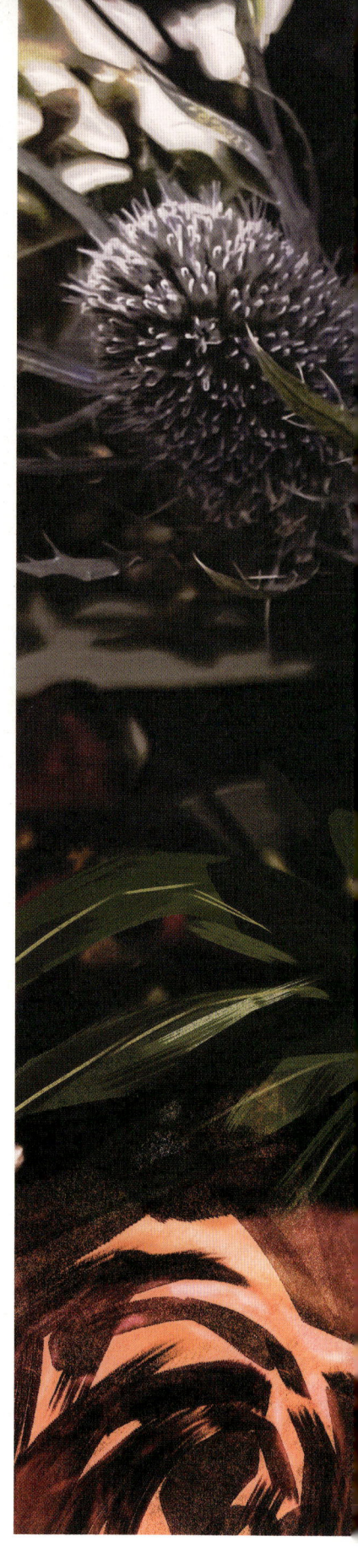

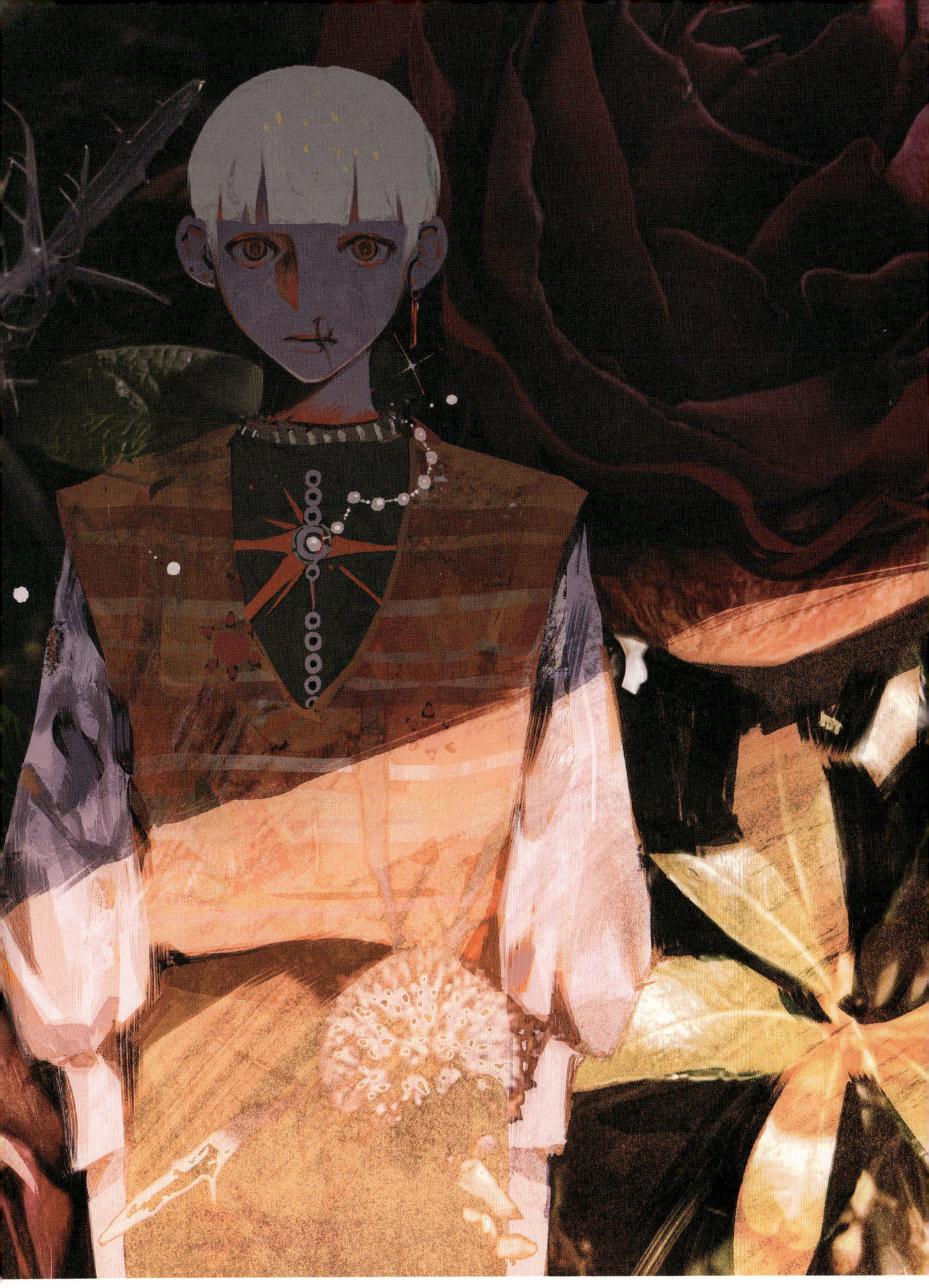

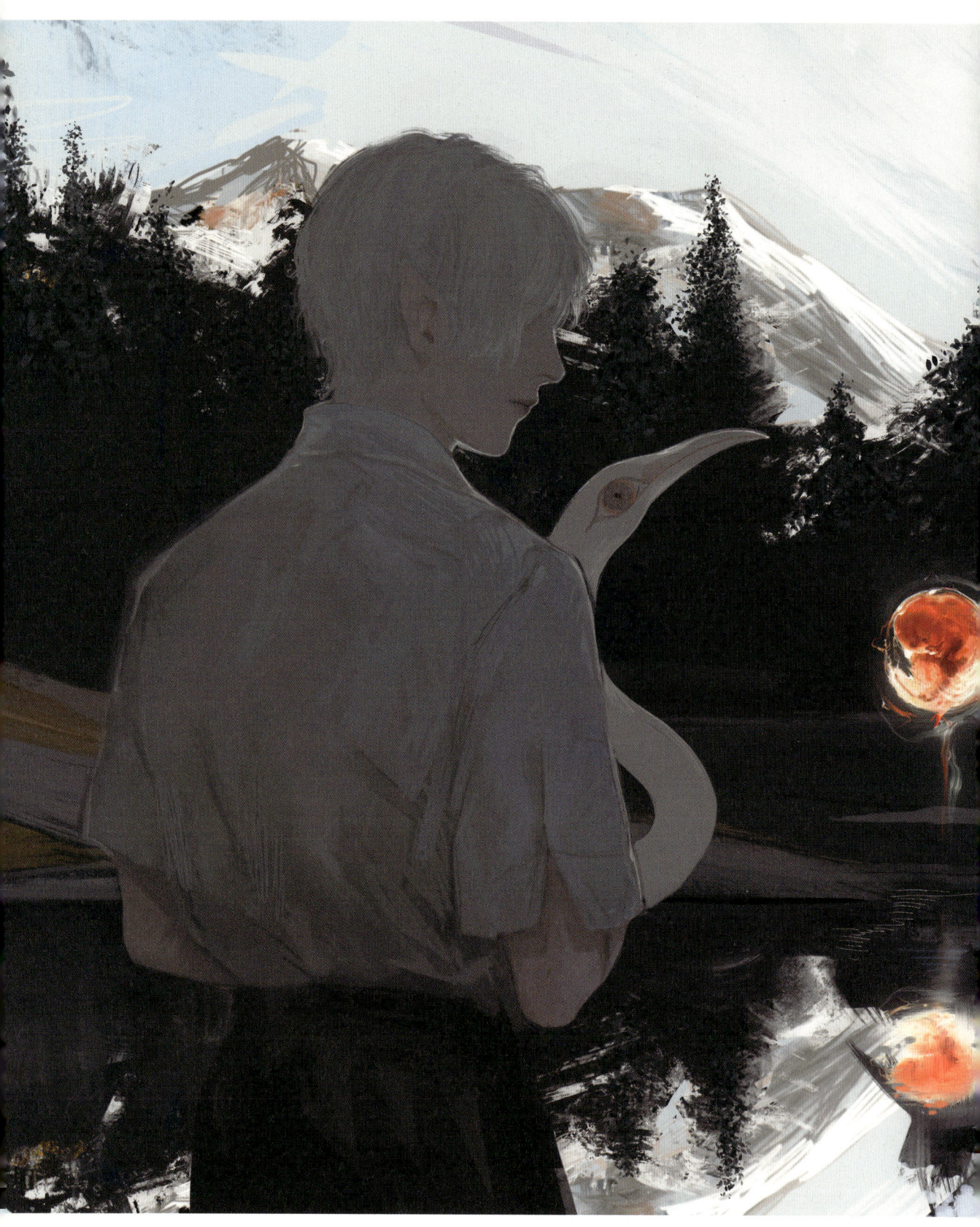

• FETAL SLEEP •

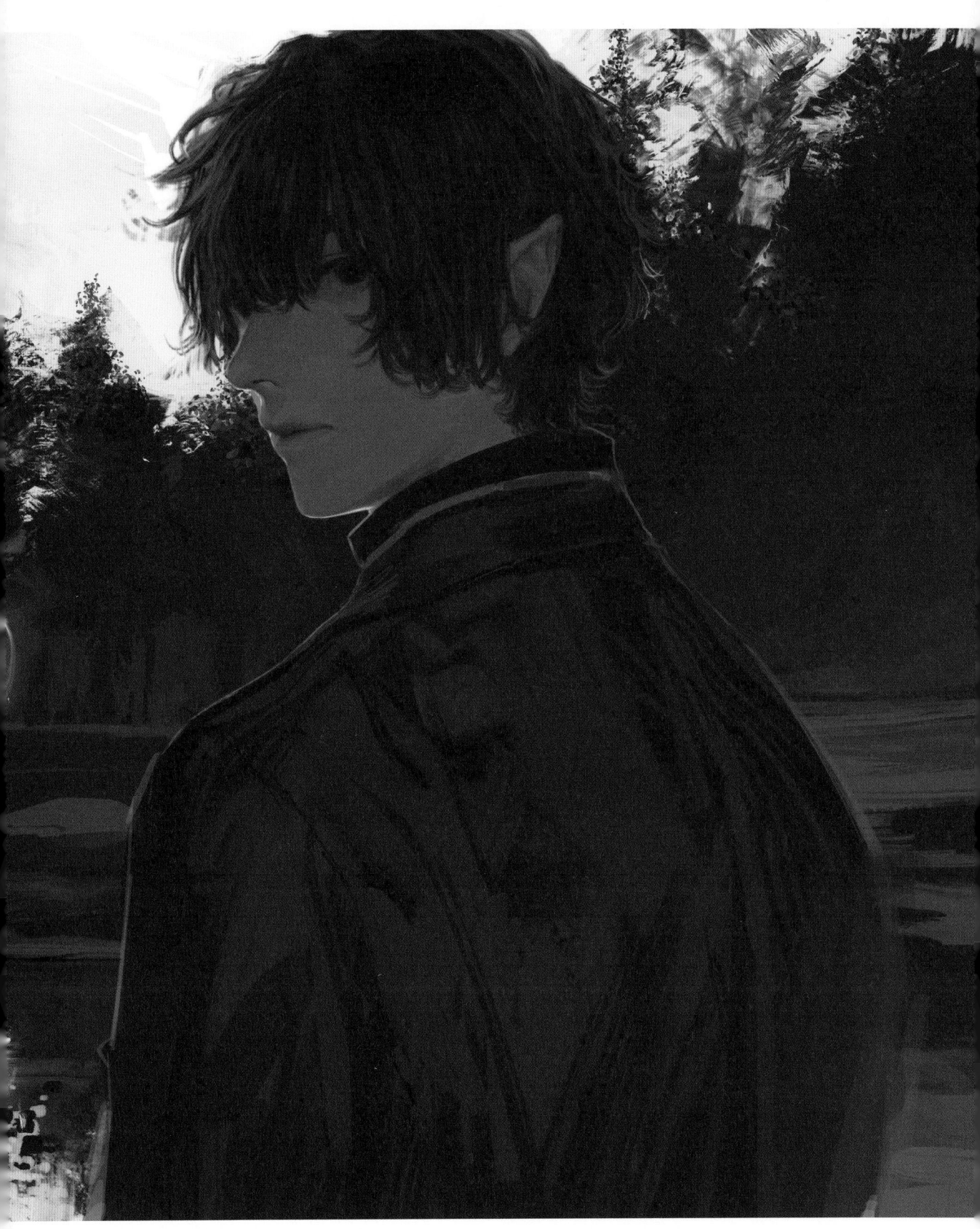

MIND GAMES

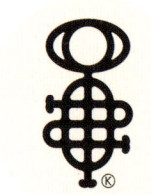

ONIKU Kuitai

Kuitai draws inspiration from lines and patterns, using them to create fantastic, colorful illustrations of the world.

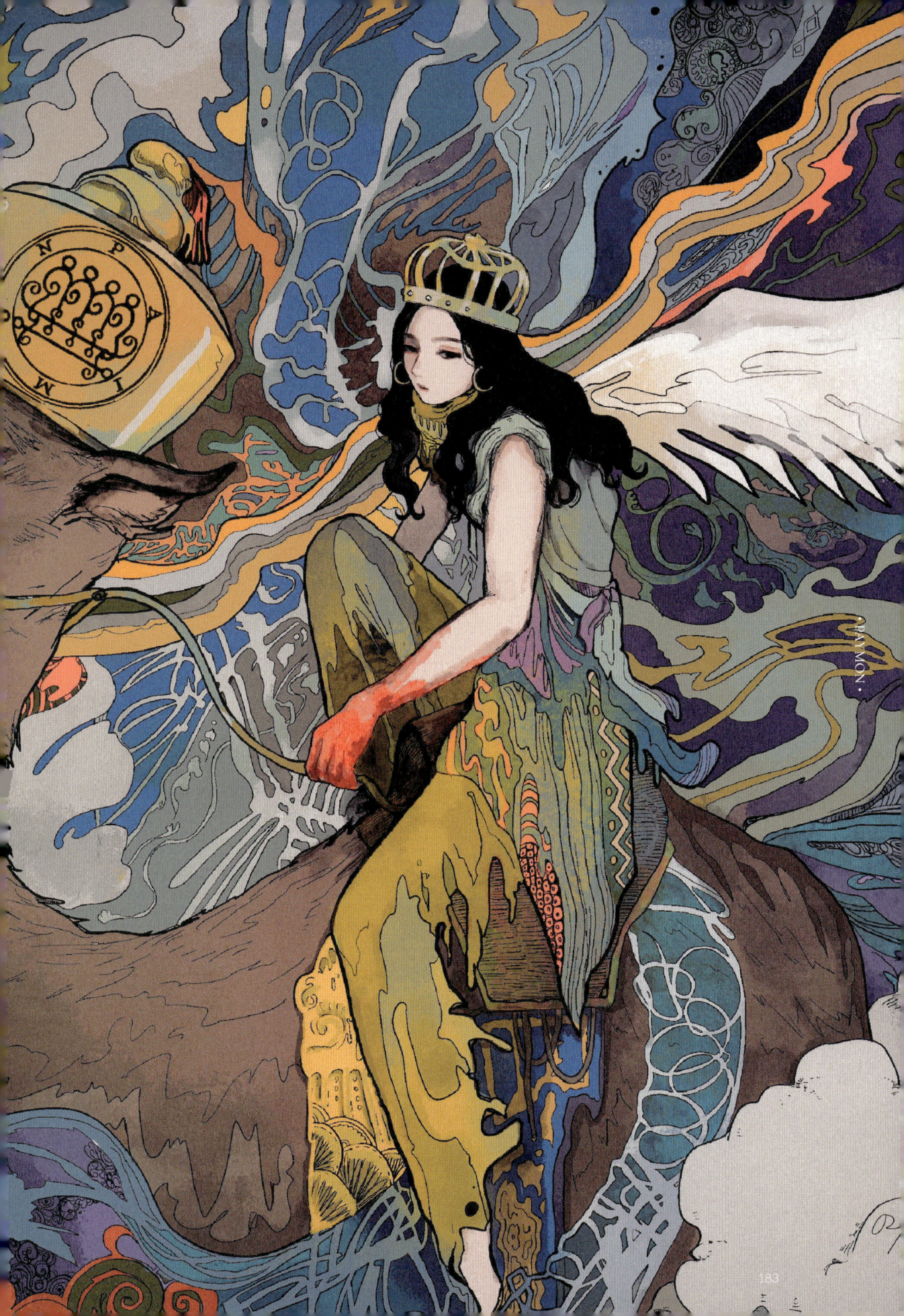

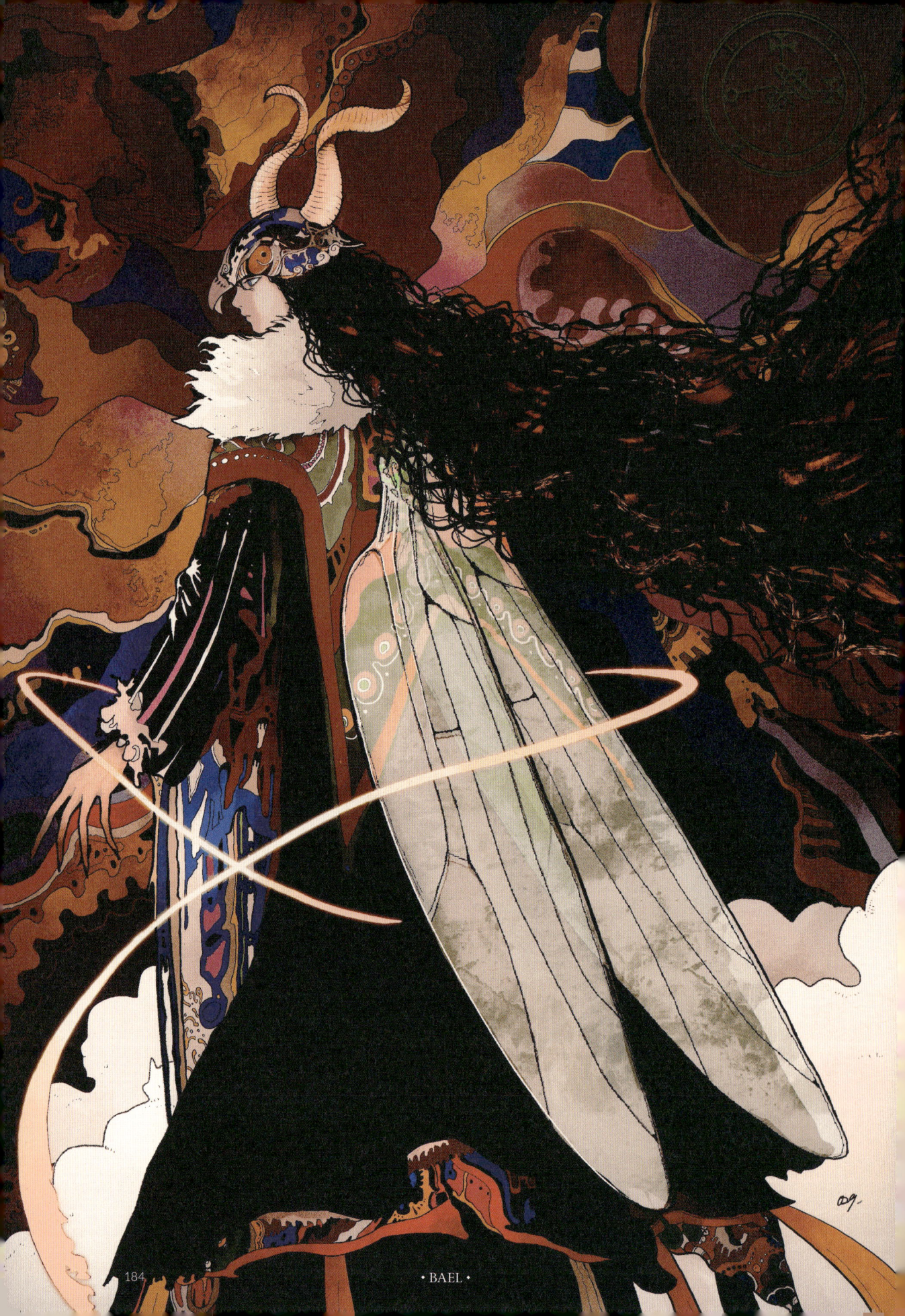

• BAEL •

Q: How did you begin your career in art? What inspired your interest in painting?

OK: I have really enjoyed looking at art since I was a little girl, from Western paintings to ukiyo-e. I am not particular about genres.

I have never studied it in earnest, but anyway, I have been doing what I love for a long time, and here I am today.

Q: Could you please describe the painting mediums you frequently use?

OK: Basically, I use Procreate on my iPad. I also like ballpoint pen drawings.

Q: Your recent work features illustrations depicting the *72 Pillars of Solomon* described in *Ars Goetia.* What is the biggest attraction of this theme for you?

OK: It was a game that led me to know about the *72 Pillars of Solomon*, but the pecking order of each demon, its coat of arms, its appearance, etc. I was attracted by the way it stimulated my imagination. So I wanted to interpret this theme in my own way.

Q: Your works use strong and rich colors. Do you have your own unique color-matching method? How do you usually choose and match colors?

OK: I imagine a richly-colored abstract painting, and I put colors on the canvas while putting together the overall balance with my senses. I rely on my own senses a lot.

Q: Congratulations on your solo exhibition at 9DAYS GALLERY in May 2024. Could you share any interesting or memorable experiences from the exhibition?

OK: Thank you very much. This was my first solo exhibition, and I was very happy to meet my fans in person. It was also a valuable experience to have them buy my works right before me.

It was very interesting that the gallery made a giclée print that matched my painting (Canson Etching Rag), and it had a wonderful texture as if it had been painted in an analog manner.

Q: Have you encountered any particularly challenging or troubling situations during your creative process? How did you overcome these difficulties?

OK: When I cannot create in any way, I stop painting and rest. If my body does not need me to draw, I first enrich my other hobbies. In my case, doing so will make me want to draw again.

Q: Your works often feature dynamic lines and intricate patterns to depict subjects. What inspires those graphical elements?

OK: I have always loved looking at kimono patterns and textiles. Knowing what meanings are attached to them has also inspired me. As for dynamic lines, I like free-flowing lines. I often use the lines as they are in the drafting process.

Q: Has Japanese culture had a significant influence on your work? Are there specific elements of Japanese culture that you particularly admire or feel proud to incorporate?

OK: I often use the vermillion color in my illustrations. The beautiful poison is not limited to Japanese culture, but vermilion is also made of a highly toxic substance, mercury sulfide. This poison is also meant to ward off evil. This vivid color is one of the things I am proud of about Japanese culture.

Q: Among your illustration works, which one left the deepest impression on you?

OK: There was a time when I only drew illustrations of women. But I got really tired of that. So I started drawing what I wanted to draw every day to enhance my inspiration. I still have strong feelings for the illustrations I created during that period. Among them, a character with a pure white face, a pure white horn, and vermilion paint is my savior.

Q: Do you plan to try different art forms or mediums in the future? Is there any creative field that you have not tried yet but have always been interested in?

OK: Up until now, I have mainly been working only with digital art. I think it would be interesting to paint this colorful art in analog form. I would also like to try my hand at large scale art.

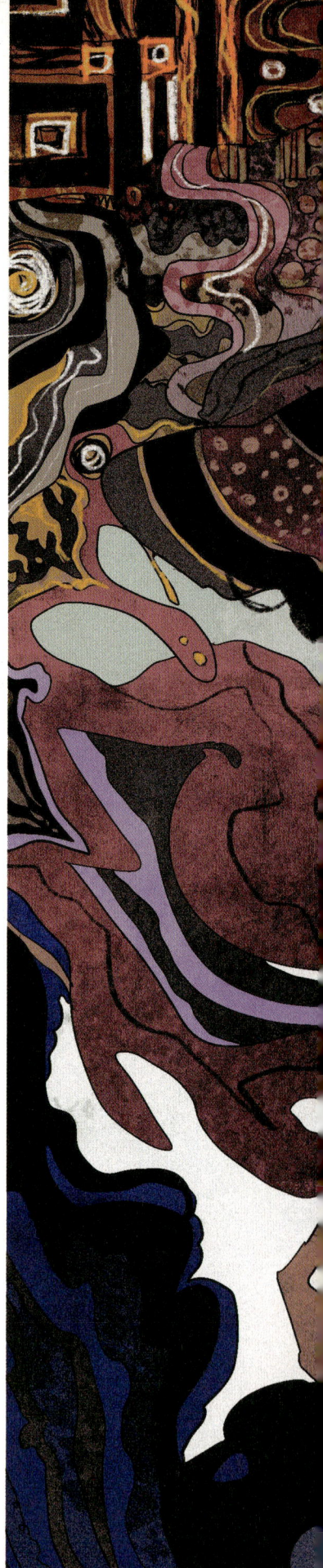

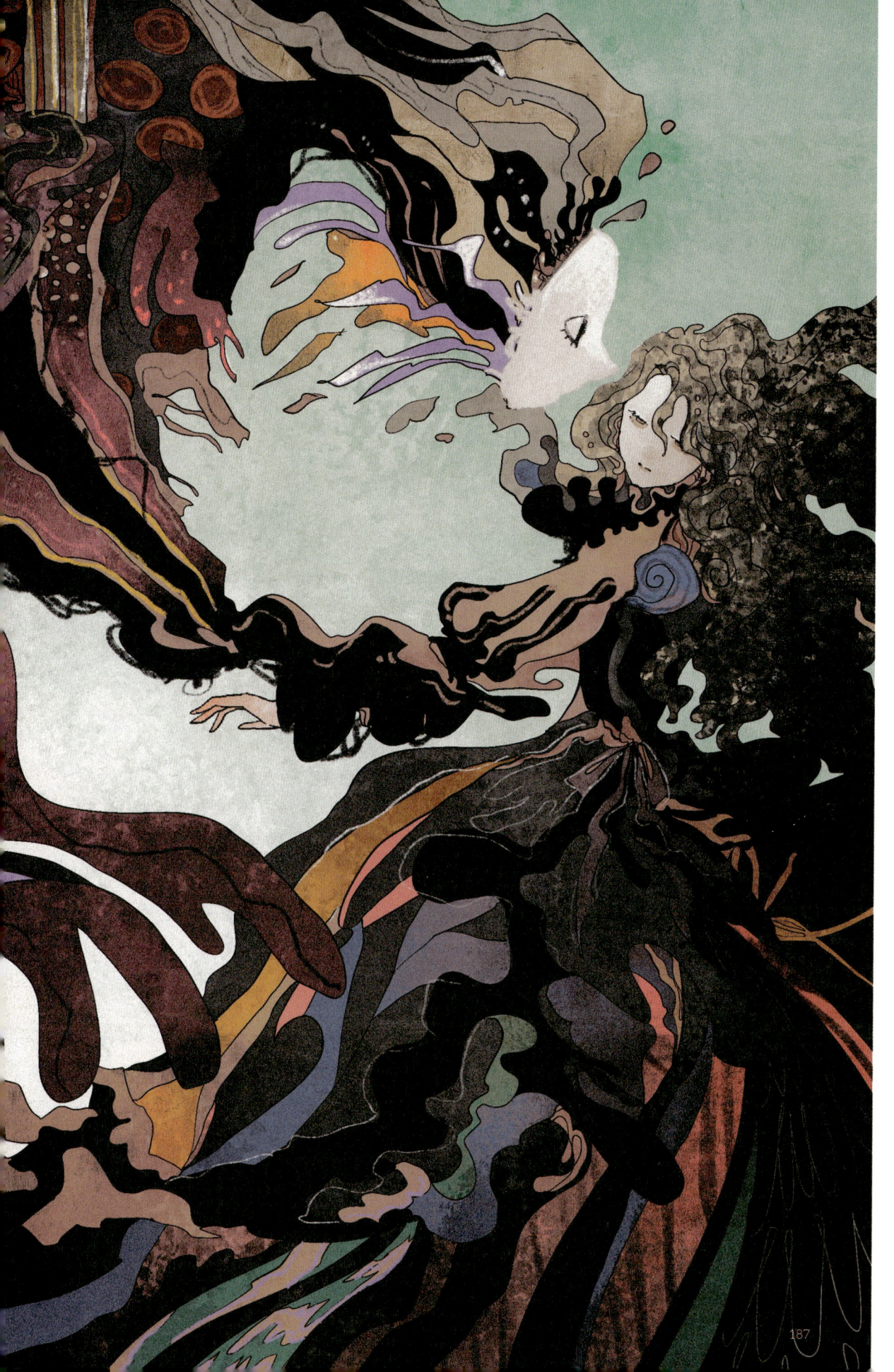

• ESCAPE •

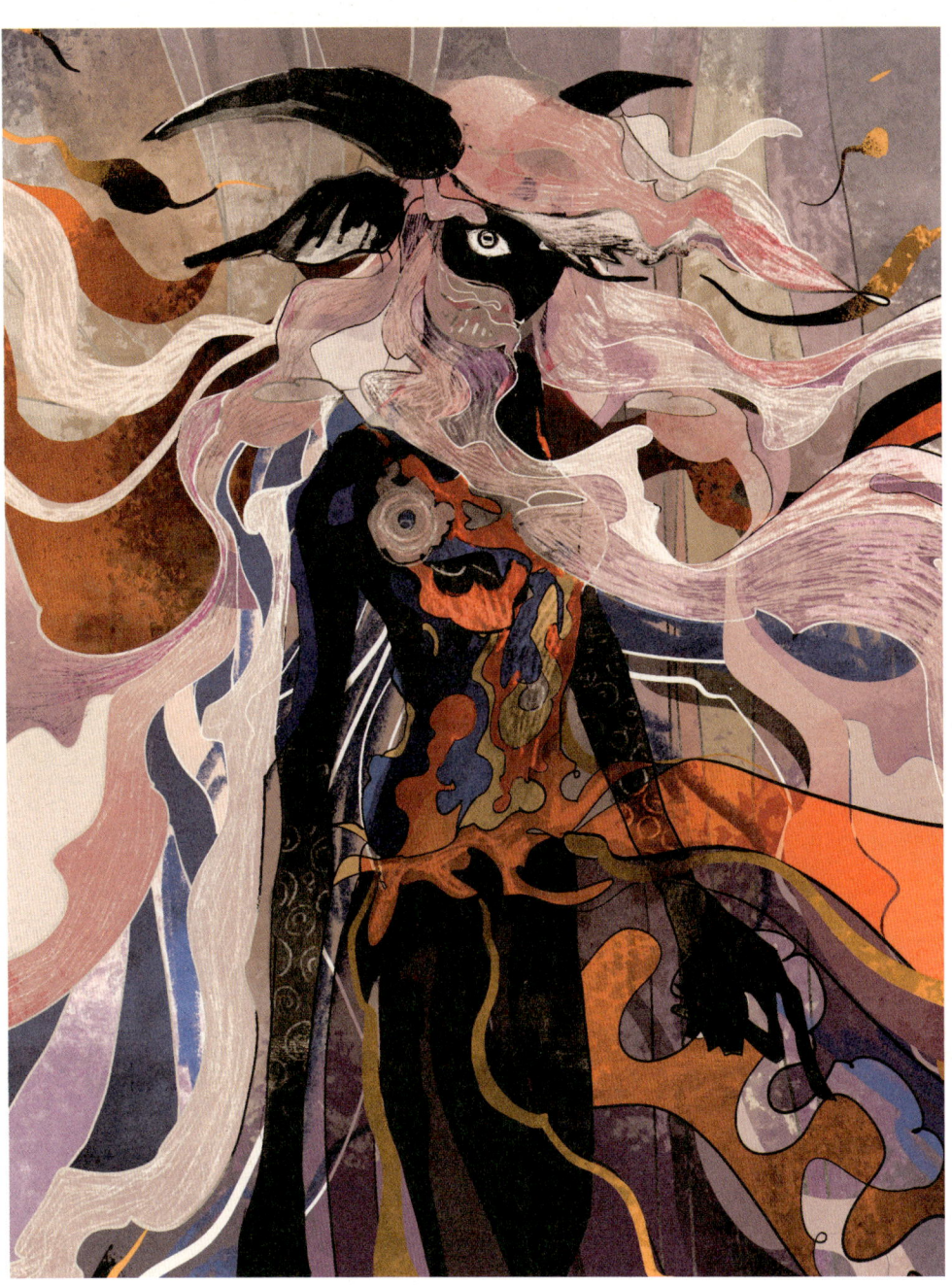

· TURBID ·

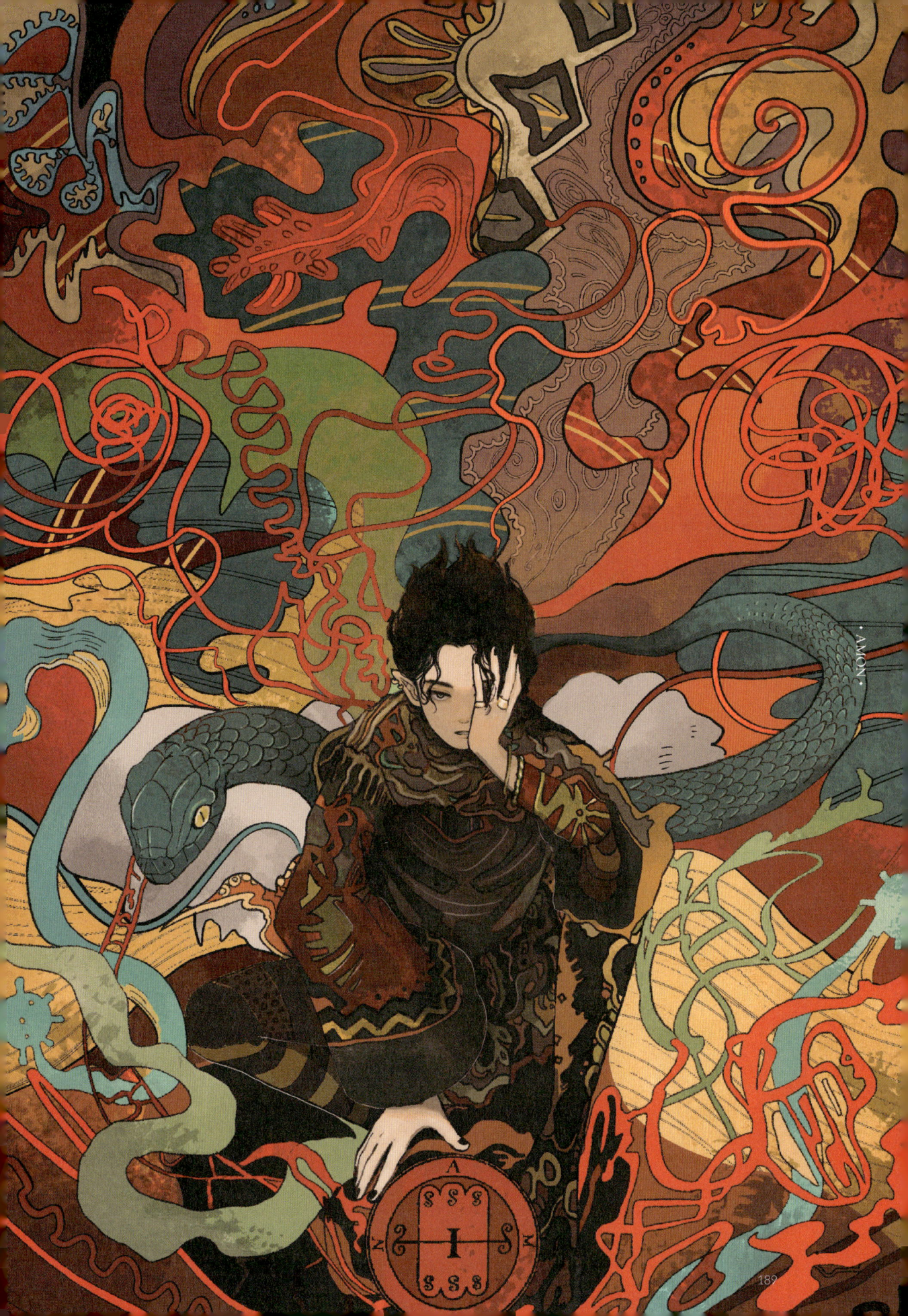

•AMON•

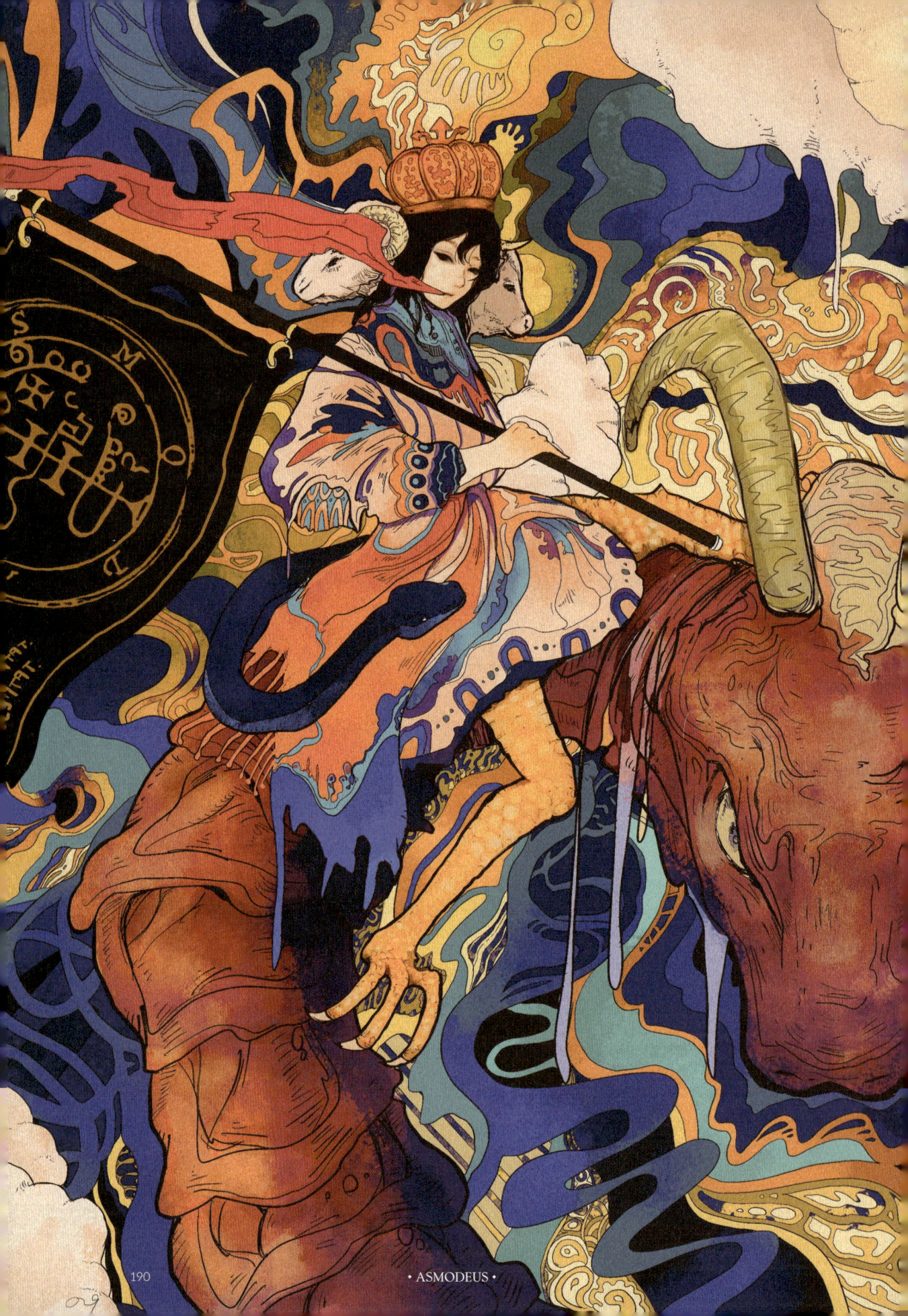

• ASMODEUS •

" I imagine a richly-colored abstract painting, and I put colors on the canvas while putting together the overall balance with my senses. I rely on my own senses a lot. "

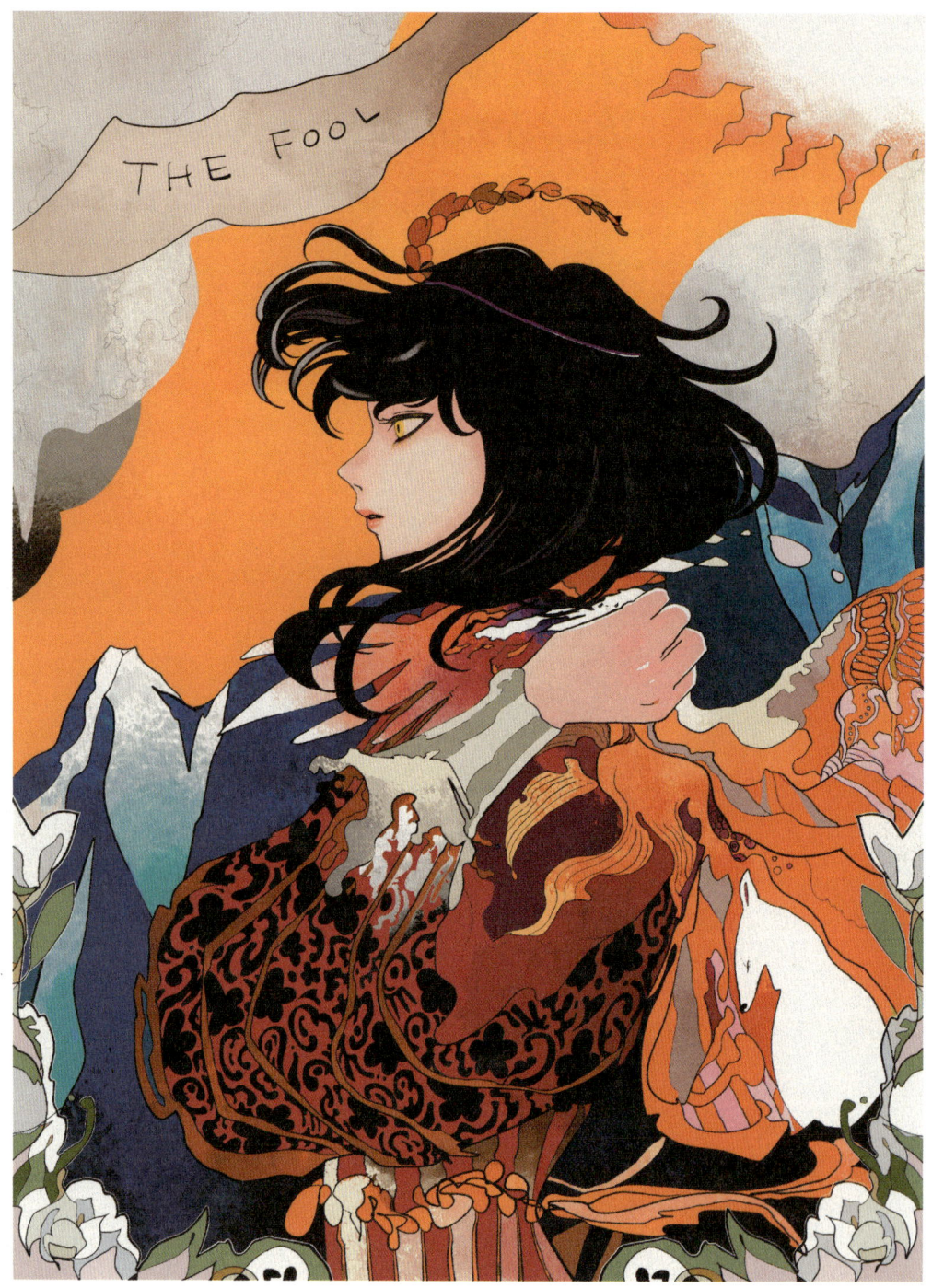

• THE FOOL •

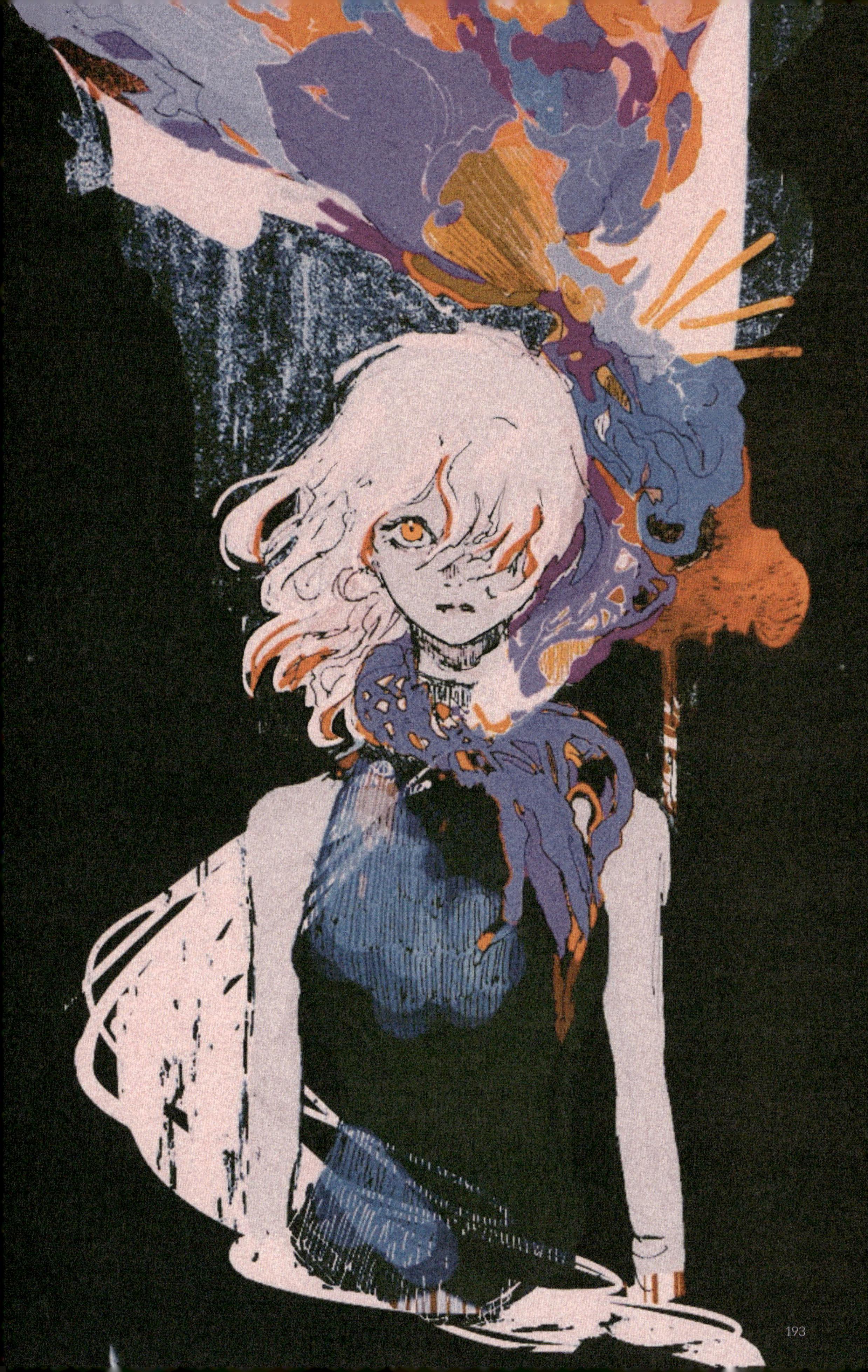

EVERYTHING IS ANIMISTIC

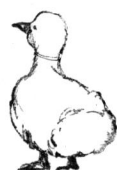

kokuno

kokuno likes to draw lines with an emphasis on flow and rhythm. She loves a world that is fantastical in every way, with special interest in themes to do with symbiosis.

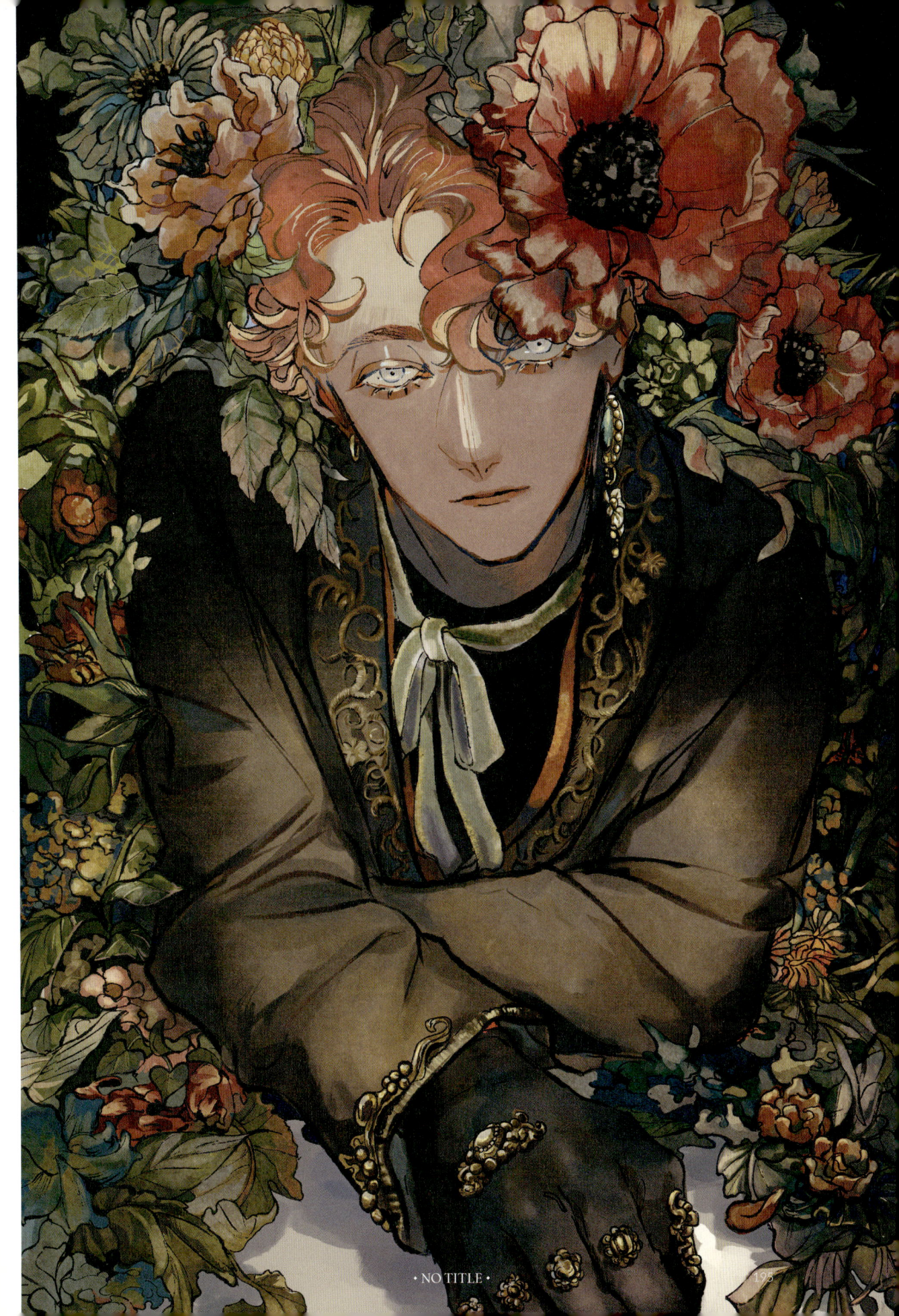

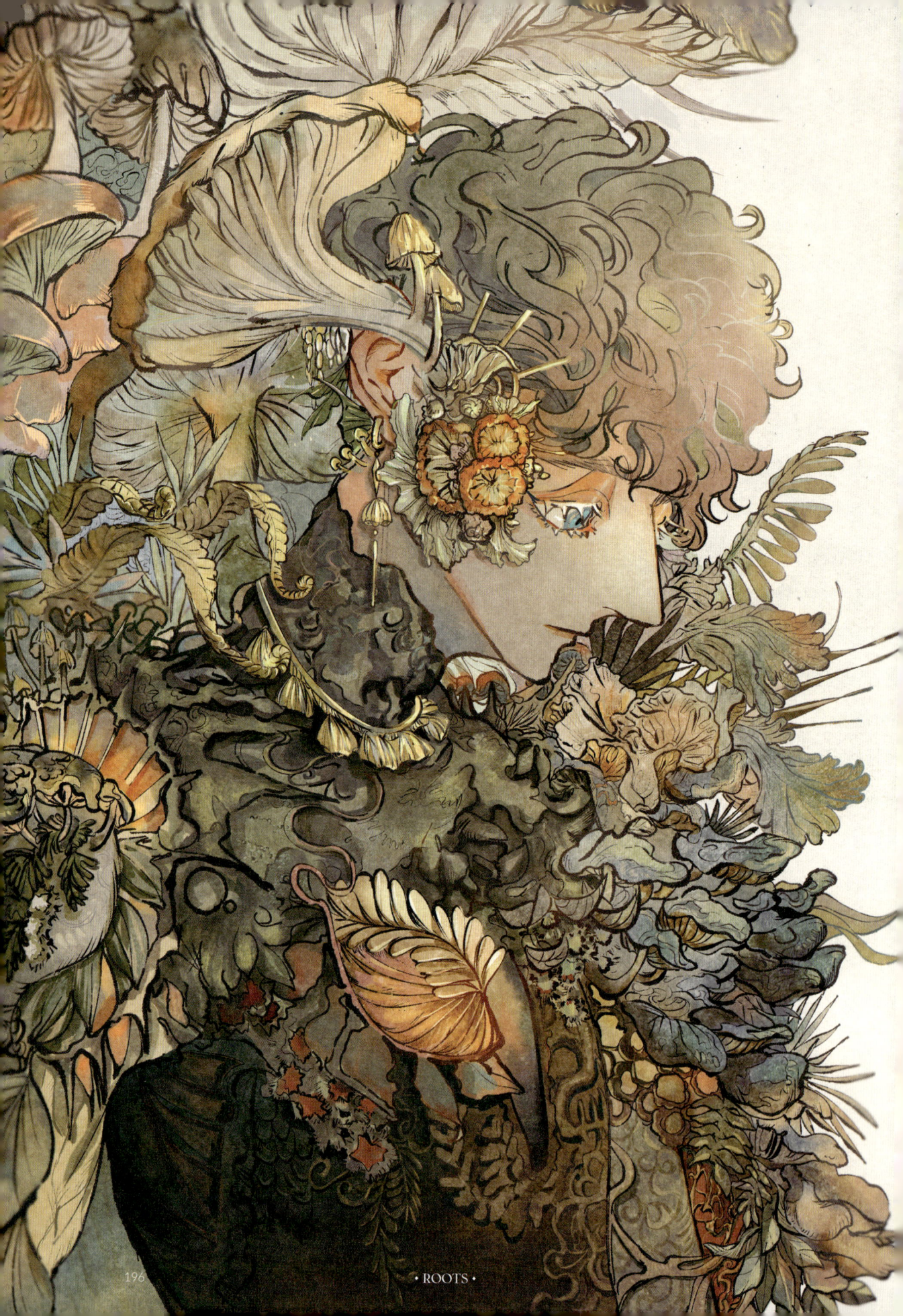

• ROOTS •

Q: How did you begin your artistic career? What initially sparked your interest in illustration?

kkn: I have been drawing pictures for as long as I can remember. From the beginning, I have been drawing original works (images in my head) and just loved the act of drawing, and before I knew it, it had become a part of my life. I have never studied painting in particular. I simply painted what I liked at that time. I have been inspired by the activities of many creatives, and I would be happy if my works could also inspire others. I started uploading my works on SNS as "kokuno" in 2020 with the thought that I would be happy if my works could also inspire others. Now, that has led me to the style of activities I am doing now. I am always grateful to everyone.

Q: Your work centers around the theme of coexistence. What does this theme mean to you, and how is it expressed in your creations?

kkn: I have always painted in my own natural way, and I want to love things as they are. I have respect for man-made things as well as for natural things, for all living things, which exist on this planet. I wish to depict all things in one piece without any separation. Paintings with multiple creatures in one picture or people integrated with plants express this theme particularly prominently.

Q: Where do you find inspiration for your work? Are there specific artists or art movements that have significantly influenced you?

kkn: I draw from all of the everyday things in life that are full of creativity: the light and shadows woven by nature, the designs that abound in every aspect of life, and the wonderful music. I have been influenced by the artists I have met, so no one in particular represents this person, but I think I am strongly influenced by the Art Nouveau style. I also like to look at fashion magazines, so I often get inspiration for color schemes, poses, and layouts from there.

Q: The details in your work are highly intricate, especially in the clothing and backgrounds. Does creating these details require a lot of time? What tools or techniques do you use to achieve such refined visual effects?

kkn: Thank you very much. The detail itself is in what I call a "one-shot" state, so it actually doesn't take that much time. I first decide what kind of motif I want to draw (rounded, curved, straight, etc.), and then I draw according to my sense at that moment. Currently, all of my drawings are basically done digitally. I usually draw lines and colors in layers under a substantial picture that is the base of the texture. Although I draw digitally, my drawing style may be very analog.

Q: The color palette in your artwork has a distinct retro feel and is remarkably harmonious. Do you have particular preferences or methods for selecting colors?

kkn: Actually, I am not very good at choosing colors. That is why I am conscious of not being bound only by rules and theories. First of all, I try to love colors that only I can choose, which are chosen based on the sense of color that I have cultivated. When I paint a single work, I decide on about two theme colors for that painting. I always try to enjoy painting, as if I am mixing paints, and I do not need to choose the same colors. Maybe that is why the paintings look colorful. When I deal with the colors, I often add light (color) rather than shadows. I think I will continue to explore color selection in the future.

Q: The motif of the sea appears frequently in your work and descriptions, such as in _Shallows_ (P200) and _Whitecaps_ (P202). What does the sea symbolize in your art, and what inspiration does it bring to you emotionally or intellectually?

kkn: The sea is everything for the painting and me. I believe that the sea is where everything ends up, so I hope to touch the sensibilities of each individual by using sea-related expressions in my work and by depicting things that are unexplained and unclear. Also, I think it is a symbol of the fluidity that I value when I draw lines. Each encounter that is born through my work is also a gift from the sea of the present world. Someday I would like to paint my idea of the sea directly as well.

Q: Did you encounter any challenges or difficulties during the creative process? What was the most challenging moment for you?

kkn: There was a period when I was seriously troubled about color selection and color application. I was troubled by the discrepancy between my ideal palette and the palette I had in my mind at the time, as well as by the discomfort of applying colors to line drawings, since I also like line drawings.

After an encounter with a certain work, I could change my mindset from coloring to painting— painting with the palette I have now, with an innocent feeling, and gradually changing my mindset to enjoy coloring.

It was a period when I reaffirmed that, first of all, try to accept everything, and a new range of expression will expand.

Q: Are you influenced by Japanese culture, such as Japanese manga, anime, ukiyo-e, etc? What influence do you think the cultural elements have on your creations?

kkn: I have been inspired by the kind of energy that Eiichiro Oda of the manga *ONE PIECE* has for his "paintings." I also admire the printmaker Hasui Kawase for his beautiful harmony of colors and the way he creates margins. All of the inspiration I receive from the works of creators who have faced the challenge of making things directly, regardless of the era, is an important source of creative energy for me.

Q: What are your expectations or plans for your future artistic creation?

kkn: I would like to continue to write honestly about what I like at any given time. And I would be very happy if my works could trigger the creative energy of those who encounter them. I would like to continue to paint many more works and someday become an artist who can hold a solo exhibition.

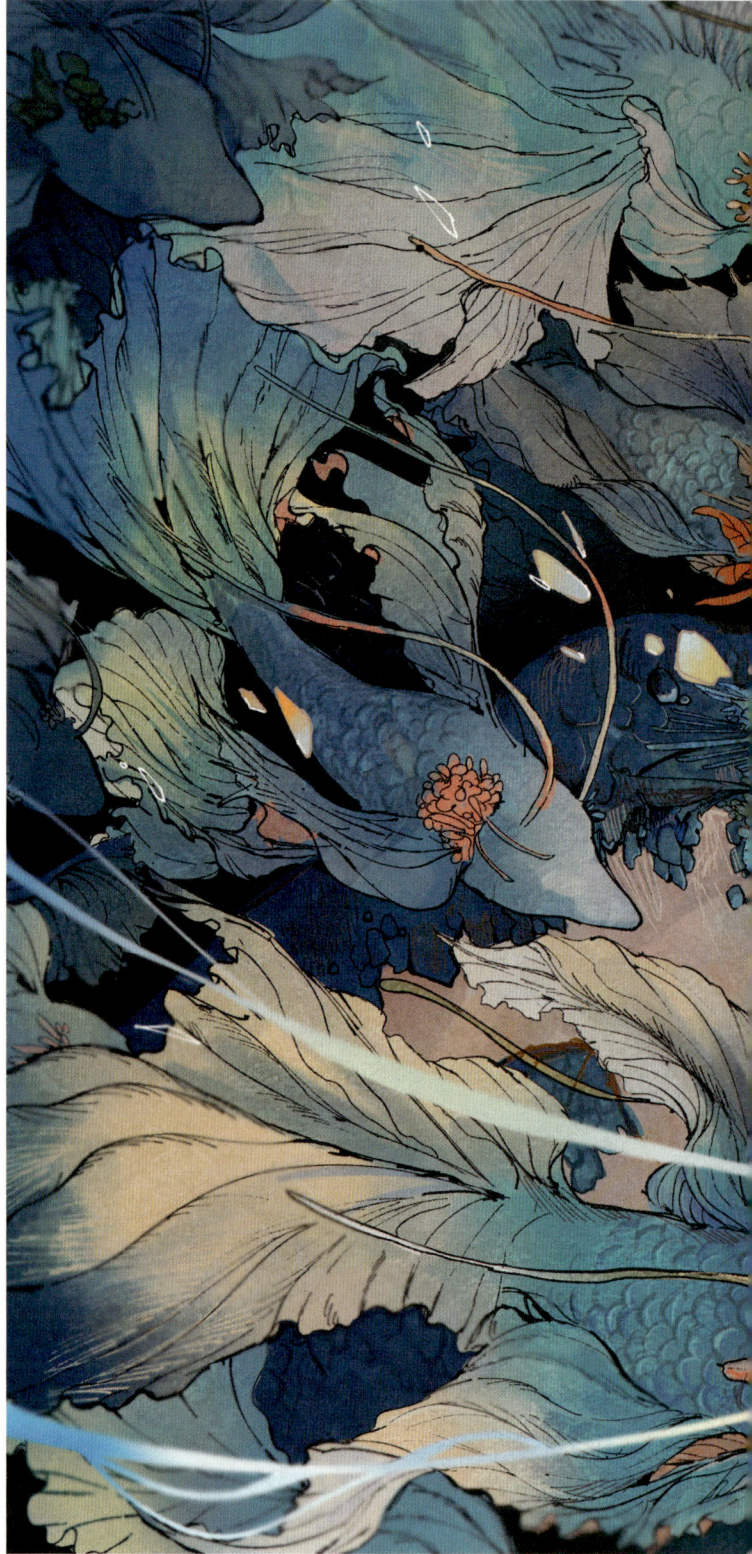

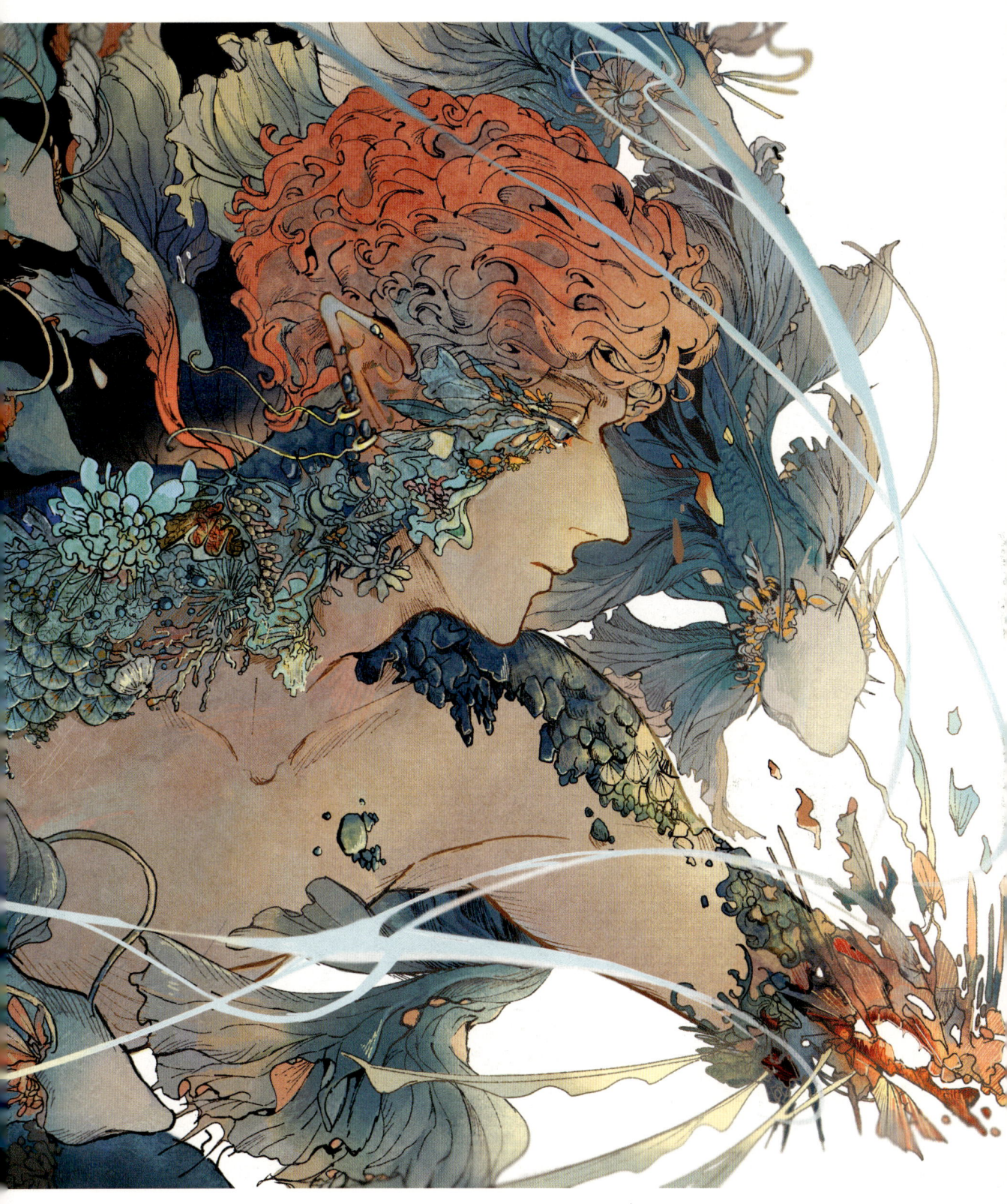

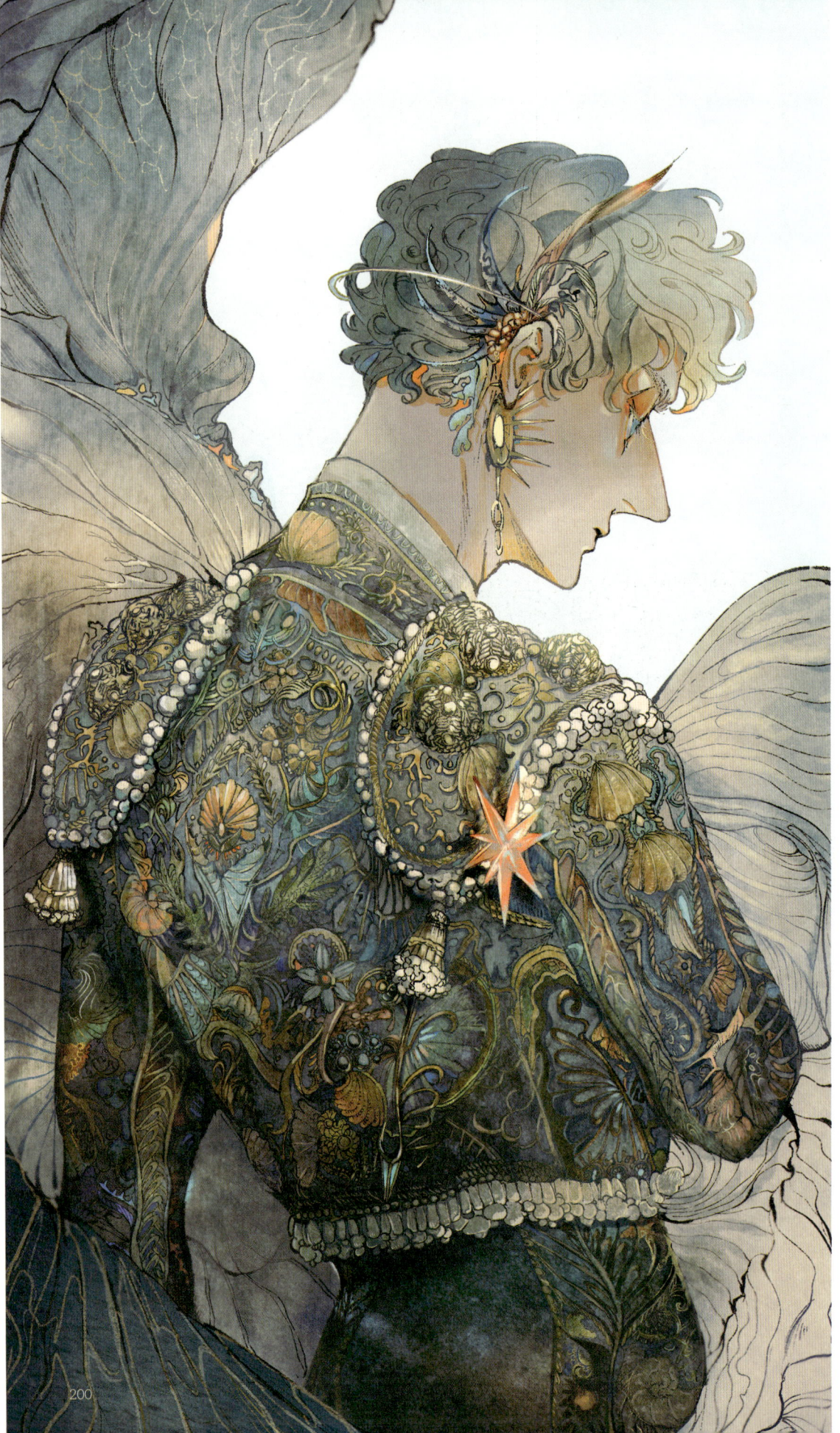

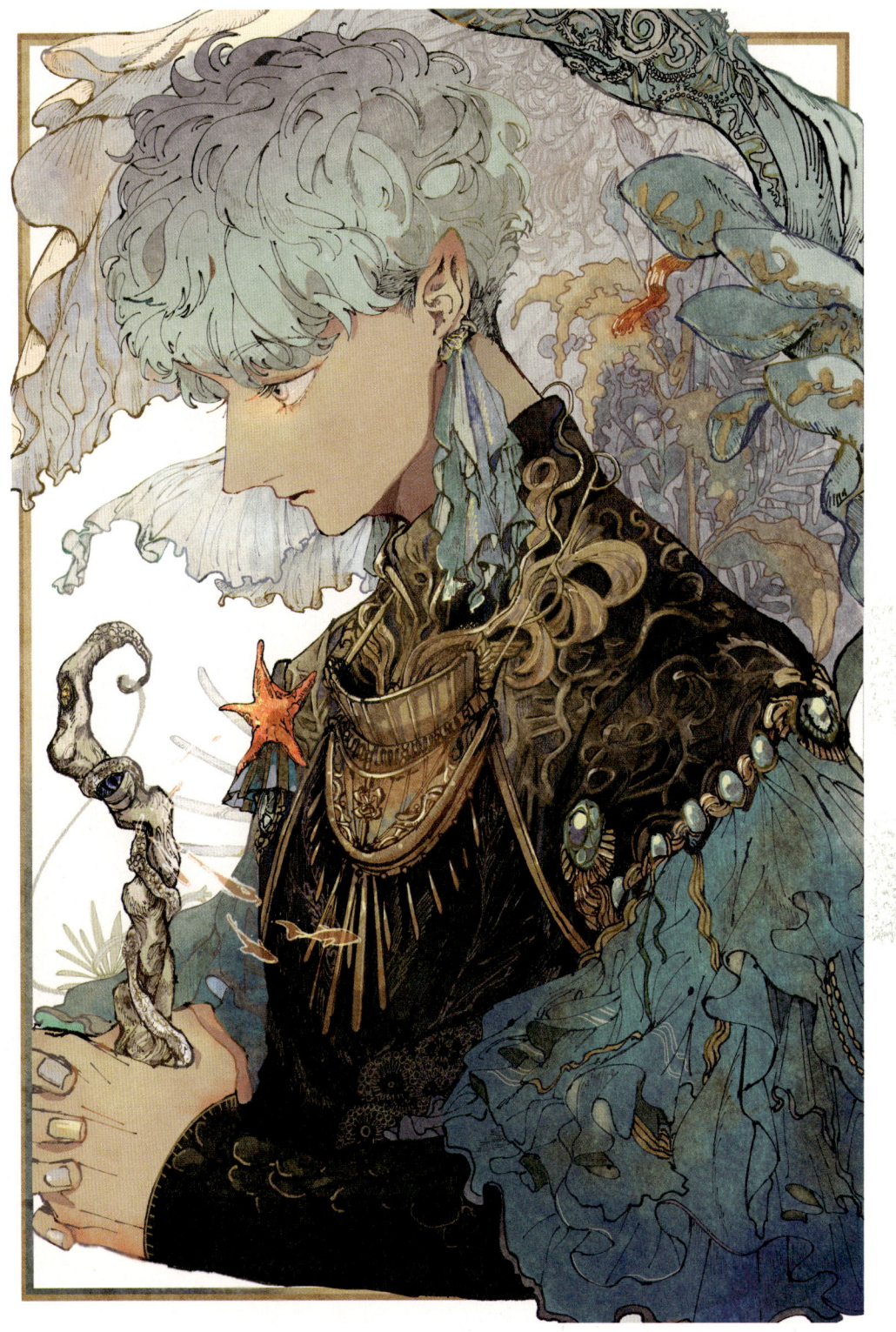

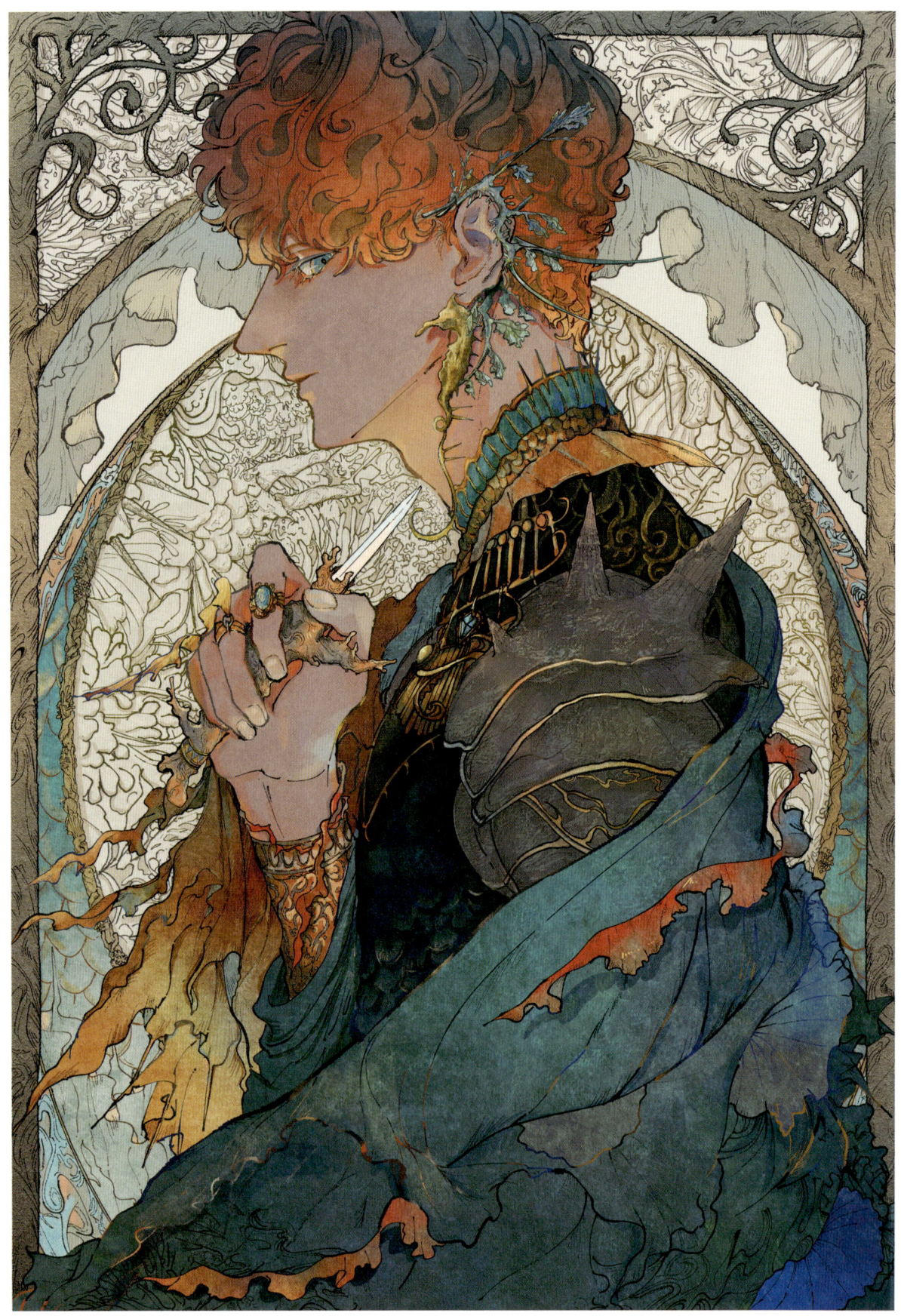

• WHITECAPS •

" I wish to depict all things in one piece without any separation. Paintings with multiple creatures in one picture or people integrated with plants express this theme particularly prominently. "

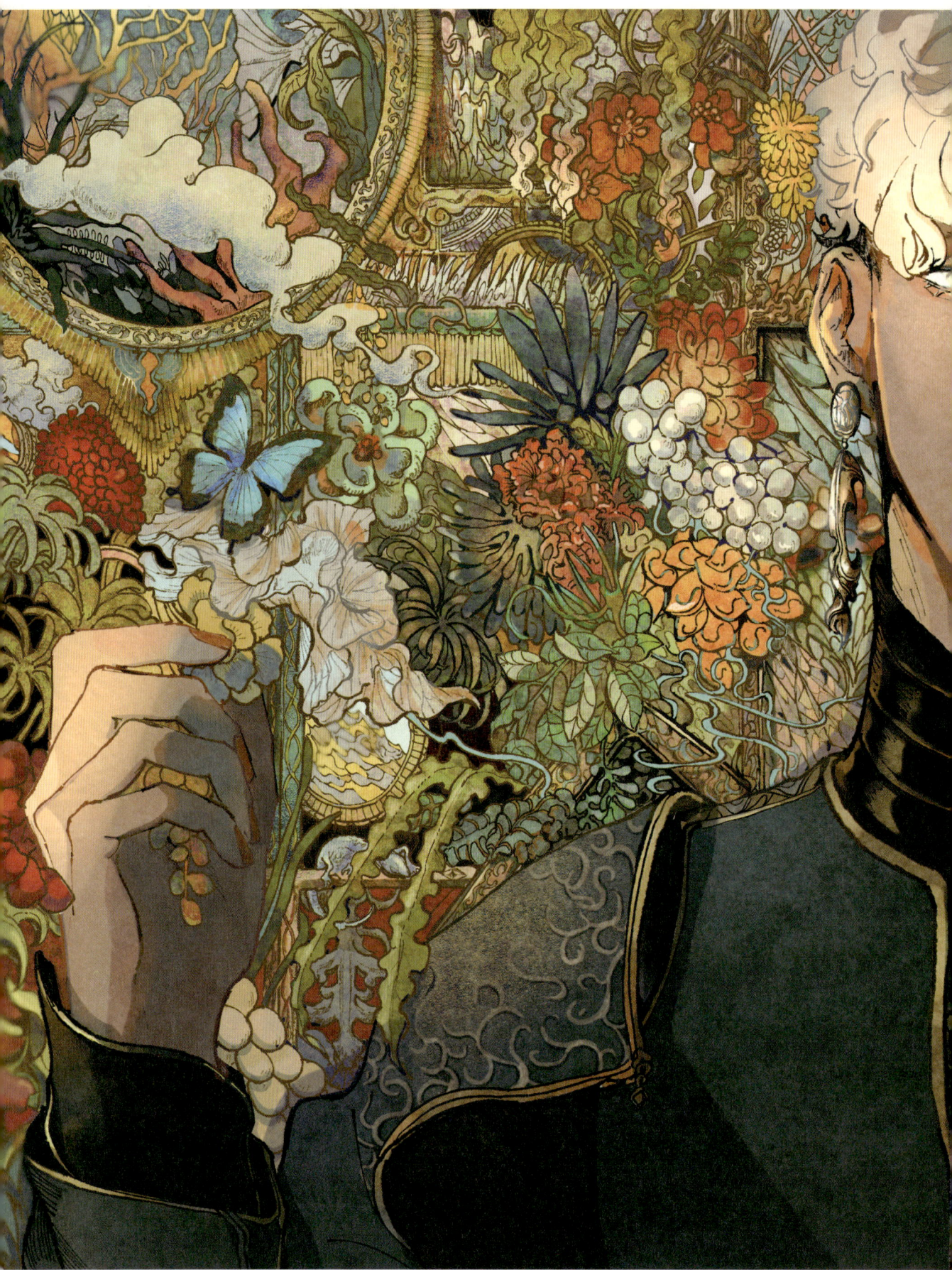

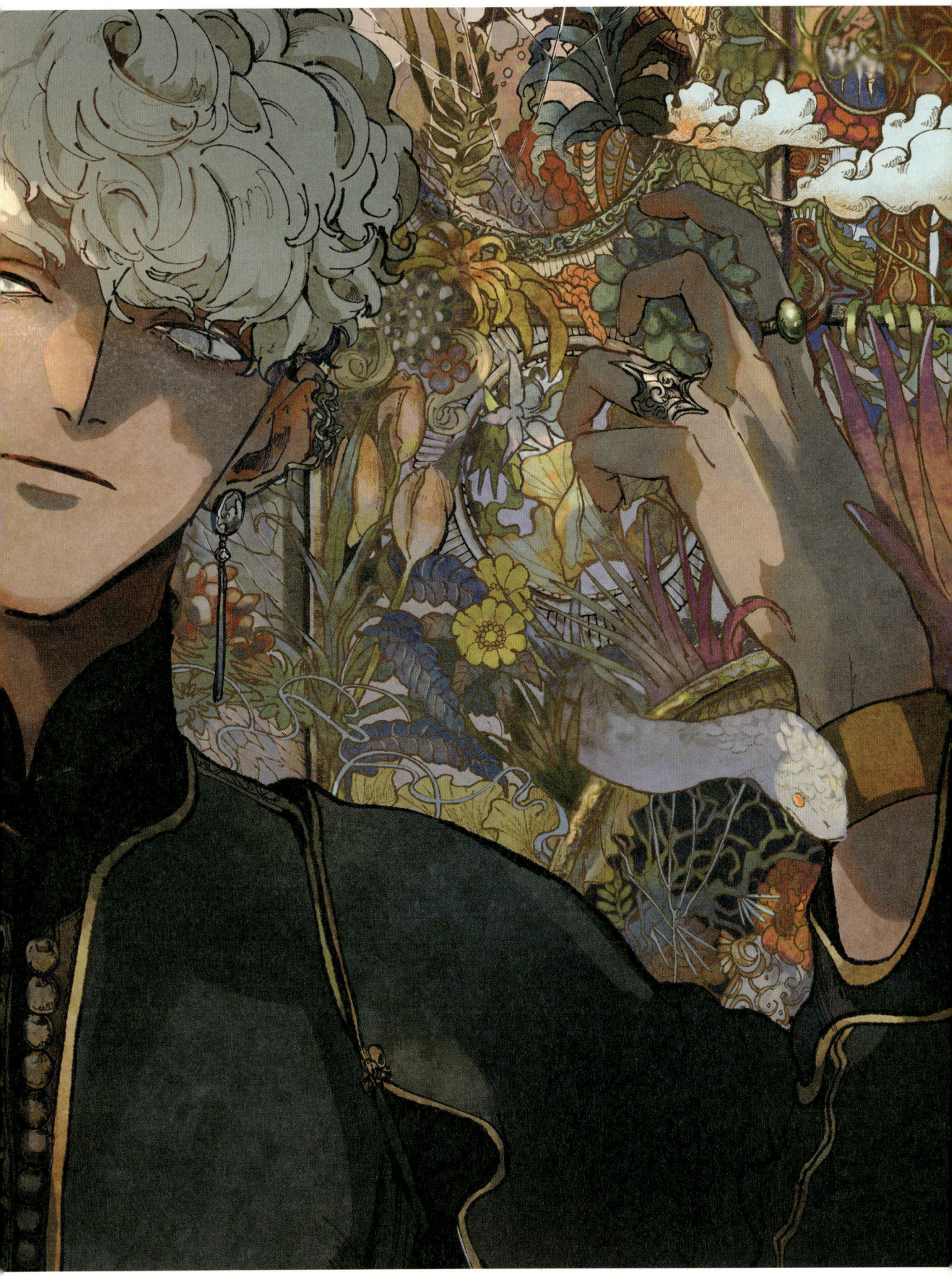

STRONG-WILLED FRAGILITY

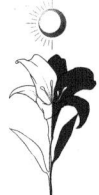

ico

Japanese-born ico started as an illustrator in 2022 and often portrays a girl with both fragility and strength. Meanwhile, ico works on music video illustrations, character design, etc.

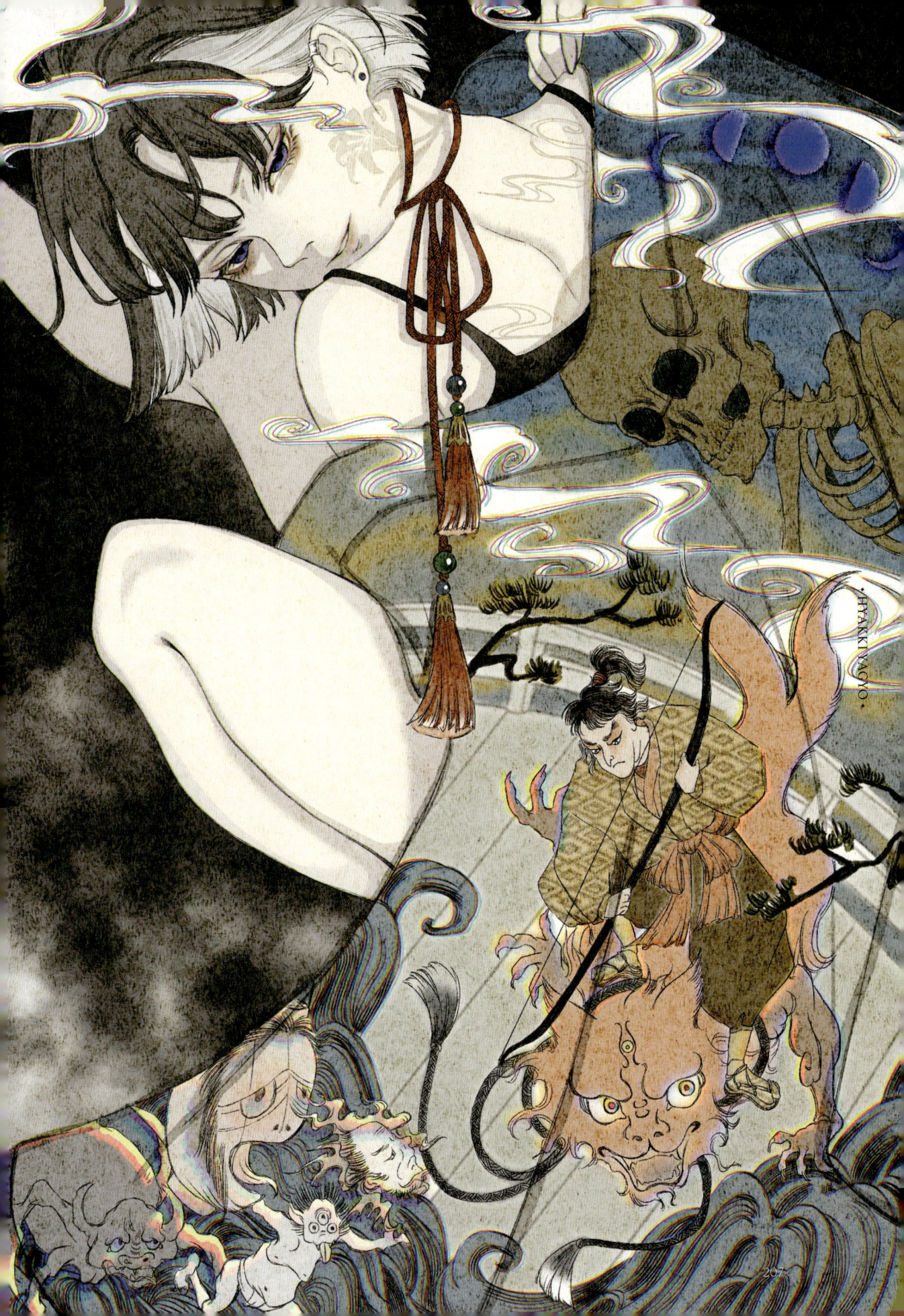

·HYAKKI YAGYO·

207

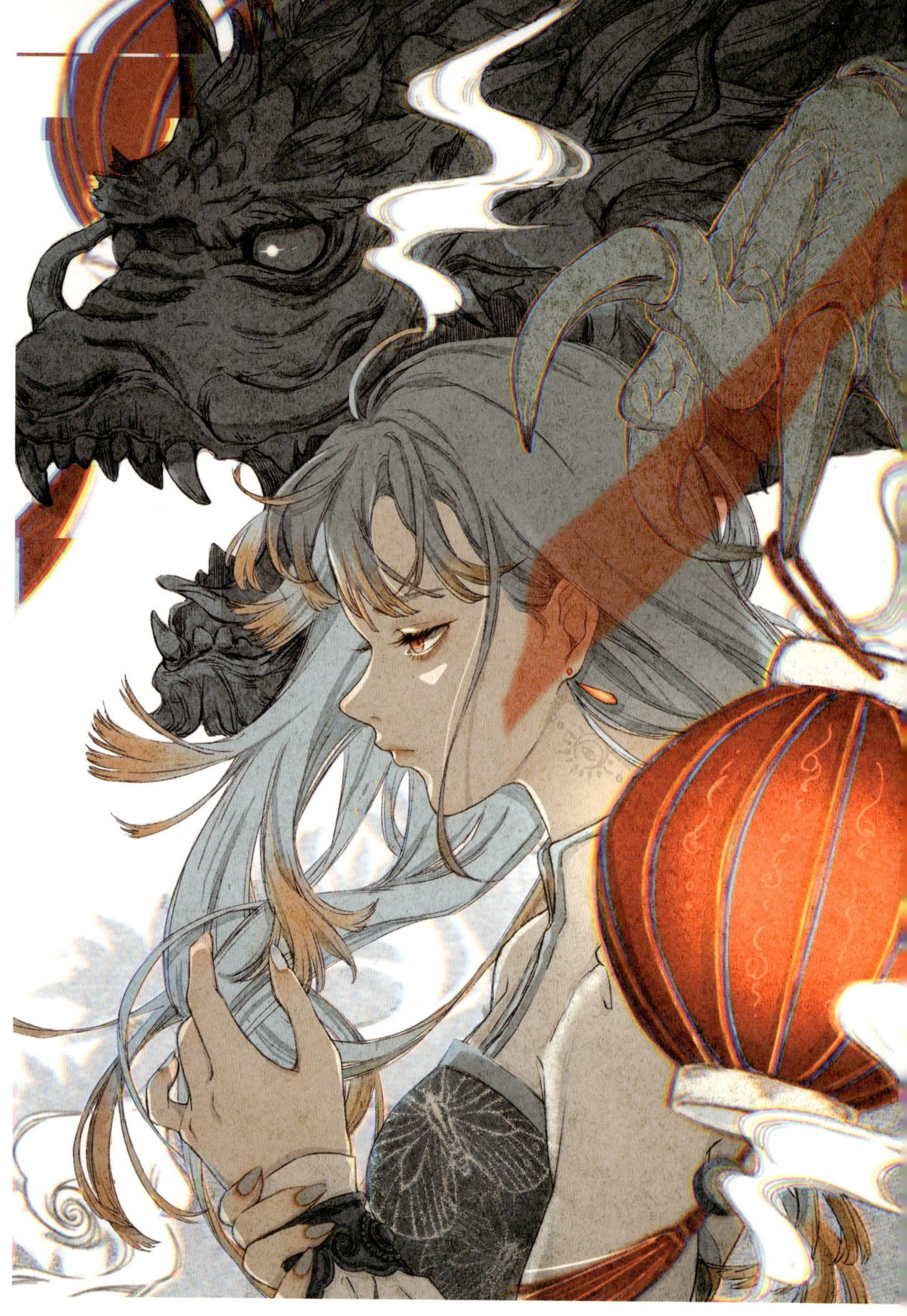

• CHILD OF HEAVEN •

Q: How did you start your art career? What inspired your interest in illustration?

ico: I grew up watching Studio Ghibli's films from a very young age, and I have loved drawing and watching them since I was a little girl. I started working in art because I strongly felt that I wanted to do a job that could move someone like Studio Ghibli's films.

Q: Can you share why you chose to feature a character who is both delicate and resilient as the theme of your work? What messages or emotions do you aim to communicate through the character?

ico: Human beings have a variety of emotions, such as joy, anger, sadness, and sorrow, but I decided to paint delicacy and strength because I want to paint pictures that are close to someone's feeling of loneliness or trying their best to live.

Q: Your work incorporates traditional Japanese elements, such as the ukiyo-e style clothing seen in the *Hyakki Yagyo* series (P207), and Japanese *yōkai* influences in *Child of Heaven* (P208) and *Unpainted Face* (P210). How do you seamlessly integrate these traditional cultural aspects into your illustrations?

ico: When I incorporate traditional patterns and motifs into my illustrations, I try to create an atmosphere that is not outdated even in the modern age by making the colors more saturated, as in contemporary illustrations.

Q: Where do you usually find inspiration for your creative work?

ico: I look at many paintings every day and have learned a lot from so many people, but the artists and production companies that have particularly influenced me are Yoshitaka Amano, Alphonse Mucha, and Studio Ghibli. I think they have in common the timeless atmosphere and charm of their characters. I would like to make an effort to draw attractive people like them.

Q: When creating illustrations for music videos and character designs, how do you balance your style with the client's requirements?

ico: When I first started this job, I had a hard time finding the right balance, but now I think I can strike a good balance by getting a lot of input from my clients and understanding exactly what they want from me while incorporating my own style.

Q: Have you faced any challenging moments during your creative process? How did you overcome those obstacles?

ico: I still often feel unsure of myself, but when that happens, I read back the messages I received from fans. Fans look at my drawings and express in words what they like about them, so I can reconfirm what I am good at. I really appreciate it.

Q: While your works *Silkworm* (P216) and *Reincarnation* (P217) may depict seemingly negative themes, they actually reflect a positive outlook. What is the main message or emotional connection you hope to convey through these works?

ico: I want to convey that although life is full of difficult events, we should never forget that there is always someone somewhere who will be there for us.

Q: Since you started your illustration career in 2022, you have achieved remarkable success in just two years. Can you share your feelings and experiences from the beginning of your creation to now?

ico: First of all, when I was a creator before I started working, I researched what kind of pictures I could draw that were unique to me, and I was very active on social networking sites. I believe that I have been able to continue working until now because of the wonderful clients I found and met through these activities.

What I pay attention to in my work is to be sincere and to always meet deadlines.

Q: What plans and expectations do you have for the future in the field of illustration?

ico: My ambition for the future is to keep painting all the time. Many people in this world feel their limitations and stop painting, so I hope to move forward while taking breaks. I would like to try my hand at private exhibitions and book cover art, which I have not tried yet if the opportunity arises in the future.

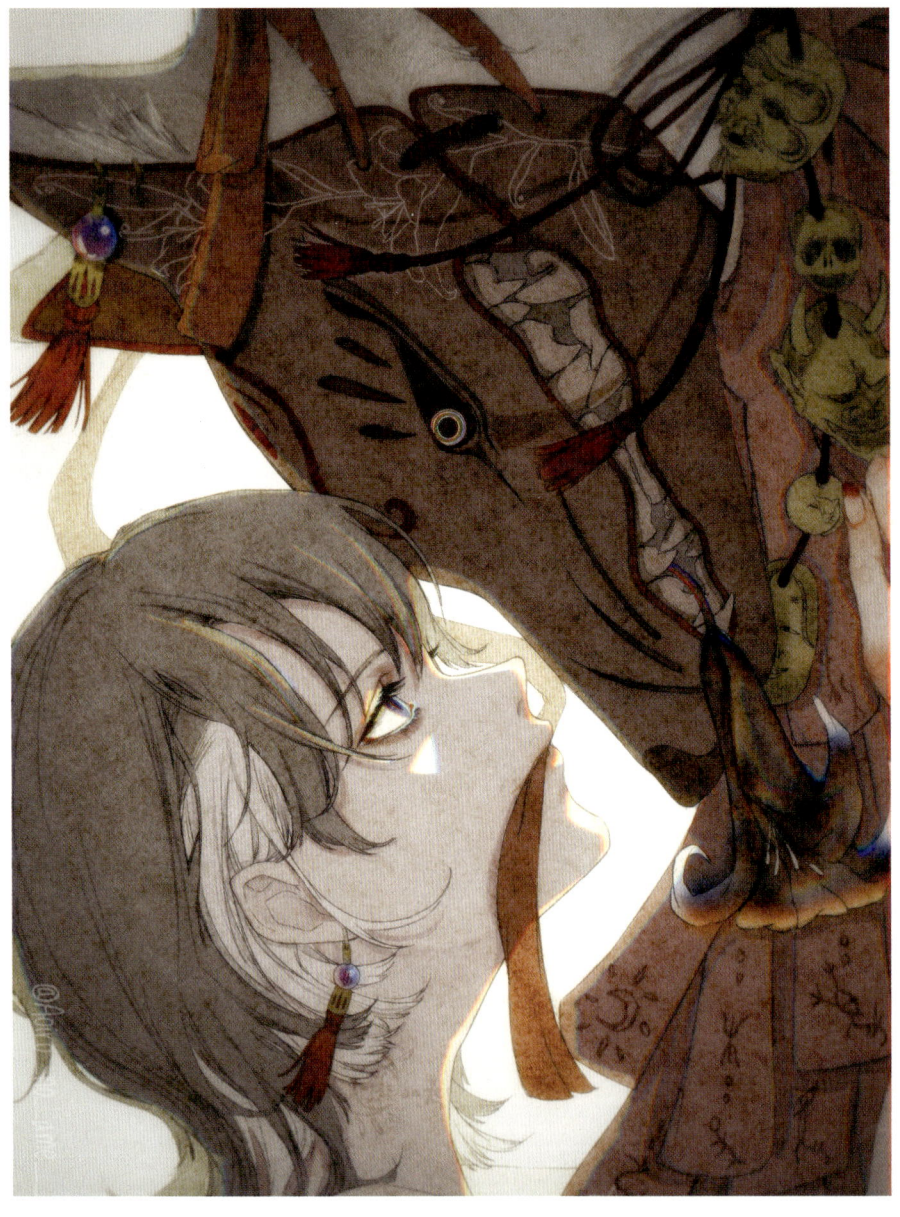

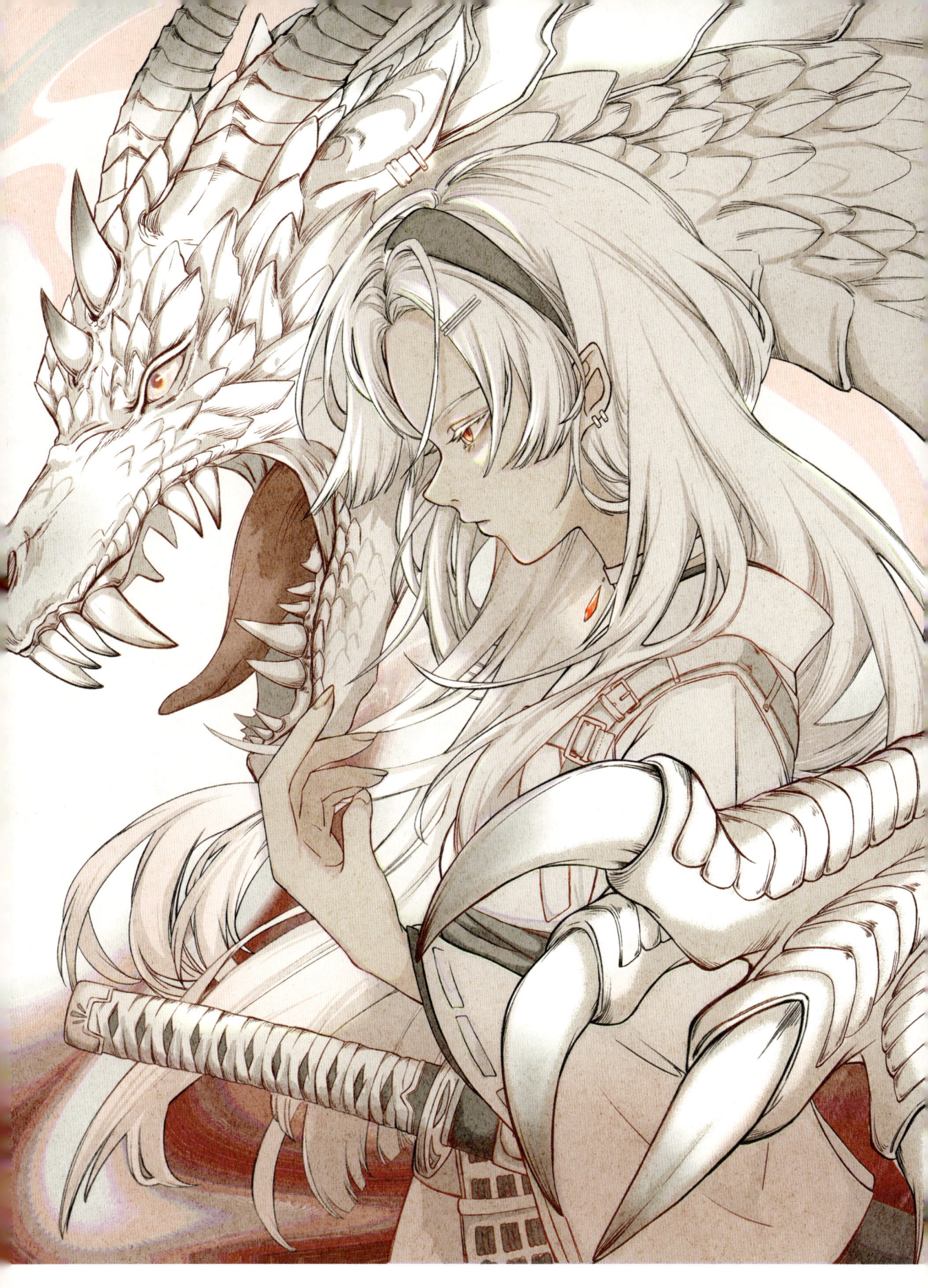

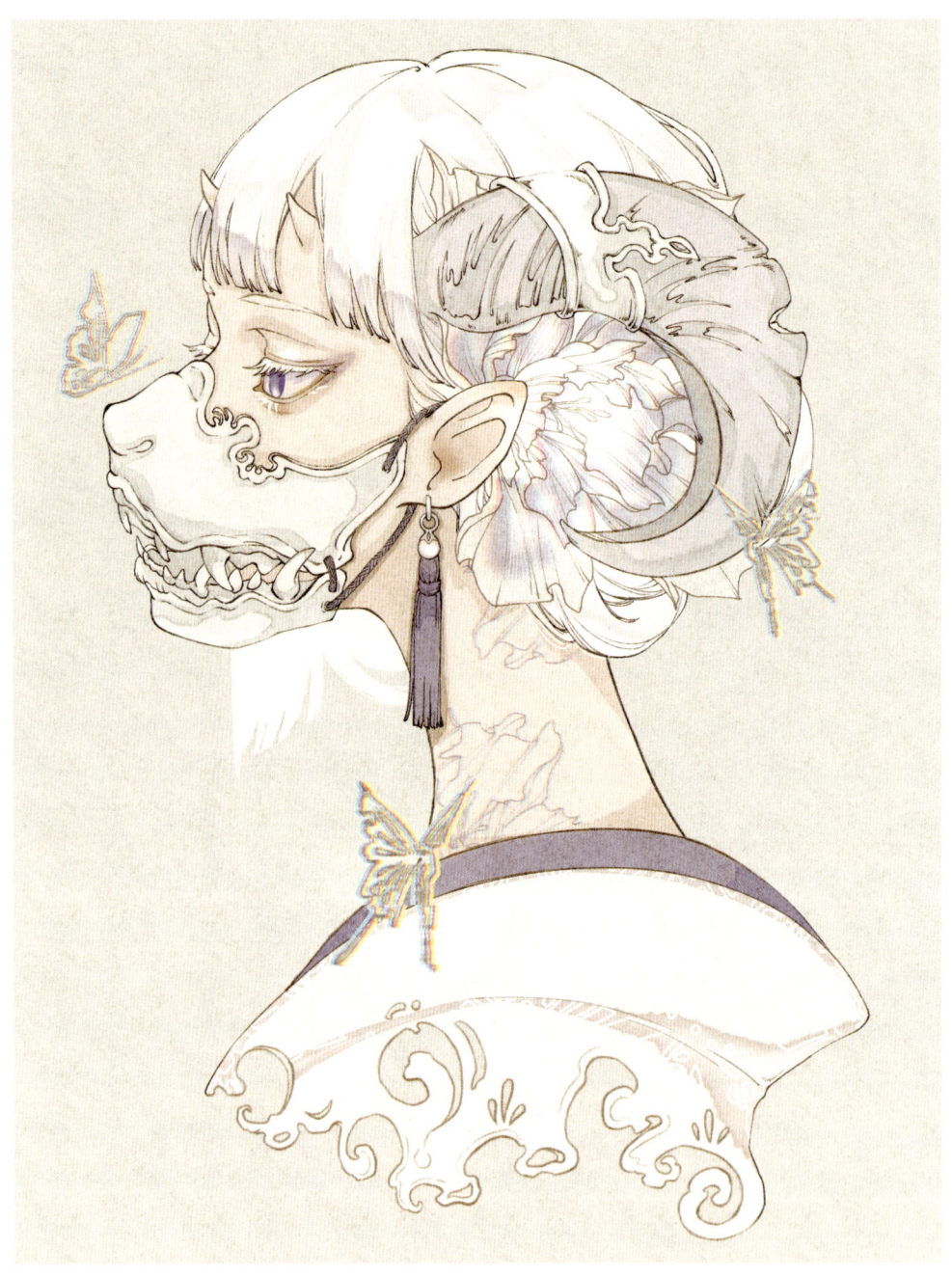

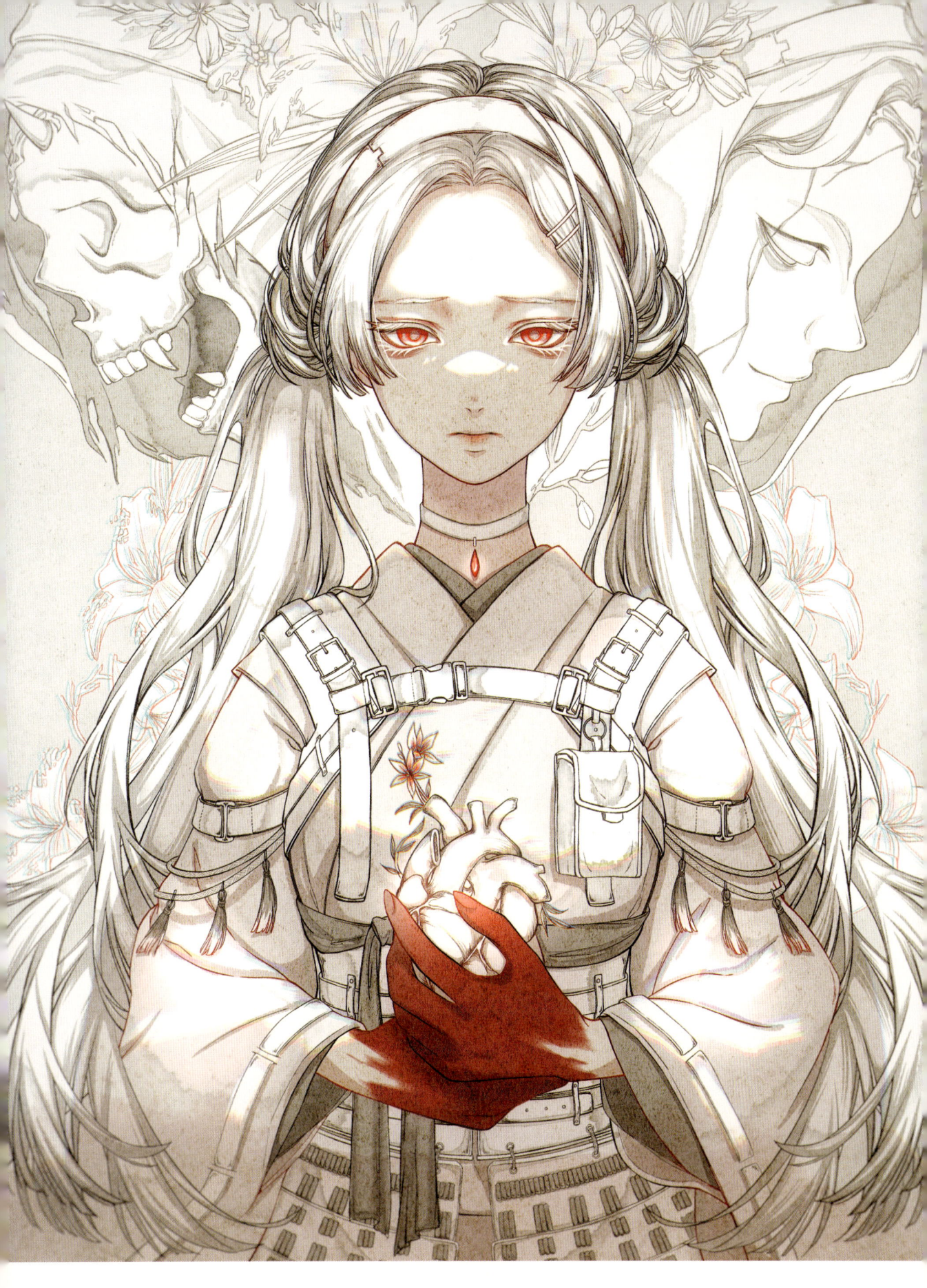

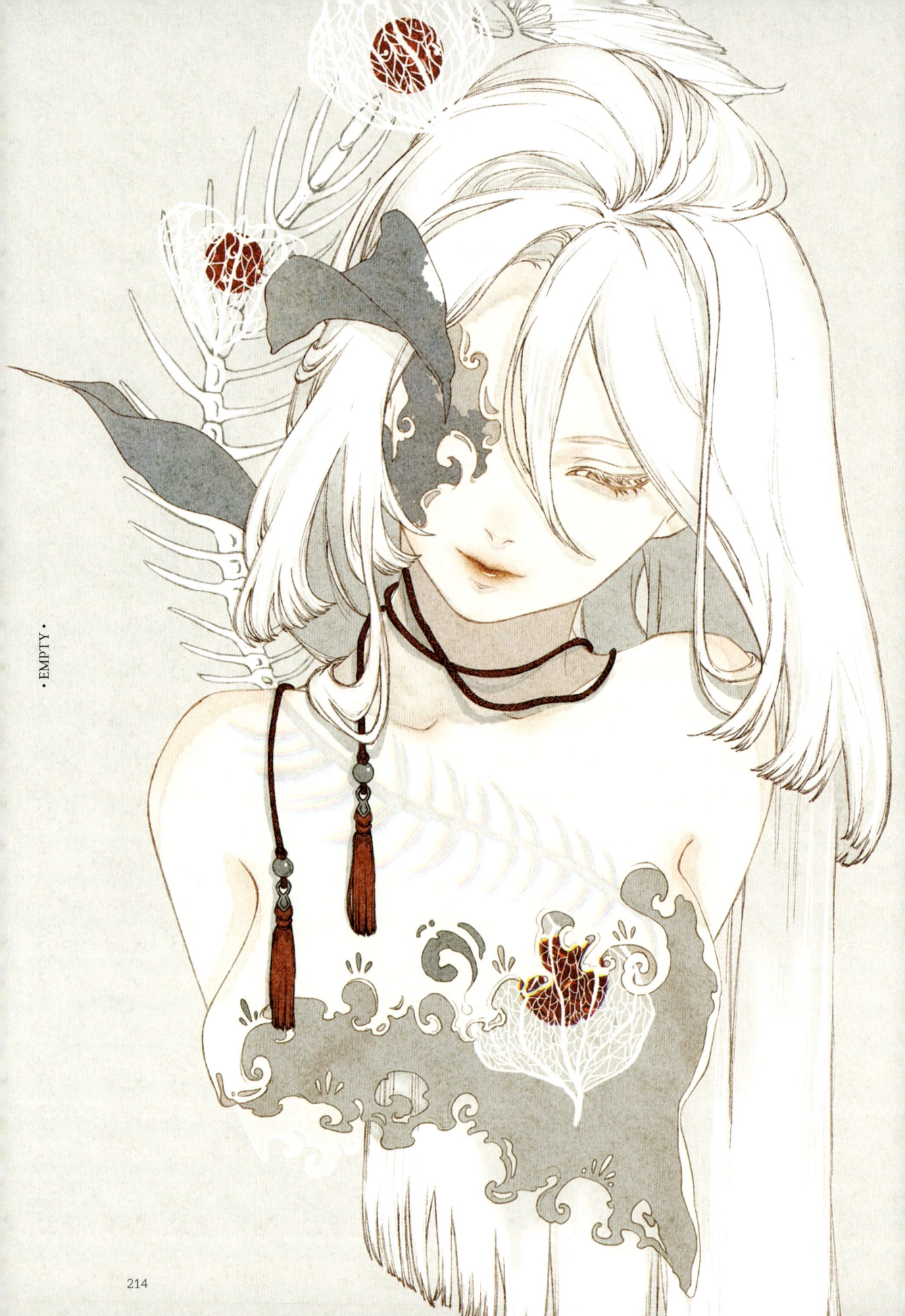

• EMPTY •

" *I want to convey that although life is full of difficult events, we should never forget that there is always someone somewhere who will be there for us.* "

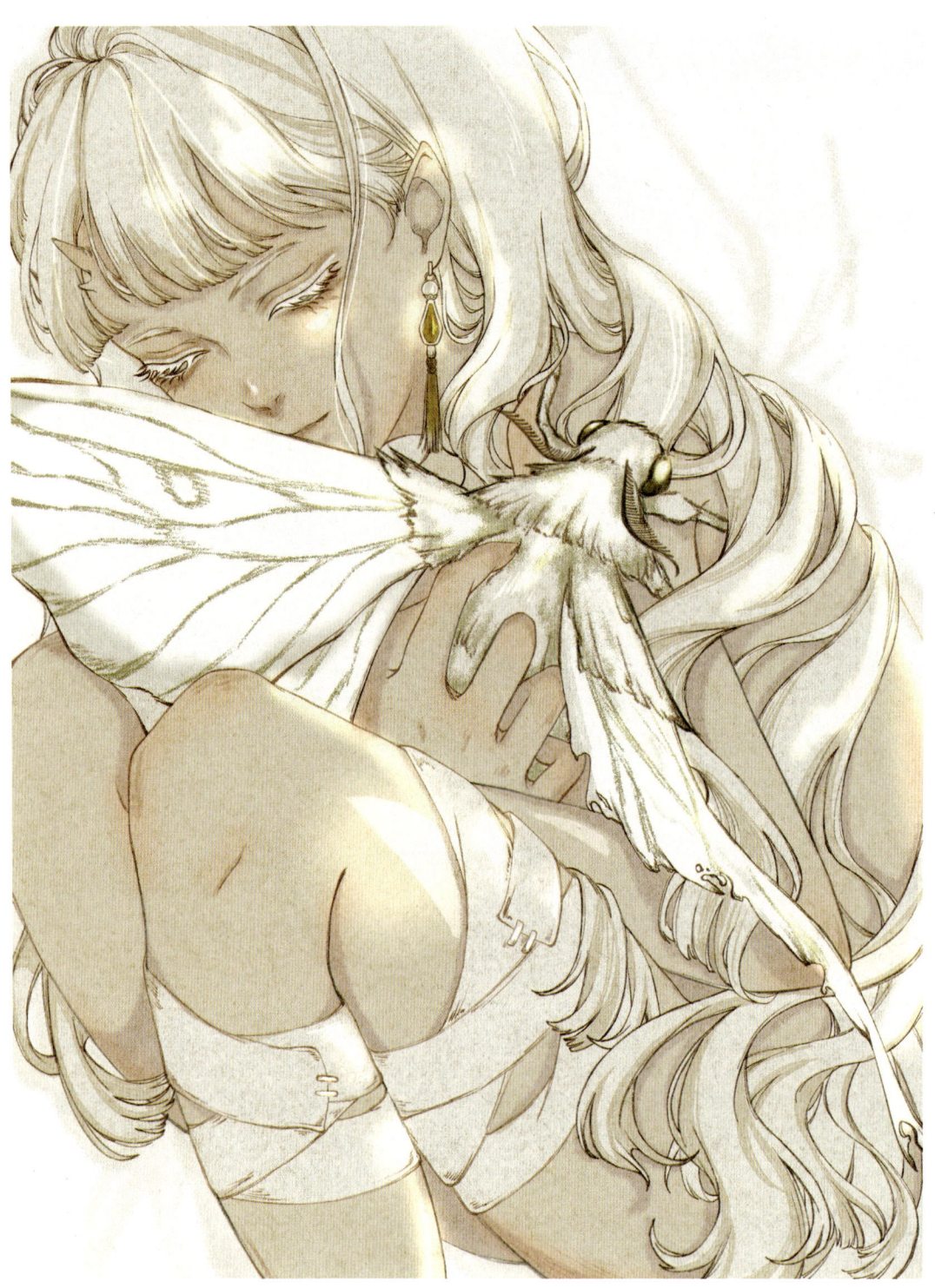

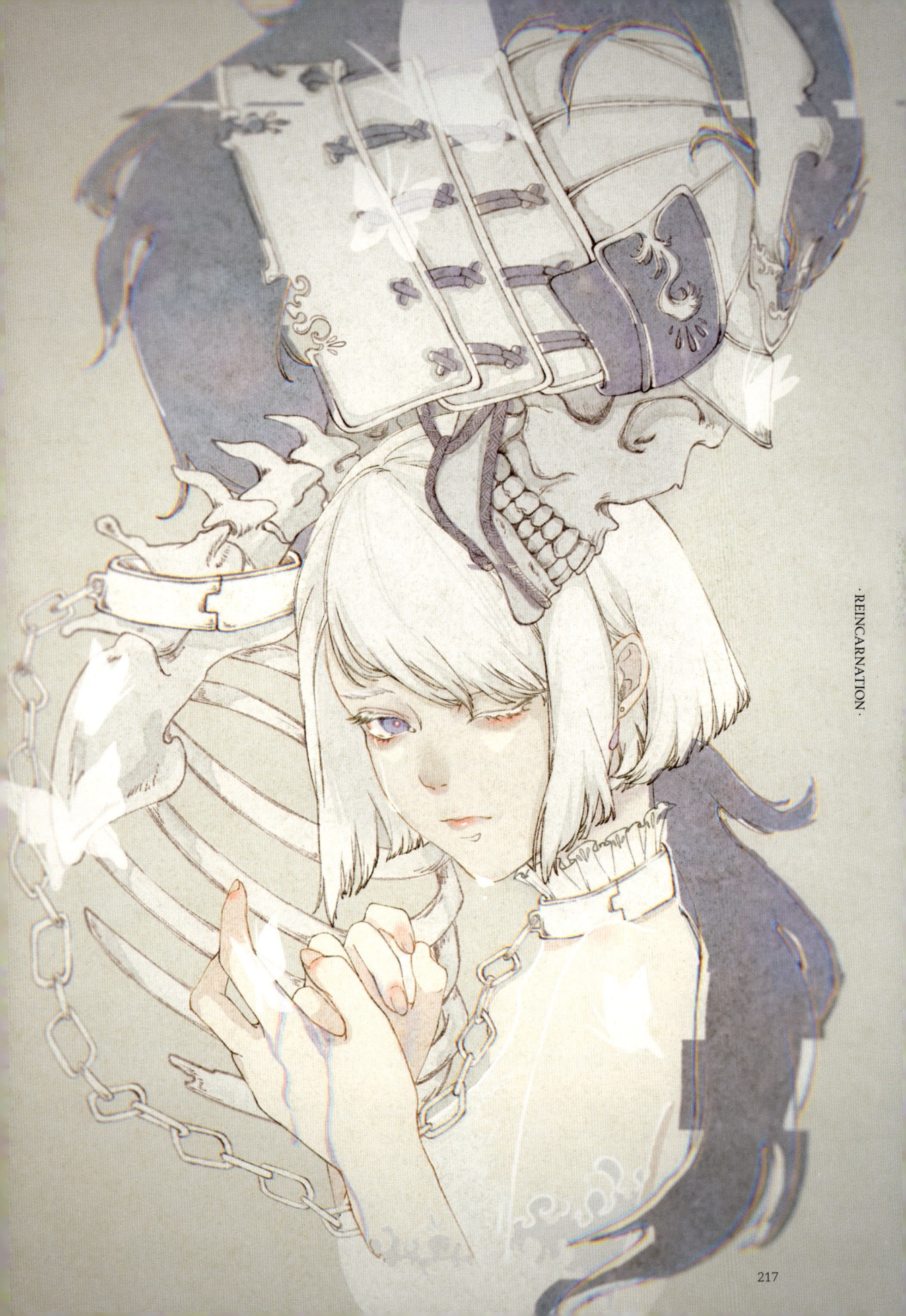

· REINCARNATION ·

ENERGY BEYOND DARKNESS

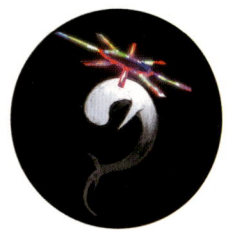

OYK

OYK has been active with her art mainly on social media since 2021. She frequently handles themes of negative emotions such as anger, sadness, and frustration to create dark works. OYK's art style is strongly influenced by Japanese *shōnen* (boys) manga, which has been familiar since childhood.

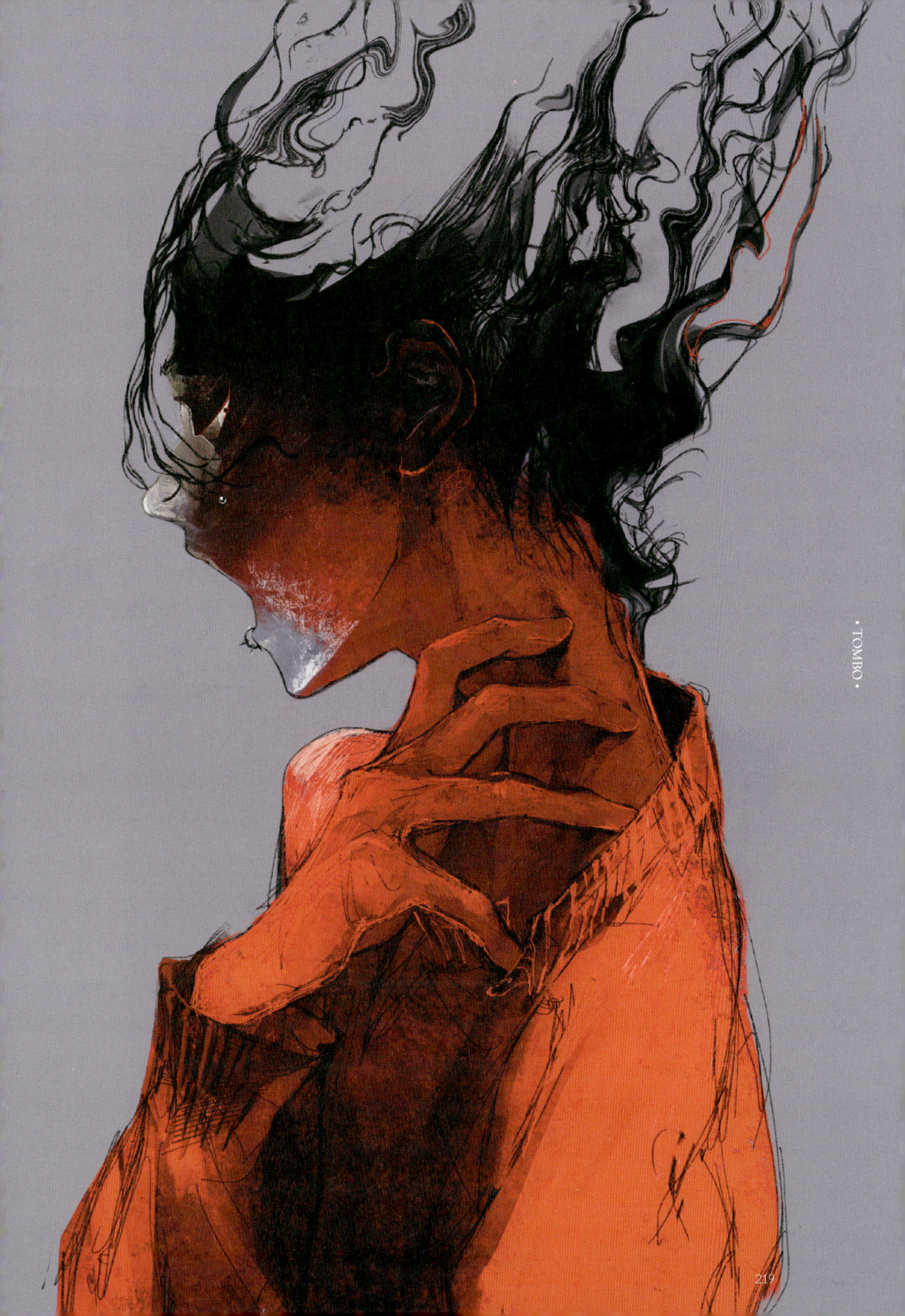

· TOMBO ·

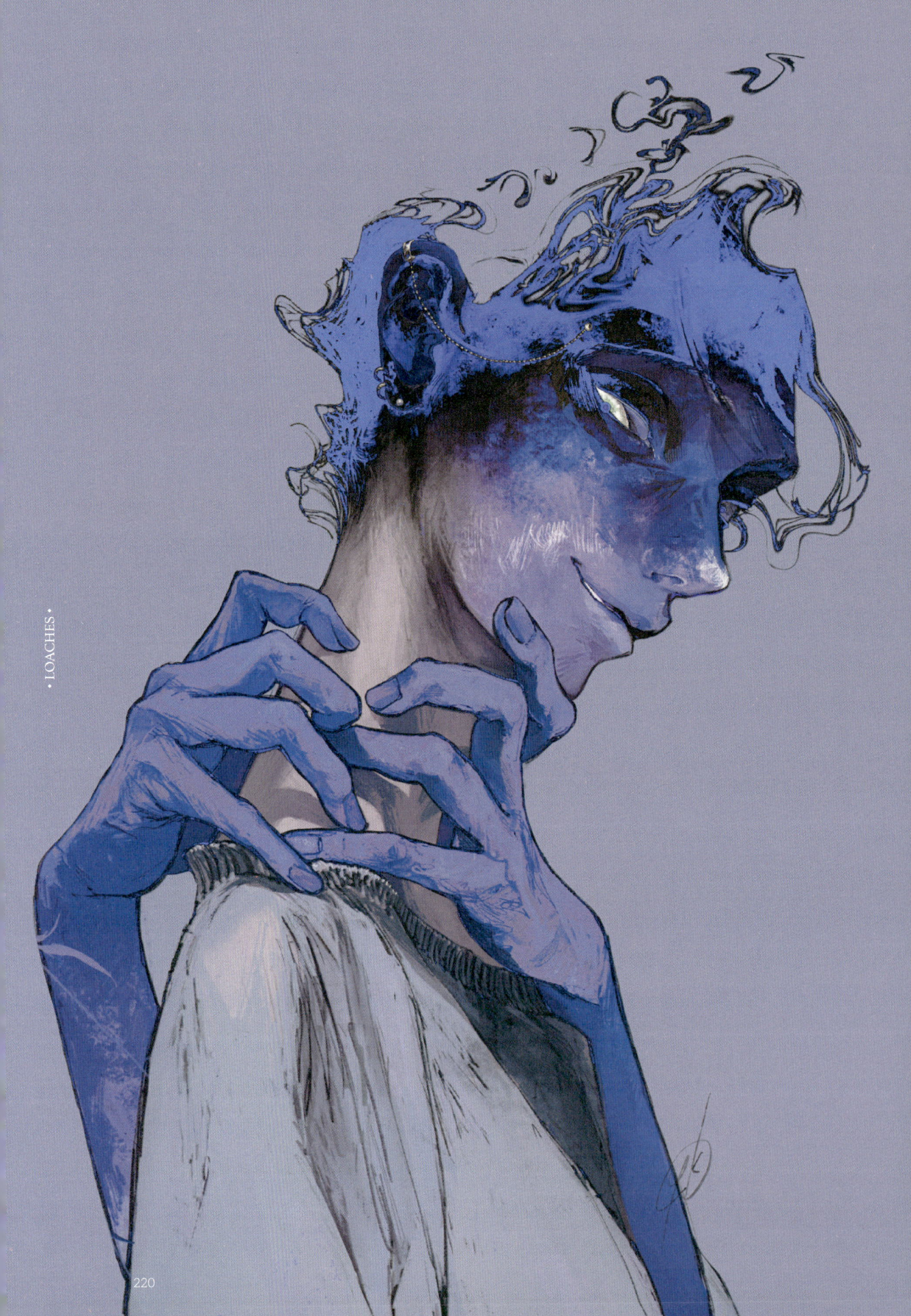

Q: Can you tell us about the origins of your passion for art? When did you begin creating dark-themed illustrations?

OYK: I think my passion for art originates from manga and anime. In particular, when I was little, I loved *Weekly Shōnen Jump*, reading the pages every week to the point where I could tear them to shreds, and I enjoyed copying them. Even now, I think one of the origins of my aesthetic sense is the *shōnen* manga from those days.

It was around 2021 that I started dealing with dark themes. At that time, I was feeling a lot of resentment, frustration, and sadness about my private matters. I had very strong negative emotions, but I couldn't let them out. So I let my emotions take over and completed my illustrations. I think that was the beginning of my current style.

Q: What specific challenges did you encounter during your creative process? How did these challenges shape and enrich the content of your work?

OYK: Since around last year, I have been facing a challenge. The challenge is how to express negative emotions. In my initial works, I simply poured out my emotions for myself. However, as more people started viewing my works, I became more conscious of the viewers and human emotions. I've been constantly thinking about whether my work needs to communicate, whether it's okay to convey negative emotions, and what I should communicate on this theme.

I'm not sure if this experiment has added depth to my work, but recently, I've started to incorporate images of vitality alongside negative ones.

Q: Your work is dominated by dark tones, which complements your subject matter. Do you have a personal color preference that you can share with us?

OYK: I like red, blue-leaning blacks, saturated reds, yellows, blues. I prefer to depict colors that are close to the primary colors by layering them on top of each other rather than applying a complex mixture of colors. As colors close to the primary colors tend to express intense emotions, I often use them in the background or as accents in areas where I want them to have meaning.

Red is often used to portray anger and other bursting emotions, blue is cold and tense, and yellow is often used to portray confusion, anticipation, and shame.

Conversely, I find it difficult to work with colors in a warm, gentle atmosphere.

I also like a rough and dry atmosphere, so I often layer each stroke with a different color on a separate layer rather than mixing various colors on one layer.

Q: What media and tools do you typically use during your creative process? How do these choices influence your work?

OYK: The equipment I use is an iPad Pro 12.9" and the app I use is Procreate.

I sometimes use the analog method in the rough drafting stage, but now I basically create everything digitally.

I have always drawn in the analog form, so the iPad and Procreate are intuitive and easy to use. I mainly use brushes with a rough impression, such as pencil and chalk.

I think that illustrations become more realistic when they have humidity and since my work often has a negative theme, I often choose brushes and expressions with a drier impression so that they don't become too realistic.

Q: In your work *Loaches* (P220), you mentioned the Japanese proverb "There is no loach under the willow tree twice." Do you draw inspiration from proverbs or literary works in your daily life?

OYK: I often take inspiration from proverbs, and sometimes I find the right proverb in the process of organizing the work after it has been made and use it as the title of the work.

I often portray my emotions in my work and don't want the viewer to recognize them. So, I try to distance the work from the viewer by quoting proverbs and using euphemistic titles for my works. I also organize my emotions by re-framing the work within the framework of a proverb or other words.

Loaches was created as a counterpart to *Tombo* (P219). Like dragonflies, I wanted to paint on the theme of small creatures, and when I was looking for just the right proverb or words, I found the proverb about loaches. This is exactly what I am doing now, and I have created a work that mocks the ridiculousness of my search for a second loach.

Q: Your works all express strong emotions. Do you think strong sadness and anger can be a source of energy? How do you balance these emotions? Which work left the deepest impression on you?

OYK: I believe intense emotions, such as sadness and anger, are one of the most important human sensations to cherish. They tend to cause negativity, but they are also great energy. I believe that the more intense the emotion, the more it is like a stake in the ground for me to know what I value and who I am.

I sublimate them exactly into art, such as illustration. By illustrating my own intense emotions, I imagine that I am organizing the emotions and converting the energy that is about to burst into energy that can be used in the long term. I wish I could use the energy that negativity starts with as energy to protect the things I care about. Illustrating is a stress release or a ritual of transformation.

My influences, in terms of expression, are the *shōnen* manga from my childhood and old Japanese artworks, but my influence, in terms of thinking, is the manga *Land of the Lustrous*.

Q: Does your active presence on social media have a positive impact on the spread and influence of your works?

OYK: Yes, I think it has been helpful. I primarily showcase my works on Instagram and X. While I do occasionally exhibit my works at shows, social media definitely allows me to reach a wider audience. I believe that many people have discovered my work through social media.

I don't think my works are easily accepted by everyone, so by utilizing social media, I can broaden the range of people who come across my works and reach those who might truly appreciate them.

Q: Any plans for the future?

OYK: I intend to continue exploring my current theme, but I believe it will gradually evolve. This is because my own interpretation of negative emotions, human nature, and the impact that art has on viewers is constantly changing.

As I mentioned in my response to the question about challenges, I am currently exploring how to depict vitality alongside negative emotions. In doing so, I feel that my perspective on emotions like anger and sadness is becoming more objective.

Additionally, beyond the theme, I want to challenge myself with various forms of depiction and expression. I plan to experiment with different mediums, both analog and digital, to find the expression that best fits the theme.

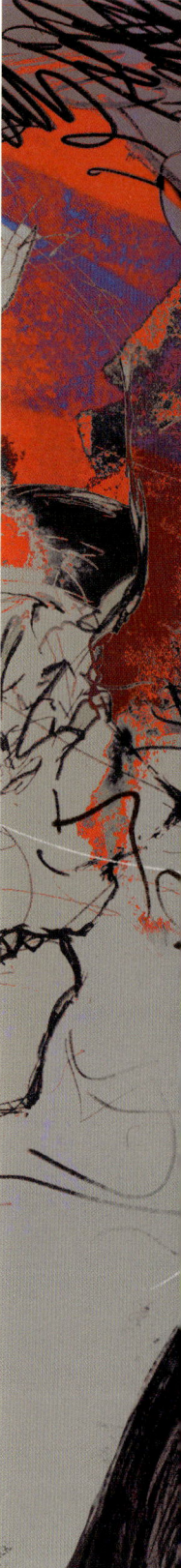

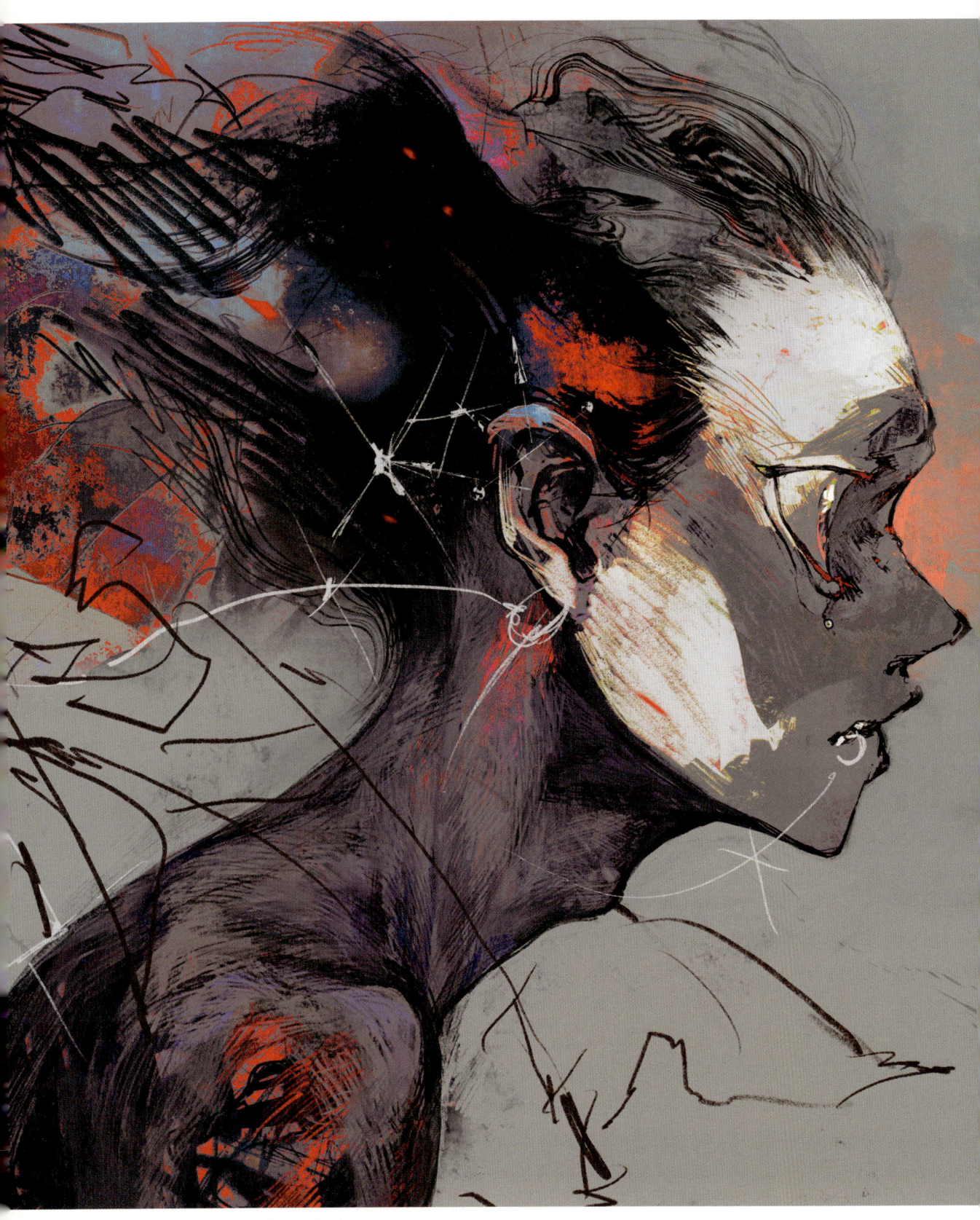

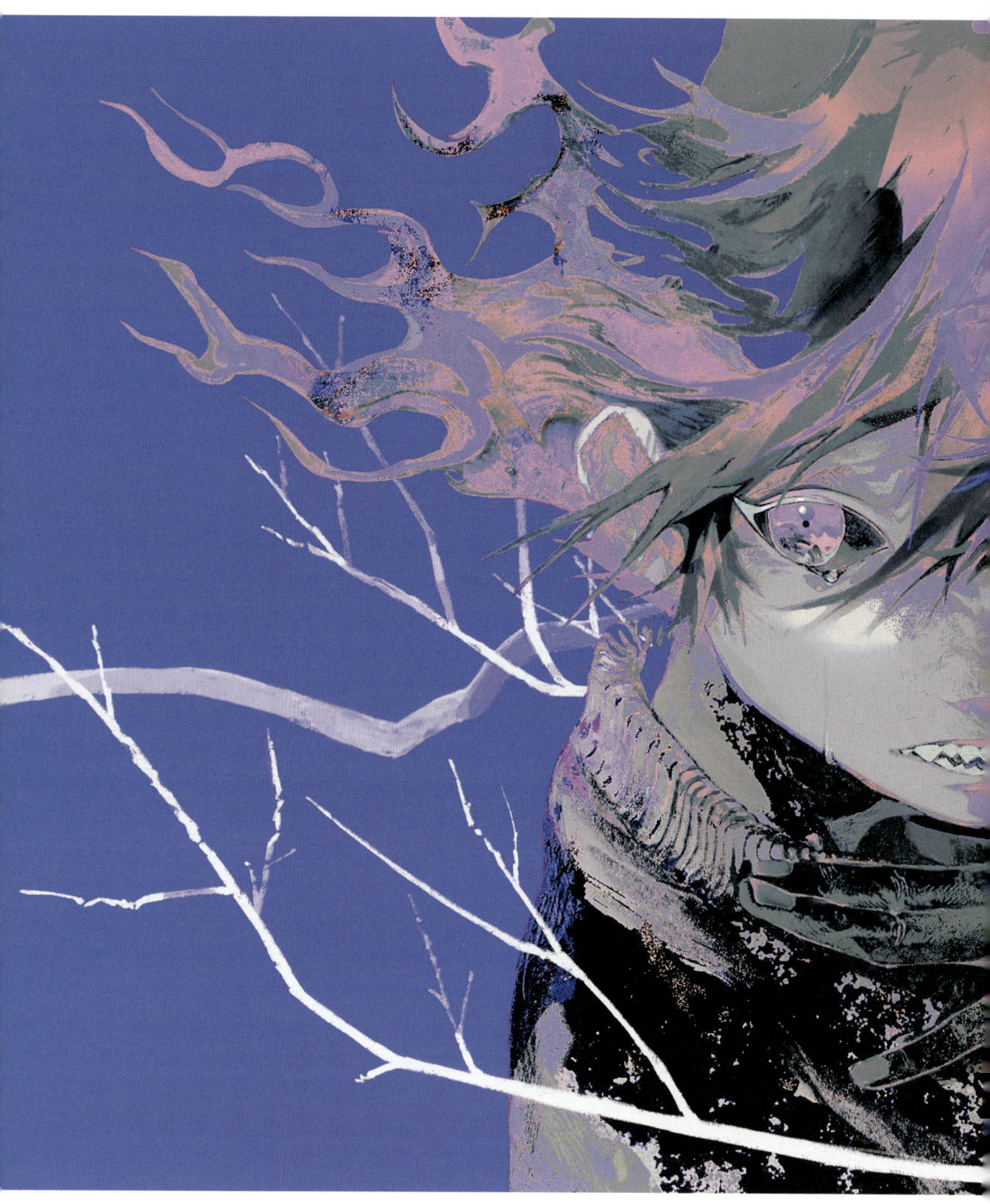

• AQUILEGIA •

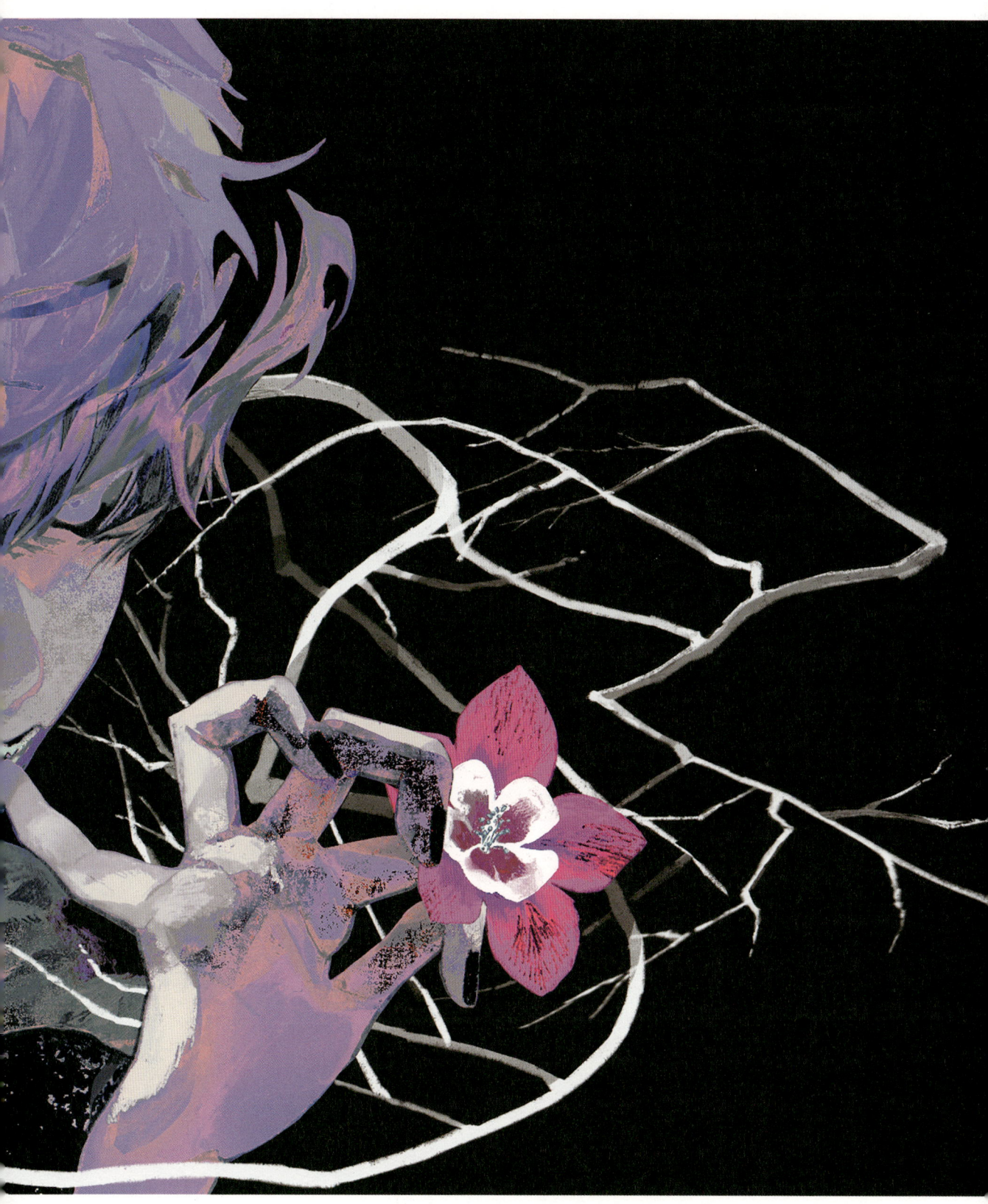

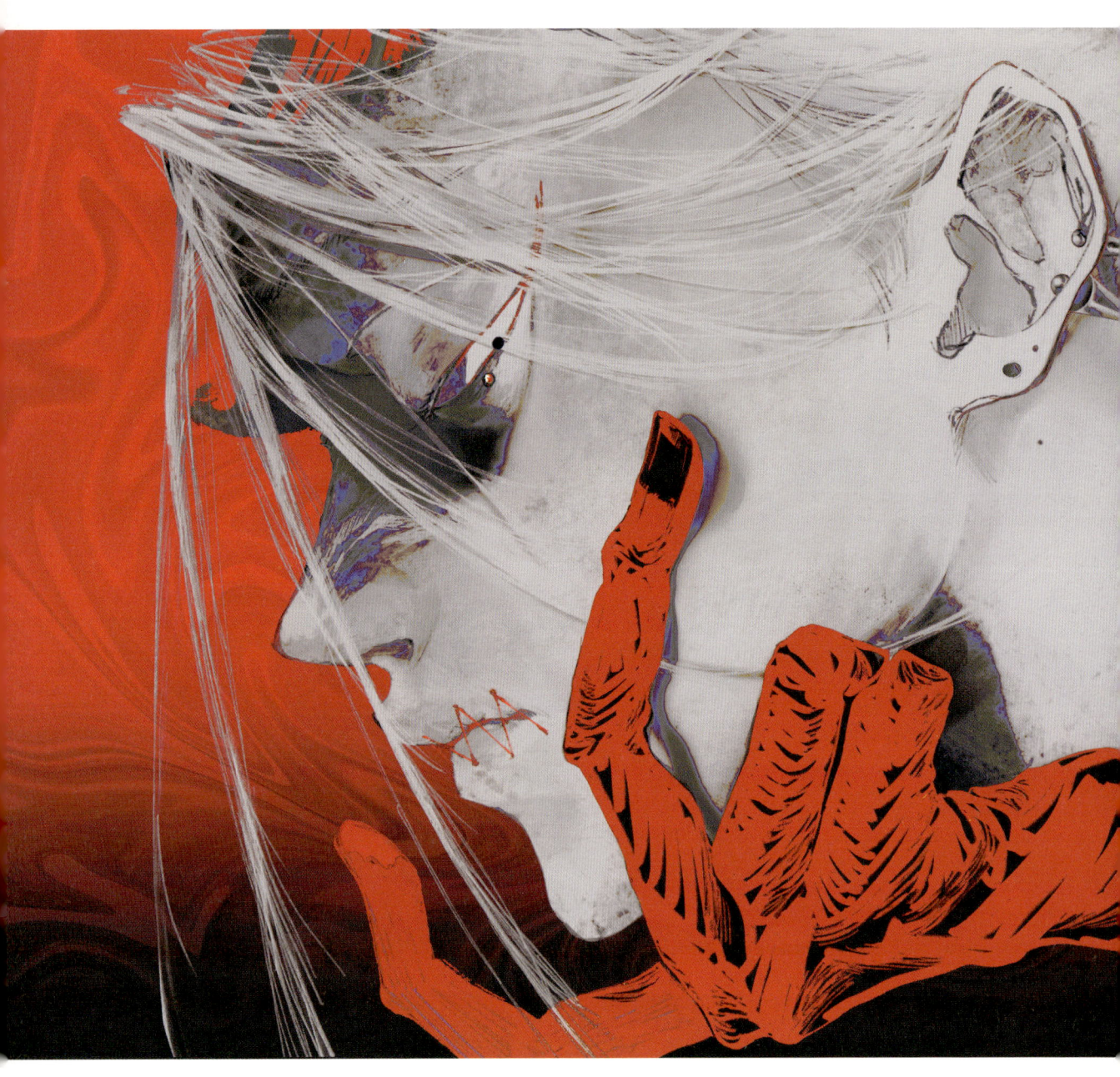

" *I believe intense emotions, such as sadness and anger, are one of the most important human sensations to cherish. They tend to cause negativity, but they are also great energy.* "

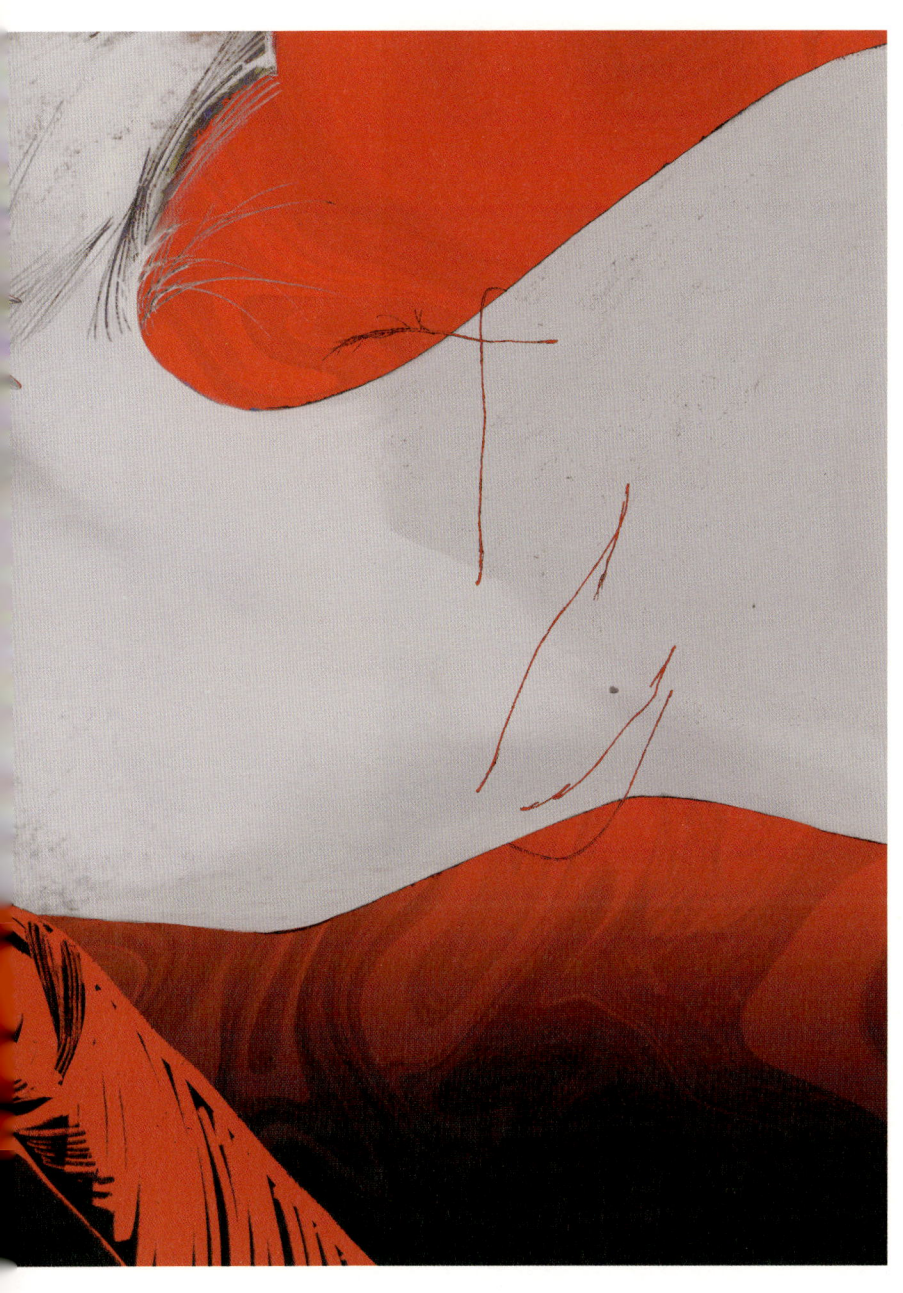

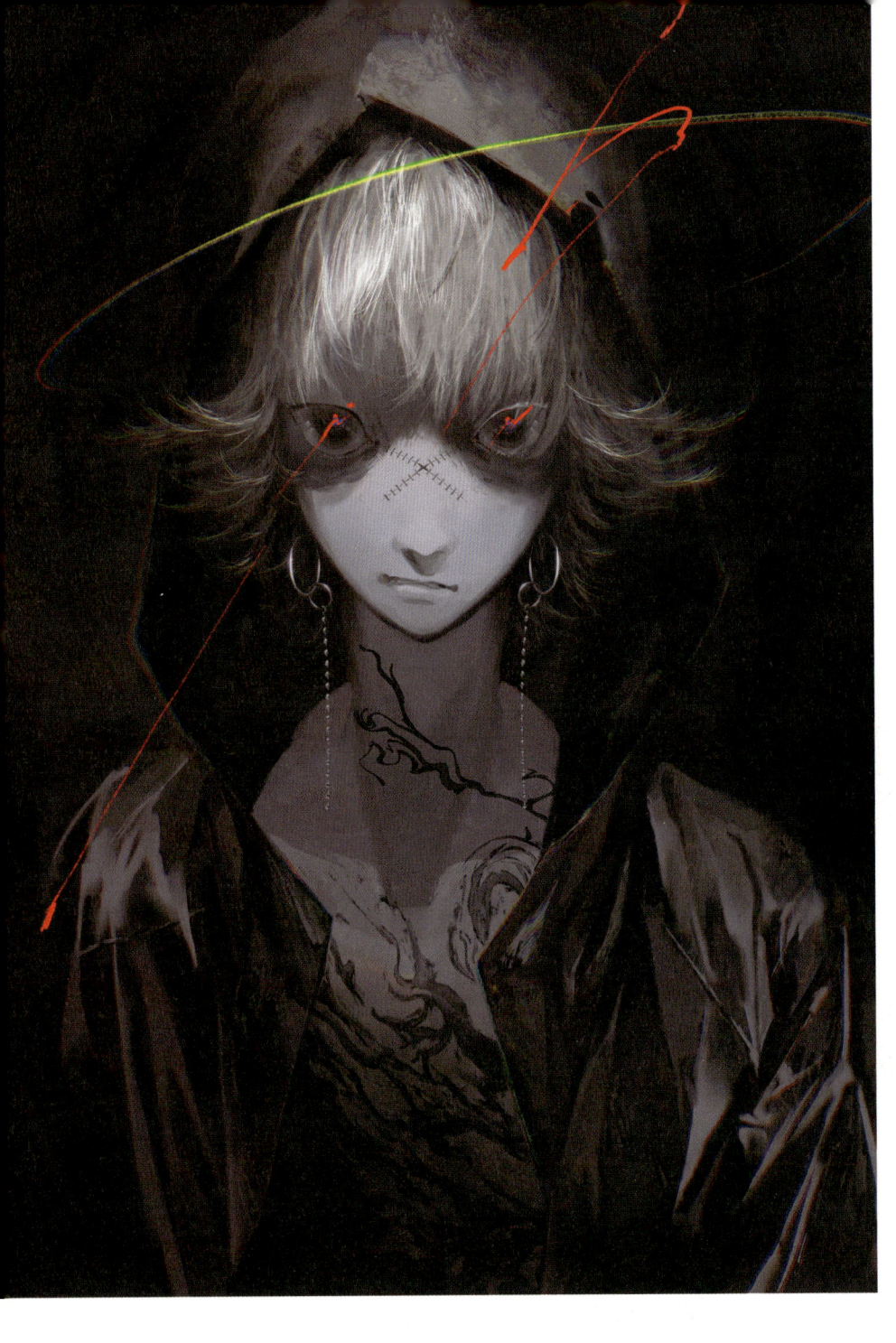

• A CORNERED MOUSE •

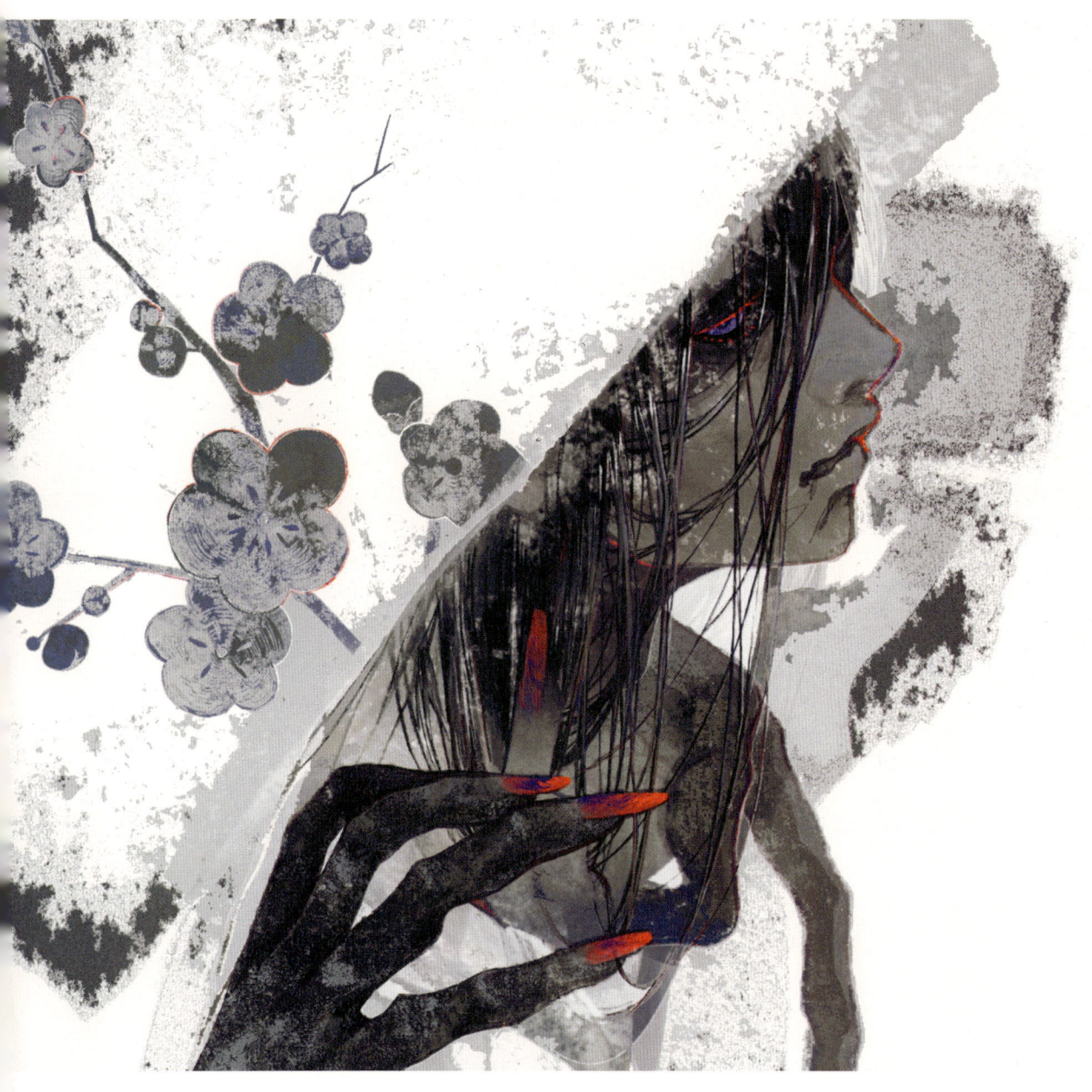

UNBREAKABLE POWER

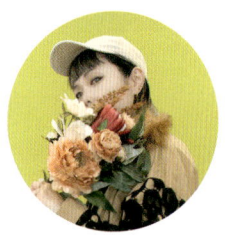

velonyca toto

She was born in 1986. She is currently
living in Tokyo and has been drawing
artwork since 2005.

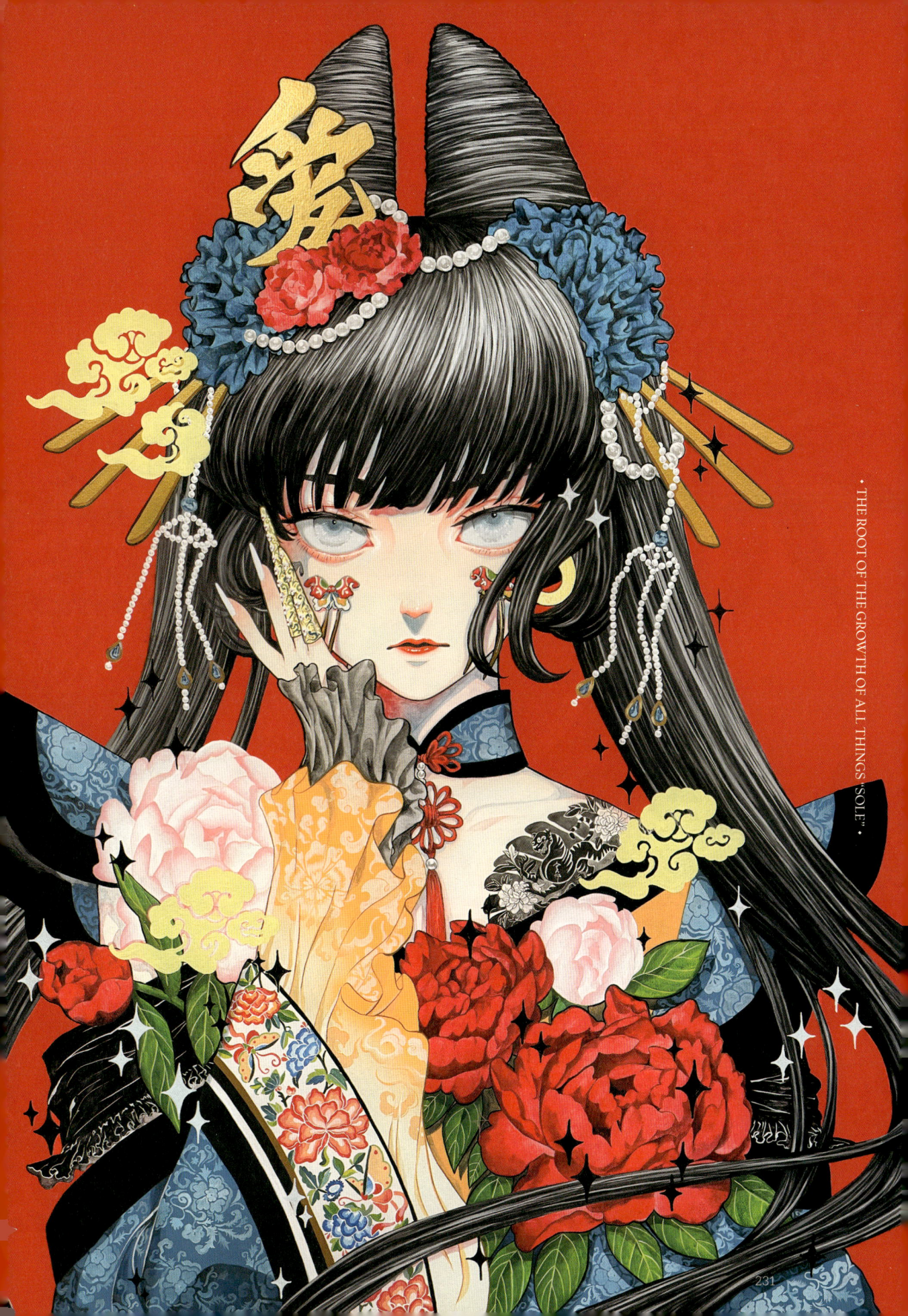

231

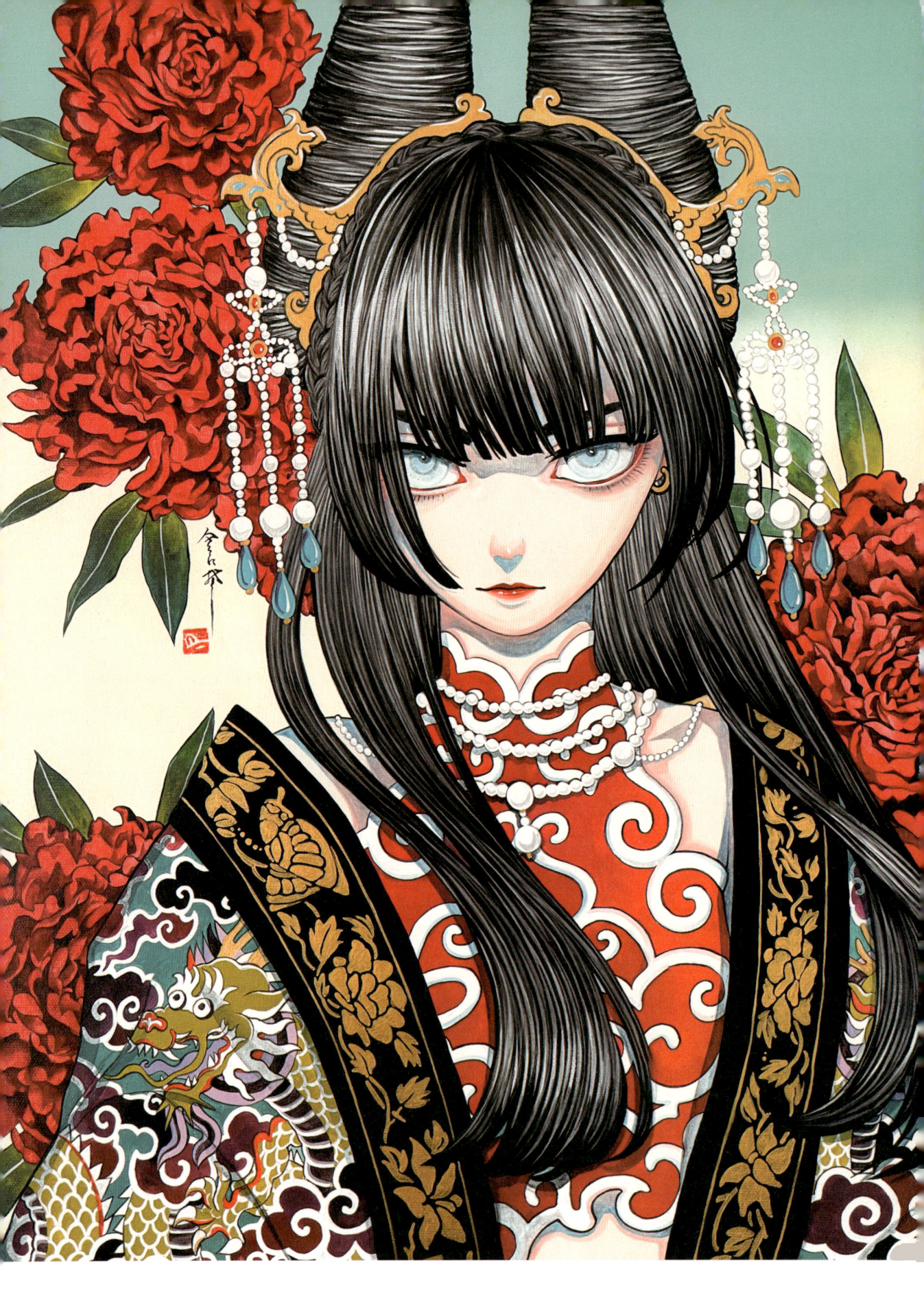

• THE ROOT OF THE GROWTH OF ALL THINGS "STELLA" •

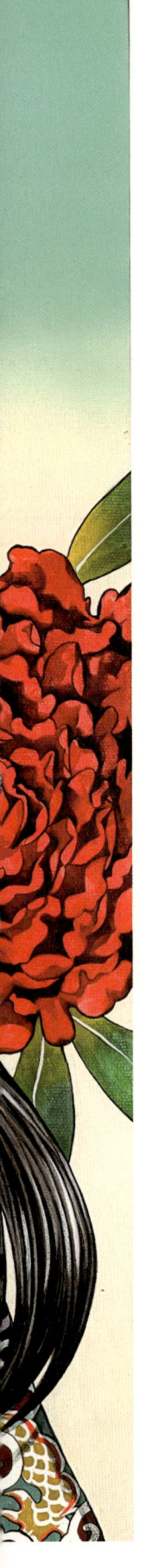

Q: You began creating art in 2005. Can you share what inspired you to start? Is there an interesting story behind it?

vt: I was a graphic designer and gallery director. As I was looking at art every day, I began to want to turn my ideas and passions into art.

During my daily time in the gallery, I realized that viewers came to see the paintings. A painting is treated like a person, it is bought and sold. I find this relationship between the painting and the viewer particularly interesting.

Q: The colors used in your works are bold and bright, especially the bright red that immediately attracts the audience's attention. Do you have any preference for color matching?

vt: I choose colors to communicate directly to the viewer. I try to use colors that will reach people who need help at a distance so that they can get the message immediately and not be bothered. People may be distressed or close their eyes. I want my art to be a beacon of hope, sometimes great anger or explosion, and I want people to feel vivid emotions close to them.

Q: You often use acrylic on canvas to create. Can you tell me why you chose this medium? And what is the unique charm of acrylic painting? Have you tried other painting methods?

vt: At first, I painted on paper. That was because paper and acrylic paint were the most familiar to me. I felt I wanted to create stronger, more robust works. That's when I decided to paint on canvas.

Q: Your series of works *The Root of the Growth of All Things* (P231, P232, P238) talk about the strong vitality of women no matter what situation they are in. As a female artist, do you hope to convey a certain emotion through these works?

vt: I have not decided on the gender of the characters. I am Japanese, so I have lived with anime and video games since childhood. In such media, men who act like women live without any sense of discomfort, and women who look like men live as women as they are. This is what I felt from the standpoint of watching them.

Of course, the author has the right to decide who the characters are. But I want you to feel free to do so.

However, what I want to convey is that they are tough and strong. Even though they are in pain, they do not stop walking and have hope.

Q: We noticed that you prefer to use mythical animals such as qilins, dragons, and tigers in your works, and also use oriental elements such as peony flowers and waves in the background. Can you tell us where the inspiration for these elements comes from? Are there any artists or art schools that you particularly like or that have the greatest influence on you?

vt: I am influenced by many video games, especially the systems part. I aim to fulfill the viewer's emotions by turning mythical creatures such as *zui-jū* (auspicious beasts) and *shin-jū* (divine beasts) into human beings and moving them around.

Many video games are played by moving the avatars of the main characters into the game world.

I hope that the art of painting, which is as unique as a human being, will start a story when it meets its viewer, who is also unique.

Many of the motifs I paint have an oriental element to them, which comes from the fact that many of the deities have strong wishes for good fortune in their daily lives. Every time there was a pandemic or an earthquake, they wished for happiness and good fortune. We believe that this sentiment is necessary for us to move forward.

By the way, video games are cheaper than hamburgers in Tokyo.

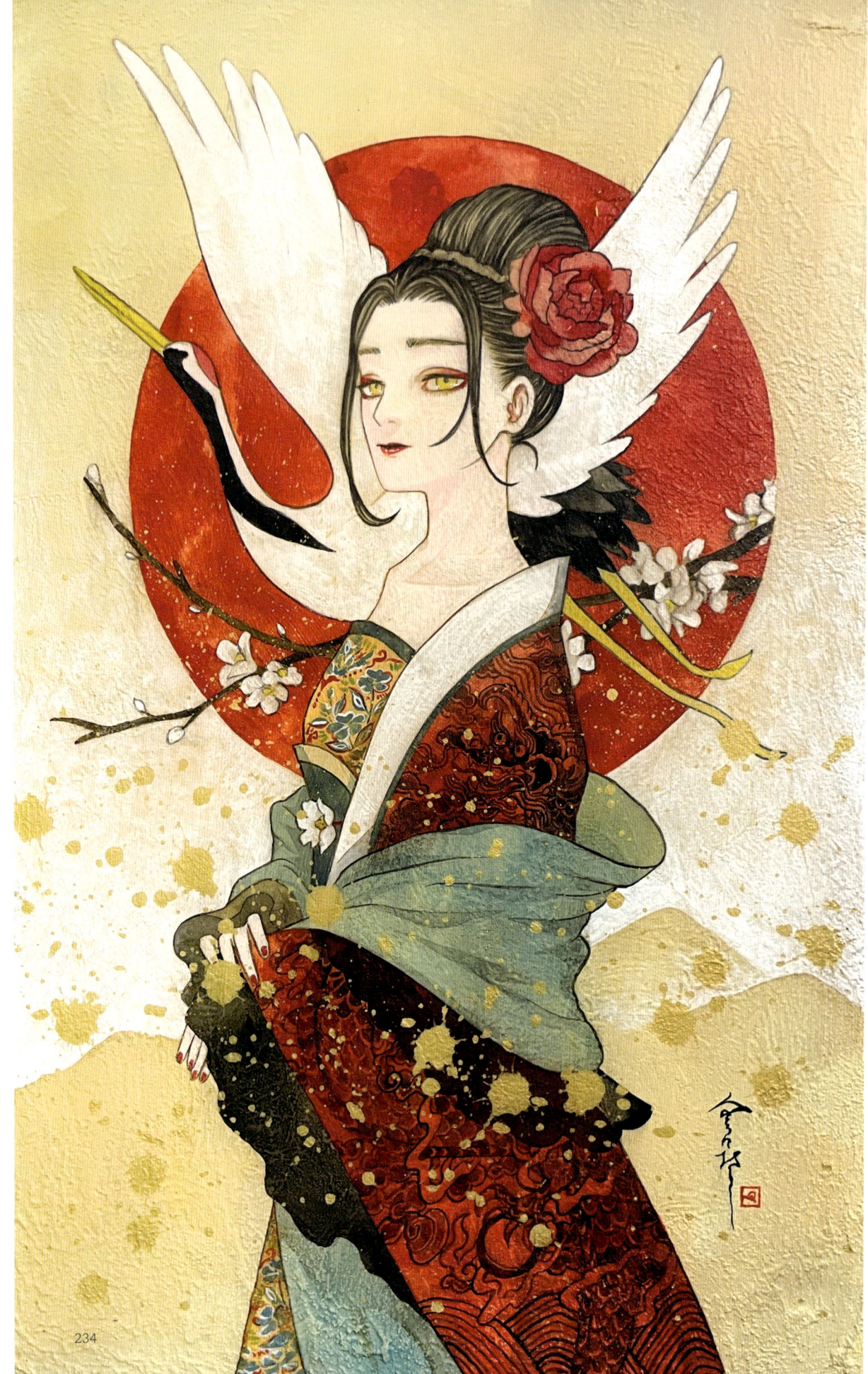

Q: You live in Tokyo. Can you tell me how Japanese culture has influenced your work? What Japanese culture are you most proud of and fond of?

vt: I love Japan. I live in Tokyo. Tokyo is in the middle of an island.

It is a small country with a well-developed Internet, and I create small works of art every day. It is a very strange feeling.

Compared to other countries, I feel very free. I like that very much.

Japanese people create a lot of movements by themselves in a short time. I am very interested in what that speed means and what this otaku culture will be like in 5, 10, or 30 years. Will art and video games get along well with each other?

Q: Did you encounter any particularly troubling or challenging things during the creative process? How did you overcome the difficulties?

vt: When the pandemic hit the world, I hated everything. I hated everything and drew many of the pictures that popped into my head. The pictures I drew were much much more powerful than anything I had ever drawn before.

During the pandemic, anxiety overcame everything in Japan. My child was one year old. My family was anxious every day. I was sick of it. I was born to be happy! I want to let everyone go! I think I strongly believe that.

I think reality is important. But everyone needed to relax a little bit away from it. I thought they should get support. I wanted to do that, just like in the movies and the games.

Difficulties always make me grow for the better. I am absolutely invincible.

Q: You display and sell your works through galleries and other channels. How do you view the relationship between artistic creation and marketing?

vt: My artistic creation is complete when it is displayed in the marketplace. It is an essential reaction.

Let's play together. Let's have fun together. The gallery is always open to everyone, the art is always exciting, and the market teaches us the reality within the market. Every day the market changes globally. Every day the main language spoken changes. It is very interesting.

I want to be a *shuku* (inn) for visitors, whether for artistic creation or the art market.

Q: Any future plans or new creative directions?

vt: I create small dolls. They are not figures or soft vinyl dolls, but wooden sculptures. I want them to be like talismans, with a different atmosphere and a very strong power to lean on. Their houses and rooms are also created with wood. Cutting the wood and making the small dolls by myself gives me a different inspiration than painting on canvas. Only one person can have (and buy) one of their little dolls. It's a wonderful thing. Please become a captive of the excitement of taking away something unique.

" *Many of the motifs I paint have an oriental element to them, which comes from the fact that many of the deities have strong wishes for good fortune in their daily lives.* "

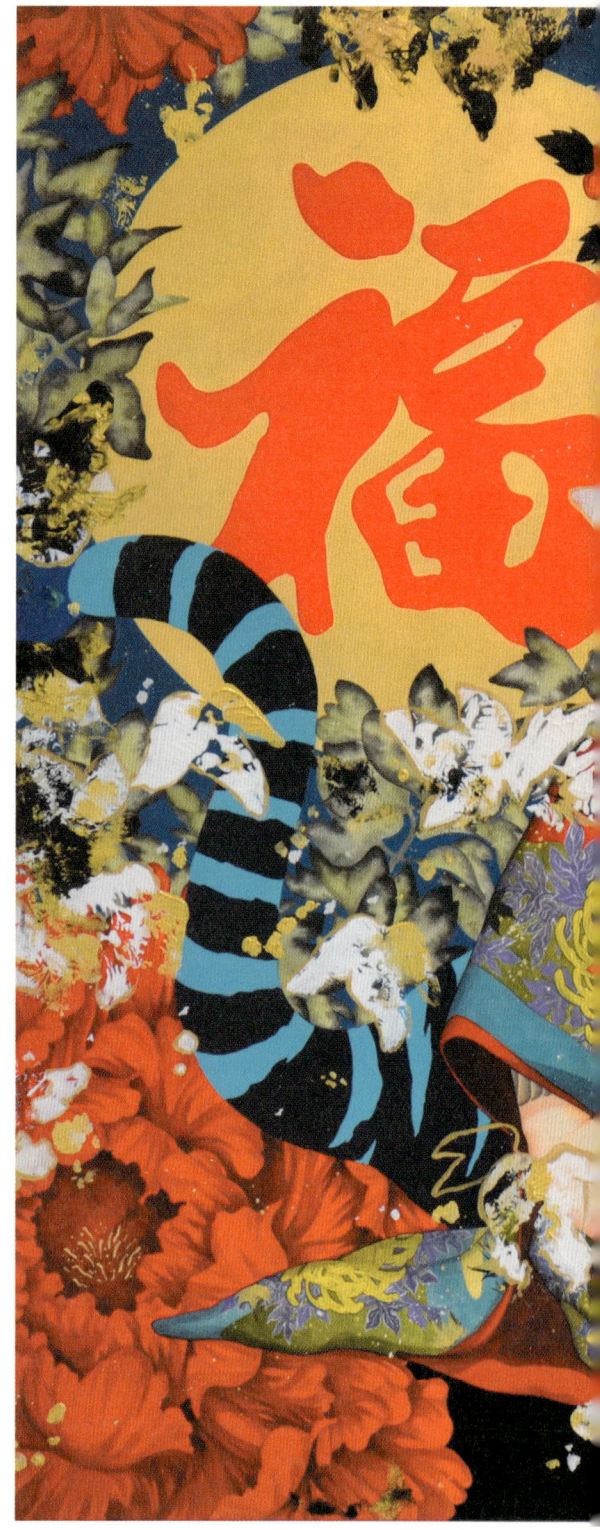

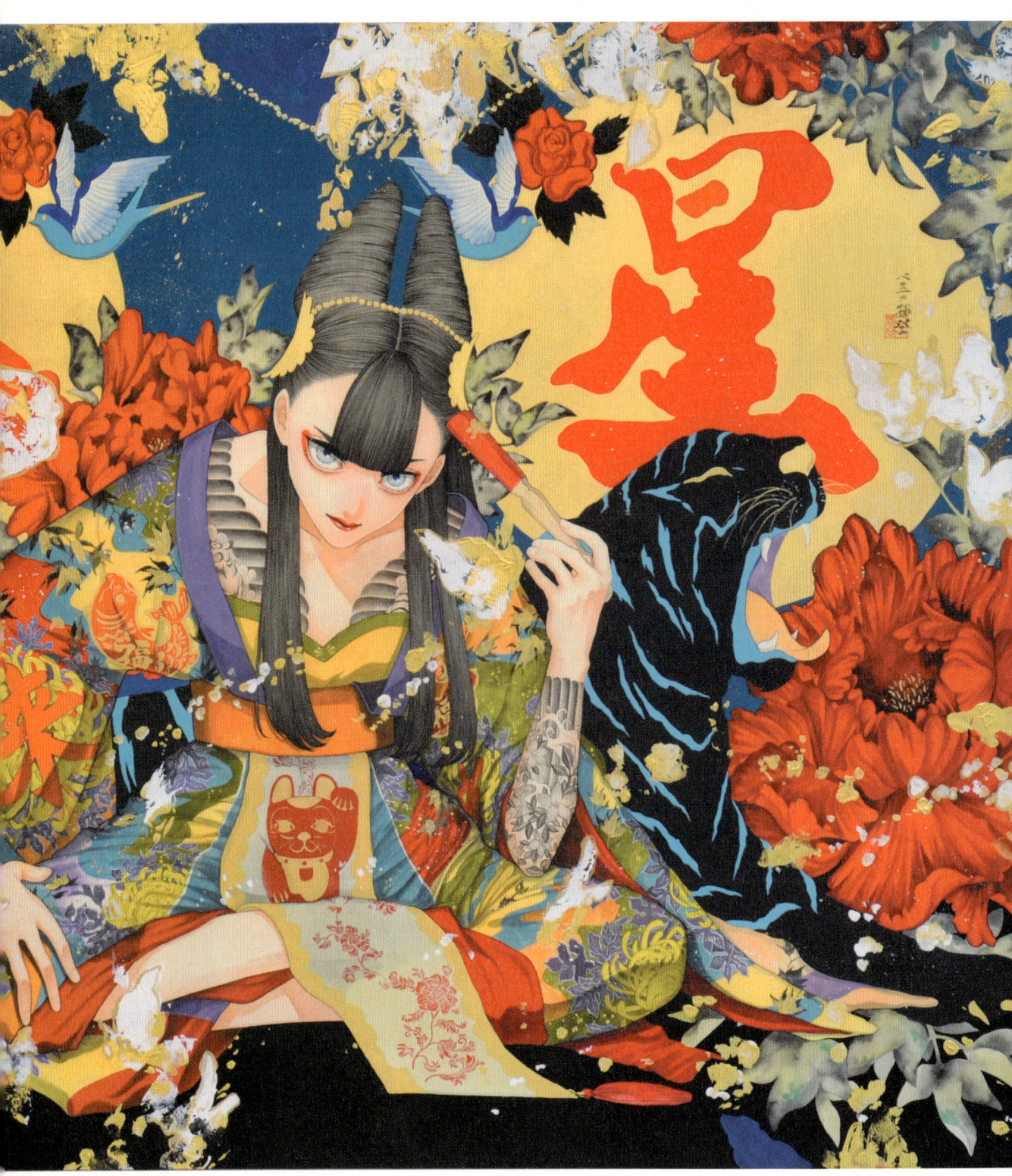

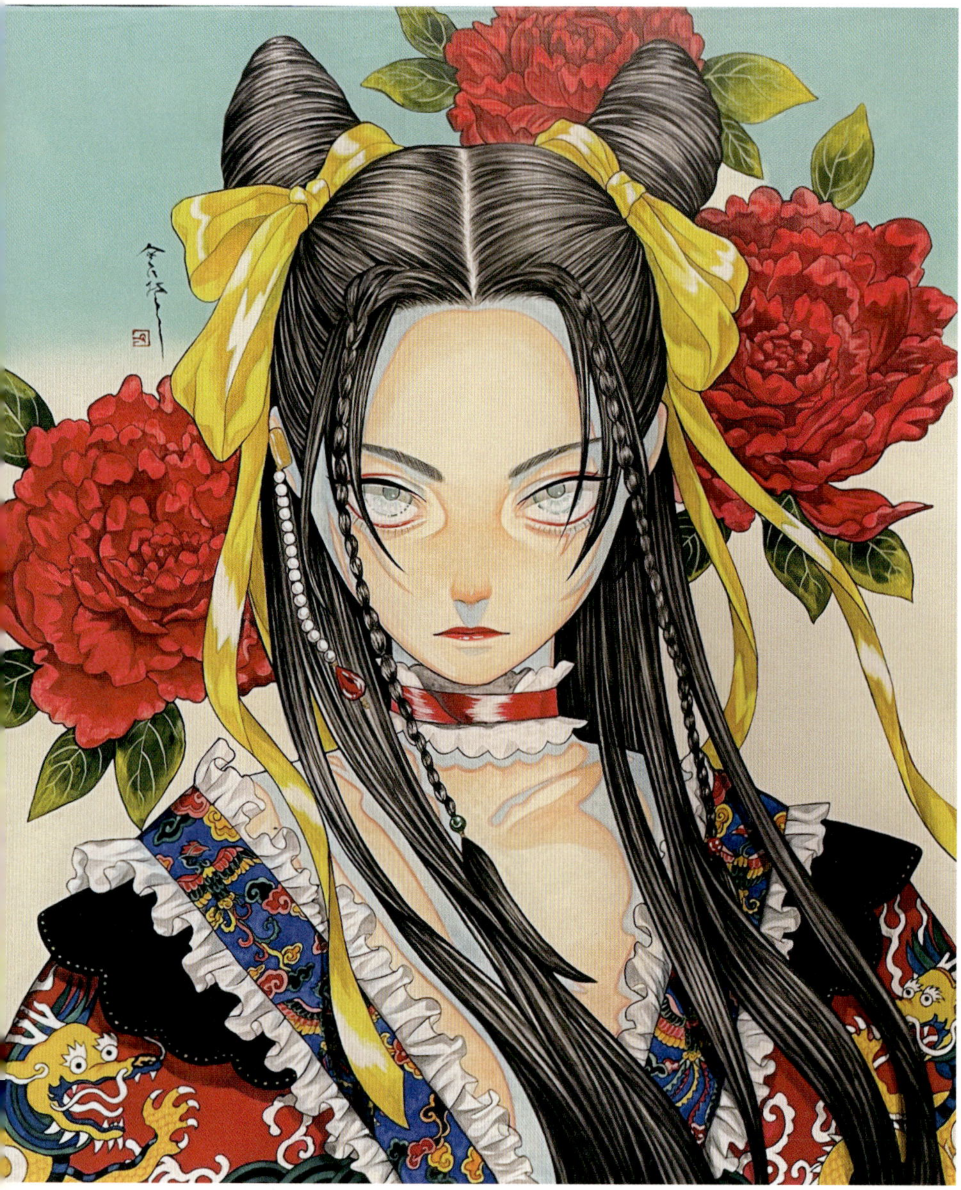

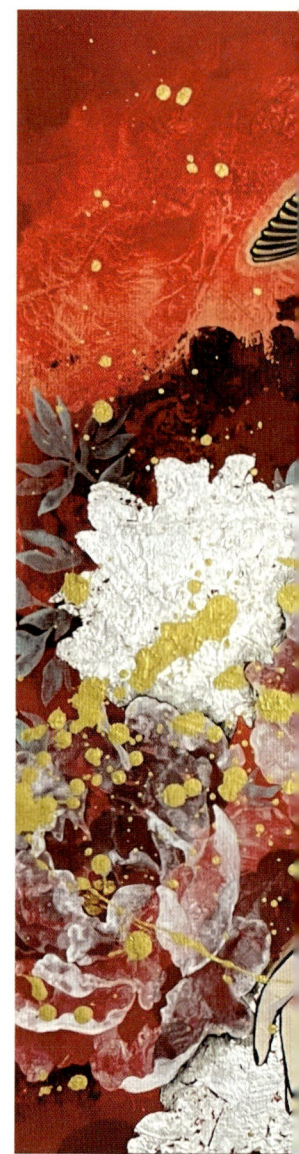

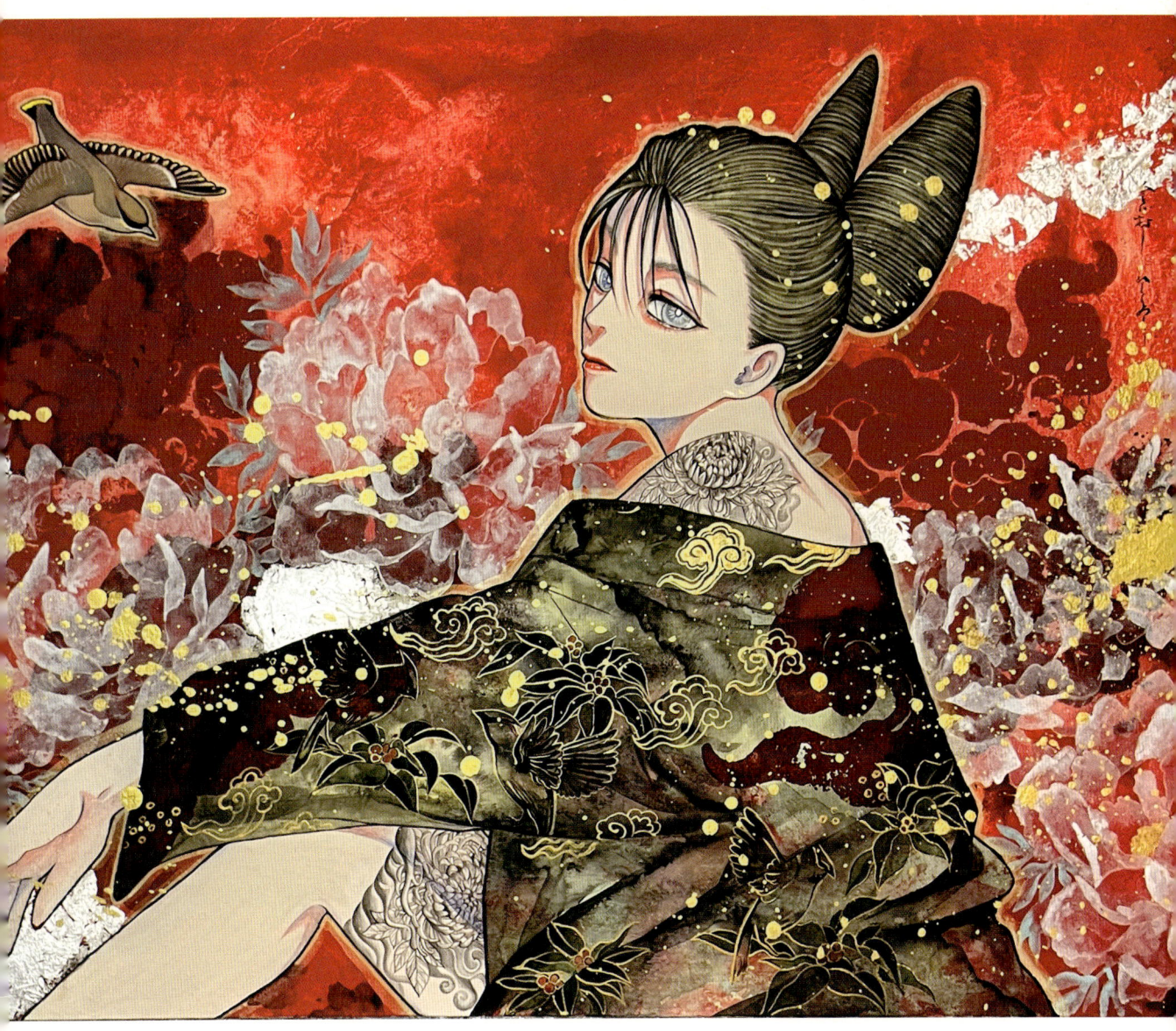

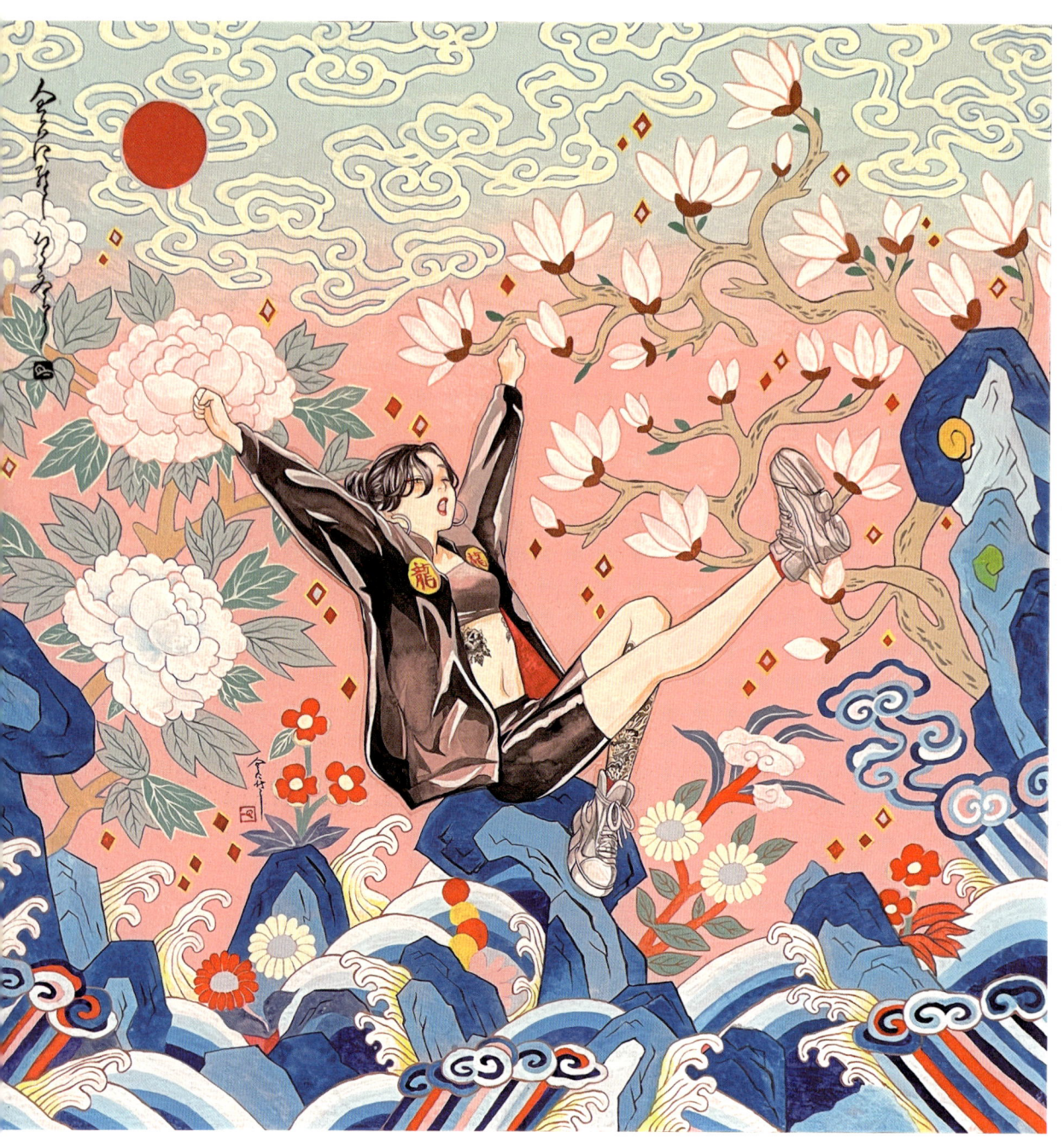

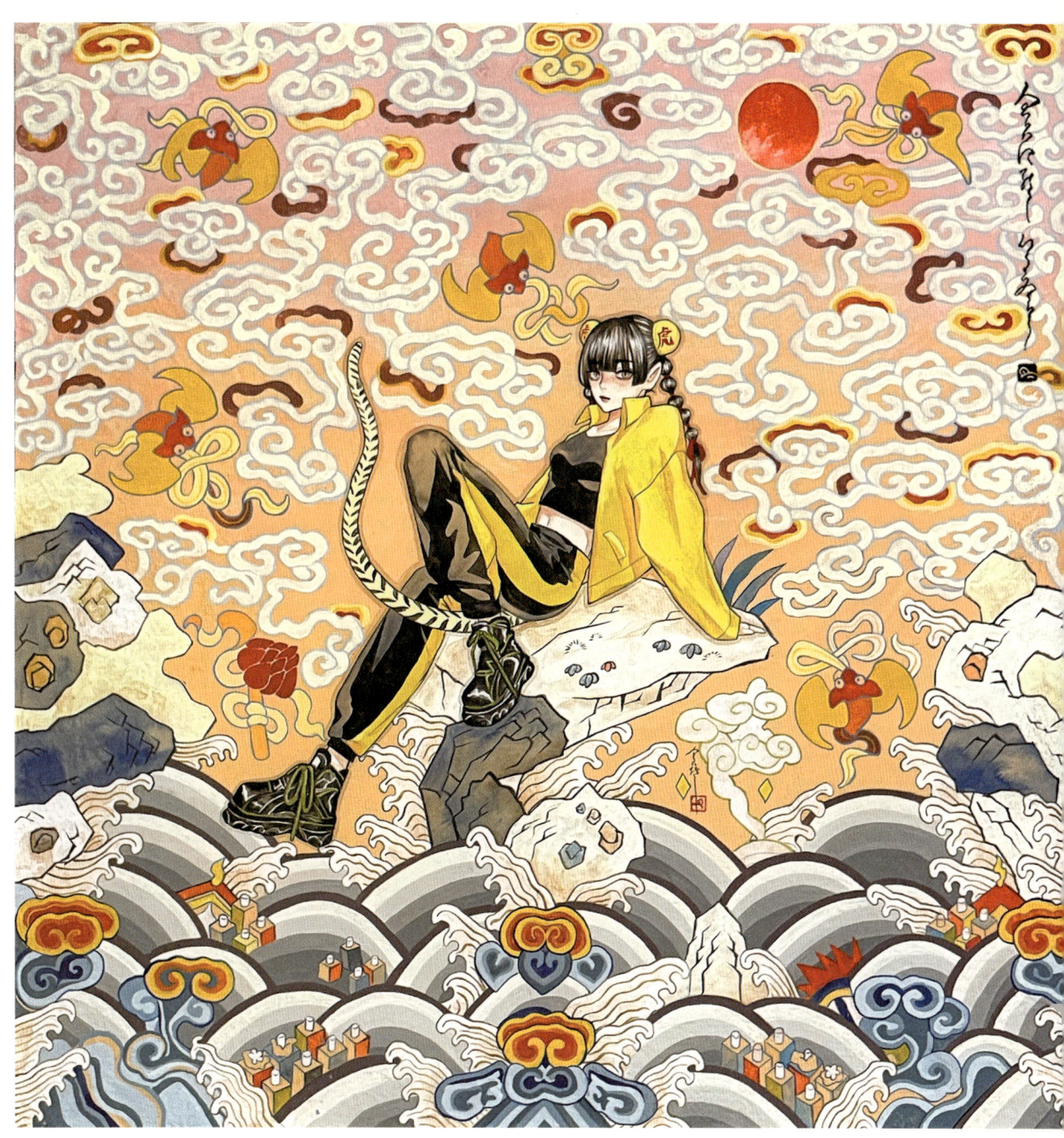

FOLLOWING NATURE

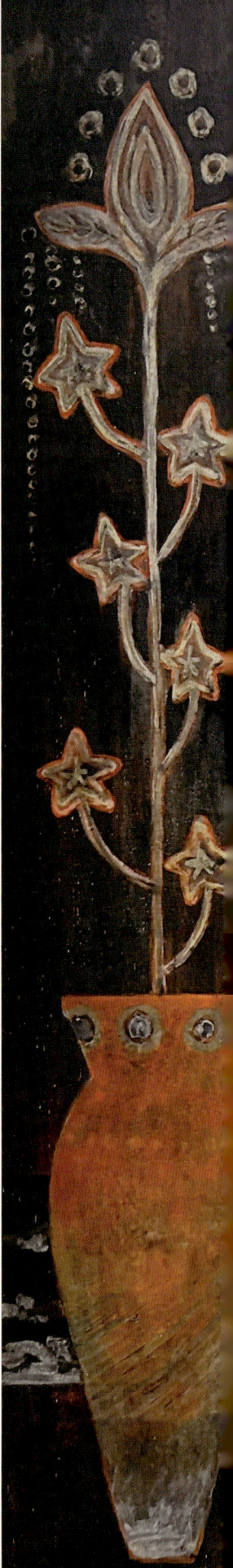

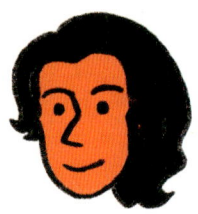

Tsurikawa

Tsurikawa creates artworks that use the theme of "the relationship between humans and beasts." She paints while thinking about how she wants to live between nature and civilized society. She loves the beautiful shapes of living things.

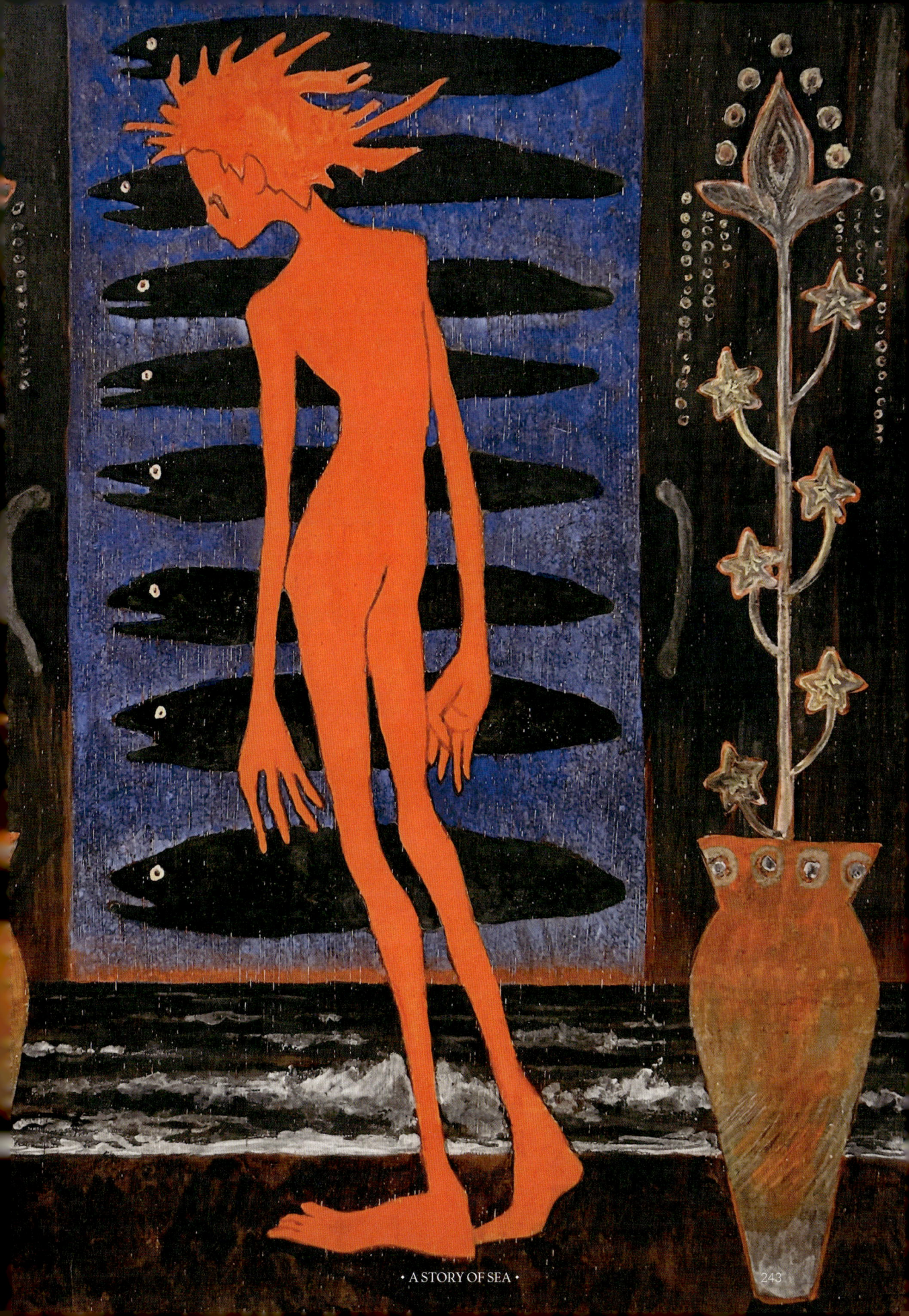

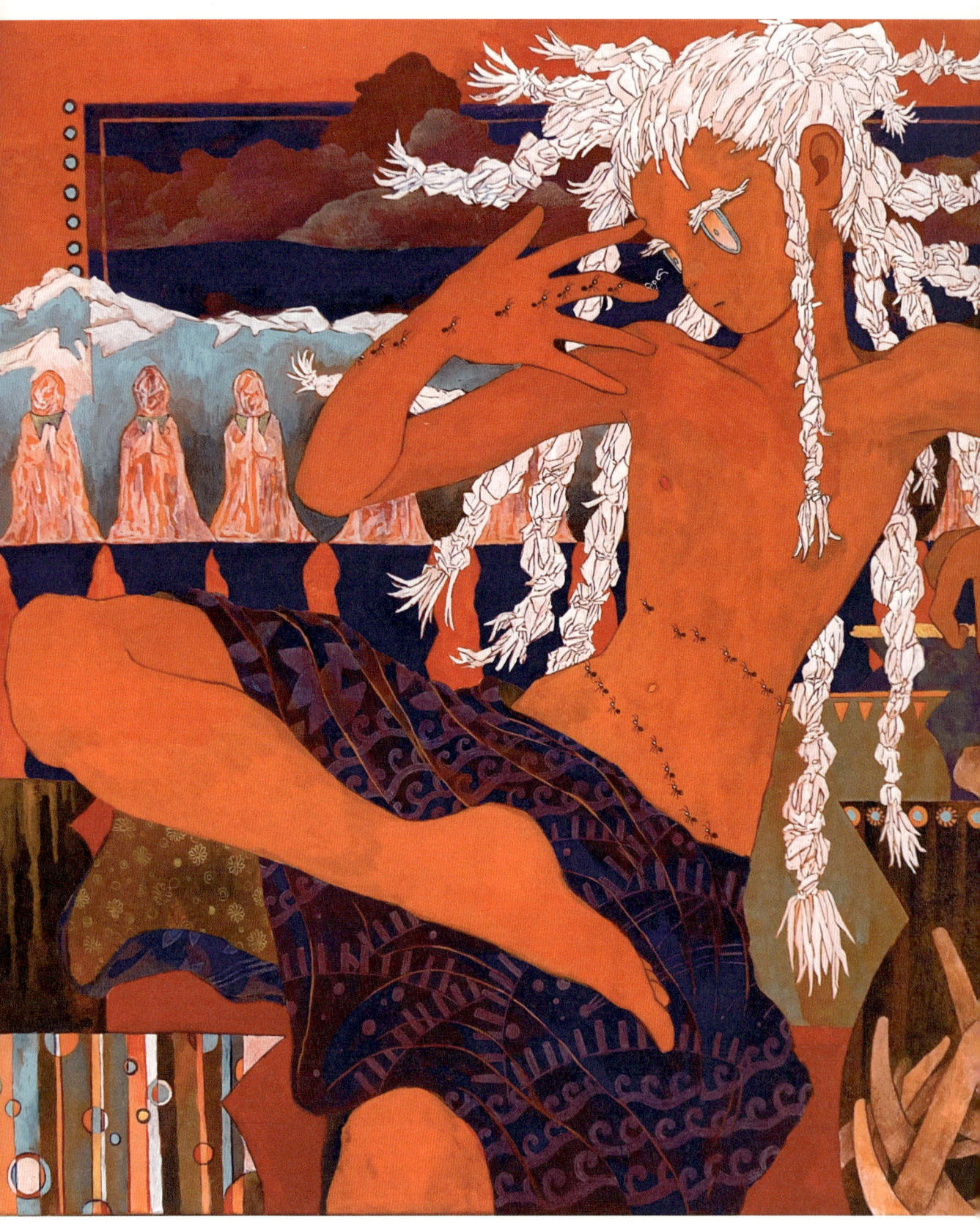

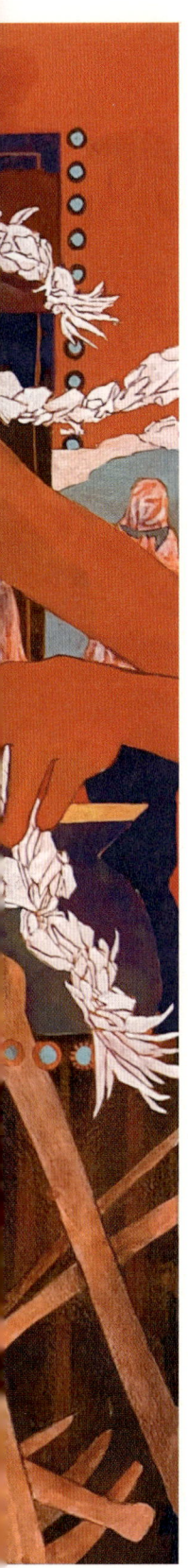

Q: **What inspired you to explore the theme of "the relationship between humans and beasts" in your artwork? What significance does this theme hold for your creative process?**

T: When I take a walk on the beach, I often see dead fish and birds that have been washed up and partially eaten by other creatures. Creatures living in nature decompose their bodies after death to become energy for other creatures, whereas, in the civilized society in which I live, human corpses are generally incinerated and placed in graves. Cremation is one of the conclusions that humans have reached over a long period due to hygienic considerations, which led me to wonder what the difference is between animals and humans.

When we are in the city, we miss the abundance of nature, but when we live in the wilderness, we sometimes prefer the lights of the city. Like animals, I have a desire to be decomposed by other creatures after death, and at the same time, I have a desire to be burned and disappear from this world without a trace. We live in a world of contradictions between the civilized world where humans live and the natural world where animals live, but we are involved in both worlds. Since I love both worlds, I go back and forth between the two and create artwork of what I think about each time.

It is not so much a theme for my paintings, but rather a theme throughout my entire life, and the creative process is just one of those processes. I love painting, but perhaps in the future, I will explore this theme in other ways of expression.

Q: **In your creative process, how do you express the relationship between nature and civilization through your paintings? How do you present the beautiful forms of living things?**

T: The area where I live is close to the bustling building districts and the sea and mountains, where I can feel both nature and civilization at once. For this reason, I make sketches around my residence and draw subjects that inspire me. Recently, I often go to the beach. So I use creatures that I find on the beach and fish that I sketched at a nearby aquarium as my subjects. Instead of depicting either nature or civilization, I always include subjects that represent both

nature and civilization in my artwork. For example, I combine subjects such as a fish carcass and a ship, or a seashell and a lantern.

Q: **Your works usually use orange-red as the color. What is your preference in choosing colors? Does orange-red have any special meaning?**

T: The coloring of the work is inspired by the color of ink in calligraphy and the vermilion color of the calligraphy signatures. Chinese ink and vermilion pigment are used in my artworks. Orange is a color that evokes the heat of the sun and life but is also associated with flesh and blood and decay. I love it as a color that allows me to imagine both life and death. I use various kinds of paints, such as acrylics and mineral pigments, to paint my works, and it is difficult for me to adjust the orange color, which is completely different depending on the paint. However, this trial-and-error process is one of the most enjoyable parts of my production process.

Q: **Your work is partly inspired by novels and music. Can you share some of that?**

T: I like to take walks on the beach while listening to music, where I make sketches and get inspiration for my artwork in the process. My favorite places are the sandy beaches of Enoshima and Kamakura, which are also the setting of *Slam Dunk*. There are also many dead fish and shells on the beach.

I listen to a wide range of music from rock to classical. My recent favorite is Kenshi Yonezu.

I like to ride in a car, and ideas for paintings come to me most when I am idly watching the scenery flow by outside the car window. I am also interested in maps and topography, and walking around the city looking at maps is an essential part of my creative process.

Q: **The work *Savior* (P244) won the 72nd National Student Art & Design Award at the Gakuten. Can you share your thoughts on the creation of *Savior*? What does this award mean to your artistic career?**

T: The theme of *Savior* is "save yourself." While attending school and interacting with various people, I came to realize that while it is necessary to seek help from someone else, the only person who can truly save you is yourself.

Savior is a work that I had been thinking about for a very long time, and because I had a well defined idea, I was able to complete it in about a week.

Winning this award was a great leap forward in my career as an artist and gave me confidence in my work. The award was an important experience in my life as an artist, as it allowed me to be involved with many people, as I was asked to produce artwork and publish books.

Q: You often explore death as a source of life in your work. What implications do you think this concept of the cycle of life and death has for modern people?

T: The idea of life and death is a gradual repetition of *saṃsāra* was a salvific concept for me. The existence of an afterlife, such as heaven and hell, has haunted me every night since I was a child, and I often found myself unable to sleep because I thought about it so much. While I was alive, it was more realistic and acceptable to me to see creatures dying and being eaten by other creatures, rather than in another world where no one can give me an answer.

But I don't think all people think this way. There are as many variations of life and death as there are living creatures. No one way of thinking is right, and each person has his or her own image of life and death, all of which should be respected. I continue to create my artwork in the hope that even one person in the audience will somehow share my thoughts.

Q: How does the natural landscape influence your visual and emotional expression in your works?

T: When I walk in nature, what comes to mind is a feeling of awe. The existence of forests, oceans, and rocks that have been created over a very long time than I have makes me feel both fear and a sense of security and respect at the same time. Especially when I walk alone at night sea, I feel fear and excitement that I do not get when I walk on the same ocean in the daytime. In the pitch-black darkness, when only the white waves are coming toward me from beyond the horizon with a loud sound, I sometimes think, "I'm going to be eaten!"

I often express this fear and emotion in my artwork because I don't want to forget it. The characters in my paintings often stare at me and smile or look at me as if they are aware of the viewers' presence, which is very similar to my image of the horizon or mountain ridges. It is a vast concept that spans both the human and animal worlds, and I believe that this awe is an emotion that both humans and animals share.

Q: As a contemporary Japanese artist, how do you think your works reflect issues or emotions in modern society?

T: I design the characters in my works in such a way that it is as difficult as possible to distinguish their gender. I feel that this is not intentional but rather an unconscious choice on my part to create human expressions that break down gender barriers. One possible reason for this is the inequality between men and women in contemporary Japan, and the fact that I often witness scenes of men and women fighting through SNS. Many of the artworks are set in the seas of Japan, but the characters are not necessarily Japanese. Rather, they are represented as "human beings" that transcend categories, such as countries and regions. I think this also reflects the fact that I have seen many scenes of conflict between races and countries. Although there have been many instances throughout history of conflict between different communities and creatures of different appearances, I believe that humanity has already had the experience to provide a reason to stop such conflicts. The desire to get along with each other since we are all living creatures in the same world is also included in the creation of this work.

Q: Any plans or goals in the future?

T: My major goal is to continue creating artwork until I die. As long as I am alive, I would like to pursue my own expression and inspiration. What I want to draw or express may change as I get older, but whatever choice I make, I hope to choose a path that I have no regrets about. As a goal that I hope to achieve soon, I would like to experiment with 3D works and interesting exhibition methods. I am secretly planning to exhibit in natural environments such as the sea or mountains, based on the theme of "between humans and beasts" and I hope that one day I will be able to realize this goal. I would like to continue to enjoy creating works of art, and I hope that this enjoyment will be conveyed to the viewers as well.

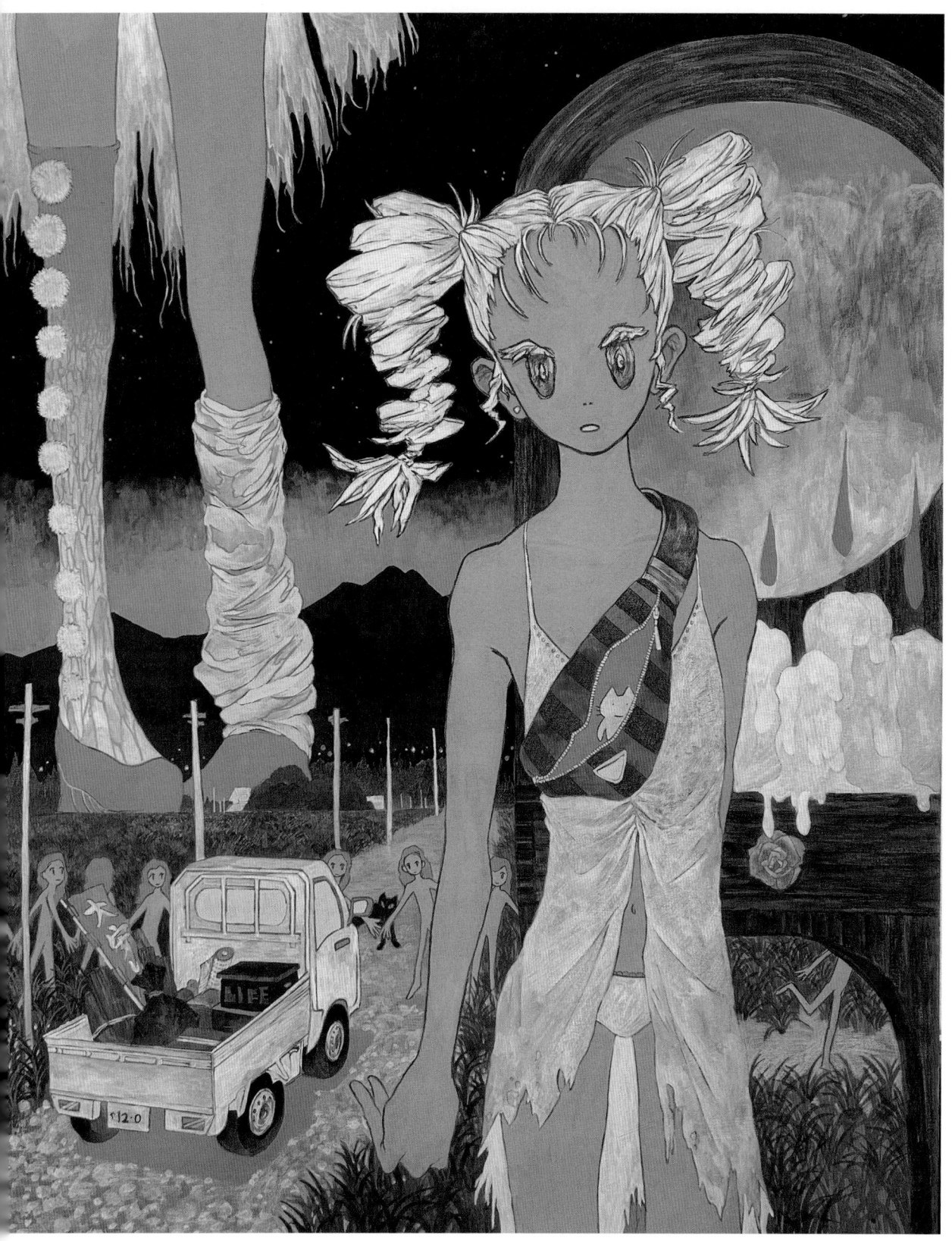

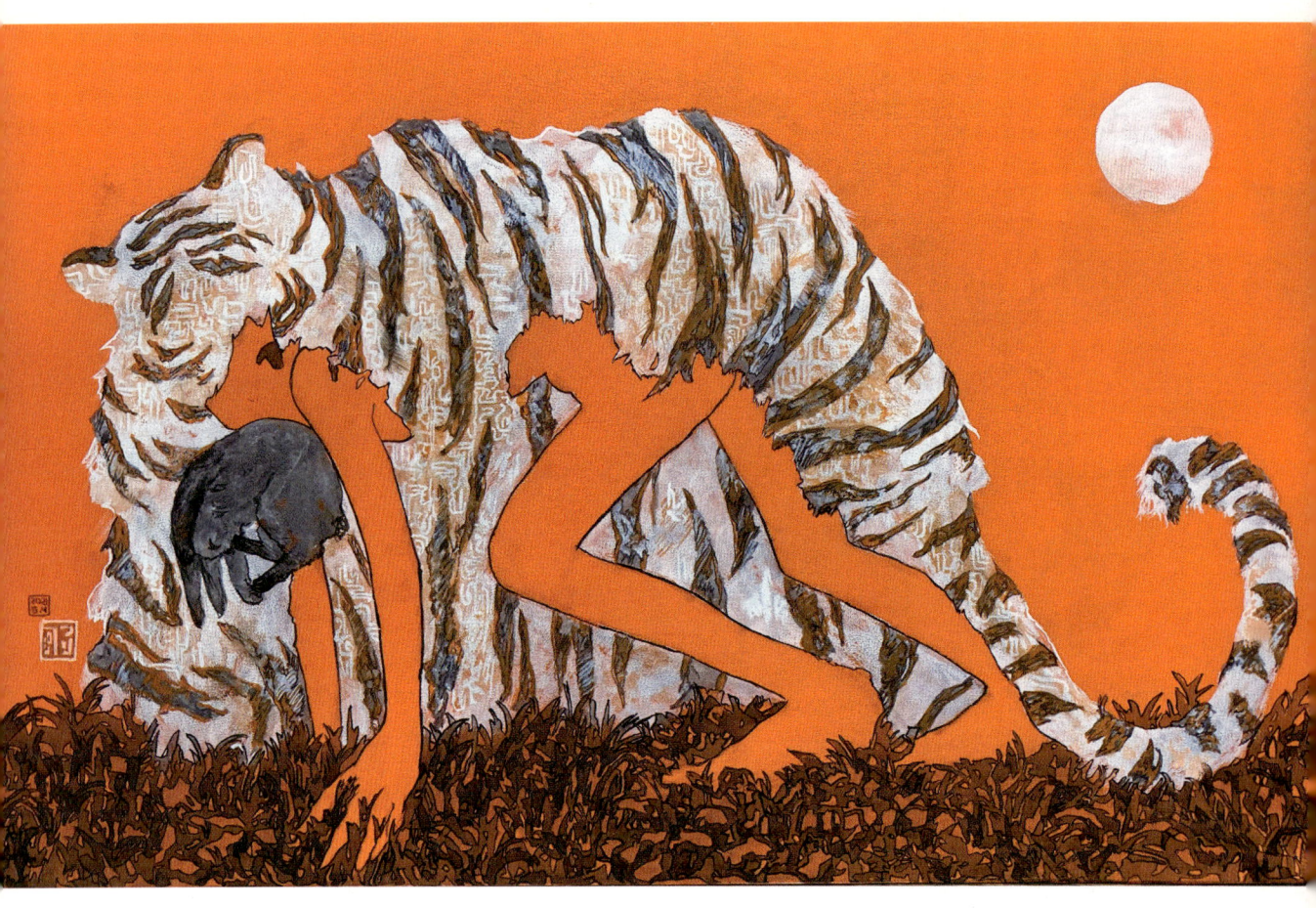

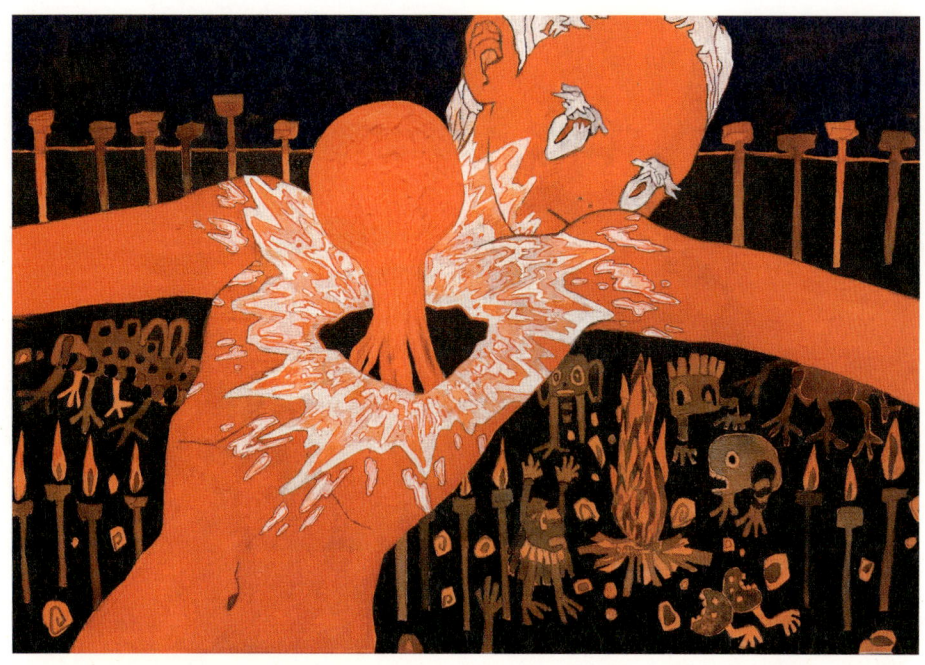

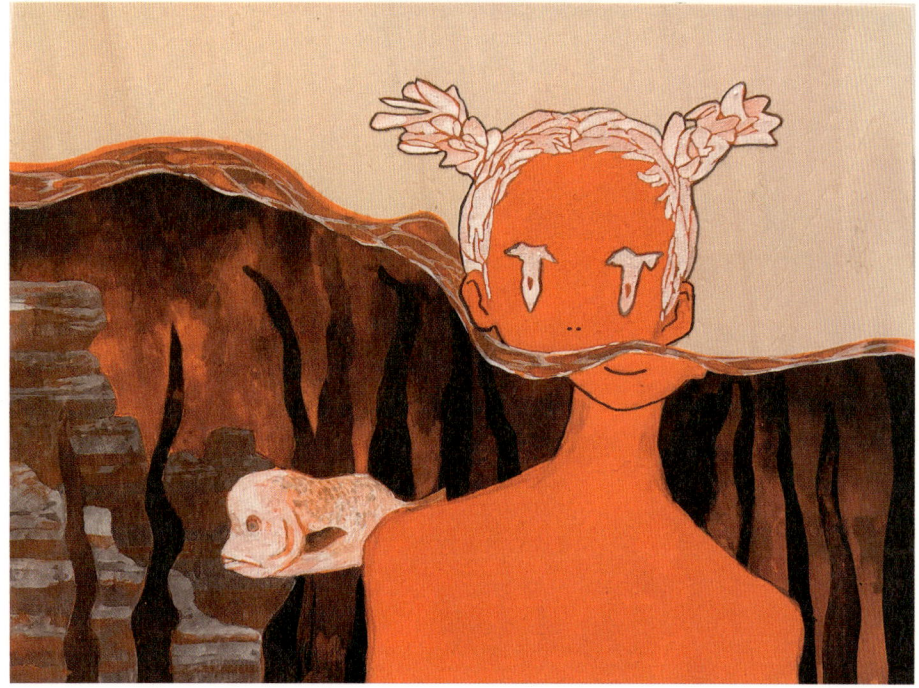

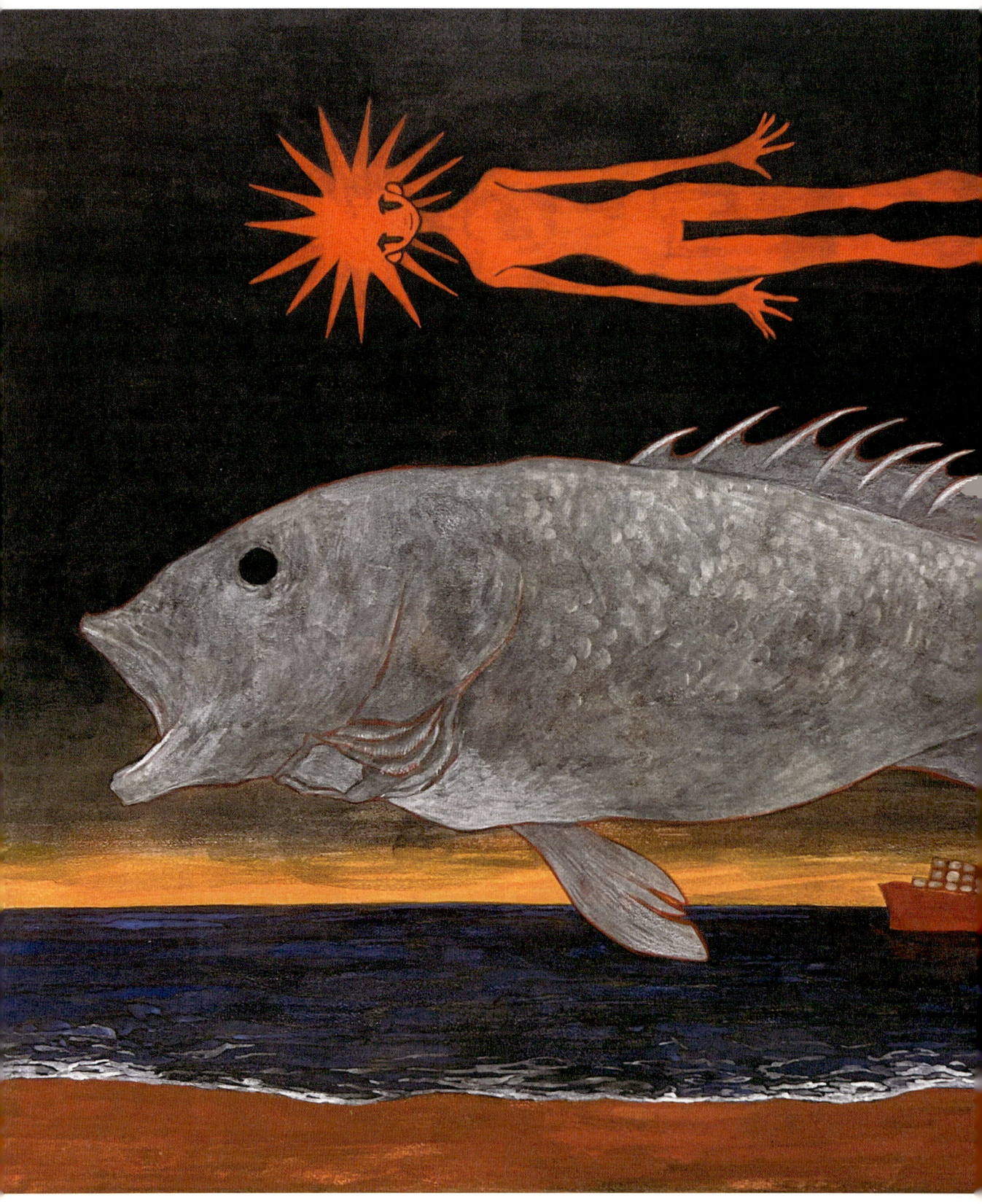

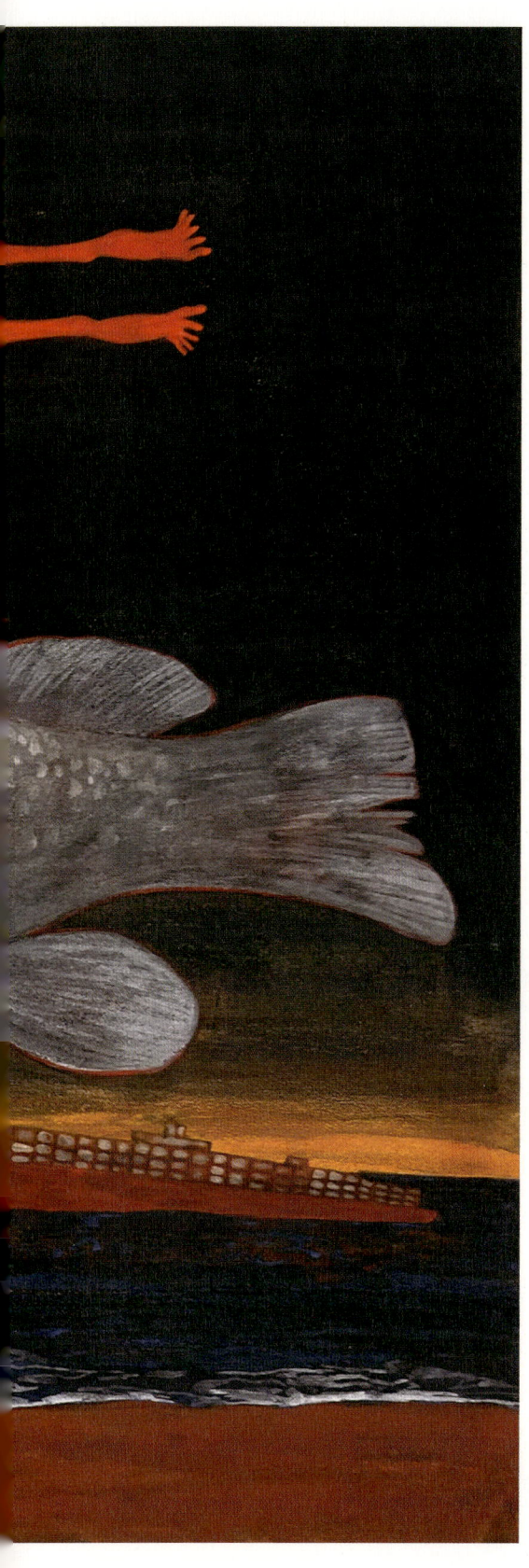

" *The existence of forests, oceans, and rocks that have been created over a very long time than I have makes me feel both fear and a sense of security and respect at the same time.* "

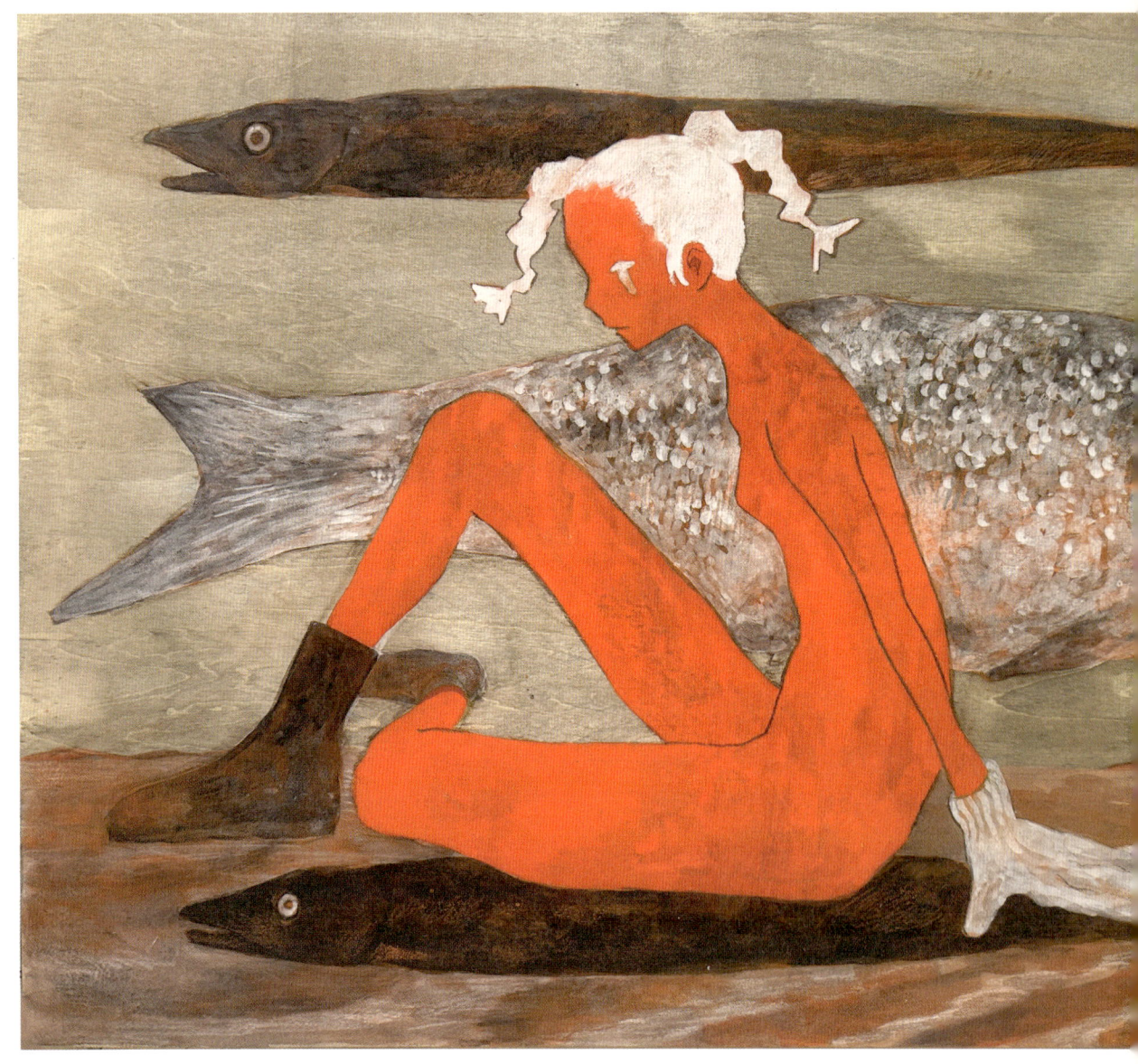

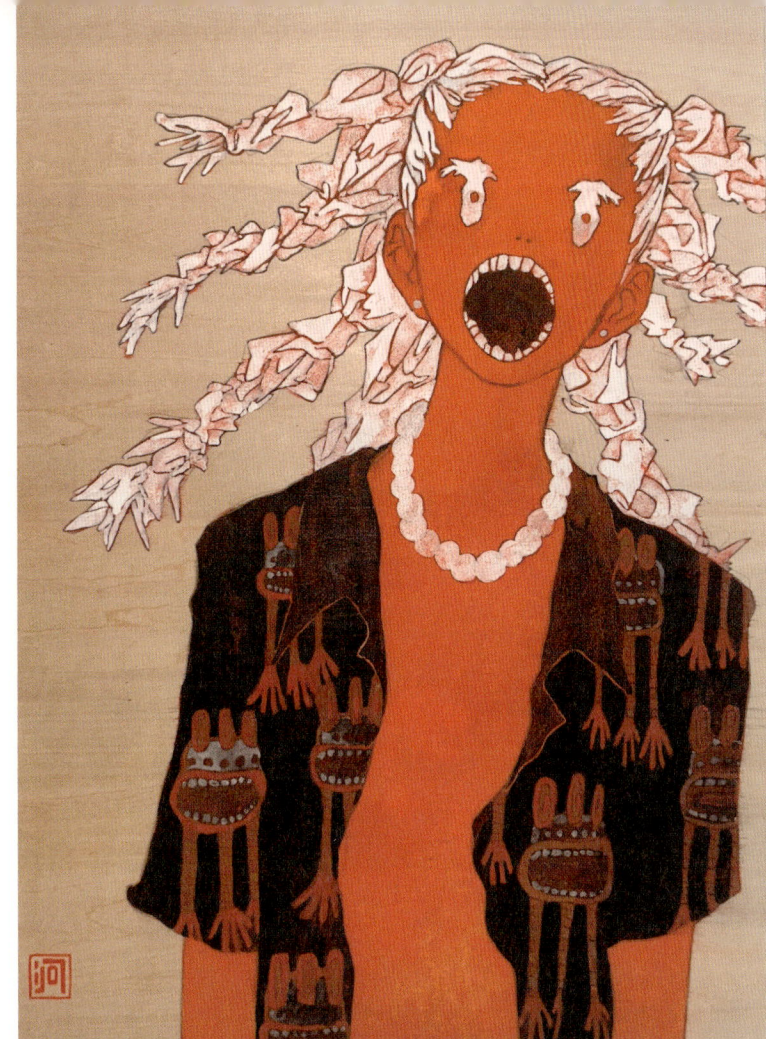

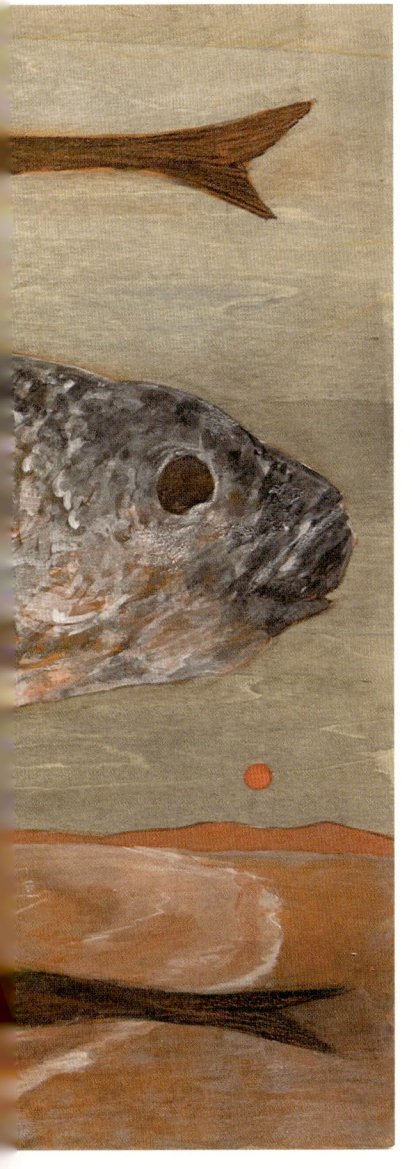

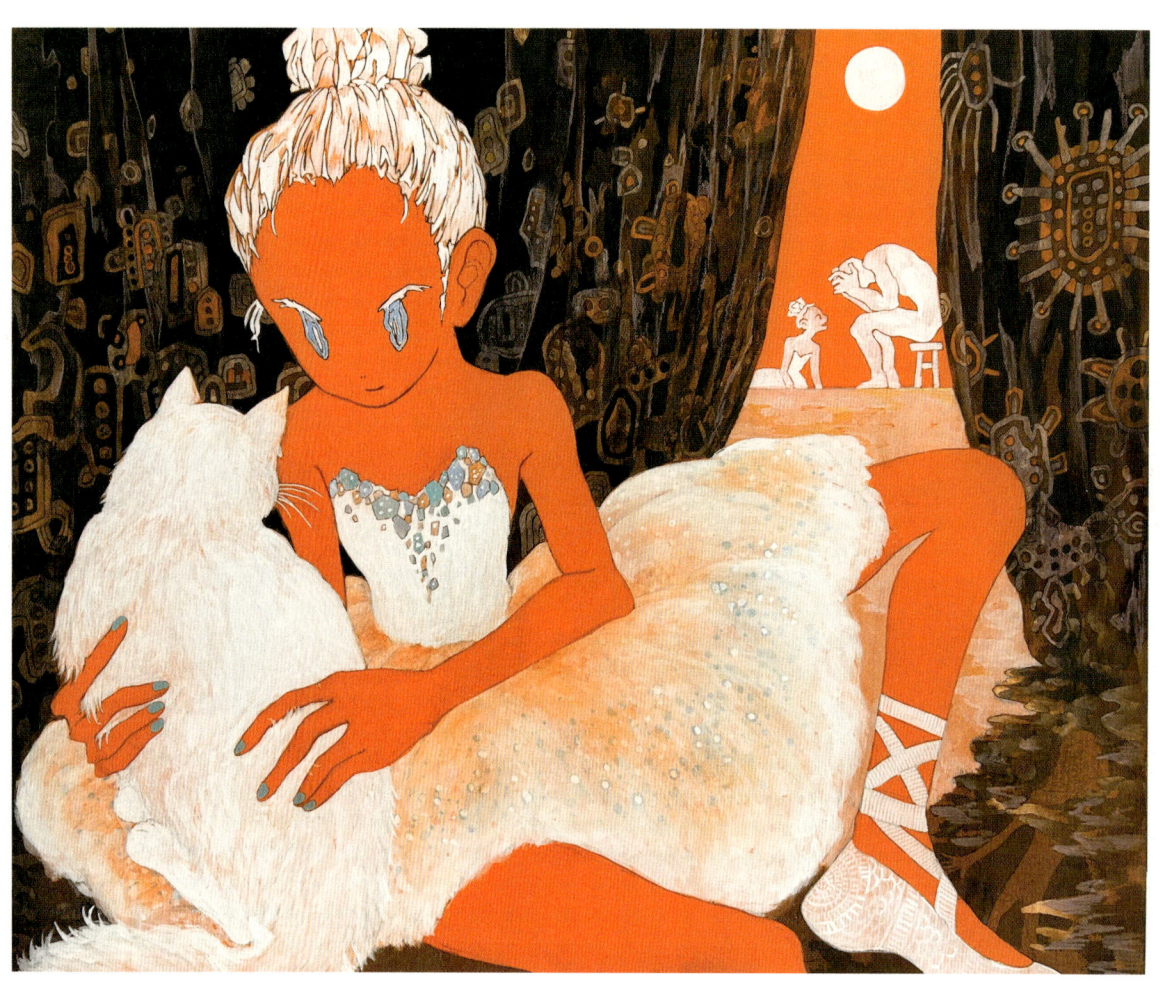

• CURTAIN •

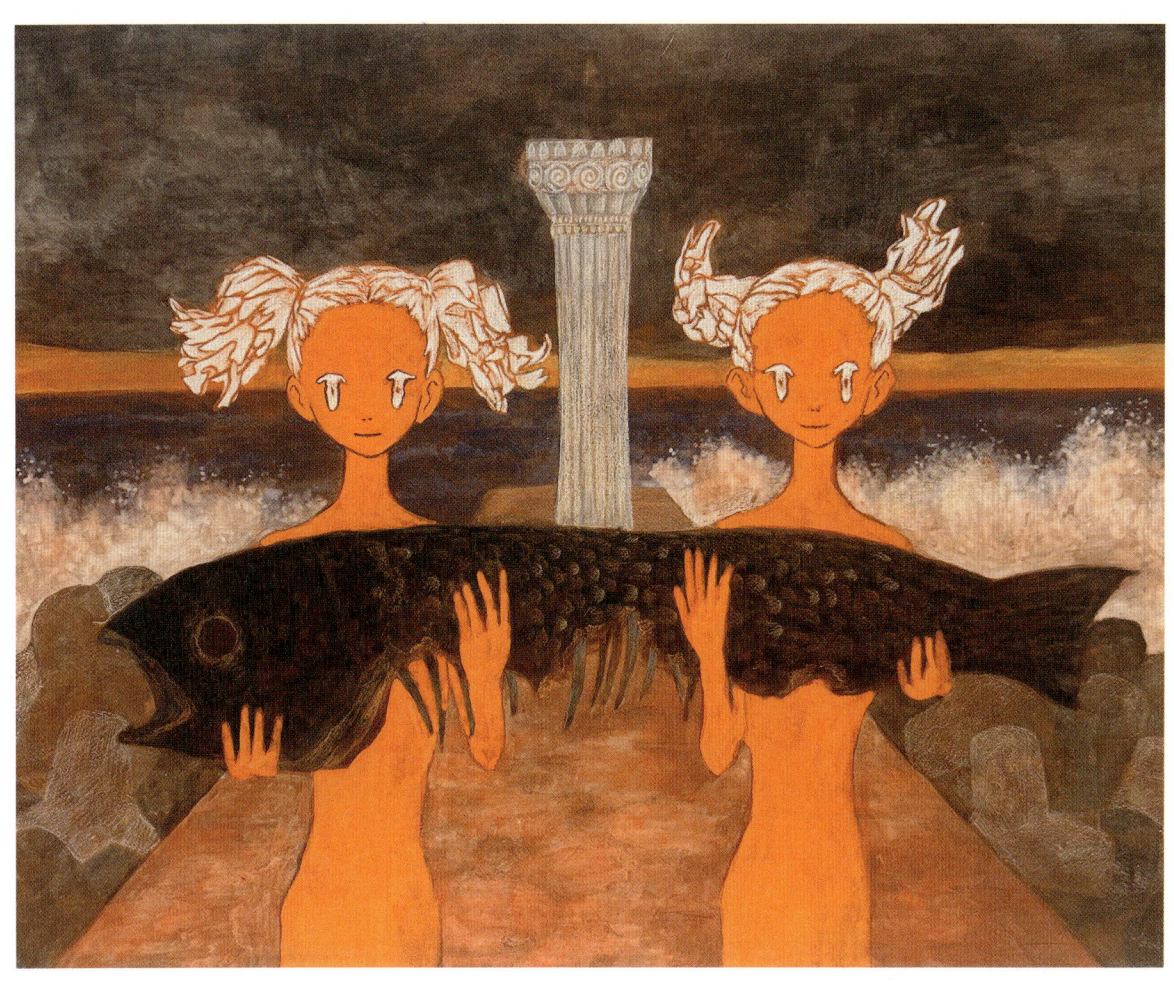

DARK ELEGANCE

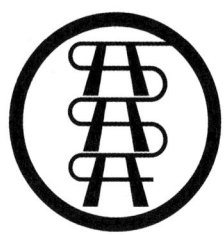

Kotaro Chiba

A freelance illustrator and artist who was born in Japan and lives in Niigata. He started printing his illustrations on T-shirts in around 2007 and later illustrations for books, magazines, and vinyl and creates portraits commissioned from around the world. He is also a graphic designer creating logos, branding, business cards, posters, flyers, etc.

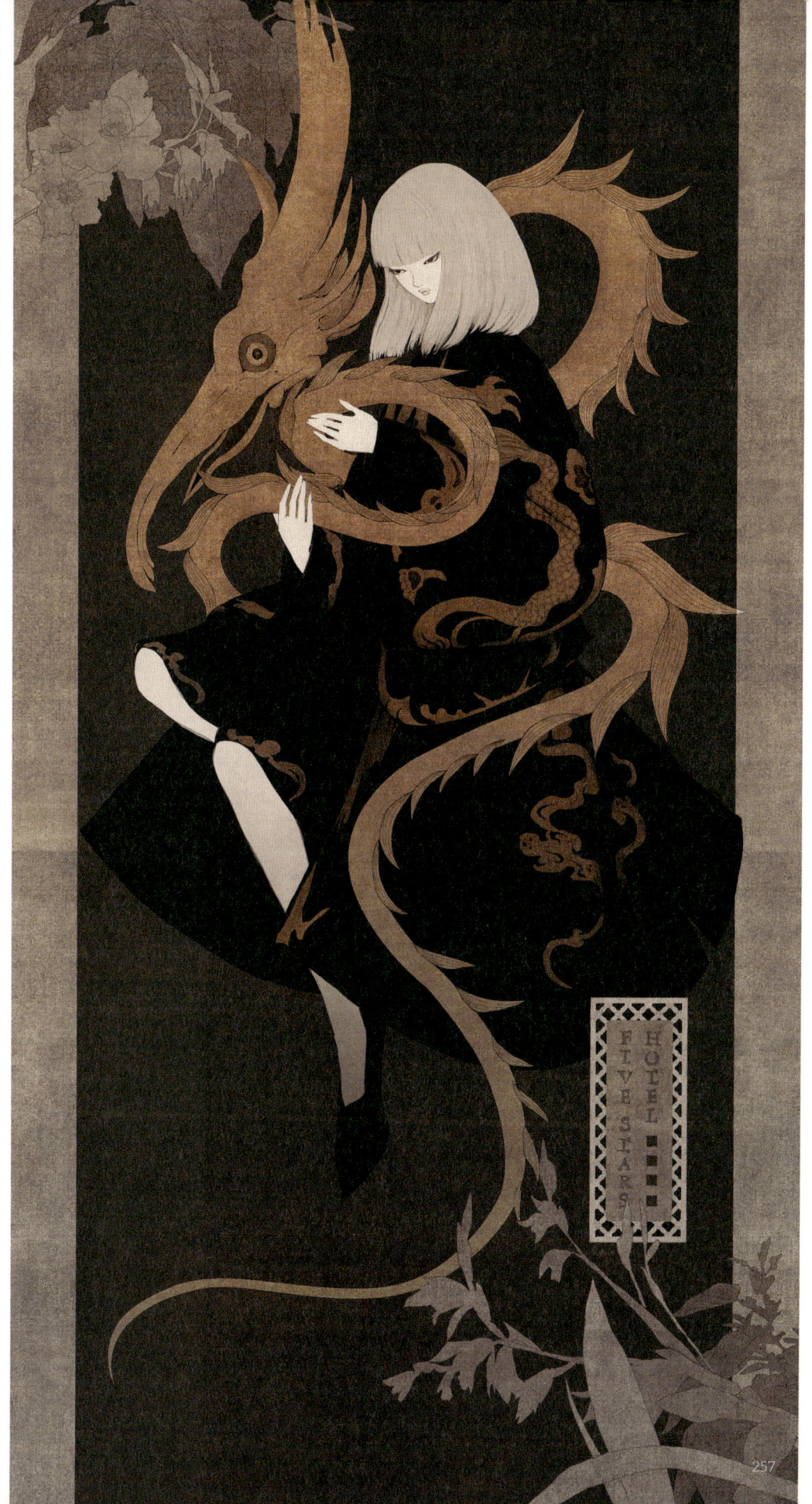

257

Q: How did you begin as a freelance illustrator? Was there any particular inspiration or experience that motivated you?

KC: I used to want to be a designer, but I couldn't get a job at a design agency, because I didn't have the aptitude to be a designer. It all started when I decided to make my own T-shirts and other items to make money.

Q: Your work mostly uses black and white tones. Is this due to personal preference, or are there other reasons behind it? How do you perceive the role of color in art?

KC: It's just personal preference. I understand that viewers will be happy if there are more colors in my work, but a simple color scheme seems to be more in line with my personality. I want to be true to myself. That's the result.

Q: Can you tell us about what influence ukiyo-e has had on you? Which part has the greatest influence on your creation?

KC: All Japanese people live in anime and manga culture. As Japanese people born and raised in Japan, we believe that we cannot escape from the Japanese cultural background. Manga is now a representative culture of Japan, but I don't have much interest in it. For me, the culture of my generation is nothing new or exciting. I'm more interested in ukiyo-e, which has a more classic look than manga. I had no choice but to refer to it as my cultural background.

Q: You often combine girls with elements of animals or skeletal imaginations in your artwork. Where do the inspirations come from? What do they represent in terms of your emotions or meanings?

KC: For me, it is important to choose the material that has the most appeal for the painting. I personally don't like horror movies or zombie movies, so I don't realize it. Simply looking for something cute or beautiful makes me feel uncomfortable with my personality. I

wasn't aware of it until now, but it took me a long time to realize it.

Q: Since 2007, you've been applying your illustrations to various mediums such as T-shirts, books, and magazines. What are the differences in your creative experiences across these mediums? What unique motivations or goals do you have for each medium?

KC: My mission is defined by the requests of my clients. It may have to be unique, or it may have to be in the style of another existing artist. The important thing is that I have to come up with a proposal that goes beyond their draft. It's something I try every time, and it's the most difficult thing to do, but it's also very exciting. Sometimes they accept it, sometimes they reject it. It's a gamble, but something interesting will only happen after this conflict.

Q: How do you deal with your two identities as a graphic designer and illustrator? What similarities or differences do you find in your work involving these two fields?

KC: I think there are no boundaries between these two fields. With the rise of the Internet, all works can now be evaluated in a virtual world, regardless of generation or region. I had assumed that for some time. In other words, I've always wanted to create something that's all about being interesting, and that's what I'm doing.

Q: As a Japanese illustrator, how do you think about Japanese manga and anime culture? How does it influence your creativity?

KC: I was greatly influenced by certain manga and anime works, but in reality, I am not interested in most manga and anime cultures. In fact, my foreign friend knows about it much better than me. However, since I was exposed to manga from an early age, I believe that I cannot escape the influence of manga on me.

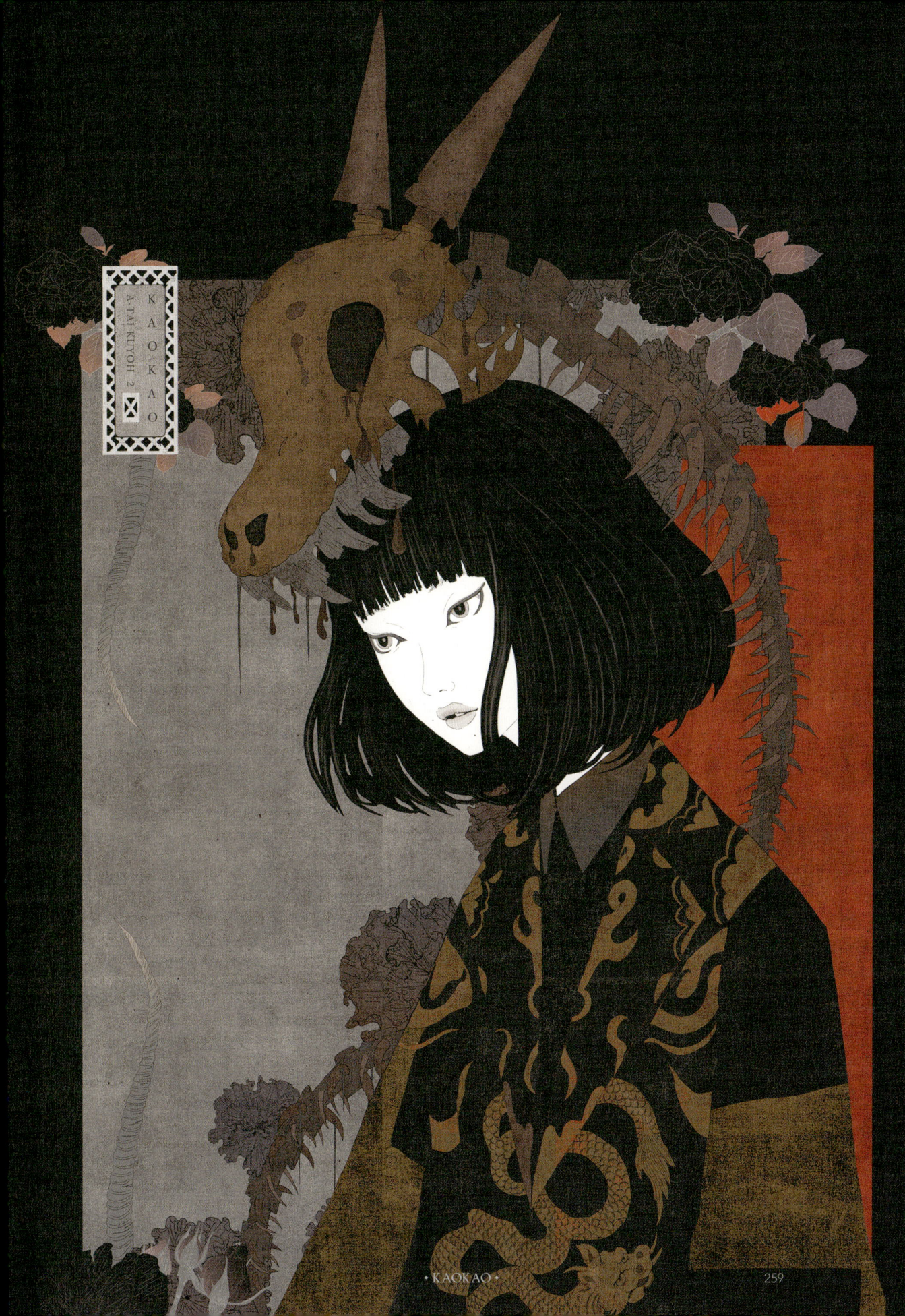

KAOKAO
A-TAÏ KUYÔH 2

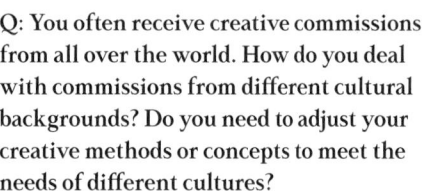

Q: You often receive creative commissions from all over the world. How do you deal with commissions from different cultural backgrounds? Do you need to adjust your creative methods or concepts to meet the needs of different cultures?

KC: I carefully consider what the client wants every time. I also study as much as I can about the cultural background. But I mostly don't have time to study it, so I try my best to know about it as much as possible. Also, the style required depends on the country. Clients may not fully understand the need for subtle changes in art style depending on culture. I will have to be flexible about it and make suggestions.

Q: What do you think is the most important thing for an artist?

KC: Stay healthy both physically and mentally. And learn how to be lazy in the work.

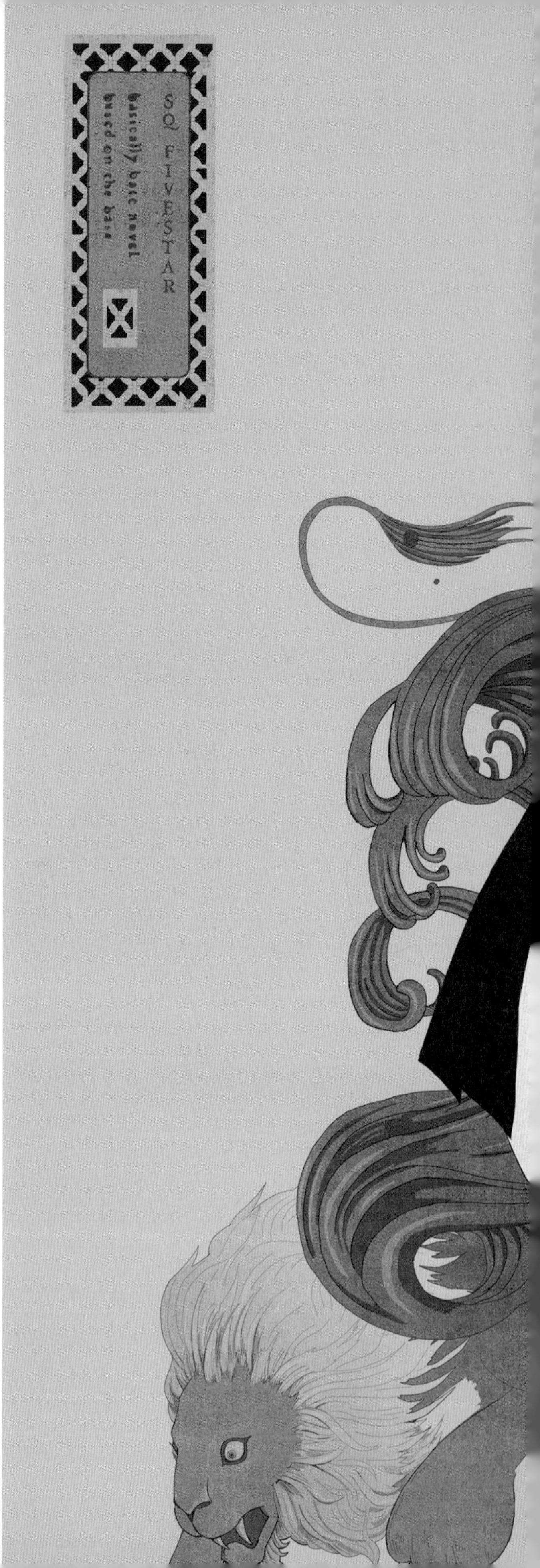

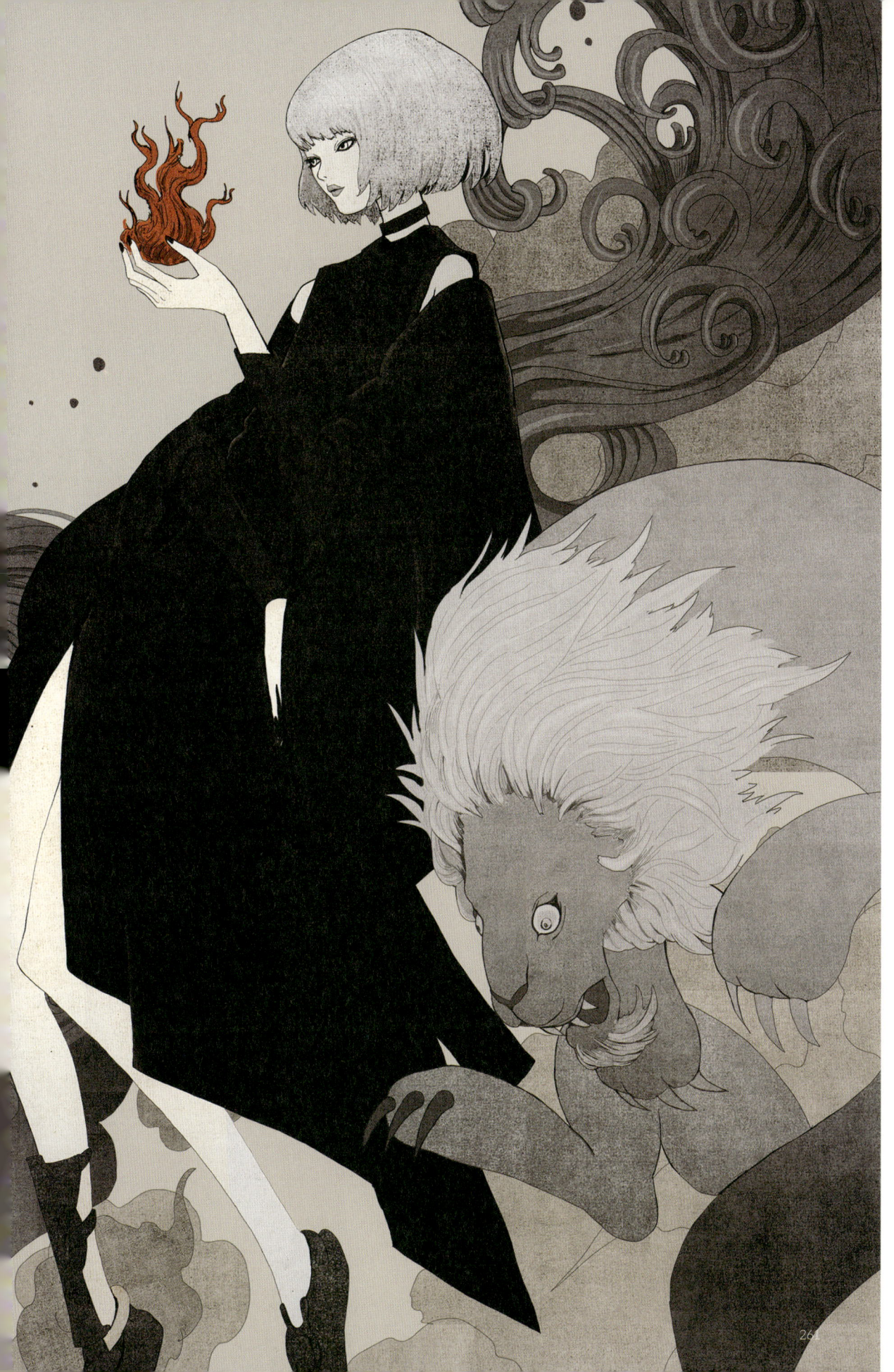

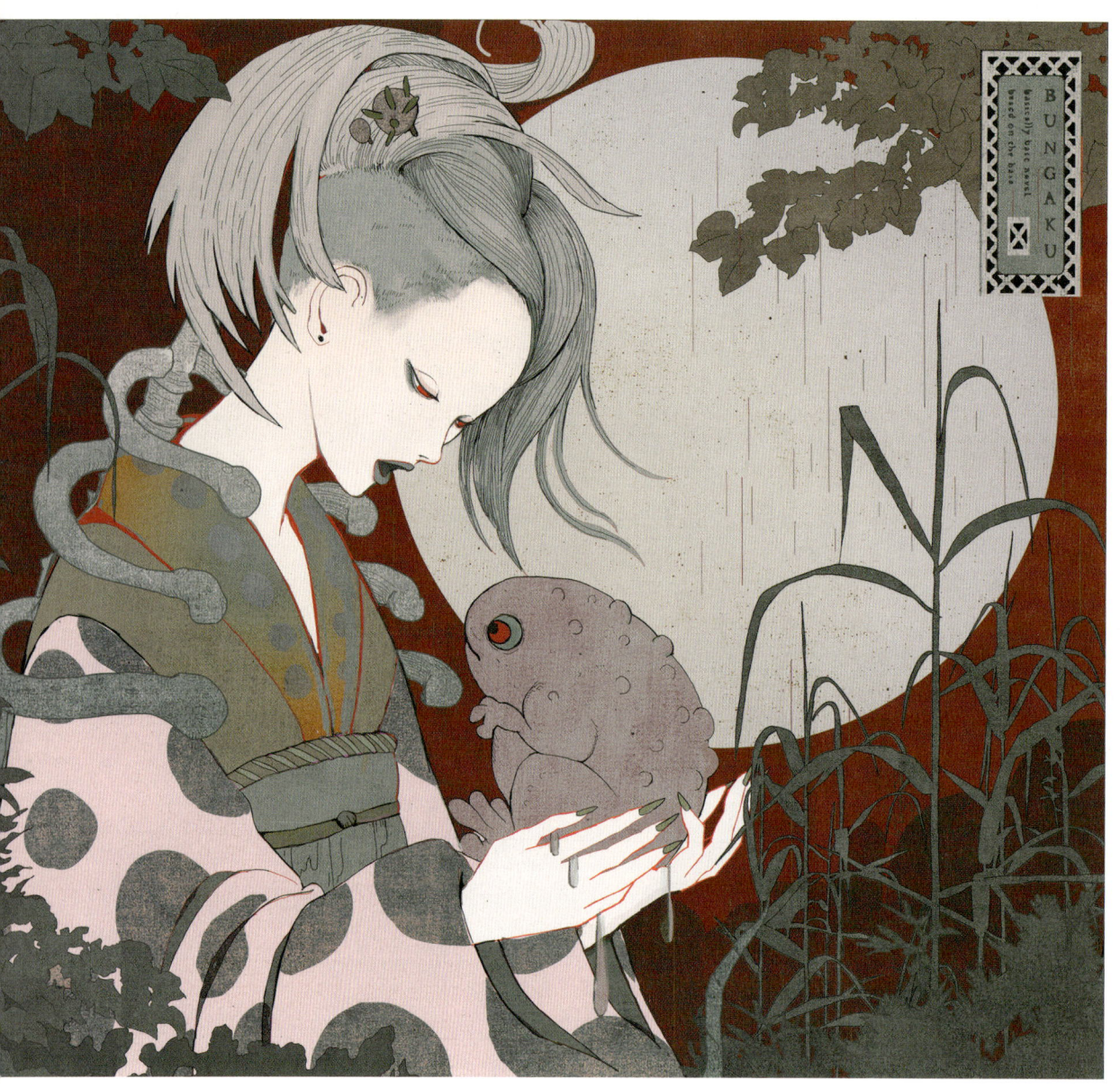

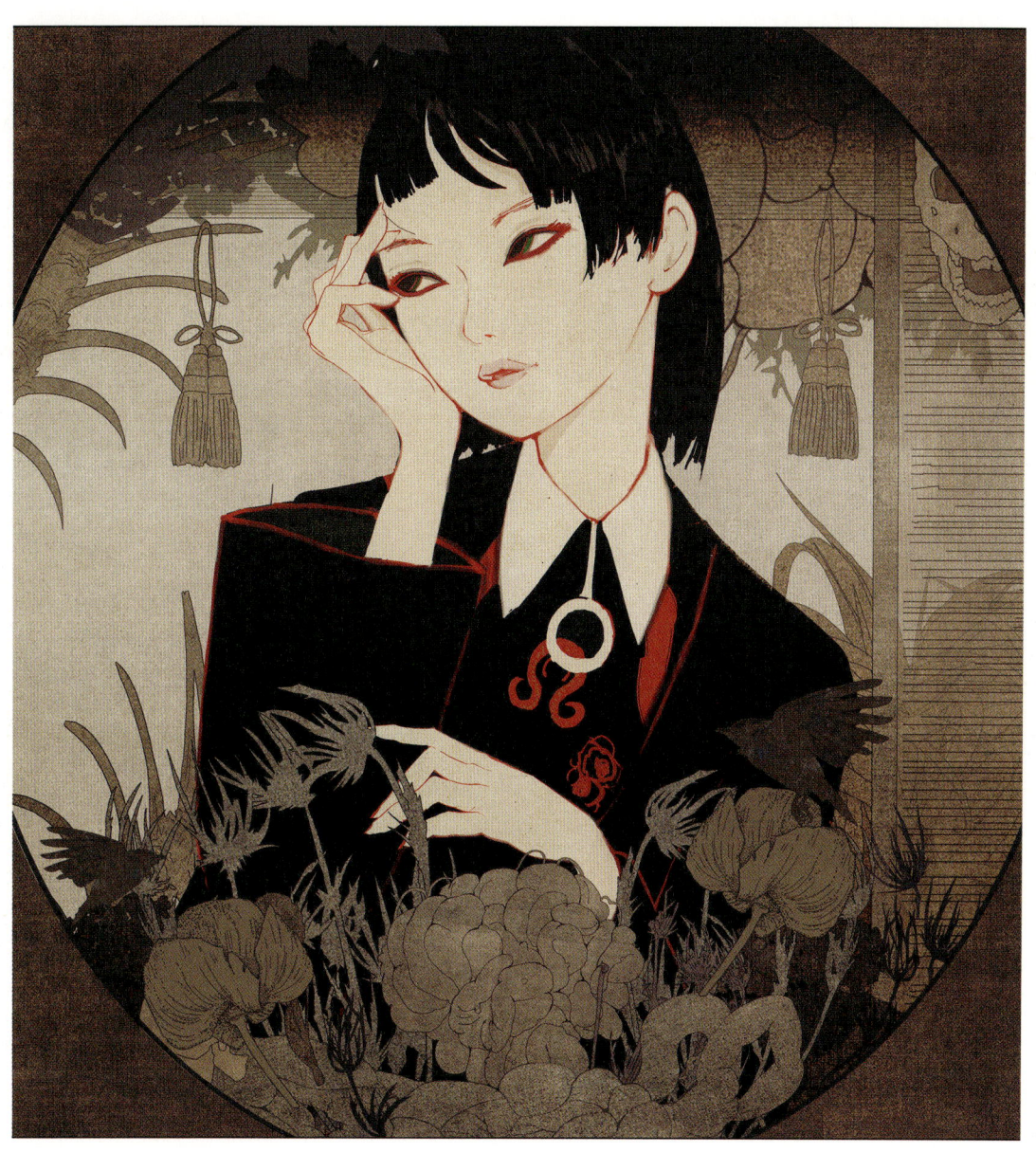

" *A simple color scheme seems to be more in line with my personality. I want to be true to myself.* "

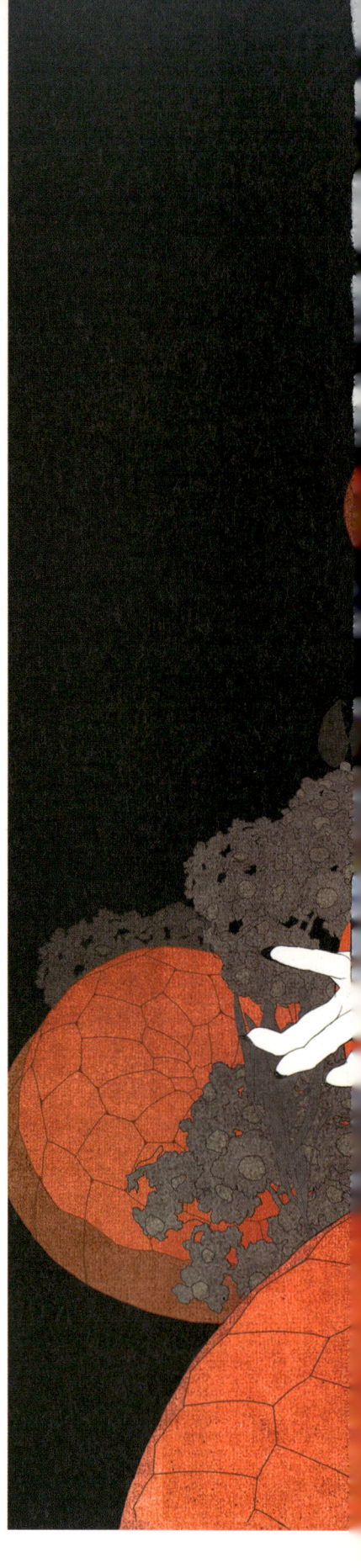

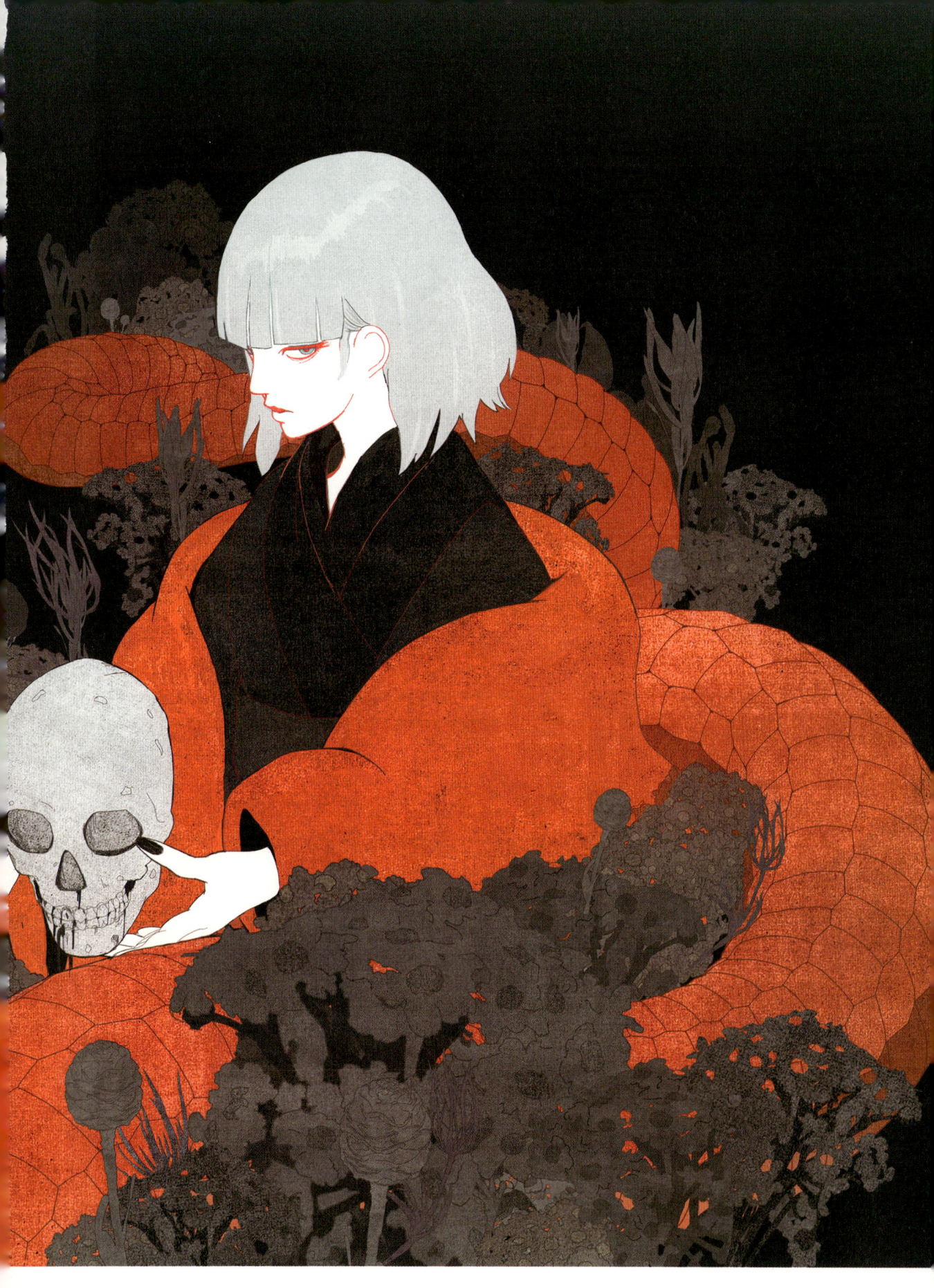

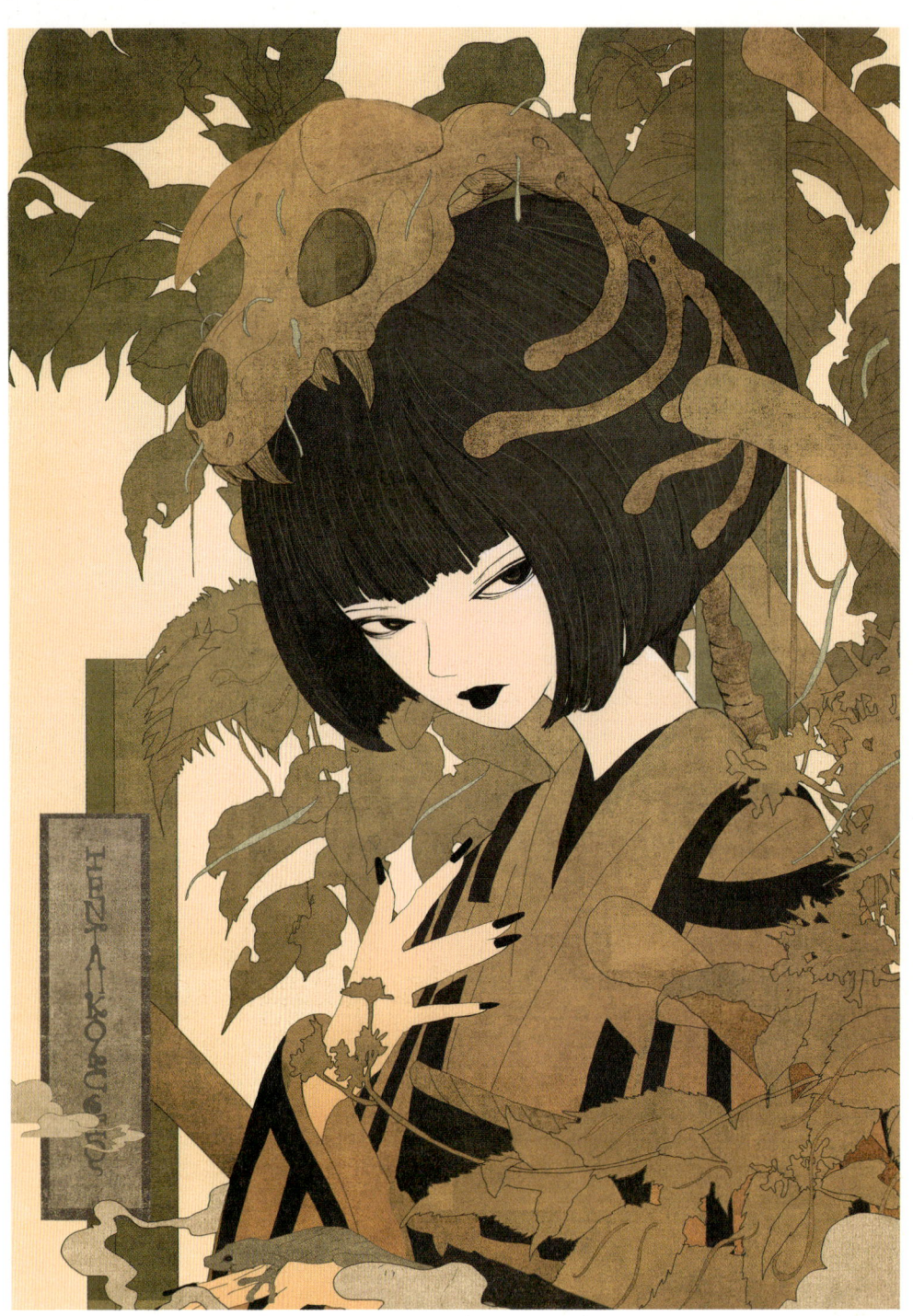

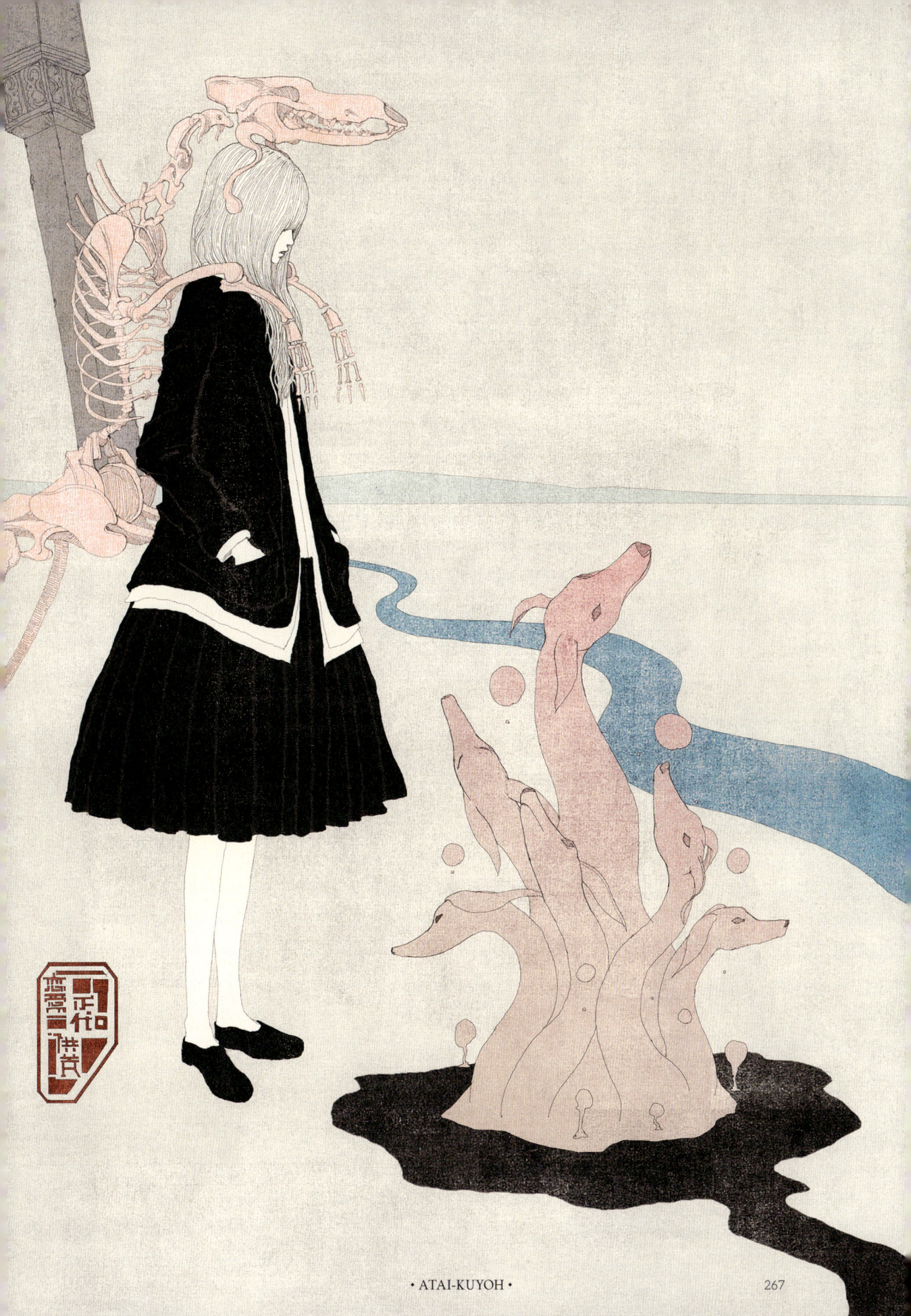

THE DARK
INTERPRETATION

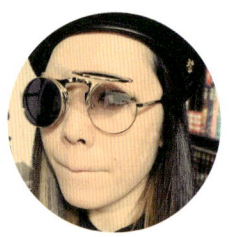

C7 (Shiina)

C7 is an artist who retrieves and combines precious fragments
accumulated in her subconscious, using primarily lines to
seamlessly blend them into a unified whole.

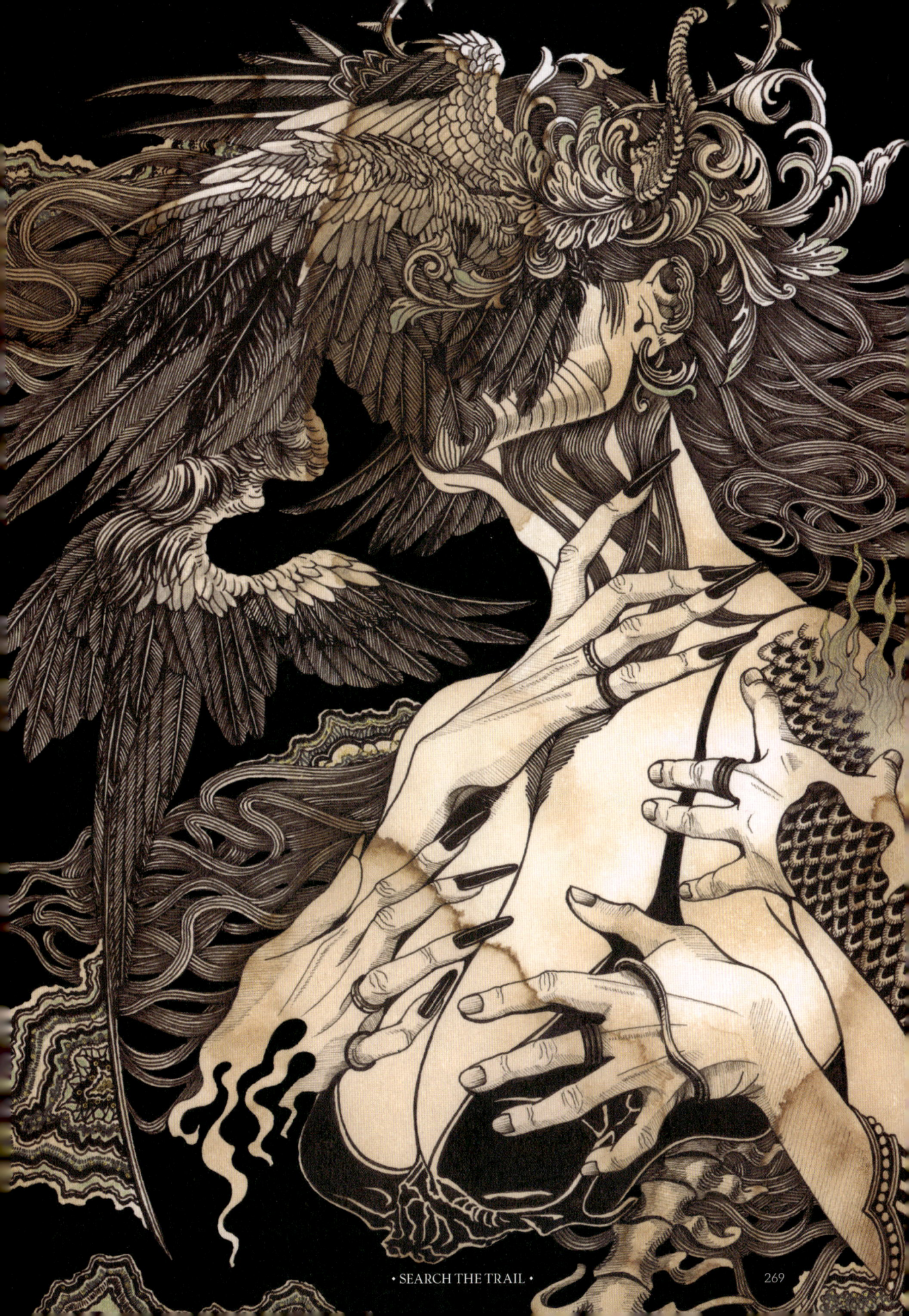

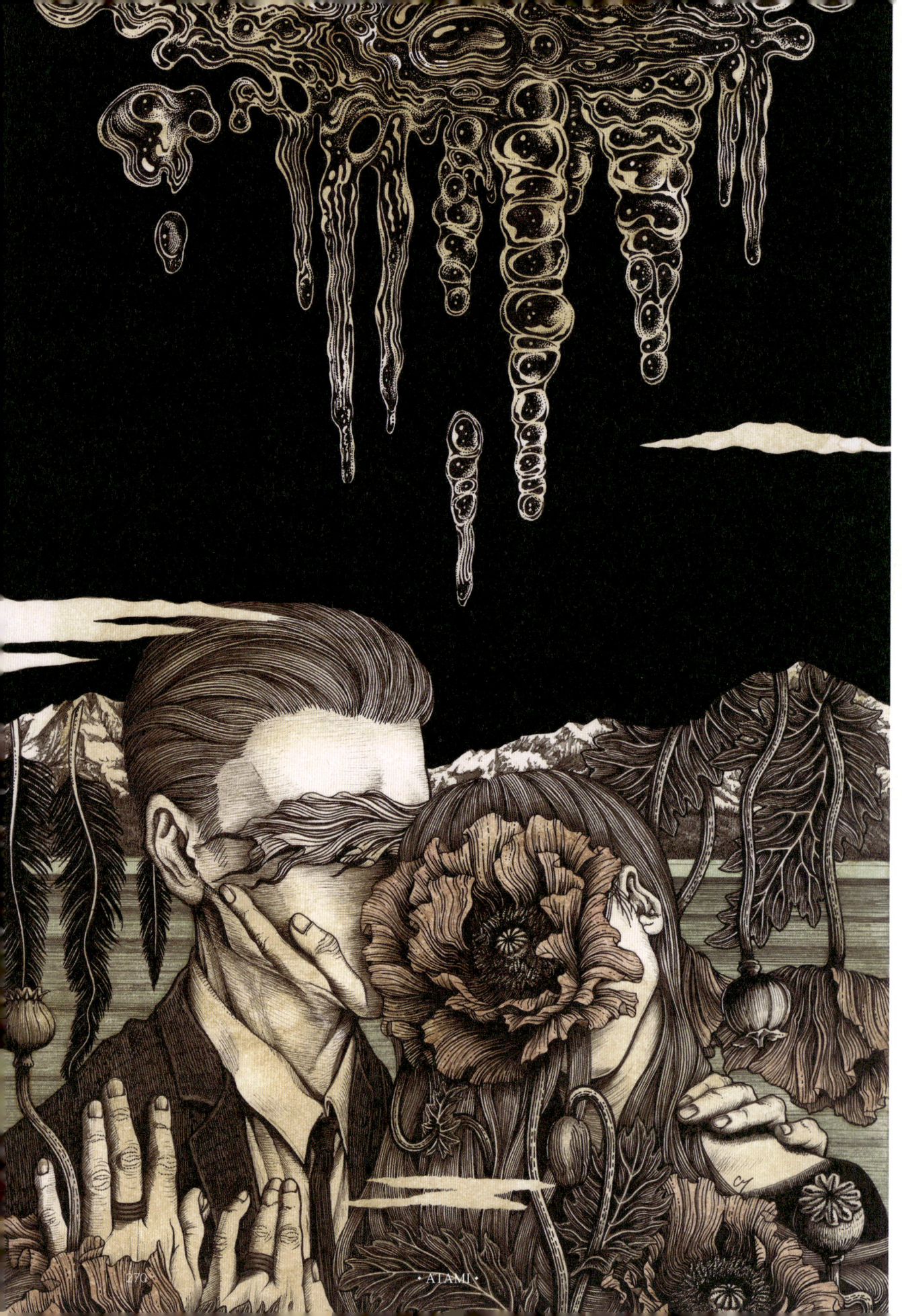

· ATAMI ·

Q: Can you share a little bit about your creative process? Are you self-taught, or did you go to art school? What inspired you to become an artist?

C7: I graduated from Tokyo Designer Academy's Artist Department, majoring in Illustration.

After that, I worked as a print-related designer for a few companies. But then I was invited by a friend from my school days to start exhibiting in a rented gallery, and from there I began to receive more invitations from galleries to plan exhibitions and take part in art fairs overseas.

Q: You use ink and coffee as creative media in your works, which give the works a unique texture, especially the coffee staining, which creates a retro and natural atmosphere. Meanwhile, your works are relatively restrained in the use of colors, and bright colors are relatively rare. Can you share how you choose these creative media? And in the creative process, do you have some specific habits or preferences to achieve these unique effects?

C7: I use the same coffee that I normally drink. Because I want to feel closer to my work. As for colors, I value hues that make me feel at peace. I realized that the green accent color was the same as the color of a painting that had been hanging at the entrance of my parents' house since before I was born.

Q: What are the themes of your works? In the creative process, do you use painting to explore or solve your inner emotions and problems? Do these works carry your unique emotional expression?

C7: The general themes are dreams and death. I am barely able to survive by thinking about and protecting myself and those closest to me. I want to capture the essence of anxiety by facing death in advance, which comes to everyone, and delving into its absolute fear.

I combine fragments of my everyday unconscious and subconscious to amplify the images, and by diving deep within myself, I draw to understand something that influences the outside world.

Q: How do you view the relationship between your works and the audience? Nowadays, many artists tend to leave the right of interpretation of their works entirely to the audience, believing that the audience's interpretation is also an indispensable part of the work. How do you understand this view? In your creation, is the audience's interpretation equally important to you?

C7: The truth is that only I know, and no one else can invade it; sometimes I put secrets into my paintings that I don't want to share with anyone, so I hope people will interpret them however they like. Because of this, my works belong only to me, and at the same time, they belong only to that person. Being able to hear free interpretations also allows me to enjoy getting in touch with the viewers' thoughts through my works.

Q: How do you stay inspired? Are there any artists or art movements that have deeply influenced you?

C7: I keep a record of my dreams. I also find it fascinating to observe how we misperceive the shapes of things when our consciousness is unclear due to fatigue or drowsiness. I love all kinds of music and movies, and I grew up reading horror manga from a young age. I think I've been influenced by surrealism.

Q: How do you usually promote your works? How do social media or exhibitions help you promote your works?

C7: Since the schedule of exhibitions and art fairs is set throughout the year, I create works while considering the size and number of pieces according to the scale.

The number of visitors to my exhibitions has increased thanks to the use of social media.

When people come to my exhibitions after finding me online, I think it's great that they can sense that I'm creating paintings that go beyond just looking at pictures.

Q: As an established artist, what advice would you give to those who are just starting in art?

C7: Although you may not feel like you have achieved success, I hope you will not be swayed by other people's criticism and will remain true to all of your irresistible desires.

Q: What are your expectations and goals for the future? What new breakthroughs or explorations do you hope to achieve in your artistic journey?

C7: I would like to think more smoothly and freely about the connections between objects, thoughts, and atmospheres.

I am also interested in when people's emotions are stirred, so I would like to explore human psychology and incorporate it into my work.

I believe there are still more art materials and textures that suit my senses and line drawings, so I will continue to experiment and explore.

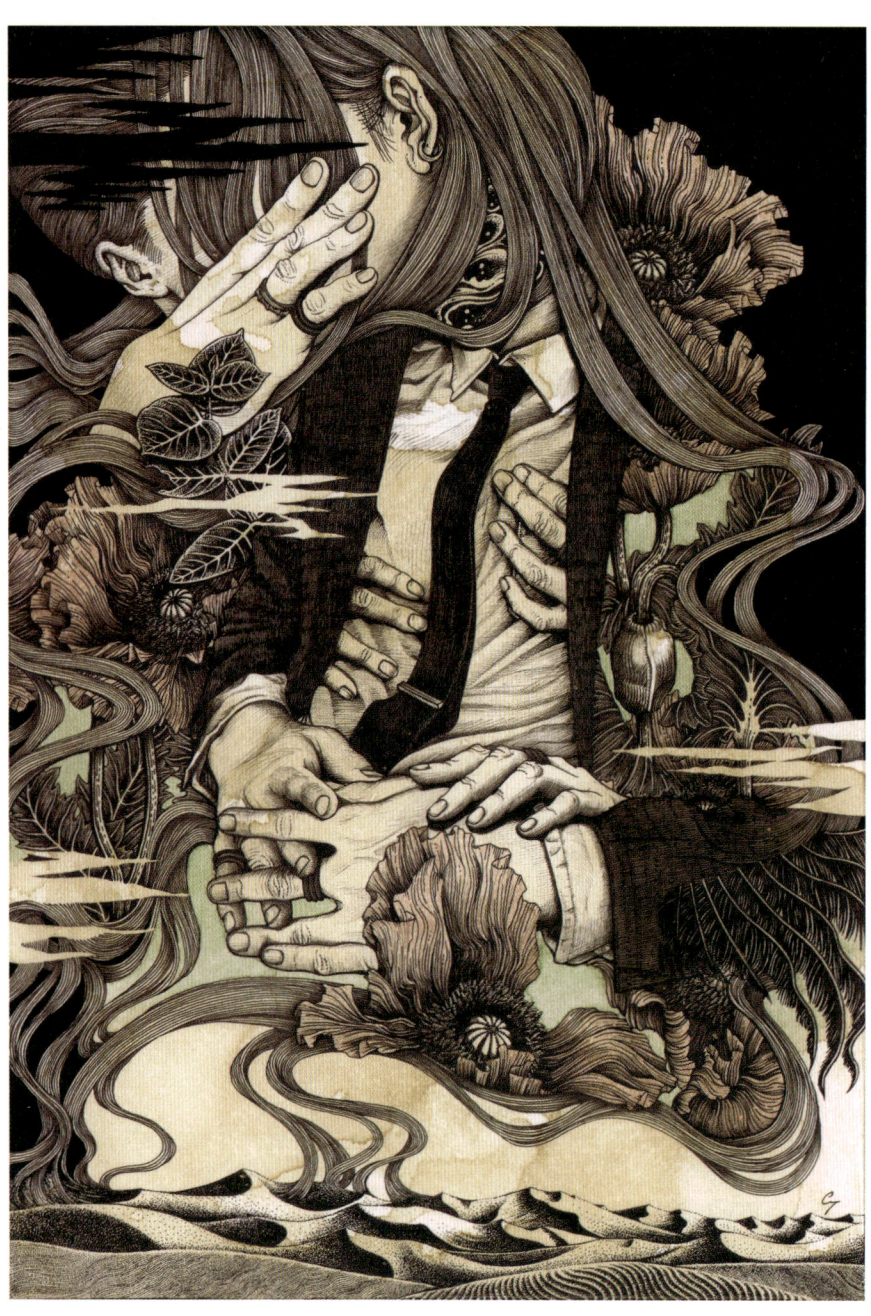

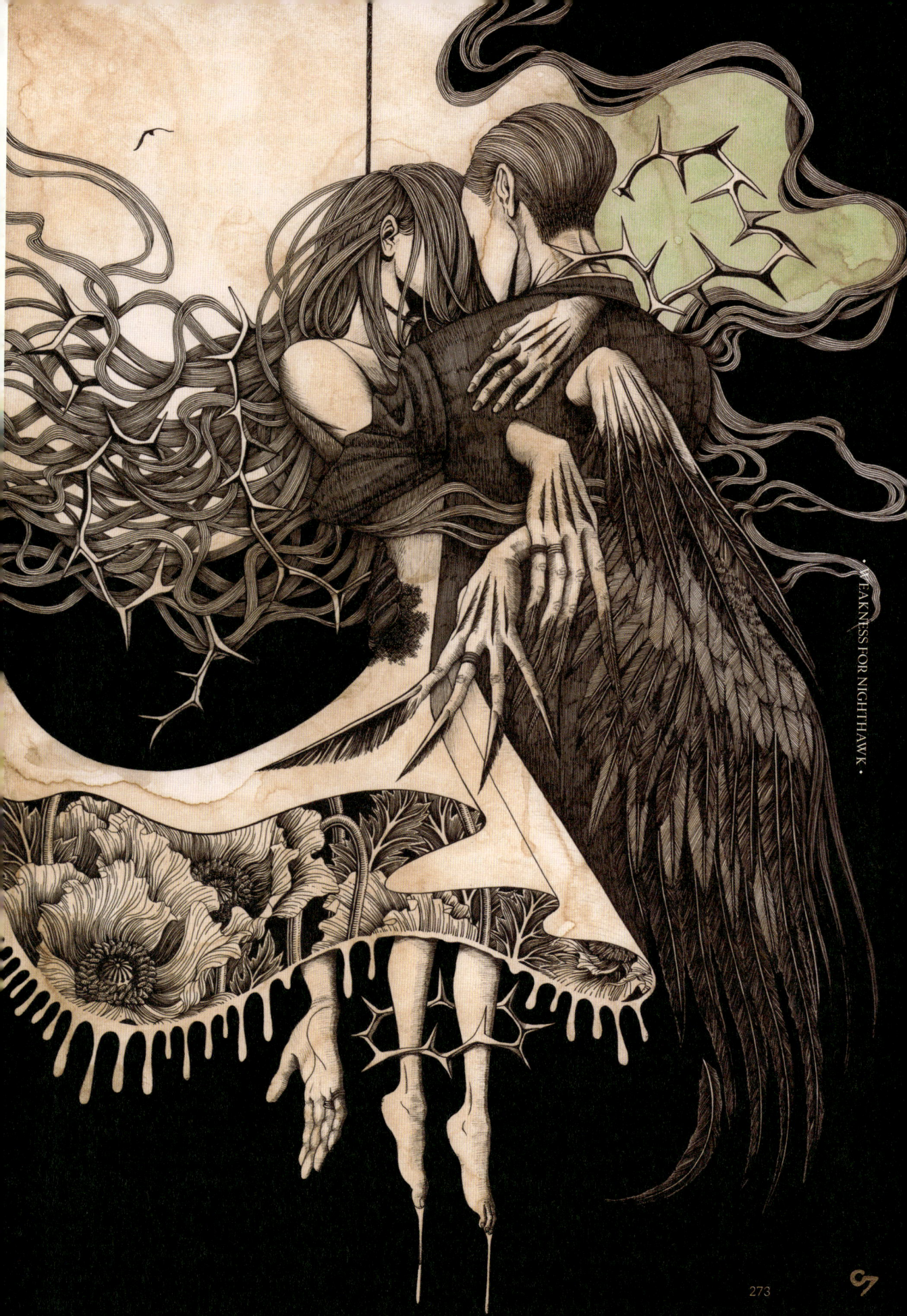

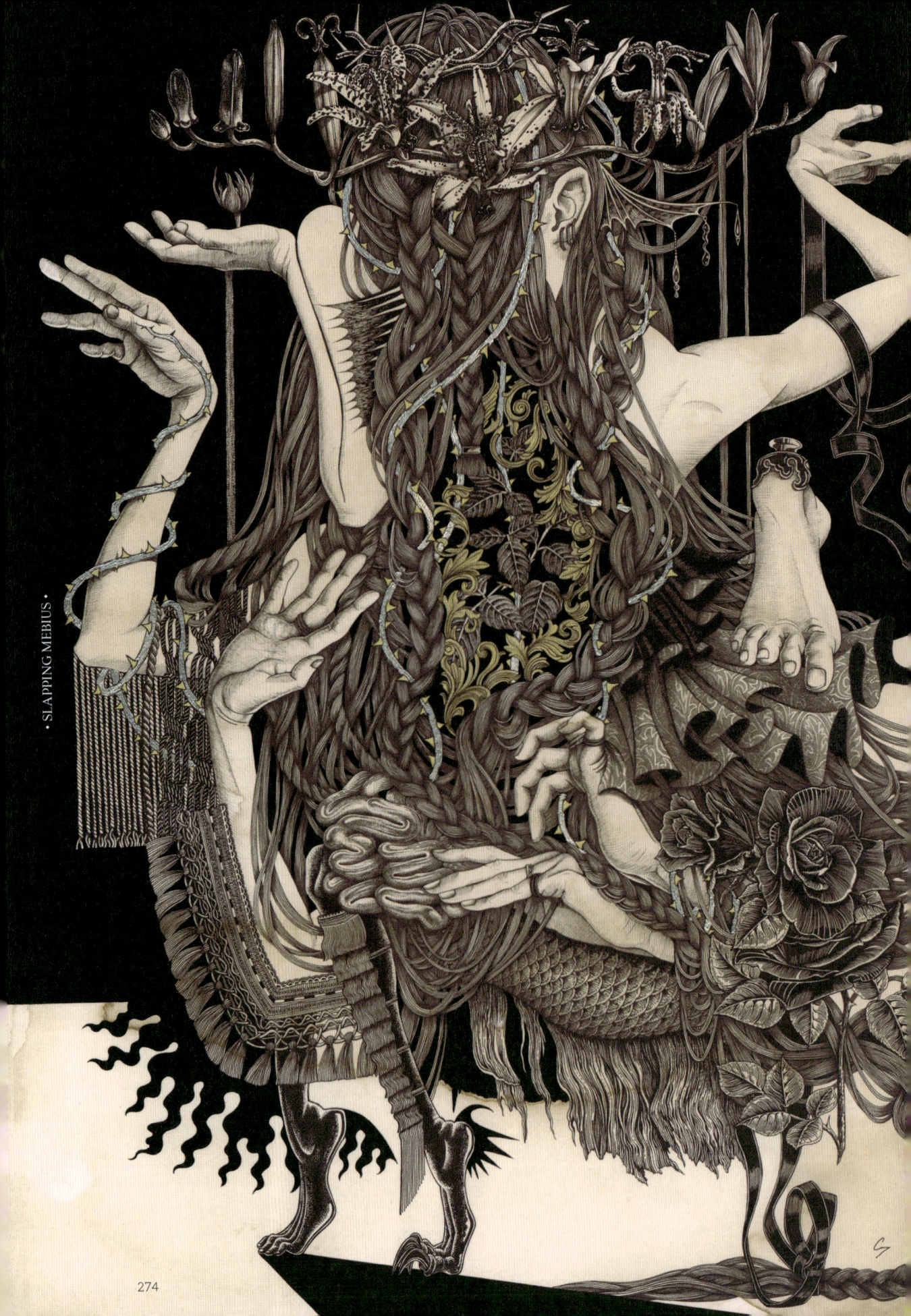

" *I combine fragments of my everyday unconscious and subconscious to amplify the images, and by diving deep within myself, I draw to understand something that influences the outside world.* "

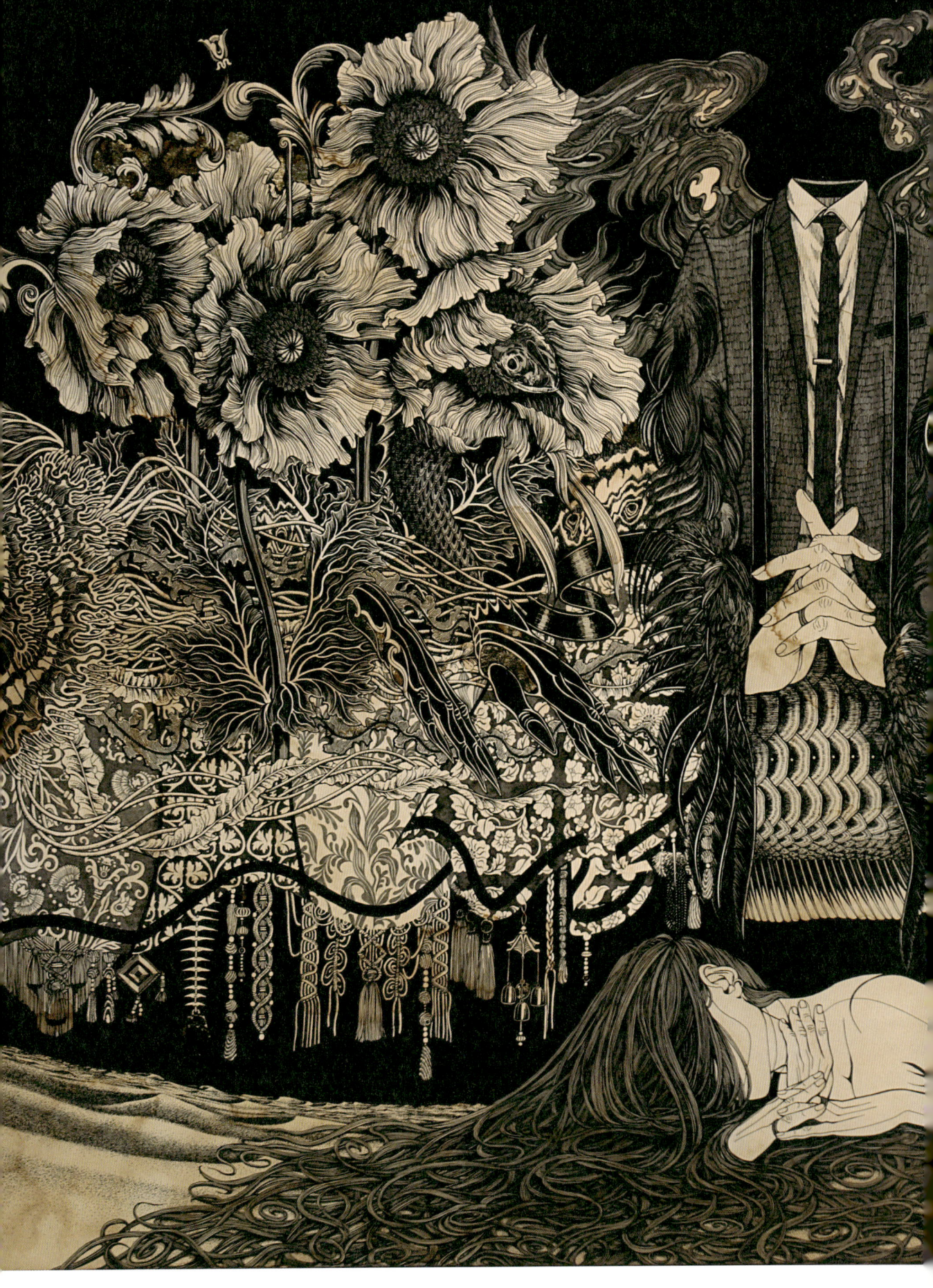

• BETWEEN THE SHEETS •

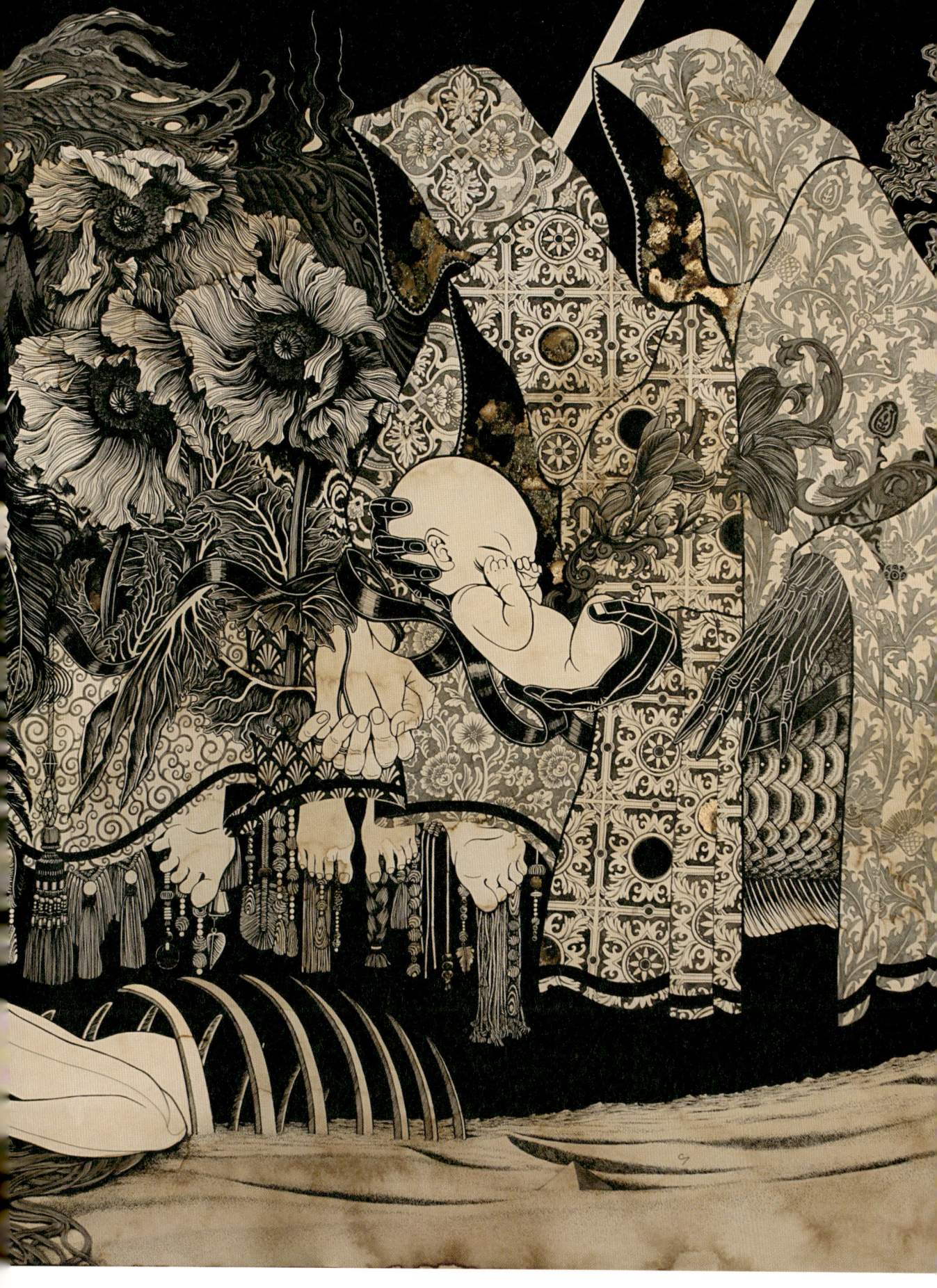

THE FEAST

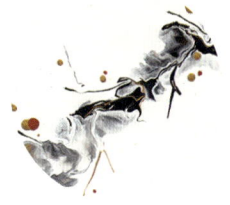

Surie

As a Japanese illustrator, she creates artwork
for book covers and music videos. Her works
are created in a flat, Japanese style of painting.

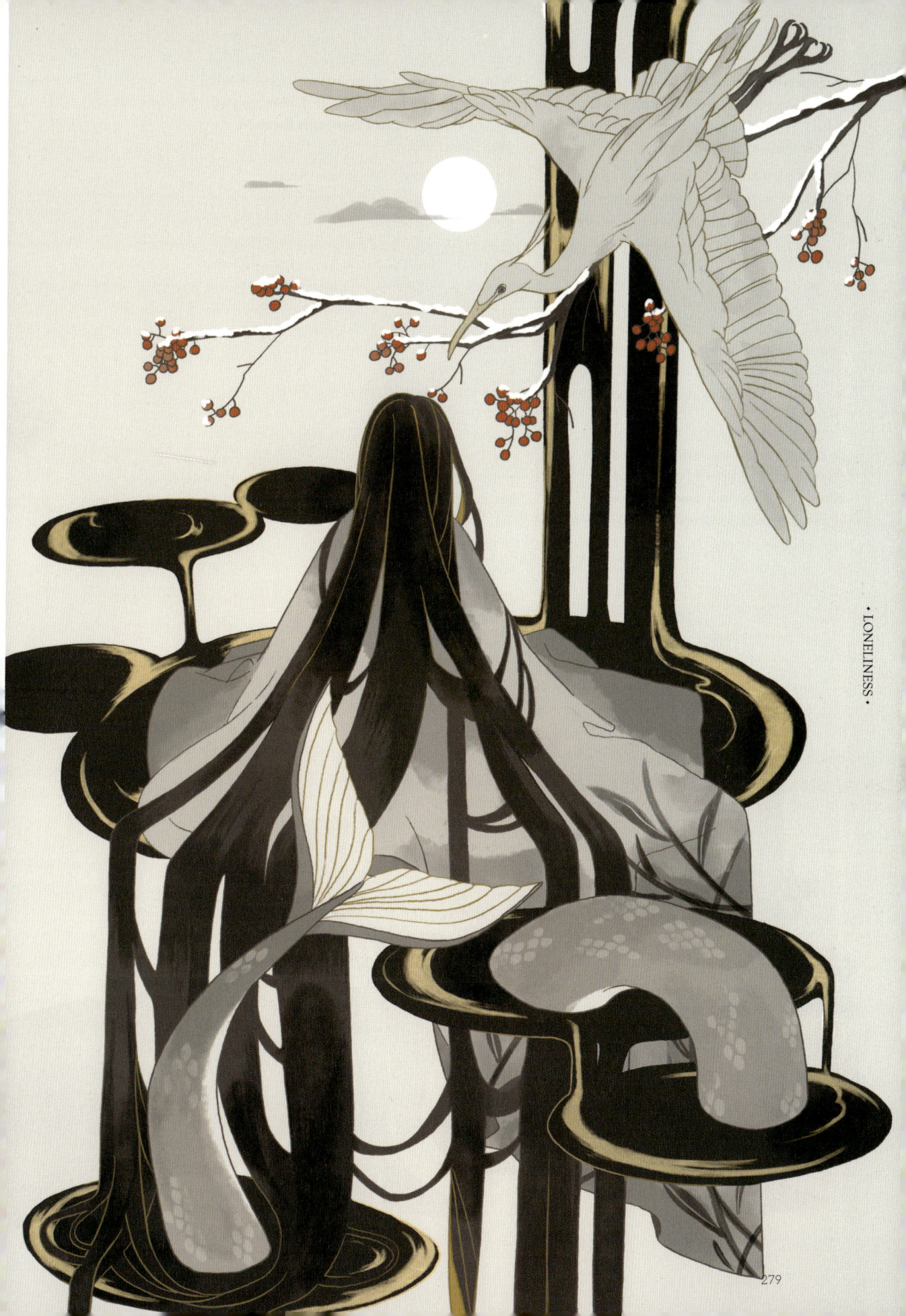

· LONELINESS ·

279

Q: **Your works cover book covers and music video illustrations, and they showcase a unique Japanese painting style. Where does your inspiration come from?**

S: My inspirations mainly come from music, books, and music videos. When I paint the illustration for work, I refer to the music, books, and music videos that are the basis of the client's request. But those are only part of my source of inspiration. I think all of the things I saw in my life are provisions of my art, such as flowers blooming in the street, winds blowing season by season, different sky colors time by time, and so many scenes. From when I got my senses to now, some things I'm feeling make my artwork.

Q: **Many of your works feature themes related to emotions. For example, the loneliness of the mermaid in *Loneliness* (P279), the sorrow of waiting in *Night of**

Waiting **(P284), and the jealousy expressed in *Chrysanthemum Feast* (P286). How do you convey these complex emotions through your illustrations?**

S: Mainly, I convey complex emotions by avoiding painting the whole face of the characters. In Loneliness, the mermaid is looking back. In *Night of Waiting* and *Chrysanthemum Feast* hair is partially covering the faces of the characters. I think people have a disposition to imagine the part of the unseen. So when I paint complex emotions, I do not paint the whole face. I constitute illustrations to be mysterious. And I convey complex emotions as another method by taking in motifs in illustrations. That's remarkable in *Chrysanthemum Feast*. Meanwhile, I painted a *hannya* (a mask used in a traditional Japanese Noh theater) and blue fire of the candle she holds. Like those, I sometimes put in motifs to be hints.

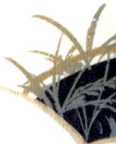

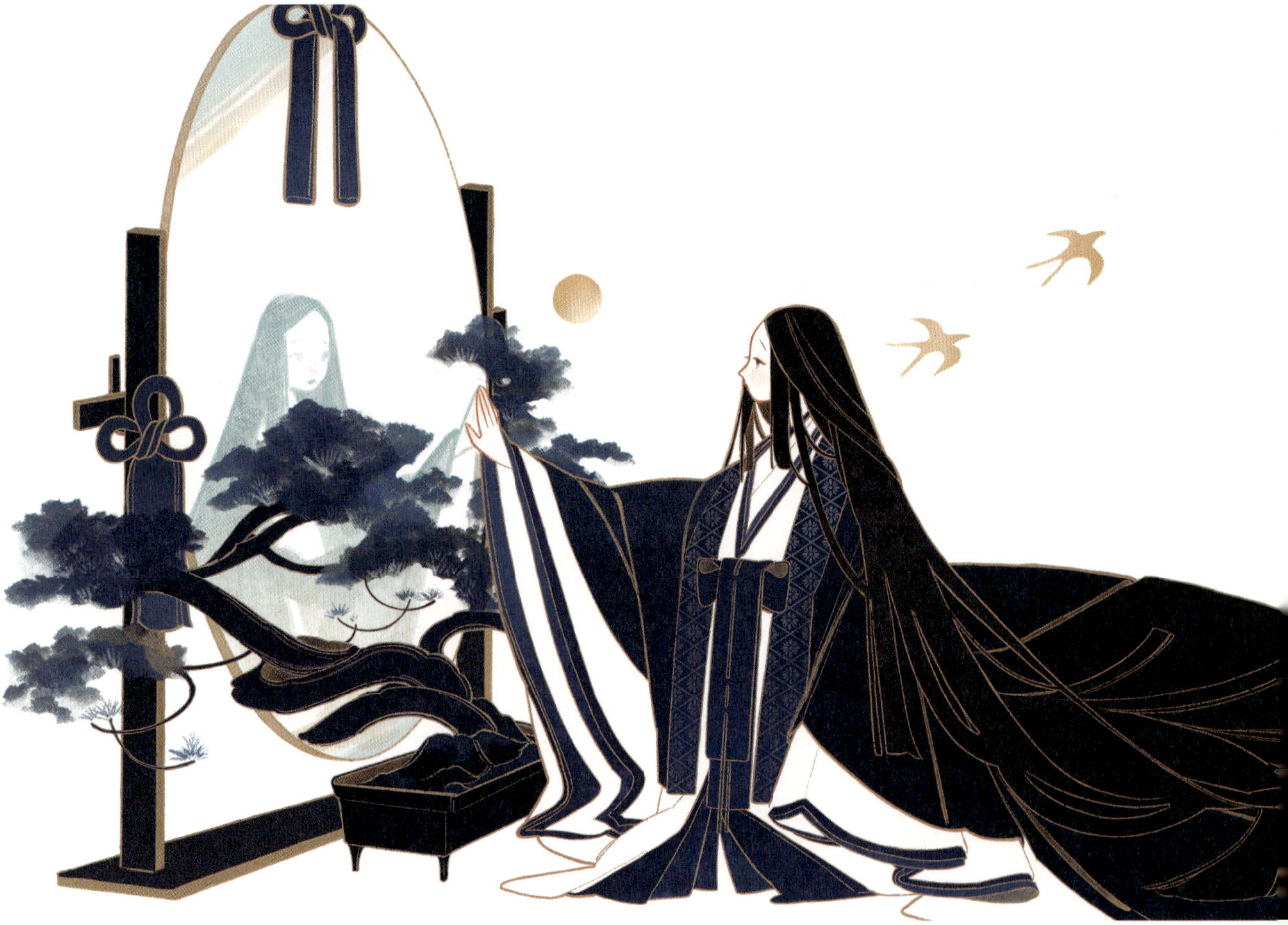

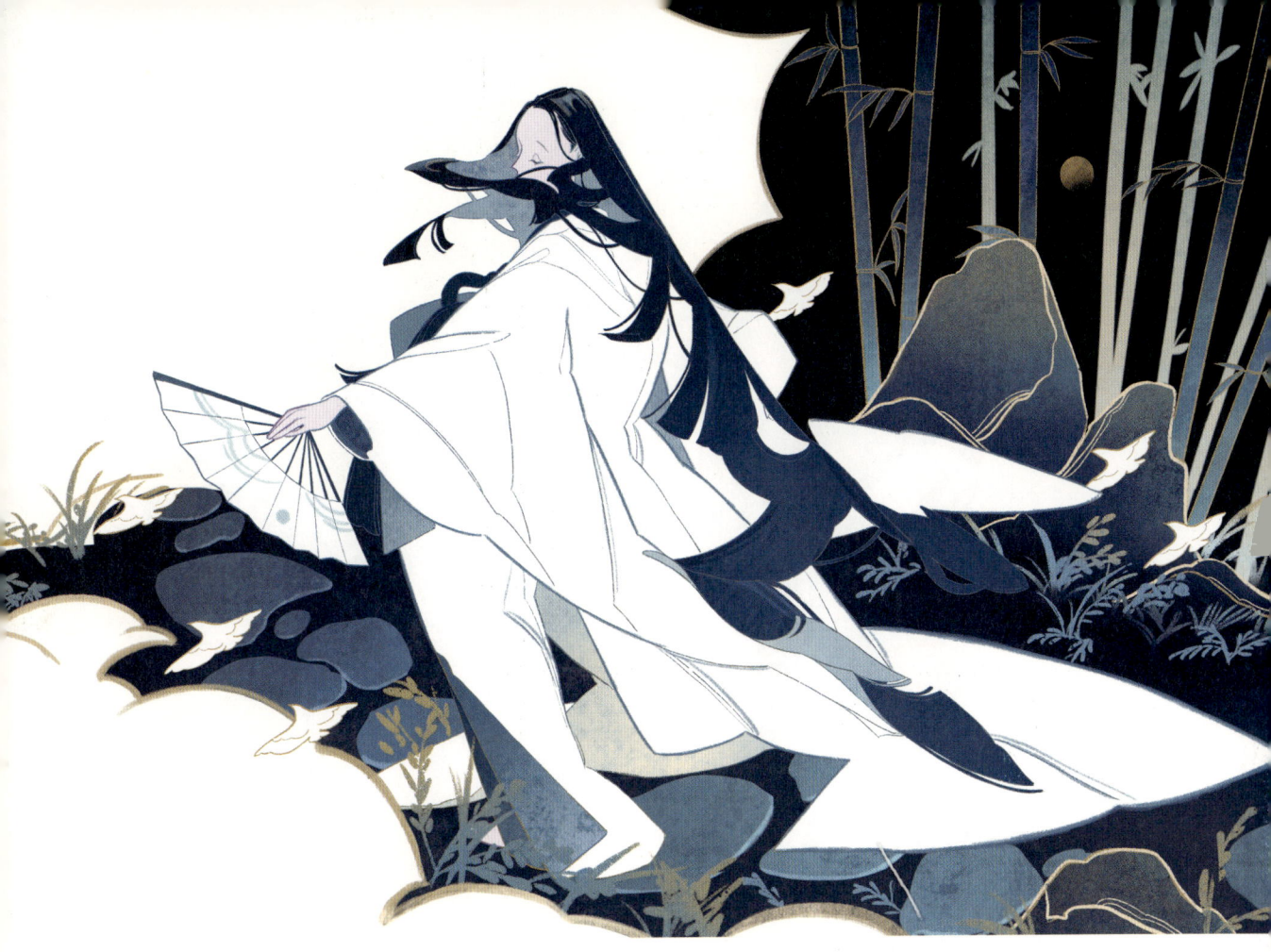

Q: You use software including Procreate, Photoshop, and Illustrator. Can you share your experiences using these digital drawing tools? What do you think are the differences between digital drawing tools and traditional drawing? Have you considered trying traditional hand drawing?

S: When I was a beginner, I used paper and pen. But as I wanted to draw more and more, I found those tools not convenient. The digital drawing tools are compact and easy to carry. So I can draw anywhere any time. Those tools make it easy to perform color adjustments and overlap the textures. I think even in the case of clients' requests, the digital drawing tools are very convenient. For those reasons, digital drawing tools can offer many benefits to creators. But through continued use of digital drawing tools, I've come to realize that traditional tools are more than just inconvenient. Those tools give me some feeling. That is the friction of the paper, the feel of the hand, the texture of the paper, the drawing feeling of the pen, etc. Those feelings can't be obtained with digital painting tools. So sometimes, I want to paint with traditional tools.

Q: How do you think being active on social media helps your work spread and gain influence? What role do these platforms play in your artistic practice?

S: I think social media has expanded my world. Because of that, I have a lot of companies and fans. Thanks to their wider advertising of my art, I can meet clients who need me. And, those social platforms make me more creative. Because I can see art by so many creators there. There are illustrations, photos,

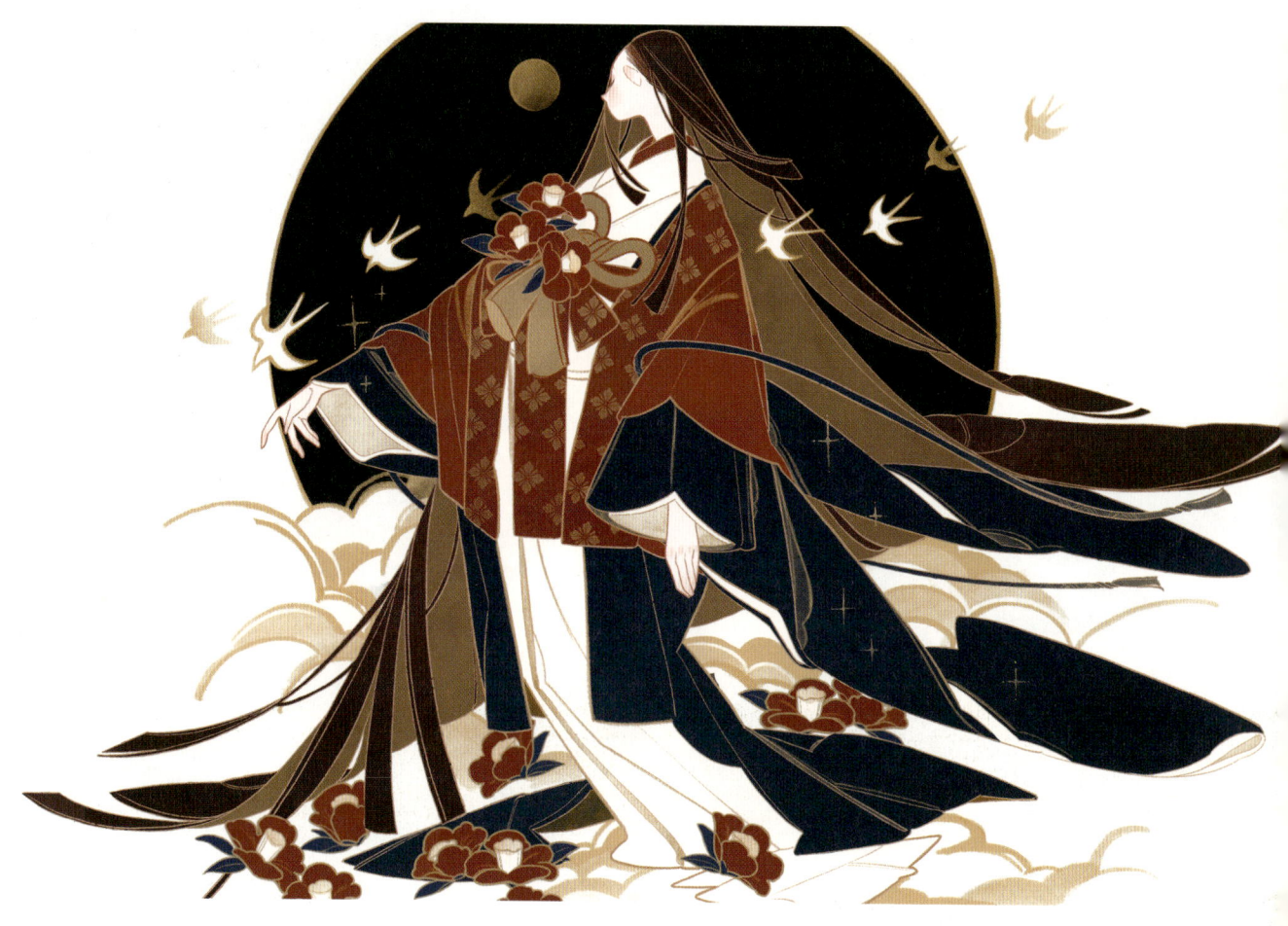

objects, and some others. Sometimes, I want to paint an illustration, when I see art made by other creators. Other creators' art gives to me some impact. My artwork is not made only by myself. My artwork is made thanks to so many people's help.

Q: As an excellent illustrator with experience in working with a variety of books, packaging, and music videos, can you share how these commercial illustration projects have influenced your creation? What insights or experiences can you share from these collaborations?

S: I think these experiences made my artwork more precise. When I make artwork for myself, I can choose what to paint. But for client work, I have to paint a variety of things. Also, there are some differences between paintings for a variety of books, packaging, and music videos

and paintings for social media posts. They vary in size, color system, and layout, and I think size is the most important. The canvas size is different, and the impression you get from the illustration is different. To deal with these differences, I have to paint with various precisions and things. From what I learned, my artwork has become more precise.

Q: How did your experience studying graphic design influence and connect your later illustration creation?

S: Currently, graphic design studies have not had much influence on my illustrations. If I must say, it's only when I draw book covers and other works that I can anticipate where the designer will put the title. But these have taught me how to compose in terms of art itself. I often draw illustrations with a lot of margin, and when I draw them, I think about the shape of the margin. Therefore, I can create sophisticated illustrations. I think that margin is as important as objects, especially in illustrations with a lot of margin, and I tend to think this way when studying graphic design.

Q: Your works incorporate many Japanese themes and elements. How do you combine traditional Japanese culture with modern painting styles? Which of these cultural elements do you like best?

S: I think my works are particularly texture oriented. When I color and draw lines, I choose brushes with analog texture. This makes my works look like *Nihonga* (lit. pictures of Japan), Japanese ink wash painting, and ukiyo-e. When I choose colors, I often choose colors with low saturation and brightness. This art technique is my imitation of ukiyo-e. In addition, I also imitate Japanese gold lacquer, often using a color that looks like gold as dots. Each cultural element is my favorite, but I often use ukiyo-e

and *Nihonga* as the basis of art techniques. I think Japanese culture is simple, beautiful, and kind. These make people relax. I want to incorporate its atmosphere in my artwork.

Q: How do you see the future development of Japanese illustration? What new plans or creative directions do you have?

S: I think the future development trend of Japanese illustrations is unstable. Because illustrations drawn by AI are becoming popular in Japan today. When people question the value of the existence of creators, I feel uneasy about not being able to foresee the future but having to determine the current situation and think about how to survive in the future. In addition, I hope to spread my illustrations overseas in the future. Not limited to the Japanese style, I want to try various illustration styles. Therefore, in addition to my current illustration work, I must continue to learn and practice new styles.

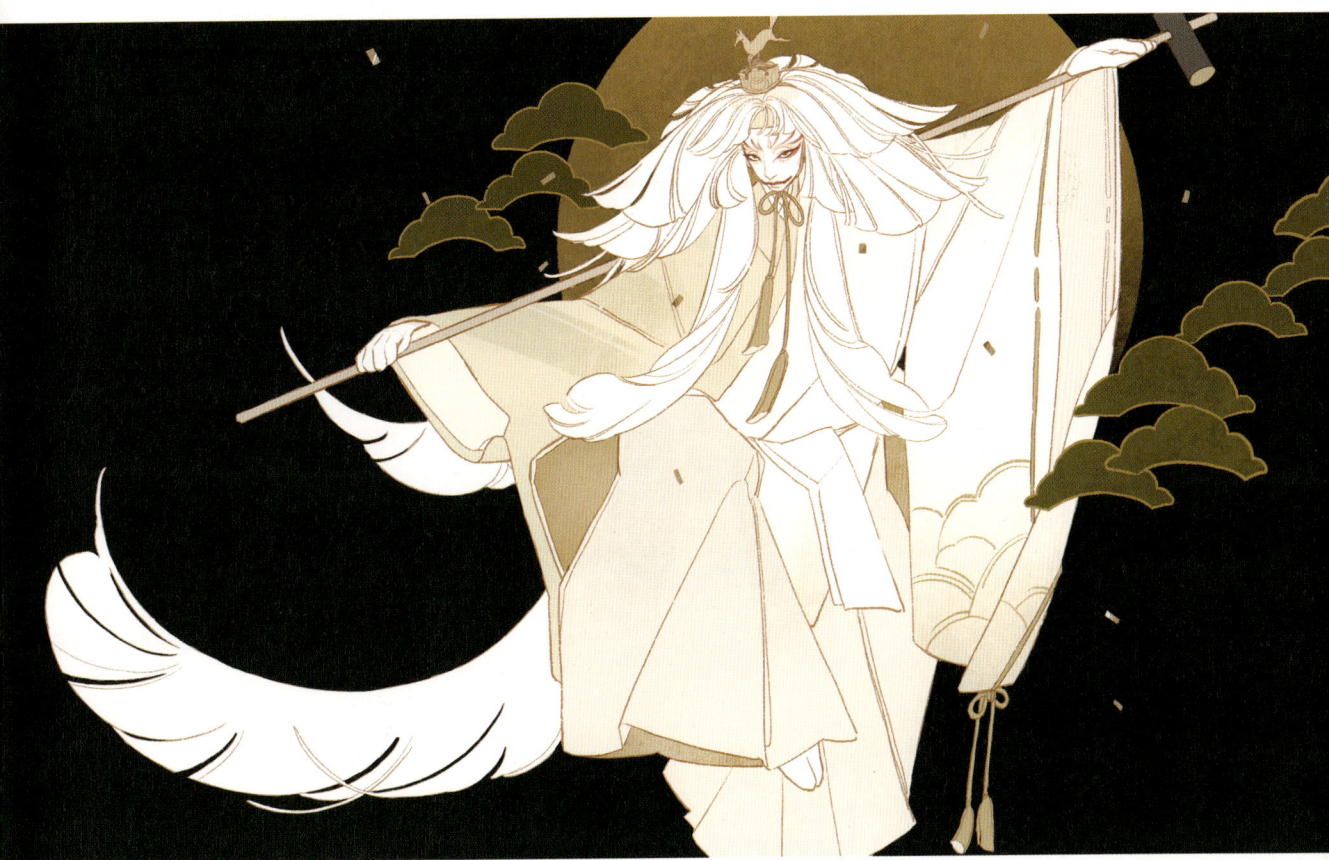

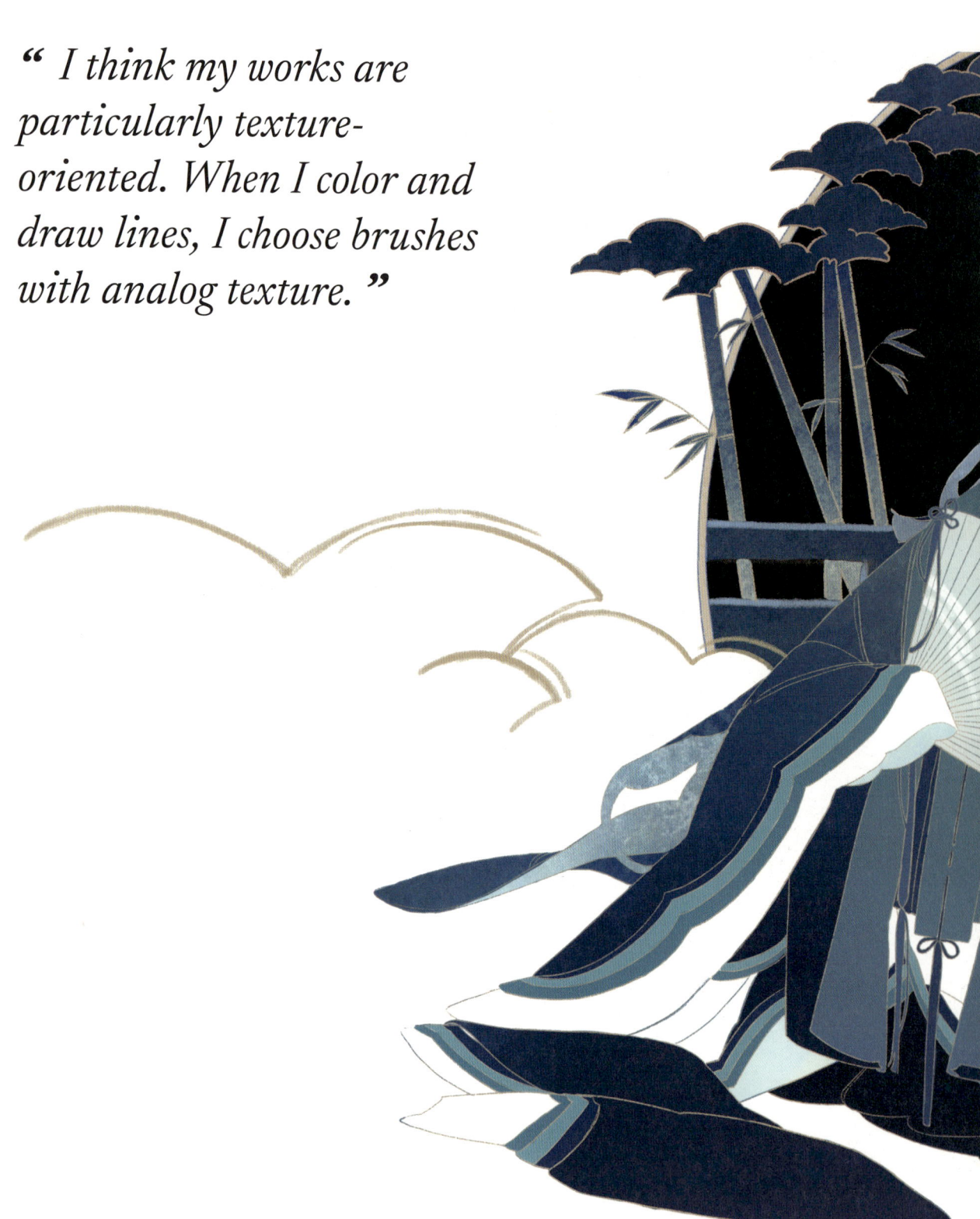

" *I think my works are particularly texture-oriented. When I color and draw lines, I choose brushes with analog texture.* "

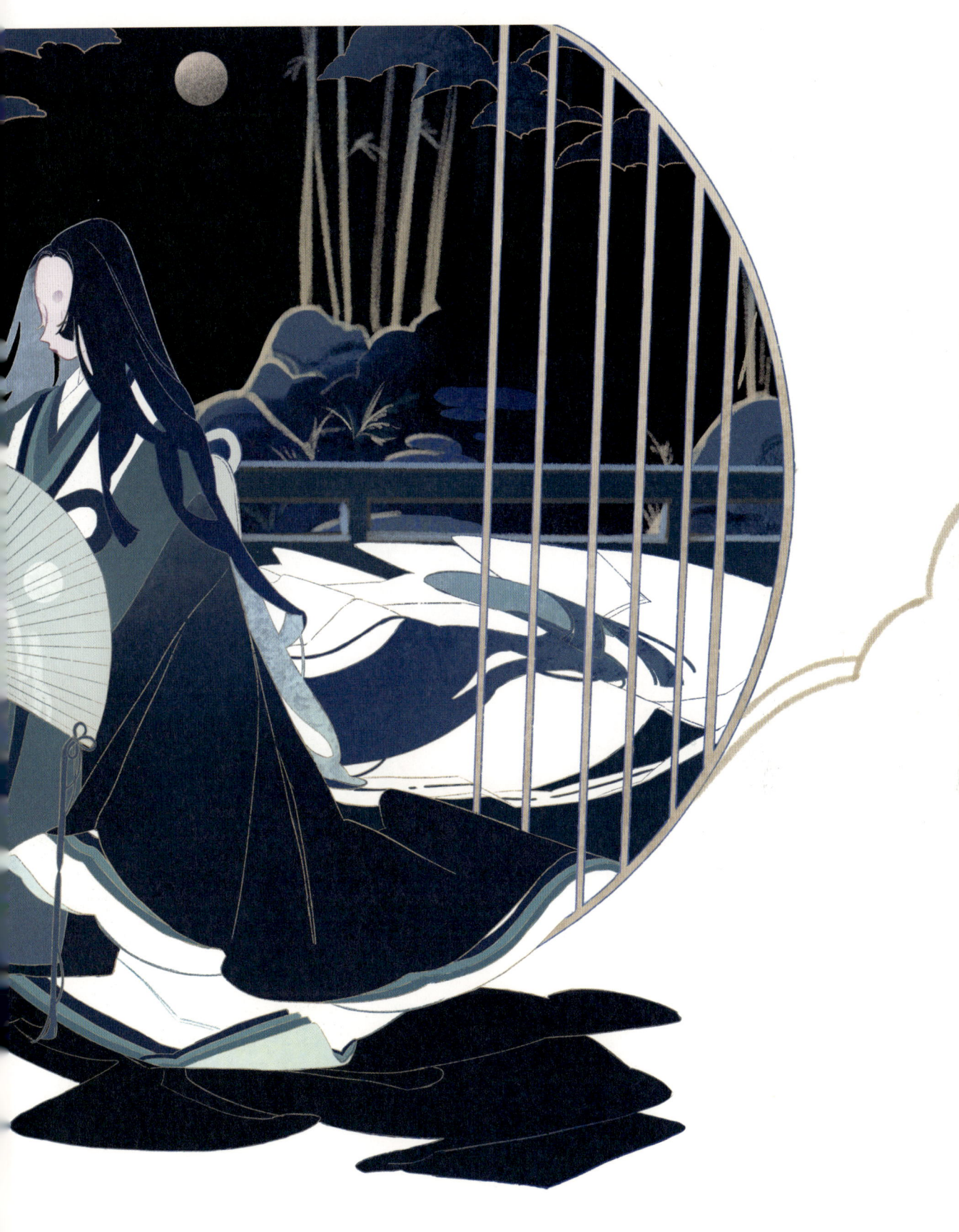

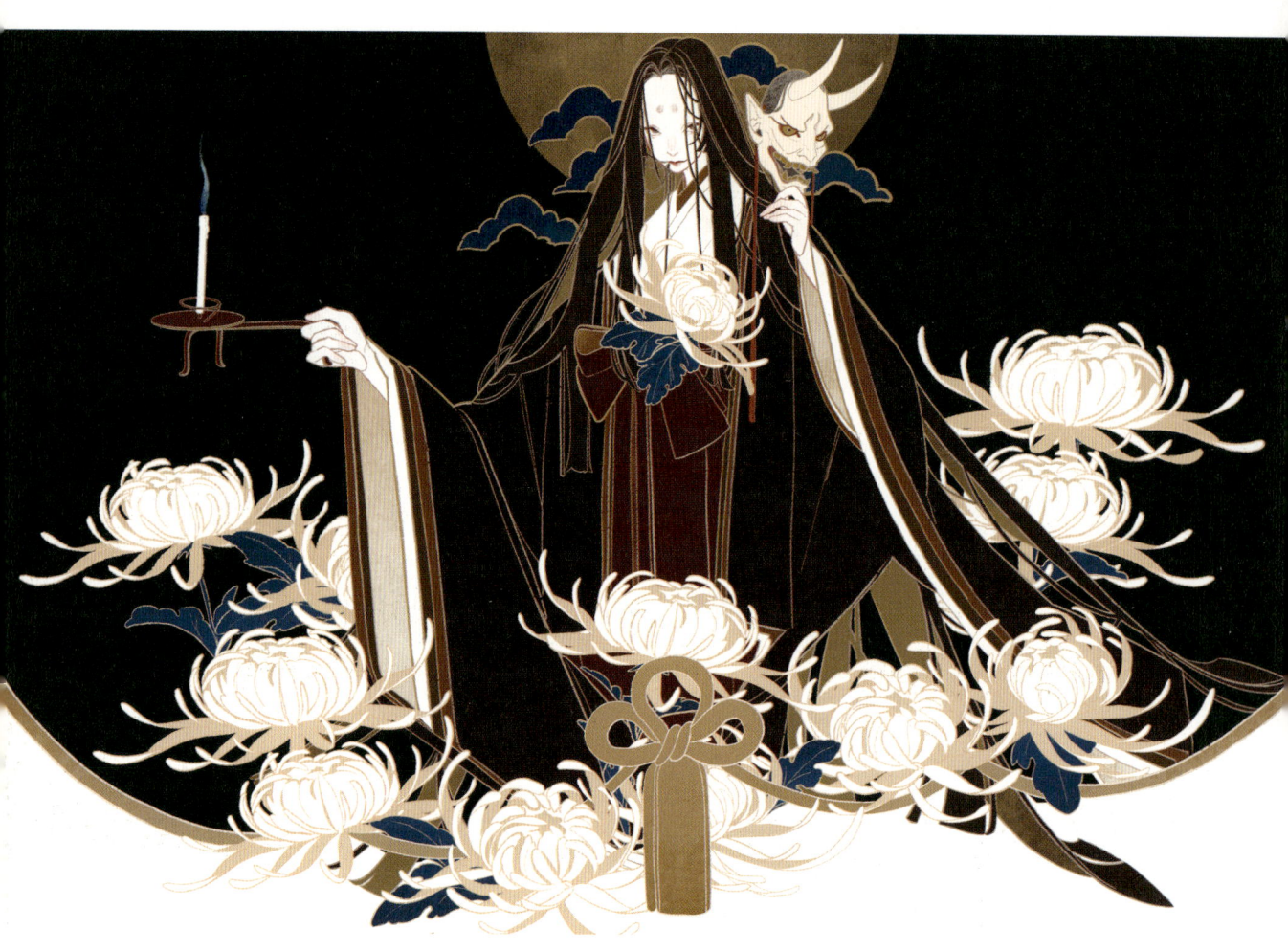

• CHRYSANTHEMUM FEAST •

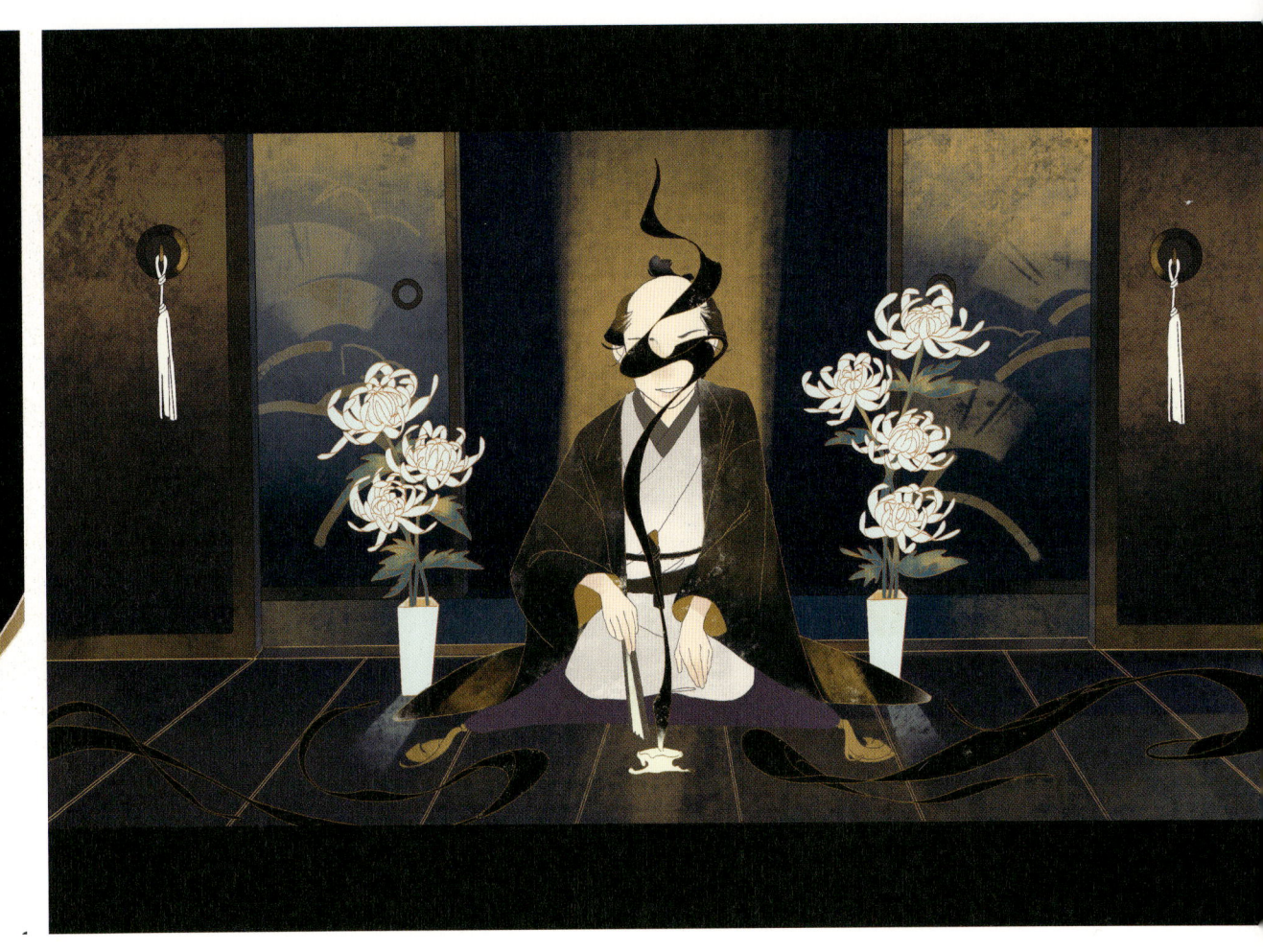

ARTWORKS INFO

Kazuhiro Hori

P011   DEPENDENCE
Two girls are leaning against a large skull. Their surroundings are filled with sweet food. Both girls look empty and lifeless. However, they have no energy left to fight against it.

P013   NECROSIS
The girl is trying to strangle the other girl facing her. That girl seems to accept it and may even want it. Perhaps they are the same person. Is that what she wants—to be fulfilled? To be free from reality?

P014   EMPTY
The girl wants to fill the world with what she loves. And that hope is seemingly fulfilled. But will the result really make her happy?

P016   SANCTUARY
Everyone has things they don't want others to step on or interfere with. However, protecting this sanctuary is difficult. And you never know who might invade or when. The intruder may not mean any harm, but they will invade regardless. The girl does her best to protect the important things to her.

P017   WAVE
Needless to say, this work is a homage to the ukiyo-e of Katsushika Hokusai.
The waves are replaced with whipped cream, the boat with a girl, and Mount Fuji with strawberries. The things that surround the girl are essentially things that she likes and with which she wants to satisfy herself, but in contrast to this, a mass of desire is threatening to engulf her very existence. However, she does not know how to resist it and accepts it with resignation.

P019   SWEET LIFE
The girl is sitting in a daze. Her eyes are not very strong and unfocused. She is surrounded by her favorite stuffed animals and sweets, but her heart is never satisfied. Instead, the world seems to express a feeling of emptiness. She seems to accept this situation.

P021   PIETÀ
At first glance, the space is filled with fluffy, warm stuffed animals. But the hands of the stuffed animals are entwined with the girls. The hands, however, are not tightly constricted, but are ready to be unloaded at any time. The image sources are Michelangelo Buonarroti's *Pietà* and Katsushika Hokusai's ukiyo-e.

Sakuma Yuka

P035   TRACE
Becoming an adult means erasing all traces of your girlhood.

P036   APPEARS AND DISAPPEARS
Sadness and joy come in turns.

P038   DREAM THAT IS UNDERMINED
Everyday life is effortless. We are deprived of thought because we are only given it. We can no longer distinguish between dreams and reality.

P040   NOSTALGIA
Like an octopus entangled, there are memories that will not disappear in me. At a moment's notice, the memories come back to life, and each time they do, my heart goes sweetly numb.

P041   SELF-AWARENESS AND BUDDING
We all know the tightness of being classified as something. The girl also has strong and robust horns. That is what it means to be oneself.

P043   IMMATURE PIECE
Lotus flowers are beautiful even when grown in the mud. It will be stronger and nobler than other flowers. The girl is still a bud. She will become a big flower despite her ordeal.

P044   LAST FLIGHT
The last time I entrusted my feelings to a bird and watched it fly away.

P045   PLEASE DON'T CRY
Do not look to others to resolve your grief. My grief must be healed by me.

Miki Katoh

P073   BURNING RED OF FOX SPIRIT
It is time to prepare for the midnight festival now.

P074   HIDAKA RIVER
At the end of passion and obsession.

P076   BLESSING WIND
To preach the gospel with wind.

P078   KIRIN AND RAINBOW
The soaring kirin brings the gospel.

P080 RAINMAKER
The dragonlord's princess prays for rain.

P082 CHERRY BLOSSOM STORM FOR SECRET LOVERS
We belong together over and over.

P083 BAKU'S DREAM
The *baku* (tapir-like supernatural beings) dispels nightmares and brings the gospel.

Takahito Izumi

P085 RED JAPANEASE UMBRELLA
When the woman suddenly looked upon the sky, the snow that had stopped just a moment ago started falling again. The woman's red umbrella stands out vividly in the achromatic snowy landscape. The contrast is pleasant. Among Japan's four seasons of spring, summer, fall, and winter, winter is quiet and beautiful.

P086 TOKYO YUKATA GIRL WITH CAT
The summer festivals are a traditional summer feature in Japan. A young girl and a cat dance enthusiastically to the sound of festival drums. In the back, an old man and a cat are peeking out from behind the *sudare*. *Sudare* is something made of bamboo, reed, etc., woven together with gaps in between. It is a piece of traditional Japanese summer décor used as indoor partitions and sunshades.

P088 KIMONO GIRL
A woman wearing a red kimono with a camellia pattern stops reading midway through and becomes lost in thought. In other words, it is like a Japanese version of Jean-Honoré Fragonard's famous painting *A Young Girl Reading*. Her kimono pattern is retro, but she is a modern beauty. The artist says that he enjoys reading during the long autumn nights.

P090 YUKATA BEAUTY
Yukata (bathrobe) is a traditional Japanese summer kimono. In the case of this picture, the navy pattern on the white background looks cool, and the yellow *obi* (sash) is a nice accent color. The figure of a woman tying her *obi* with her back to her mirror is somehow as gorgeous as the artist thinks.

P091 JAPANEASE SUMMER GIRL
A young woman sits on an *endai* under a cotton rose and enjoys the cool evening breeze. *Endai* is a long chair made of wood or bamboo and is a Japanese-style bench. Ukiyo-e prints from the Edo period often depict beautiful women relaxing on *endais*.

P093 UKIYO-E GIRLS CRAZY ABOUT A SMARTPHONE
Japanese high school girls are at the fore of the latest Japanese culture. Although this painting depicts modern high school girls, it is reminiscent of ukiyo-e. Ukiyo-e are woodblock prints and hand-painted paintings depicting the daily lives of people during the Edo period. One of the most popular types of ukiyo-e is *bijin-ga*, which depicts beautiful women. Ukiyo-e is characterized by bright colors and bold compositions. It is a representative art emblematic of Japanese culture.

P094 WARD OFF PANDEMIC
Japanese high school girls became a bodhisattva. The bodhisattva is a warm-hearted person who is willing to self-sacrifice in order to help people achieve enlightenment or save others. Her appearance is truly one filled with compassion. She continues to pray today to save people from disasters, such as infectious diseases and wars.

P095 DUEL ON GOJO OHASHI BRIDGE
The setting is Gojō Ōhashi Bridge in Kyoto. It's an interesting battle between Musashibō Benkei and Ushiwakamaru (later Minamoto no Yoshitsune) took place during the Heian period. It's where it was. The battle between the two contrasting characters, Benkei, who is large and strong, and Ushiwakamaru, who is nimble and agile. In this painting, Benkei is carrying modern weapons such as rocket cannons, and Ushiwakamaru is depicted as a modern-day high school girl wearing a sailor suit.

Ryohei Shimazaki

P097 HELL COURTESAN AND THE GIRL
When the artist saw Kawanabe Kyosai's *Hell Courtesan*, he had an idea of a girl in a uniform imitating the Hell Courtesan. So he drew this piece. The strip of paper represents a smartphone, and the *obi* (sash) represents a backpack. The Hell Courtesan appears to be gazing at the girl.

P098 MAIDEN'S PHOENIX
An homage to Katsushika Hokusai's *Woman with a Cat*. Instead of the cat, the maiden holds a phoenix that Hokusai painted in another work. The phoenix and the maiden are depicted as one, and the phoenix's tail is water-like, but it also gives the impression that it is flowing from within the maiden's body. The kimono pattern is *Shinobu grass* (squirrel's foot fern). There are also falling autumn leaves on the white band, giving an image of the autumn season.

P100 A DREAM BANQUET OF THE DRUNK BEAUTY
An homage to Katsushika Hokusai's *The Drunk Beauty*. The small creatures on the lacquered shelf are having a party around a pot, but this is a hallucination seen by a drunk woman. The kimono pattern is inspired by the Rinpa school of autumn grass. The artist wanted the *obi* (sash) to have a modern look. The sake in the bottle is now empty, and the plum branch is placed in it.

P102 PUPPETEER
An homage to Li Song's *The Knick-knack Peddler* in the Southern Song Dynasty, China. The demon is a depiction of the artist himself. The artist collects women's body images like dolls (objects) as subjects and depicts himself using them in his works. At the bottom of the leftmost basket is the fragile ego that lurks deep within the artist. On the right are things around him that he collects as subjects for his works. He collects materials as motifs for the creation of his works in daily life.

P104 WOMAN IN THE SNOW
An homage to Katsushika Hokusai's *Tiger in the Snow* and Kawanabe Kyosai's *Hell Courtesan*. It depicts a woman running through the snow with *Otafuku* (lit. much good fortune) on her shoulder. The running woman is likened to *Benzaiten*, one of the Seven Lucky Gods, and six other Seven Lucky Gods are depicted on the kimono pattern. He depicts a woman who is bound, struggling to get out of something, and running with all her might toward salvation.

Ichiraku Studio

P107 DOKURO GAESHI
This piece depicts an Iga ninja performing the art of *Gashadokuro* (skeletal giants).

P108 SARUTOBI SASUKE
A painting depicting Sarutobi Sasuke performing the *Kirigakure no Jutsu* (hiding mist technique) on the banks of a river.

P110 FALCON AND WOMAN
A portrait of a female falconer.

P111 SHINOBI
A portrait of a ninja who controls lightning.

P113 MASK NINJA VS MONSTER
This painting depicts a masked ninja performing a *yōkai taiji* (monster extermination).

P114 DOROBŌ
A portrait of a *dorobō* (thief).

P115 TORA TORA
A depiction of a ninja performing the fire *ninjutsu* (ninja's martial art strategy).

P116 OBAKE, KYŪBINOKITSUNE, BAKE NEKO
These three female portraits show in order: ghost, nine-tailed fox, and the changed cat.

Shihori Hattori

P119 AFFECTION / ATTACHMENT
This piece is part of a three-part series inspired by a story from the classic Japanese literature *Uji Shūi Monogatari*, which tells of a revered monk, Ichijō-ji Sōjō, and his beloved disciple. In this artwork, the disciple does not appear; instead, the monk is shown holding a ceremonial helmet. The monk's expression reflects a deep reverence for the memory of his disciple, intertwining the solemnity of his religious devotion with a tender sense of nostalgia. This quiet moment captures the profound human connection that underlies the tale.

P120 FRESH GREEN
Created as part of a zodiac-themed calendar series for the Year of the Rooster, this piece represents *Seimei*, one of the 24 solar terms in the traditional Japanese calendar marking the peak of spring. The artist employs a playful visual metaphor by transforming the rooster's comb into tulips, offering a fresh perspective on the conventional rooster motif. This innovative approach brings a humorous element to the traditional subject matter while maintaining its seasonal significance.

P123 DARK MOON ON YEAR'S END
This piece, also part of the rooster calendar series, draws inspiration from the Japanese New Year's Eve tradition where the moon is said to hide (*tsuki-kakure*). The artwork features the *Onagadori*, a Japanese national natural monument known for its extraordinarily long tail feathers that can grow up to four meters in length. The artist utilizes this majestic bird's elegant form to convey the solemnity of the year's end.

P124, P125 TURTLE MAN & CRANE MAN
These two paintings depict a man adorned with a turtle and a crane, both of which are cherished symbols of good fortune in East Asia. The background is stamped with gold leaf, which not only conveys the auspicious intent but also incorporates the space creation style typical of traditional Japanese paintings. The composition serves as a reminder of the interconnectedness between these symbols and the structure of the world.

P126 GRAVE VISIT
It is a self-portrait of the artist visiting the cemetery to pay respects at her deceased grandfather's grave. The tomb is dark at night, evoking a sense of eerie mystery, but what is actually present is a mischievous monkey. When the artist lifted the stone, her grandfather, whose ashes had been interred, emerged from inside, and she was able to meet him face to face. The use of ink and light colors expresses the dim darkness of the entire painting.

Natsuki Urushihara

P129 HER SCENERY (2018)
The way she poses and flaunts her charm is both endearing and mocking. As she grows up, various desires emerge along with her innocent thoughts. The shining stars, the hole leading to the abyss, and the scenery of day and night inverted in the heavens and the earth represent such duality. As one grows up, one can no longer remain pure, and the artist depicted this landscape as a scene of hope that accepts and celebrates such changes.

P131 HER SCENERY (2018)
The azure forest, which symbolizes the beautiful thought that lies within her heart, is placed at the location of her heart, depicting it as a view of the inner thought influencing the world. The thought circulates through the world from her fingertips and then merges with her again. The artist depicted the thoughts that were sent out to the world and the echoes that were returned from the world, resulting in her great growth.

P132 HER SCENERY (2017)
The way she sits comfortably and gazes into the distance was felt to be a view of her future. By arranging the movement of clouds descending from the distant sky and the various events they bring about around her, the artist depicted the scenery as a prayer for happiness in an unpredictable future.

P134 SUMMER OF SCENERY
The euphoric midsummer sleep seemed to overlap with the mountains being cloaked and assimilated by the swirling clouds. The artist prayed and painted this happy image to last forever.

Mika Nitta

P137 DIALOGUE
Mika Nitta's drawing style is inspired by ukiyo-e. This work shows a representative piece from a series depicting a girl and an imaginary creature. The various expressive lines and subdued color saturation create a nostalgic view of the world that seems to come from somewhere in the past. It is like a myth passed down from generation to generation.

P138 PRISM
A different space where light reflects diffusely. There, plants grow and crystals begin to grow. If you listen carefully, you can

hear the sound of their growth. The girl is soothed by the sound as she spins the thread. The work depicts a world full of life force from thin and minute things.

P140 OXYGEN

This work is a piece about humans and nature. Imaginary creatures are the figurative representations of a larger nature. The girl is breathing and surrendering as if she is infused with some kind of energy. There is an atmosphere of mystery and magic.

P142 STAND BY ME

A creature with its body repaired in places and a girl with her eyes closed. She may be blind. Each body is connected by a thread, indicating that each being is in a relationship of mutual support. We always lose something in our lives. However, this work expresses the artist's thought that sometimes it can be a strength that enables us to be close to others.

P145 LAST LAND

The atmosphere is somber as if the end is in sight, but the light shining through and the new flowers blooming give the impression of a beginning. The large moon, which seems to be an egg, shines a gentle light on the bones. The theme of this work is that death is not the end but the beginning of life.

P146 SECRET GARDEN

A girl holding something and a girl with farming tools. The girl on the left appears to be a grave keeper. The girl on the right is holding a corpse or a secret...? Amidst the colorful patterns and flowers that give the impression of glamour, there is an air of disquiet between the two girls. The society we live in also has its own hidden sins behind the glamor.

Hanae Nakajima

P149 VISITOR

This work is based on the theme of "gift," which not only means a tangible gift but also refers to talent or ability. The artist drew it with the image of her looking forward to receiving a gift before she was born.

P150 SKY FORECAST

People express the weather in the sky by incorporating it into their clothes and decorations.

P153 LOOKING FOR FACES

This work was inspired by the scene where Peter Pan searches for his shadow and Son Goku's clone technique. The artist drew Son Goku looking for and encountering his alter ego (shadow).

P154 UNDERWATER EXCURSION

This work reflects the artist's admiration for free fish swimming underwater. She drew twins looking at the fish as if it were a cake.

P157 FOAMY RAIN

The artist created this design based on the image of a mermaid and her love, based on the tear-like rain that falls in the distance and the flamingo, which is said to be a symbol of love.

P158 IN THE BLUE SPARKLE

This work was inspired by the brightest star, Sirius.

P159 TRAVELING OF STARS

This work is based on the dream the artist had while she was sleeping, which turned into a lotus that grew from her back and became a flower pot, imagining herself traveling around the stars in her dreams. It is a dream that influences reality and contains a wish that will eventually become a reality.

P160 DREAM

The artist drew an angel dreaming in the darkness and a flamingo dwelling in her heart.

Tsubonari

P163 TORI

An illustration for a New Year's greeting card in the year of the Rooster. After having the opportunity to see an old painting of a rooster drawn by a Japanese artist in the 18th century, Itō Jakuchū, the artist explored fusing it with aesthetic and decadent images. The illustration features a mysterious-looking boy as the main subject, but with the luxurious feel of *maki-e* (sprinkled picture), it avoids becoming too dark. The artist intended to symbolize the beginning of a vibrant year.

P164 LUO

A part of the *Banquet of Dolls* series featuring the *Butterfly Boy*. He is among the highest-ranked *dorei* (slave) and is owned by the trading company.

P166 ASSASSIN BOY

A boy from a family of assassins. He uses *kiseru* (smoking pipe) as a weapon. He is a resident of *Antengai*. He is rich in emotions and unable to kill people. He lives in a pleasure district.

P169 MIND'S EYE

An artwork in the early days after the artist began creating with dark themes. The artist was studying techniques of Japanese traditional gold lacquerware called *maki-e* and was inspired by combining it with illustrations of aesthetic motifs.

Kaihara

P171 NO TITLE

The artist continues drawing as if scratching in the darkness.

P172 PORTRAIT

Raise it, with the beat of fire in your hands.

P176 THE GREAT GOAT OF THE MORNING STAR

The feeling of his hand touching it certainly had meaning.

ONIKU Kuitai

P183 PAYMON

Paymon is one of the demons of demonology and the ninth demon of the *72 Pillars of Solomon* described in *Ars Goetia*.

P184 BAEL

Bael is one of the demons of demonology and the first demon of the *72 Pillars of Solomon* described in *Ars Goetia*.

P187 ESCAPE

Take her by the hand and lead her away.

P188   TURBID
Turbid is the true beauty.

P189   AMON
Amon is one of the demons of demonology and the seventh demon of the *72 Pillars of Solomon* described in *Ars Goetia*.

P190   ASMODEUS
Asmodeus is one of the demons of demonology and the thirty-second demon of the *72 Pillars of Solomon* described in *Ars Goetia*.

P192   THE FOOL
She is a completely unplanned wanderer who walks around completely unrestrained, not even aware of other cards. The eccentricity of her costume is reminiscent of a clown.

P193   CATHARSIS
Release the emotions you've been holding back.

kokuno

P195   NO TITLE
This personal work is an image of a place where light does not reach and hides within. That may be why the flowers blooming there look so vivid.

P196   ROOTS
The origin is always present in everything. The image of this personal work is that all beings end up in the same place. The use of green, which is not normally used, is also impressive.

P199   AIRFLOW
Something invisible to the eye but certainly exists. It is your will. It is a piece of work that expresses the idea that "I am the one who wills it." (Contributed illustration ©Shutugen Garou / Creator's Show Up Gallery)

P200   SHALLOWS
The movement of the waves, the glimmer of light. This personal artwork was inspired by the image of a shallow, where something hidden deep inside can be seen and hidden.

P201   SHIRUBE
He and the artist were thinking about "unasaka (the end of the sea)." The thoughts just happened to meet. The artist called her personal work "shirube (guide)."

P202   WHITECAPS
This work is based on the concept of "things wandering in the sea." It was created with an awareness of movement in stillness. His eyes, looking straight at us, seem to have made up their minds. (Contributed illustration ©Shutugen Garou / Creator's Show Up Gallery)

P204   EMPTY THEORY WORLD
In every world, there are walls, all of which are connected by fantasies. This personal work is filled with that idea. It represents the relationship between the artist and the picture.

ico

P207   HYAKKI YAGYO
The artist painted this picture to show the history of the battle between *yōkai* and humans in Japan and to help people imagine whether the young girl is a human or *yōkai*.

P208   CHILD OF HEAVEN
The artist likes quiet but strong-willed individuals. She would be happy if people who see her paintings could sense some strong will in life and living. This picture was painted with that will in mind.

P210   UNPAINTED FACE
The artist painted this picture to reflect on her true self. The dog-like creature facing the woman is wearing a mask, perhaps because it cannot face its true self. The artist hopes one day, she can love herself.

P211   WHITE REAPER "DETERMINATION"
The artist wanted to tell a story about a girl who was born pure white and gentle despite her race as the god of death and how she accepts her destiny and life. The dragon is her only friend. The painting is in two parts and another part is titled "Conflict."

P212   EDGE
The artist thinks her life is made up of meeting many wonderful people. For some reason, when she thinks of encounters, she thinks of the shape of a circle. She painted this picture because the animal with the circle shape was a sheep.

P213   WHITE REAPER "CONFLICT"
The artist wanted to depict a story about a girl who was born pure white and gentle despite her race as the god of death and how she accepts her destiny and life. She still has a lost look on her face, and the artist thinks she's about to travel and decide how she wants to live her life.

P214   EMPTY
One of the words in the language of the devil's lantern flower is "falsehood." The artist painted this picture thinking that people from all walks of life hide their loneliness and try to put on a smile.

P216   SILKWORM
The silkworm, an insect, has wings but cannot fly. At first glance, it may seem sad, but the artist painted this picture with the desire to love even such a somewhat lacking self.

P217   REINCARNATION
The first impression of this picture may seem to be a bad ending, but it depicts a single-minded couple who continue to have feelings for each other even after being reborn.

OYK

P219   TOMBO
In Japanese, the word tombo is written as " 蜻蛉 " and means both "dragonfly" and "mayfly." This work is inspired by the mayfly. The artist wanted to depict the fleeting life of a mayfly along with a sense of anger.

P220 LOACHES

As a Japanese proverb goes: "There is no loach under the willow tree twice (柳の下にいつも泥鰌はおらぬ)." It means "Just because something went well once, it doesn't mean it will succeed again if repeated." This painting is a self-deprecating reflection on the idea that even if one finds luck on social media once, it doesn't mean it will continue successfully.

P223 I KNEW. I WASN'T THERE.

This painting depicts the swirling emotions of anger, sadness, and regret that come after disappointment. Intense sadness and anger are powerful negative emotions, but they can also become a significant source of energy. I hope to move forward correctly while embracing my strong emotions.

P224 AQUILEGIA

The artist depicted emotions that are tightly bound and the sadness and anger that have nowhere to go. Unable to control these intense emotions, the artist feels a desire to disappear, yet foolishly, she also wants to attain something beautiful. This is the theme of the painting.

P226 AUN

This work was inspired by "A-un." "A" is said to be the sound of the beginning, and "Un" the sound of the end. In this piece, the character's mouth is stitched, preventing them from making either sound. Without a beginning or an end, everything swirls within them, unable to escape, leading to feelings of resignation, anger, and self-disappointment.

P228 A CORNERED MOUSE

The artist created this work based on the proverb "Even a cornered mouse will bite a cat (窮鼠猫を嚙む)." The meaning of the proverb is that a cornered mouse will fight back against the cat. The artist wanted to depict the emotions of the cornered mouse.

P229 BOUND TO THE BEYOND

The character's costume is modeled after traditional Japanese bridal attire. It depicts a scene where the character goes to marry a monster and leaves this world. The character is painted with sadness, resignation, and melancholy.

velonyca toto

P231 THE ROOT OF THE GROWTH OF ALL THINGS "SOLE"

These girls exert themselves with a strong will to live, no matter what their circumstances. The artist feels that this is the fundamental beauty of life. This girl is named after the Sun.

P232 THE ROOT OF THE GROWTH OF ALL THINGS "STELLA"

These girls exert themselves with a strong will to live, no matter what their circumstances. The artist feels that this is the fundamental beauty of life. This girl is named after the Stars.

P234 SENKAKU

Senkaku is written as " 仙鶴 " and means the crane on which a hermit rides. Cranes are also used as a symbol of marital harmony, as they harmoniously spend their lives together as husband and wife. Cranes are also revered as symbols of longevity, virtue, and ability. The artist created this piece with the hope of depicting a symbol of good things through her.

P237 FUSHINRAIRAI

The artist drew this picture with the Chinese zodiac signs together with the *fu-shin* (people who bring good fortune). The artist wishes that many good things will come to you. 2022 was the Year of the Tiger.

P238 THE ROOT OF THE GROWTH OF ALL THINGS "FLOS"

These girls exert themselves with a strong will to live, no matter what their circumstances. The artist feels that this is the fundamental beauty of life. This girl is named after the Flowers.

P239 RED

This artwork represents the energy of a person. The flowers represent positive and negative emotions. He/she lives in a swirling energy, exposed to those emotions and the atmosphere. In the midst of all this, a sparrow reaches him/her. Sparrows are auspicious birds that bring long family fortunes and prosperity to descendants. In a life filled with anxiety and hope, he/she will find solace in the sparrow.

P240, P241 THE MANDARIN SQUARE: DRAGON & TIGER

These works are modeled after the Mandarin Square of the Ming and Qing dynasties in China. The dragon, tiger, and qilin are each placed to depict how they are still living and breathing in human society today.

Tsurikawa

P243 A STORY OF SEA

When I saw a dead moray eel washed up on the beach, I felt that death was closer to the beach than in the city. Death is not only sad but also a source of sustenance for the living. Living things continue to exist in a great cycle of life and death.

P244 SAVIOR

This work won the 72nd National Student Art & Design Award at the Gakuten, a large-scale public art exhibition that has been held in Japan for over 70 years. The theme of this work is "What is salvation." The ants crawling on the body resemble a person seeking help from God. People may consider it salvation to look to God and find the challenge and solution within themselves.

P247 THE SETTING SUN

Inspired by a song by a band the artist likes, the title is taken from the song *The Sun That Never Sets* by a Japanese band "climbgrow." When the artist saw the orange sunset through the dark and heavy clouds, she wished it would last forever.

P248 TRANOI NIENOU

This work was inspired by Atsushi Nakajima's novel, *Sangetsuki* (The Moon Over the Mountain). It expresses the erosion of the spirit by a ferocious beast. There are many differences between humans and wild animals, but the artist believes the difference between humans and beasts in this picture is "whether or not they are aware of their own cruelty."

P249 FIRE BALL

The fireball represents the soul of life. As living creatures are active, heat is always generated and flows to the body's surface. The artist created this work so that she would never forget the feeling that she was alive.

P249 BORDER LINE

The worlds of the sea and land are very different. Fish living in the sea and humans living on land may have different ways of thinking and common sense. The theme of this artwork is the shifting consciousness of creatures between the sea and land.

P250 THE SUN NEVER SETS

Inspired by the song *The Sun That Never Sets* by a Japanese band called "climbgrow." When the artist saw the orange sunset through the dark and heavy clouds, she wished it would last forever.

P252 HELLO GOOD BYE

In the ocean, waves are coming in and going out. This work depicts these waves as "hello" and "good-bye." The title of this work is also taken from the song *Hello Goodbye* by the Japanese band "climbgrow."

P253 LOUDER!

The artist sometimes feels the urge to scream louder. She is afraid to actually yell, so she lets the person in the painting yell for her.

P254 CURTAIN

Beyond the serene world lies a world of chaos, full of impulse and madness. This work depicts the suffering that seems to be hidden by curtains but cannot be concealed.

P255 MARRIAGE

The artist painted this work because she thought this is what marriage is like, and she thinks that two people waiting for death together is the ultimate love.

C7 (Shiina)

P269 SEARCH THE TRAIL

Close your eyes and sharpen your sense of touch. No matter how much you explore the surface of the body, gravity cannot be found.

P270 ATAMI

Someday, I will bury the layered memories in the garden along with their warmth.

P272 SLOW DANCE WITH YOU

Matching our steps with our breath, we share a sense of connection—like the beautiful patterns in the sand, renewed each night.

P273 WEAKNESS FOR NIGHTHAWK

To hold on to what was precious, having a weakness was necessary.

P274 SLAPPING MEBIUS

Resisting all continuous eternities, I move forward, linking together ideals.

P276 BETWEEN THE SHEETS

A place at the farthest edge of sleep, wrapped in the soft, warm touch and the flickering embrace of fleeting fantasies.

Surie

P279 LONELINESS

A lonely mermaid. She is the only mermaid living in the winter lake. Maybe that's more lonely than people can imagine. This illustration is the artist's imagined Japanese ink painting with a low saturation color. She used a color resembling gold as an accent.

P280 REFLECTION

A woman who is talking to herself in the mirror. She is staring at herself in the mirror with intelligent eyes. What is she asking for herself? That's only she knows. The artist used refreshing colors to express her loneliness and intelligence. And she used a gold-like color as an accent and a contrast.

P281 NIGHT BREEZE

A woman walking in the garden at night. In this illustration, she is dancing with a cool breeze. The artist expresses coolness with many cold colors. The illustration is composed to emphasize the depth of the scene and to share the need for coolness on a very hot summer day. Her intention is to share this feeling with those viewing the work.

P282 FLYING SWALLOW

An illustration of swallows and a woman. Swallows are flying beautifully in the night sky. The young woman is yearning for the beautiful, free-flying swallows. The artist imagined the swallows' colors. She chose a limited palette of red, dark blue, and white. To create a flow in the illustration, the direction of the swallows and the woman are the same, and the flow of clothes and hair is moving in the other direction.

P283 PLUM BLOSSOM FLOWERS

The ghost of plum blossom is an old story in Japan. That story is about the ghost of plum blossom following the exile of her lover. People call the story "Legend of Tobiume (flying plum)." In this illustration, the artist drew the character's sad feeling of love. She chose pale colors to evoke the sad atmosphere.

P284 NIGHT OF WAITING

A woman waiting for her loved one. This illustration is paired with *Night Breeze*. As the woman is waiting for her lover on a chilly night, the artist chose to suggest the temperature with cold colors as a way to share her empathy for the subject's loneliness with viewers of the work.

P286 CHRYSANTHEMUM FEAST

An illustration of the jealousy of women. In Japan, there are varieties of chrysanthemums that bloom in disorder. They can't support the weight of their flowers, so they need to be supported artificially. The Japanese call them *kuruigiku*, or "the mad chrysanthemums." The artist focuses on such a chrysanthemum and creates a woman driven mad with jealousy that despite herself. who went mad with jealousy that she couldn't help herself.

P287 SHINIGAMI

Shinigami is the Japanese Grim Reaper. There is an old story about the *shinigami* in Japan illuminated by a Japanese play called *Rakugo* (lit. story with a fall). This illustration depicts the storyteller of *Rakugo*. *Shinigami* is a story with an atmosphere of horror, so the artist expressed it in a dark color. To obscure the main character in this illustration, the artist covers his eyes with the smoke of the candle.

INDEX

ACKNOWLEDGMENTS

We would like to express our gratitude to all of the artists for their generous contribution of images, ideas, and concepts. We are also very grateful to many other people whose names do not appear in the credits, but who made specific contributions and provided support. Without them, the successful compilation of this book would not have been possible. Special thanks to all of the contributors for sharing their innovations and creativity with all of our readers around the world.